State, Law and Family

State, Law and Family:

Family Law in Transition in the United States and Western Europe

MARY ANN GLENDON

Professor
Boston College Law School

1977

NORTH-HOLLAND PUBLISHING COMPANY

AMSTERDAM – NEW YORK – OXFORD

NORTH-HOLLAND PUBLISHING COMPANY – 1977

Library of Congress Catalog Card Number: 76-54929
North-Holland ISBN: 0-7204-0574-2

Published by:
NORTH-HOLLAND PUBLISHING COMPANY
AMSTERDAM – NEW YORK – OXFORD

Distributors for the U.S.A. and Canada:

ELSEVIER NORTH-HOLLAND, INC.
52 VANDERBILT AVENUE
NEW YORK, N.Y. 10017

Library of Congress Cataloging in Publication Data

Glendon, Mary Ann, 1938–
  State, law, and family.

  Bibliography: p.
  1. Domestic relations – United States. 2. Domestic
relations – Europe, Western. I. Title.
K670.G44   346'.73'015   76–54929
ISBN 0–7204–0574–2

PRINTED IN GREAT BRITAIN

IN MEMORY OF
Sarah Frances Pomeroy
and
Martin Francis Glendon

FOREWORD

In 1972 I published a book entitled Marriage Stability, Divorce and the Law. When I started work on that book in the middle 1960s, change was already under way in the field of divorce. From an event of comparatively rare occurrence divorce had grown into a mass phenomenon. But little of that development was visible in the laws of divorce and divorce procedure. In the main, they still stood as they had been written in the 19th century. They had widely become inappropriate for the new reality, but traditional ideology was too strong to allow basic change in the law of the books. So what prevailed for decades was a contrast between the law of the books and the law in action, a compromise between the forces of conservation oriented to Christian traditions held to be inviolable and "modern" individualism oriented to the right of pursuit of happiness, a compromise that was worked out not in the halls of the legislatures but in the rooms of the divorce courts. So the main theme of the book was the description of this compromise, inquiry into its causes, and the demonstration of the futility of promoting, or even protecting, marriage stability by rendering divorce difficult or impossible. As I was working on the book, the old law of the books began to change. The new ideology began to find expression in more or less radical reform statutes such as those of England, Italy, New York or California or the 1970 draft of the Uniform Law on Marriage and Divorce of the National Conference of Commissioners on Uniform State Laws. So I had to include in my book a chapter entitled The Liberal Breakthrough. That very chapter indicated that the adaptation of the statutory texts to reality had at last begun. What has happened in the few years since the completion of my manuscript has gone way beyond even the realities of that time. The law of divorce is undergoing a rapid and fundamental change.

Change, rapid and fundamental, has also been characteristic of the field of Interspousal Relations. On the presentation of this field in the International Encyclopedia of Comparative Law the author of the present book and I have been cooperating for some six years. In that work we had to cope with a peculiar problem. When we thought we had finished the presentation and analysis of a major problem, a new law would come out in one country after another, a law that would affect not only minor details but the very fundamentals; and where there were no new constitutional amendments, international conventions, or statutes, the changes were finding expression in judicial practice. In the course of continuously developing industrialization the position of women changes in society and, as part thereof, the roles of the partners in the marital relationship. That change is finding ready expression in the laws.

In the present book Mary Ann Glendon places the changes of special aspects of family life and family law into the broad and comprehensive context of an inquiry into the transformation of the relation between the family and the state. In this work she makes explicit what has long been felt more or less vaguely. By systematically putting together a vast number of details from all branches of family law, she makes us see what is presently under way. The family and the state, both basic institutions of society, are changing their roles in the fulfillment of human needs. More and more functions that were once performed by the family are taken over by the state. Yet some of the ancient functions of the family are not only preserved, but their need for performance by the family is felt with increased urgency. In consequence, the compulsory machinery of the state has come to be applied more extensively in matters of education, care of the young, the old and the helpless, while it is in the course of being withdrawn from attempts to regulate relationships that are believed to need freedom if they are to come to full fruition.

This process of transformation is illuminated by placing the individual phenomena in the contexts of coherence, of history and of supra-national observation.

Two points are elucidated by the historic perspective. Regulation by the state of all aspects of family life, as we have known it in the recent past, is by no means perpetual and self-evident. Creation and termination of marriage was left to be regulated by private mores in ancient Rome and, it seems, in most other parts of the ancient world. In the city-states the communities of free citizens were homogeneous in ways of life and religion, so that common convictions were strong enough to guarantee marriage and family stability; and the propertyless slaves did not count. But when Rome had expanded from a city to world empire, when non-citizens were absorbed and slavery was transformed into the colonate of serfs, regulation by an institution became necessary. In that age of decaying and dissolving state power, the institution upon which the task devolved was the universal Church. But when that institution was split by the Reformation and state power was consolidated in the age of absolutism, the task of marriage regulation fell to the state. And now, as Professor Glendon describes it, new aspects of family and marriage control are assumed by the state while many areas of traditional state regulation are returned to private determination.

Of course, the long drawn out process of substitution of a new phase did not take place everywhere at exactly the same moment and in exactly the same way. But if we look back upon this process, it constitutes a phenomenon common to all parts of Western civilization. And common to all places of Western civilization, the old ones as well as those to which that civilization is now coming to extend, is the current phase of the relation between the family and the state. In the United States we are easily tempted to look upon legal or social phenomena as matters peculiar to our country. Important insights can thus remain hidden or be obscured. Professor Glendon looks upon the subject of her inquiry as one involving the modern, developed industrialized countries. But wisely she has refrained from detailed coverage of the world. She has limited herself to the United States, England, the Federal Republic of Germany and France. In all four countries the same development is shown to be under way. It is also shown, however, that this common development has not reached everywhere the same stage in every respect, and that there is diversity in the attempts to articulate the social development in legal rules and concepts. As American lawyers we are more inclined to isolationism than our European brethren. Even if we were not always aware of the unity of Western civilization, it ought to be demonstrated to us by the simultaneity of the rise of new legal problems and new legal institutions. Product liability, environmental law, antitrust, securities regulation, consumer protection, new forms of property relations between spouses, these are just a few illustrations of legal innovations presently appearing, we are tempted to say, everywhere, in the United States, in France, in Japan, in the U.S.S.R. Of the 50 states of the United States it is often said that they are laboratories in which experiments can be, and in fact are, undertaken in the legal handling of new social problems. We could all profit if we were to study consistently the experiments not only of the sister states of the United States, but of our sister states in the realm of our common Western civilization of which the United States, France, Germany or Sweden are no less just variants than New York or Illinois. Mary Ann Glendon's work proves how fruitful such an approach can be.

The book also proves the fruitfulness of another escape from the confines of an isolated discipline. The sociological literature on marriage and the family is immense. But in all the innumerable books and articles one rarely finds an adequate consideration of the role of the law and its machinery. If they are touched upon at all, it is mostly in a vein of negative or even contemptuous critique. But how can the reality of family life and of the family's functions in society be studied if the legal aspects are neglected or distorted? The law after all does affect the lives of the members of society. We lawyers have learned that we cannot adequately describe law or adequately solve new legal problems without careful observation of social reality. Professor Glendon's book neatly illustrates how consideration of social life and its attempted regulations, legal and otherwise, can be combined for the sake of understanding. The book is addressed to students of law as much as to students of society. It clarifies the citizens' often confused view of what is actually going on in our agitated age, and it is written in such a fluent style that reading it is a pleasure.

Many of the topics treated in the book are controversial. Many of the present developments in family life and marriage appear to one as desirable progress and to another as dangerous signs of social decay. Among social scientists, including historians, the desirability or possibility of objectivity is debated. Professor Glendon has been striving for objectivity and, we believe, has succeeded.

Chicago, Illinois   Max Rheinstein

ACKNOWLEDGMENTS

The contribution to this book of my teacher and friend, Max Rheinstein, goes back 16 years when, as his student, I was first exposed to his contagious fascination with the complex interaction of law and society and to the remarkable example set by his habits of work and thought. Later, as his co-author in two major undertakings over a period of eight years, I had the extraordinary privilege of being able to observe closely a master at work on the technical intricacies as well as the grand design of an enterprise. The ideas and the methodology of the present work have their genesis in the work that I did with Rheinstein. In his characteristically generous way, though he was busy with his own work, and has been trying unsuccessfully to retire since 1968, he nevertheless found time to read and comment on every chapter of this book. In the fullest sense, the credit for anything worthwhile which may be found within these pages belongs to the teacher; the shortcomings are those of the student.

A fellowship from the Ford Foundation made it possible for me to devote my entire sabbatical year 1975–1976 to writing. A fellowship from the Radcliffe Institute for the same period made the Harvard University libraries available to me, and furnished the occasion for me to profit from the friendly interest and assistance of labor economist Dr. Hilda Kahne and sociologist Dr. Janet Z. Giele. The conclusions, opinions and other statements in this book are, needless to say, my own and not those of the Ford Foundation or the Radcliffe Institute. For his continuing support and encouragement, not only during the sabbatical year, but in all my years of teaching and writing at Boston College Law School, I am deeply grateful to my Dean and fellow property law teacher, Richard G. Huber.

For giving me the opportunity to express and test some of my ideas in public lectures and discussion, I am indebted to the Law Faculty of the Catholic University of Louvain, Belgium, and Professor Marie-Thérèse Meulders who organized the 1976 Journées d'études juridiques there in memory of the legal philosopher Jean Dabin; to Dean Patricia A. Graham of the Radcliffe Institute; and to the German Academic Exchange Service (DAAD).

Several individuals read and commented helpfully on parts of the manuscript or supplied me with useful material. My colleague Hugh J. Ault deserves special thanks for having done both in abundance. Others who were particular generous with their time or suggestions were: Mauricette Craffe of the *Service de recherches juridiques comparatives* in Paris; Andreas Heldrich and Erik Jayme, both of the Munich Law Faculty; my colleague Sanford N. Katz of Boston College Law School; Elisabeth A. Owens of the Harvard Law School; Jacob W. F. Sundberg of the Stockholm Law Faculty and Dr. Vivian Fox of the Boston State College History Department. Able, tireless and resourceful research assistance in the preparation of this publication was furnished by Edwin T. Hobson and Gregory F. Kishel while they were students at Boston College Law School.

I am grateful to the Virginia Law Review Association and the American Association for the Comparative Study of Law for permission to reprint excerpts from the following articles: Glendon, Power and Authority in the Family: New Legal Patterns as Reflections of Changing Ideologies, 23 Am. J. Comp. L. 1 (1975); Glendon, The French Divorce Reform Law of 1976, 24 Am. J. Comp. L. 199 (1976); Glendon, Marriage and the State: The Withering Away of Marriage, 62 Va. L. Rev. 663 (1976). The permission of the International Association of Legal Science to reprint excerpts from the following chapter prepared for the International Encyclopedia of Comparative Law is also gratefully acknowledged: Rheinstein & Glendon, The Effects of Marriage, Ch. 4 International Encyclopedia of Comparative Law, A. Chloros ed. (to be published in 1977).

Edward R. Lev read the manuscript more than once from beginning to end, and greatly enriched it as to both form and substance. But his contribution to this work lies above all in his supporting, sharing and always keeping fresh the belief that marriage and the family are not only worth writing about but also worth living. We have both had some help sustaining this belief from our daughters, Elizabeth Ann Glendon Lev, Sarah Pomeroy Lev and Katherine Glendon Lev.

Chestnut Hill, Massachusetts   Mary Ann Glendon
September 1976

TABLE OF CONTENTS

Table of Contents

LIST OF ABBREVIATIONS

Note on form and style of citations: The basic system of citation followed throughout is that of the rules developed by the Hamburg Max-Planck Institute for Foreign and International Private Law for the International Encyclopedia of Comparative Law. In cases not covered by these rules, American and English citations are in the form of the Uniform System of Citation (published by the Harvard Law Review Association), and French and West German citations are in the forms commonly used in those countries.
Translations: Translations of quoted material were made by the author except where otherwise indicated.

1. Frequently Cited Works

Bassett	Bassett, The Marriage of Christians – Valid Contract, Valid Sacrament?, in The Bond of Marriage. An Ecumenical and Inter-disciplinary Study 117 (W. Bassett ed. 1968).
Beitzke	G. Beitzke, Familienrecht (17th ed. 1974).
Bénabent	Bénabent, La liberté individuelle et le mariage, Rev.trim.dr.civ. 1973, 440.
Bouscaren & Ellis	T. Bouscaren & A. Ellis, Canon Law: A Text and Commentary (4th ed. 1963).
Brissaud	J. Brissaud, A History of French Private Law (R. Howell transl. 1912, orig. publ. 1904–1908).
Bromley	P. Bromley, Family Law (4th ed. 1971).
Carbonnier, Mémoire	Carbonnier, La question du divorce: mémoire à consulter, D.S. 1975. Chr. 115.
Carbonnier, 1 Droit civil	J. Carbonnier, 1 Droit civil (10th ed. 1974).
Carbonnier, 2 Droit civil	J. Carbonnier, 2 Droit civil (9th ed. 1972).
Carbonnier, Flexible droit	J. Carbonnier, Flexible droit (1971).
CACSW Report	Citizen's Advisory Council on the Status of Women, The Equal Rights Amendment and Alimony and Support Laws (Dept. of Labor, Washington, D.C. CACSW Item 23–N, 1972).
Clark CB	H. Clark, Domestic Relations. Cases and Problems (2d ed. 1974).

Clark HB	H. Clark, The Law of Domestic Relations (1968).
Cretney	S. Cretney, Principles of Family Law (1974).
Dörner	H. Dörner, Industrialisierung und Familienrecht: Die Auswirkungen des sozialen Wandels dargestellt an den Familienmodellen des ALR, BGB, und des französischen Code civil (1974).
Drinan	American Laws Regulating the Formation of the Marriage Contract, 38 Annals Am. Acad. Pol. & Soc. Sc. 48 (1969).
Eekelaar	Eekelaar, The Place of Divorce in Family Law's New Role, 38 Mod. L. Rev. 241 (1975).
Elston, Fuller & Murch	Elston, Fuller & Murch, Judicial Hearings of Undefended Divorce Petitions, 38 Mod. L. Rev. 609 (1975).
I Esmein	A. Esmein, Le mariage en droit canonique v. I (2nd ed. by Génestal 1929).
II Esmein	A. Esmein, Le mariage en droit canonique v. II (2nd ed. by Génestal & Dauvillier 1935).
Field of Choice	The Law Commission, Reform of the Grounds of Divorce: The Field of Choice (1966).
Finer Report	Report of the Committee on One-Parent Families (Finer Report), 2 vols., Cmnd. No. 5629 (1974).
Foster	Foster, Marriage: A "Basic Civil Right of Man," 37 Fordh. L. Rev. 51 (1968).
Foster & Freed, Divorce Reform	Foster & Freed, Divorce Reform: Brakes on Breakdown?, 13 J. Fam. L. 443 (1973–1974).
Foster & Freed, Unequal Protection	Foster & Freed, Unequal Protection: Poverty and Family Law, 42 Ind. L. J. 192 (1967).
Freed & Foster	Freed & Foster, Taking out the Fault but not the Sting, Trial Magazine, April 1976, 10.
Glendon, Separate Property	Glendon, Is there a Future for Separate Property?, 8 Fam. L. Q. 115 (1974).
Glendon, Family Power & Authority	Glendon, Power and Authority in the Family: New Legal Patterns as Reflections of Changing Ideologies, 23 Am. J. Comp. L. 1 (1975).
Goode	W. Goode, The Family (1964).
Gottlieb	B. Gottlieb, Getting Married in Pre-Reformation Europe: The Doctrine of Clandestine Marriage and Court Cases in Fifteenth-Century Champagne (unpubl. Ph.D. dissertation, Columbia University, 1974).

Helmholz	R. Helmholz, Marriage Litigation in Medieval England (1975).
Hübner	R. Hübner, A History of Germanic Private Law (Philbrick transl. 2d ed. 1918; orig. publ. 1913).
Hunt	D. Hunt, Parents and Children in History: The Psychology of Family Life in Early Modern France (1970).
Jeanmart	N. Jeanmart, Les effets civils de la vie commune en dehors du mariage (1975).
Jolowicz	H. Jolowicz, Historical Introduction to the Study of Roman Law (2d ed. 1967).
Kahn-Freund	Kahn-Freund, On Uses and Misuses of Comparative Law, 37 Mod. L. Rev. 1 (1974).
König	König, Sociological Introduction, in IV International Encyclopedia of Comparative Law Ch. 1 (A. Chloros ed. 1974).
Krause, Int. Encyc.	H. Krause, Illegitimacy, in IV International Encyclopedia of Comparative Law (A. Chloros ed. 1976).
Krause, Illegitimacy	H. Krause, Illegitimacy and Social Policy (1971).
Lindon	Lindon, La nouvelle legislation sur le divorce et le recouvrement public des pensions alimentaires, J.C.P. 1975. I. 2728.
Markovits	Markovits, Marriage and the State: A Comparative Look at East and West German Family Law, 24 Stan. L. Rev. 116 (1971).
Marty & Raynaud	G. Marty & R. Raynaud, I Droit Civil (2) (2d ed. 1967).
1 Mazeaud	1 H. & L. Mazeaud and J. Mazeaud, Leçons de droit civil v. 3 (M. Juglart ed. 1967).
4 Mazeaud	4 H. & L. Mazeaud and J. Mazeaud, Leçons de droit civil v. 1 (3d ed. 1969).
Müller-Freienfels, Ehe und Recht	W. Müller-Freienfels, Ehe und Recht (1962).
Müller-Freienfels, Equality	Müller-Freienfels, Equality of Husband and Wife in Family Law, 8 Int. & Comp. L. Q. 249 (1959).
Neuhaus	Neuhaus, Zur Reform des deutschen formellen Eheschliessungsrechts, FamRZ 1972, 59.
Noonan	Noonan, Novel 22, in the Bond of Marriage. An Ecumenical and Interdisciplinary Study 41 (W. Bassett ed. 1968).
Pollock & Maitland	II F. Pollock & F. Maitland, History of English Law (2nd ed. 1898, reprinted 1923).

Putting Asunder	Archbishop's Group, Putting Asunder: A Divorce Law for Contemporary Society, The Report of a Group Appointed by the Archbishop of Canterbury (1966).
Rheinstein, Family and Succession	Rheinstein, The Law of Family and Succession, in Civil Law in the Modern World 27 (A. Yiannopoulos ed. 1965).
Rheinstein, Int. Encyc.	Rheinstein, The Family and the Law, in IV International Encyclopedia of Comparative Law Ch.1 (A. Chloros ed. 1974).
Rheinstein, M.S.D.L.	M. Rheinstein, Marriage Stability, Divorce and the Law (1971).
Rheinstein, Willamette Symposium	Rheinstein, Division of Marital Property, 12 Willam. L. J. 413 (1976).
Rheinstein & Glendon, Decedents' Estates	M. Rheinstein & M. Glendon, The Law of Decedents' Estates (1971).
Rheinstein & Glendon, Int. Encyc.	M. Rheinstein & M. Glendon, Marriage: Interspousal Relations, in International Encyclopedia of Comparative Law Ch. 4 (A. Chloros ed., to be published in 1977).
Ripert & Boulanger	I. G. Ripert & J. Boulanger, Traité de droit civil (1956).
Ross & Sawhill	H. Ross & I. Sawhill, Time of Transition: The Growth of Families Headed by Women (1975).
Saint-Cyr	Saint-Cyr, De l'union libre au mariage à travers l'article 301 al. 1 du Code civil, D.S. 1975. Chr. 123.
Samuels	Samuels, Financial and Property Provision, 5 Fam. L. 6 (1975).
Schmidt (1963)	Schmidt, The "Leniency" of the Scandinavian Divorce Laws, Scand. Stud. L. 7 (1963) 107.
Schmidt (1971)	Schmidt, The Prospective Law of Marriage, Scand. Stud. L. 15 (1971) 191.
Stöcker	Stöcker, Zur Kritik des Familienvermögensrechts, NJW 1972, 553.
Stoljar	S. Stoljar, Children, Parents and Guardians, in IV International Encyclopedia of Comparative Law Ch. 7 (Chloros ed. 1973).
Sundberg, Louvain Report	Sundberg, Swedish Family Law, in *Actes des VIIIme Journées d'Etudes Juridiques Jean Dabin* (to be published in 1977).
Sundberg, Marriage or No Marriage	Sundberg, Marriage or No Marriage: The Directives for the Revision of Swedish Family Law, 20 Int. & Comp. L. Q. 223 (1971).
Sundberg, Nordic Laws	Sundberg, Nordic Laws, in Das Erbrecht von Familienangehörigen in positivrechtlicher und

	rechtspolitischer Sicht 31 (v. Caemmerer et al. eds. 1971).
Sundberg, Recent Changes	Sundberg, Recent Changes in Swedish Family Law; Experiment Repeated, 23 Am. J. Comp. L. 34 (1975).
Weber	M. Weber, Law in Economy and Society (M. Rheinstein ed. 1954).
Winch	Winch, Family Formation, in X International Encyclopedia of the Social Sciences 1 (1968).

2. Periodicals

A.B.A.J.	American Bar Association Journal
Am. J. Comp. L.	American Journal of Comparative Law
Anglo–Am. L. Rev.	Anglo–American Law Review
Ann.dr.	Annales de droit
Calif. L. Rev.	California Law Review
Corn. L. Rev.	Cornell Law Review
Curr. Dig. Sov. Press.	Current Digest of the Soviet Press
Curr. Leg. Prob.	Current Legal Problems
D.	Recueil Dalloz de doctrine, de jurisprudence et de legislation
D.H.	Dalloz. Recueil hebdomadaire de jurisprudence
D.S.	Recueil Dalloz Sirey
Gonz. L. Rev.	Gonzaga Law Review
Fam. Coord.	The Family Coordinator
Fam. L.	Family Law
Fam. L. Q.	Family Law Quarterly
FamRZ	Zeitschrift für das gesamte Familienrecht
Fordh. L. Rev.	Fordham Law Review
Gaz.Pal.	La Gazette du Palais
Ghana L. J.	Ghana Law Journal
Harv. L. Rev.	Harvard Law Review
Iowa L. Rev.	Iowa Law Review
Ind. L. J.	Indiana Law Journal
Int. & Comp. L. Q.	International and Comparative Law Quarterly
J. Fam. L.	Journal of Family Law
J. L. Reform	Journal of Law Reform
J. Leg. & Pol. Soc.	Journal of Legal & Political Sociology

J. Pol. Econ.	Journal of Political Economy
J.C.P.	Juris-Classeur Périodique (La Semaine Juridique)
JZ	Juristenzeitung
La. L. Rev.	Louisiana Law Review
L. & Contemp. Prob.	Law and Contemporary Problems
L.Q. Rev.	Law Quarterly Review
Mod. L. Rev.	Modern Law Review
New L. J.	New Law Journal
NJW	Neue Juristische Wochenschrift
N. Y. U. L. Rev.	New York University Law Review
Nw. U. L. Rev.	Northwestern University Law Review
Fam. L. Rptr.	Family Law Reporter
Ohio St. L. J.	Ohio State Law Journal
RabelsZ	Rabels Zeitschrift für ausländisches und internationales Privatrecht
Rev.fr.opin.pub.	Revue française de l'opinion publique
Rev.trim.dr.civ.	Revue trimestrielle de droit civil
Scand. Stud. L.	Scandinavian Studies in Law
Stan. L. Rev.	Stanford Law Review
Tex. L. Rev.	Texas Law Review
Tul. L. Rev.	Tulane Law Review
U. Chi. L. Rev.	University of Chicago Law Review
U. S. F. L. Rev.	University of San Francisco Law Review
Utah L. Rev.	Utah Law Review
Wash. L. Rev.	Washington Law Review
Yale L. J.	Yale Law Journal

3. Codes, Statutes and Collections of Judicial Decisions

A.2d	Atlantic Reporter, Second Series (West Publishing Co.)
BGBl.	Bundesgesetzblatt (Statute Book of the West German Federal Republic)
BVerfG	Bundesverfassungsgericht (West German Supreme Constitutional Court)

BVerwG	Bundesverwaltungsgericht (West German Supreme Administrative Court)
Cal. Rptr.	California Reporter (West Publishing Co.)
EheG	Ehegesetz (West German Marriage Law)
EheRG	Erstes Gesetz zur Reform des Ehe-und Familien-rechts (West German Marriage and Family Reform Law).
F.2d	Federal Reporter, Second Series (West Publishing Co.)
F. Supp.	Federal Supplement (West Publishing Co.)
Fam. L. Rptr.	Family Law Reporter (Bureau of National Affairs)
French C.C.	French Civil Code
French Penal C.	French Penal Code
GleichberG.	Gesetz über die Gleichberechtigung von Mann und Frau auf dem Gebiet des bürgerlichen Rechts of 18 June 1957 (West German Sex Equality Law)
German C.C.	West German Civil Code (Bürgerliches Gesetzbuch of 18 August 1896)
J.O.	Journal Officiel de la République Française. Lois et Décrets. (Statutes and Decrees of the French Republic).
KRABl.	Amstblatt des Kontrollrats in Deutschland (Ordinance Book of the Allied Control Council in Germany).
N.E.2d	North Eastern Reporter, Second Series (West Publishing Co.)
N.W.2d	North Western Reporter, Second Series (West Publishing Co.)
N.Y.S.2d	New York Supplement, Second Series (West Publishing Co.)
P.2d	Pacific Reporter, Second Series (West Publishing Co.)
PStG	Personenstandgesetz (West German Civil Status Law)
Prussian General C.	Prussian General Code of 1794 (Allgemeines Landrecht für die Preussischen Staaten)
RGBl.	Reichsgesetzblatt (Statute Book of the German Reich until 1945)
S.W.2d	South Western Reporter, Second Series (West Publishing Co.)

StGB	Strafgesetzbuch (West German Penal Code)
UMDA	National Conference of Commissioners on Uniform State Laws, Uniform Marriage and Divorce Act of 1970 (with 1971 and 1973 amendments)
U.S.	United States Supreme Court Reports (U.S. Govt. Printing Office)

LEGAL AND SOCIAL INSTITUTIONS

I. Legal and Social Change

Beginning in the middle 1960s, there has been an unparalleled upheaval in the family law systems of Western industrial societies. Legal norms which had been relatively undisturbed for centuries have been discarded or radically altered in the areas of marriage law, divorce law, the legal effects of marriage and divorce, the legal relationship of parent and child and the status of illegitimate children. At the same time, through other areas of law, not ordinarily thought of as "family law", such as public assistance, social security and tax laws, the State has come into increasing contact with aspects of everyday family life, and has assumed a number of functions formerly performed by the family. The process of change continues. Taken together, these legal changes reveal a significant change in the posture of the State with respect to the family as expressed through law, that is, through that set of norms for regulating human conduct which are sanctioned by governmental action. This change equals and surpasses in magnitude that which occurred when family law matters passed from ecclesiastical to secular jurisdiction in most Western countries in the age that began with the Protestant Reformation. The change is characterized by progressive withdrawal of legal regulation of marriage formation, dissolution and the conduct of married life, on the one hand, and by increased regulation of the economic and child-related consequences of formal or informal cohabitation on the other.

Striking as they are, these legal changes are themselves but an aspect of the fact that society itself is in flux. Changes in the nature of wealth and property, changes in the economic and social roles of women, increased longevity and the ease and availability of contraception, are just some of the factors which have had an effect on the seemingly eternal yet ever-changing institution of the family and its frequent concomitant, the more polymorphous and changeable institution of marriage. What seems to distinguish the events of the present period from that process of change in marriage and family behavior which has taken place continually in the past is the rapidity with which the roles of the sexes, the relations of the age groups, the marriage relation, the structure of the family and the bases of society itself are being transformed.

This book will explore, on a comparative basis, the processes of legal and social change in various areas of private and public family law, and the gradual but radical change that is consequently taking place in the relationship of the State to the family, with special emphasis on the laws of England, France, the United States and the Federal Republic of Germany. The legal changes in each of these countries will be examined in their immediate social (using this word to include economic and political) context. Where appropriate and helpful in illuminating developments in the principal countries under discussion, recent changes in the law of other Western countries will be mentioned.

But beyond the effort to describe the current legal evolution in its social context, this book will also attempt to locate this evolution within its historical context. It is through bringing a historical, as well as the comparative legal, perspective to the current period of rapid and profound change in laws affecting the family that the relation of the current period to the whole process of juridification of family relationships can be illuminated, and the true nature of the present set of changes revealed.

Before embarking on such an all-encompassing study, however, it is essential to call to mind Max Weber's observation that enacted legal norms are only one mode of regulation of conduct in the social order, one which has appeared on a large scale rather late in history as a characteristic component of that process of rationalization and consociation which has gradually penetrated all aspects of social life.[1] It is a mode, as Weber pointed out, whose effectiveness varies greatly. Most of this book is concerned with changes in those elaborate sets of enacted legal norms which make up the family law of England, France, the United States and West Germany. A study of these changes will, however, cause us to wonder how norms of enacted law came to regulate marriage and family matters once governed only by other social norms, for example, those of convention, custom, ethics, or religion. When this question is answered, we will have a clear view of what is actually happening in the evolution of Western laws affecting the family. Such a perspective on our current situation is impossible to achieve without tracing the process of juridification from the struggle of the Christian church to establish the principle of indissolubility of marriage, to the State's eventual assumption by default after the Reformation in most countries, not only of the task of regulating marriage and family matters, but also of that elaborate set of canon law rules which has remained the basis of Western family law systems until the current period of change set in.

While this book will be primarily concerned with the sets of formally enacted legal norms which make up the family law of each country, it is essential to begin by remembering that in these societies, as in every society, there is and always has been a set of *de facto* family relationships which can never exactly correspond to the set of enacted norms and which has borne more resemblance to the legally enacted norms at some times than it has at others. In fact, one way of viewing the current period is as one of intense change in the content of both of these sets, and in their relationship to each other. Different from, but related to, these changes which are presently occurring in the laws affecting the family and in the behavior which makes up the social institution of the family itself, is still another sort of change. This involves the *ideas* which are widely held about the legal and social institutions of marriage and the family. It is from this process of interaction among legal, social and ideological change, that a major shift has begun to emerge in the posture of the State with respect to the family as expressed through its laws.

The purpose of this first chapter is to prepare the mind for the type of inquiry this book seeks to conduct. We must start by distinguishing clearly for analytical purposes between the institutions which a particular legal system may classify as "families" or "marriage" and that type of social conduct which an anthropologist or sociologist might call family or marriage behavior. To identify even the legal institutions of family and marriage is, as we shall see, by no means an easy task, since within a single system these terms are often variously employed for different purposes. But the task is vastly more difficult when it comes to identifying what constitutes family or marriage behavior in society. One can, however, make certain general observations. Family and marriage are pre-legal institutions. They were not invented by, but are inherent in the human species, although not peculiar to it. Law-makers dealing with these institutions can only act through linguistic formulation and systematic summary of behavior which is to a large extent unconscious.[2] This process has often resulted in the production of legal norms which are "ideal types", not only in Weber's sense of theoretical abstractions from reality, but in the sense of values which may or may not correspond to underlying social reality.[3]

Although, intuitively, based on our individual experiences, we may tend to think of marriage as preceding the family, in fact it is the family which is the primary institution.[4] Some form of the family, as a discrete group within the horde, can be found in all human, and many animal societies. However, marriage, in the sense of a highly individualized heterosexual relation, is said to be barely visible in the simplest human cultures, the hunter-and-food gatherer societies.[5] It is useful, especially in contemporary society where marriage does not necessarily involve procreation, to distinguish for theoretical purposes between the family as a social group which includes more persons than the marriage partners (if any), and marriage, which may or may not coincide with the existence of a family.[6]

The fact that the family is the primary institution does not exclude the fact that the family has existed in a variety of forms. Indeed, it seems that no society known to us has had only one family type.[7] On the other hand, the range of family types and, for that matter, of the forms of marriage has not been very wide.[8] Yet the fact that the range has not been wide, has not precluded a constant process of change which results in the development and emergence of family forms new at least to the societies in which they emerge.[9] But this process of change is slow, slower in the case of family forms than it is for marriage forms.[10]

To find and keep the thread through the mass of detail that lies ahead, it is essential to keep in mind the distinction between legal and social phenomena, between the institutions described and elaborated in the enacted law, and marriage and family behavior in the underlying society. To this end, we begin this book with a series of meditations on social and legal institutions. These three introductory subsections have been characterized as meditations because they are contemplative in nature, designed to invite reflection about the problems to be treated by this book and to prepare us for the kind of analysis that will be necessary if we are to find our way through the complex legal and social phenomena dealt with here. First there is a schematic meditation; then a meditation on a play by John M. Synge which raises most of the problems treated in Chapters 2 and 3 of this book; and, finally, a historical meditation on the law of Italy.

II. Legal and Social Institutions: Three Meditations

A. Legal Marriage and Marriage-Like Institutions

Let there be a set of men and women married to each other according to the rules of the legal system to which they are subject. Call this Set A. Now let there be a set of men and women cohabiting with each other in unions entered with some idea of duration and openly manifested to the relevant community. Call this Set B.

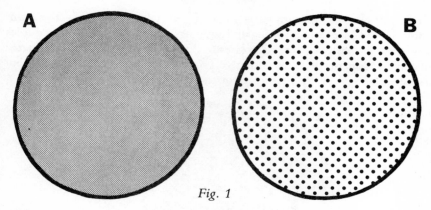

Fig. 1

Note that in Set A marriage is whatever the legal system says it is.[11] The contents of Set B call for more lengthy comment. In constructing Set B as the set of heterosexual unions which are undertaken with some idea of duration and in which the partners attest formally or informally to the relevant social environment (relatives, neighborhood, clan, community, sib, or society at large) that they consider themselves as belonging together, I have attempted to include within it behavior that a sociologist or anthropologist might describe as "marriage behavior".[12] The element of intended duration does not mean that the unions in Set B are necessarily permanent or even enduring, nor, as this set is constructed, need the unions it contains be sexually exclusive or even monogamous. I am here following the family sociologist René König in using the factors of intended duration and attestation to help to get over the difficulty of defining what turns a sexual relation into "marriage".[13] It must be acknowledged, however, that the imprecision of these terms leaves some cases that will be hard to classify. Thus constructed, Set B includes a wide variety of formal and informal unions, some of which are recognized by the legal system and some not.

Now notice, that while it will be useful, and indeed essential, for us to distinguish in theory between the set of *de jure* marriages on the one hand and the set of *de facto* marriages or marriage-like behavior on the other in the countries which will be the principal objects of our study, the two sets overlap (see Fig. 2).

The intersect of Sets A and B is the set of *de facto* unions which are stamped as legal marriages by the State, which in modern Western societies is the social control organization with a juridical monopoly of marriage and divorce. The part of Set A which does not intersect with Set B contains those men and women between whom a legal marriage bond exists, but who are not in a *de facto* union with each other. In everyday experience, then, this would include separated but legally undivorced couples and those couples between whom the *de facto* union but not the legal bond has been terminated by what was once called "poor man's divorce", i.e. absenting oneself without procuring a legal death certificate for the marriage.

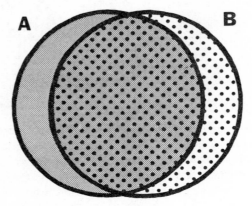

Fig. 2

That part of Set B which does not intersect with Set A, includes all those *de facto* unions as defined above which are not recognized as legal marriages by the legal system. In everyday experience in the countries under consideration, this would include cohabitation without compliance with the formalities established by the State for formation of a legal marriage, both by those who have no interest for one reason or another in complying with formalities, and by those who are not eligible for one reason or other to comply. In this group, for example, we would commonly find those cohabitants, chiefly young, who find that legal marriage, at least at their stage of life, has no advantages to offer them, and those cohabitants who are prevented from forming a legal marriage because of the existence of a prior undissolved legal marriage of one or both of them.[14] Set B would also include persons cohabiting after religious marriages not recognized as legally valid by the State, for example, in countries like France and West Germany where civil marriage is compulsory.

Actually, in the four countries whose law will be examined in this book, the overlap between Sets A and B is considerable, as the diagram above in rough fashion indicates. Most marriage behavior still takes place within the framework of legal marriage. Ease of divorce helps keep that part of Set A which does not intersect with Set B small. But as to that part of Set B which does not intersect with Set A, *de facto* but non-legal unions, there seems to be a recent increase, as we will see in Chapter 3. This change does not mean that all forms of cohabitation meet with social approval, but the borderlines between sexual conduct which is socially approved and that which is disapproved are in flux.

The fact that, increasingly, a great deal of marriage behavior in Western societies has ceased to be oriented to legal norms has become so much a readily observable fact of life in recent years, that it is perhaps hardly necessary to point out that the content of Sets A and B and their relation to each other vary from time to time and from place to place. How wide these variations can be becomes even more apparent when we step out of our immediate historical and cultural context.

In Western Europe prior to the Reformation, for example, there was *no* Set A of legal bonds created in compliance with secular norms of the State.[15] Rather, we would have to speak of those marriages recognized as such by the norms established by other social control organizations, chiefly those of canon law. When the State first assumed jurisdiction of matrimonial causes, it simply applied ecclesiastical norms. Even today, many men and women in England, France, the United States or West Germany, consider themselves subject to the systems of law of the Church of England, the Roman Catholic Church or to Islamic or Jewish law although these systems are now independent of the State, and their law of marriage is not recognized by the State, except to a limited degree in England. For such persons, for whom marriage is not, as it was for Luther, "a worldly thing", it becomes relevant to construct a Set C, the set of marriage bonds established according to the law of the religious group of one or both parties, a set which overlaps but does not precisely coincide with the sets of legal and *de facto* marriages (Fig. 3).

In countries where religious family law is still important, such as Egypt, Israel, or India, it is not normally the case that legal regulation of marriage coincides only accidentally with religious regulation. We are accustomed in the West to systems of direct marriage regulation through legally enacted norms of the State. But this is no more the universal mode of regulation in the world today, than it was the mode of regulation in the European past. In the modern world, where pluralistic societies pose acute problems of which behavior patterns and value judgments ought to be enshrined in the law, it is useful to distinguish, as Max Rheinstein does, between the *Occidental* and *Oriental* patterns of regulation of family matters.[16] In that *Occidental* pattern which is familiar to Americans and Europeans, the effort has been made to fashion legal rules which correspond to the ideas or behavior which are common to all the groups and subgroups of which the society is composed, or, which increasingly do no more than define the limits of permissible diversity within which individual choice may be exercised.

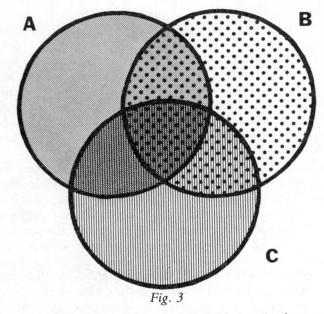

Fig. 3

That response to pluralism in society which Rheinstein characterizes as the *Oriental* pattern of regulation leaves the marriage and family relations of each member of each of the definable groups in society to be governed by the religious or customary law of that group. Thus, in many African and Asian countries, as well as in Israel, such matters as marriage and divorce are regulated by norms or Hindu, Islamic, Jewish, or other religious, or customary or tribal law, depending on one's group affiliation.[17] In these *Oriental* systems, Set A *includes* Set C, plus the customary laws of definable groups following their own well-defined patterns.

It is important to notice, however, that the *Oriental* pattern of marriage regulation is today tending to become a mode of legal regulation exercised by the *State*, albeit in an indirect fashion. It thus stands in contrast, together with the *Occidental* mode, to the situation in which the State does not regulate marriage at all: where, in other words, Set A is the empty set.

This empty set is not merely a theoretical construction. One need not reach back through the mists of time to eras when the State in the modern sense did not exist in order to produce examples of societies in which marriage and family matters have been left completely to regulation by norms of convention, custom, ethics or religion. As we will see in Chapter 7, this was the state of affairs in pre-Reformation Europe. It was largely the state of affairs in Roman times. It was, briefly, the situation which existed in the Soviet Union under the 1926 Family Code of the Russian Republic. One of the major concerns of this book can be stated as the inquiry whether or not the direction of the current period of change in the family law of all or some of the countries to be examined here is toward the emptying of the set of legal marriage relationships. Is it true, as a Swedish family law expert has said, that legal developments in his country have been marked by the disappearance of a positive interest in marriage as an institution?[18] If so, has Sweden, as has so often been the case in family law up to now, marked out the course which other Western countries sooner or later will follow?

This is one of the questions this book will address. But before leaving this schematic introduction three final observations are in order. First, it should be kept in mind that the same kind of distinctions here drawn on the theoretical plane among marriage, *de facto* marriage, and unions recognized as "marriages" under religious or customary laws, can also be developed for other institutions which are both legal and social. Thus, for example, later on, it will be important to distinguish among legal divorce, *de facto* termination of "marriage" and religious or customary termination of marriage bonds recognized by religious or customary law. Second, as we examine the effect of rapidly changing mores upon older legal norms, we will notice that as the legal set falls more and more out of correspondence with actual marriage behavior in society the outlines of a "shadow institution" within the set of *de facto* unions become more and more discernible. This "shadow institution" differentiates itself from other *de facto* unions by its resemblance to the prevalent type of legal marriage in all but the formalities required for its creation. It increases in extent and importance to the point where the legal system one way or another must take account of it and where the relationship among the sets is profoundly altered. Finally, besides the distinction here developed between marriage as a legal institution and marriage as a social institution, it will be useful throughout this book to keep in mind another distinction, one lying entirely within the realm of legal regulation, the distinction in legal effect between the status of being married and the status of being unmarried. Here, too, we will see that far-reaching changes are taking place.

B. What is Marriage?

The title of this section does not really await an answer, but rather a reformulation of the question along the lines suggested by the preceding schematic subsection. It is illuminating to attempt this exercise in the context of a one-act play by John M. Synge called *The Tinker's Wedding*.[19]

Consider the following facts: Michael Byrne and Sarah Casey are tinkers, gypsy-like travelling menders of metal household utensils. Their association began one day at Rathvanna, when Michael hit Sarah "a great clout in the lug", after which she came along with him "quiet and easy...from that hour to this present day". By the time the action of the play takes place Sarah has been "going beside [him] a great while, and rearing a lot of them". The action is set in motion by Sarah's sudden, firm and persistent demand, backed up by a threat of leaving, that she and Michael be married by a priest. We can infer from their spirited and affectionate banter that Sarah's demand is not a reaction to any trouble which has arisen between Michael and herself. Besides, we are told she is "thriving, and getting [her] good health by the grace of the Almighty God". As the play opens, Michael has already agreed to give in to Sarah's desire for a wedding, although he does not understand it, and he is putting the finishing touches on her wedding ring. Thus all that remains to do is to find a priest and get married.

But things are not so easily arranged. A priest is found, but he summarily rejects the request of the tinkers that he marry them for no fee and give them a bit of silver into the bargain to pay for the ring. He will, however, make them a special price of one pound. Even after prolonged bargaining, his final offer is 10 shillings and a gallon can which Michael has almost finished making, such a little sum as, the priest says, "wouldn't marry a child". He is unmoved by the tinkers' claim of poverty, unkindly pointing out that the tinkers are reputed to steal "east and west in Wicklow and Wexford and the County Meath". The deal is struck and the appointment made for the next day. But alas, during the night the temptation overcomes Michael's old mother, Mary, to exchange the can at the local pub in order to get a "pint for her sleep". She puts a couple of old bottles in the sack which contained the can so as to put off the moment of reckoning with Sarah. When the priest opens the sack the next day and finds the bottles he thinks that Michael and Sarah have tried to deceive him. He flatly refuses to marry them for ten shillings without the can. After increasingly harsh words are exchanged, the play ends with the priest thrown into a ditch, with Sarah's wedding ring placed on his finger. Michael's mother, who feels a little guilty about things – but not too guilty – has the last word: "[I]t's a long time we are going our own ways – father and son and his son after him, or mother and daughter and her own daughter again – and it's little need we ever had of going up into a church and swearing."

There are a number of interesting questions to ask of this little tale. It is Sarah's desire to get "married" which precipitates the action. But are not Michael and Sarah already married? Mary's concluding observation suggests that Michael and Sarah were in fact married according to the long-standing customs of the subculture of tinkers. It seems that when Michael "got" Sarah at Rathvanna the two intended their union would be of some duration, and it is clear from the play that their union was openly attested to the relevant community – that of tinkers. Michael's account of how he "got" Sarah is reminiscent of description by anthropologists of "marriage by capture", but as René König points out, it seems correctly, capture is not really a form of marriage but rather a form of "wedding".[20] Thus, from a sociologist's or anthropologist's point of view, the "Tinker's Wedding" may actually have taken place when Michael hit Sarah a clout in the lug and carried her off. If one can say that the union of Michael and Sarah constituted behavior which a sociologist, if not a lawyer, might call "marriage", is this the only sense in which they are married? In Ireland, at the time of the play, that is under the Act of Union in force from 1802 to 1921, if Michael and Sarah were married in the eyes of the Church, then they were married in the eyes of the State. There is no doubt that Michael and Sarah would have been married in the eyes of the early Church since, until the Council of Trent made the presence of a priest mandatory in 1563, Christians, like other people, could form marriages simply by exchanging consents and cohabiting.[21] But the decree of the Council of Trent may not have been applicable to Michael and Sarah. In the first place it applied only to marriages of *baptized* persons. Yet the priest in Synge's play repeatedly refers to the "heathen" state of the tinkers and at one point says explicitly, "I'm thinking you were never christened, Sarah Casey". If, in fact, Michael and Sarah were never christened, then their marital status under canon law has nothing to do with the Council of Trent. In the view of the Church, marriage is a natural as well as a supernatural institution. Thus, under canon law, marriages between unbaptized persons are fully valid, provided the crucial element of consent exists.[22] Second, even where the Tridentine formalities are required, the Church has not insisted on the priest's presence if compliance would present "grave inconvenience".[23] Grave inconvenience, it is said, can arise from poverty.[24]

Why then, if Michael and Sarah are already married in one or two senses of the word, should it be of importance to the State, to the Church, or to the parties, that another "wedding" should take place and that they should be "married" in another sense? If we ask this question from the point of view of the State and the Church, we fall upon a point of great significance for our inquiry into current processes of legal and social change. In the case of Michael and Sarah, tinkers in Ireland at the turn of the century, the answer is clear that neither the State nor the Church had much interest in their marital status. They belong to what Max Rheinstein has called the "neglected groups" of society and the law.[25] Rheinstein has pointed out that historically family law has paid little attention to the concerns of the poor and of such ethnic minority groups as the Indians of Latin America or the Afro-Americans of the United States. So far as the common law of England was concerned, propertyless individuals came to the attention of the legal system principally as objects of the criminal law. As Rheinstein correctly observes, one of the great trends which is presently transforming the law of the family is that of paying increasing attention to the needs and demands of hitherto neglected groups. But we are running ahead of our story. Suffice it to say here that Synge's priest makes it clear that he considers tinkers to be outside the scope of his sphere of action and interest and that in fact he is as puzzled about why Sarah wants to get "married" as are Michael and his mother. He considers them different from "my own pairs living here in the place". When, during their haggling over the price of the wedding, Sarah begins to cry at the thought that she will never get married, the priest remarks in a surprised fashion, "It's a queer woman you are to be crying at the like of that, and you your whole life walking the roads." Later he muses, "It would be a queer job to go dealing Christian sacraments unto the like of you."

When we turn to the question of why Sarah, a member of a neglected group, with its own customary way of marrying, seeks nevertheless to be married in some other sense, we have a number of theories to choose from. But the theory which probably would be the first suggested in similar circumstances today can be rejected immediately. Certainly Sarah has no thought of improving her economic position or "legitimizing"[26] her children through bringing herself within the framework of legal rights and duties attaching to marriage. Nor does Synge, who spent four years in the West of Ireland absorbing its culture, give us the slightest indication that Sarah thought marriage by a priest was somehow related to the salvation of her immortal soul. Rather, it seems that she is concerned about the social approval of groups other than tinkers. After she is "married", the thinks, "there will be no one have a right to call me a dirty name and I selling cans in Wicklow or Wexford or the city of Dublin itself". But it is Mary Byrne who sums it all up, inspired no doubt by the necessity of putting the best light on the situation which she herself has brought about. To Michael, still fearful about Sarah's earlier threat to leave him if he doesn't "marry" her, she says, "And you're thinking it's paying gold to his reverence would make a woman stop when she's a mind to go?" To Sarah, who has already begun to waver, the rough boozy old woman suddenly falls for the first time into a gentle tone: "It's as good a right you have surely, Sarah Casey, but what good will it do? Is it putting that ring on your finger will keep you from getting an aged woman and losing the fine face you have, or be easing your pain?" At the end of the play, Sarah's idea of getting married is left in the ditch, together with the priest and the wedding ring. Why would a poor tinker, married and wedded in custom and the eyes of God, want in addition to be married by an official? It must, suggests Synge, have been the "changing of the moon"....

C. Law and Behavior: Rome and Modern Italy

A book about family law has, even more so perhaps than books in other areas of law, to face the problem of whether and to what extent enacted legal norms can have an effect on the social conduct they purport to regulate.[27] Certainly it is easier to see the legal norms as emerging from the widespread practices of dominant groups than it is to discern the effect these norms may have on behavior. Max Rheinstein's study of divorce law and marriage stability in a number of countries[28] has so firmly put an end to the idea that a strict divorce law can assure marriage stability in a given society or that a lenient divorce law causes marriage instability, that his conclusions, which went against widely-held beliefs at the time he was conducting his study, have now passed into the general consciousness.

History, as well as contemporary society, furnishes abundant examples of the resistance of certain types of behavior to regulation by edict. That Assuerus, who, according to the Book of Esther, established as the unalterable Law of the Medes and the Persians that the husband is the head of the household, is thought by some to be none other than the same Xerxes who sent out his soldiers with whips to beat the stormy sea into submission.[29] Yet one cannot say that enacted norms have *no* effect on behavior. There is, in fact, a reciprocal interaction whose character varies from time to time and place to place, the exploration of which is one of the tasks that lies ahead of us, and which, while latent throughout this book, comes to the surface in Chapter 7. But like the man in the nursery rhyme who had to scratch out his eyes and then scratch them in again to be able to see with a new vision (to use the image beloved by the late Karl Llewellyn), we cannot approach these obviously very difficult problems of the reflexive effect of law on behavior without first appreciating how stubbornly the form of behavior involved in family law follows its own patterns independently of what the legal system says it should be doing. Reflecting upon a thousand years of marriage in what is now Italy helps us to do this. Only the bare outlines of the Italian experience will be described here, for the story is but a fragment of the account of the evolution of Roman Law, canon law and secular law which forms the subject of Chapter 7.[30]

In the later Roman Republic and in Imperial Rome, one can say that "[M]arriage was to the Romans, as to the other peoples of antiquity, a *de facto* rather than a *de jure* matter, in the sense that two people were held to be married, not because they had gone through any particular ceremony, but because they in fact lived together as man and wife."[31] It was usual, it seems, for these marriages to begin with a ceremony of some sort: in Rome, instead of getting a clout in the lug, the bride might be lifted over the threshold of the bridegroom's house and presented with gifts of fire and water. Just as marriage began with the setting up of life in common, so it ended when the community of life was broken by either spouse. Divorce was entirely free to either party and, by the end of the late republic, we are told that it had become common, at least among the upper social classes (the only sectors of Roman society of which we have knowledge).[32] The conclusion of a Roman marriage was not a legal transaction. It was a factual event which, of course, had legal consequences.

Even after the conversion of Constantine, matters did not change quickly. "Full freedom to terminate a marriage was a rule so firmly rooted in the mores that it took centuries of Christian effort to replace it by the new principle of indissolubility."[33] For one thing, as we shall see in Chapter 7, it took some time for this doctrine to be settled in the teaching of the Church itself. At first, the post-Constantine legislation did no more than threaten to punish a husband who repudiated his wife without cause. The effort by Justinian in 542 A.D. to extend these penalties to divorce by mutual consent was so unpopular that it was repealed by his successor Justin II in 566 shortly after his ascension to the throne of the Byzantine empire.[34] Marriage became indissoluble only when, after centuries of effort, the Church gained jurisdiction over matrimonial causes for its courts. Once the Church's jurisdiction was established in the various states and kingdoms which covered the area of present-day Italy, the principle of the indissolubility of marriage became the legal norm (except for the brief period of Napoleonic rule) until December, 1970. All through the long period of legal indissolubility, however, it seems that many Italians followed the age-old custom of dissolving their unions by departure, not even bothering to take advantage of the possibility of divorce briefly introduced by French laws imposed in the course of Napoleon's conquest. By 1958, in connection with efforts at divorce law reform, estimates tended to show that the number of married couples in Italy whose life together had in fact ended was about 600,000, and that about a million inhabitants of Italy were living in irregular unions, in which one or both were legally married to someone other than the *de facto* spouse. In 1969, a report was presented to the Italian chamber of deputies which stated there were then 1,160,000 separated couples in Italy. Many of these involved the so-called "white widows" whose husbands were working in other European countries. The number of free unions, while not known, was believed to involve as many as 4 million Italians, if children of these unions were counted. Thus for a long period it seems that *unioni libere* were as well established in Italy as the principle (if not the practice) of indissolubility of marriage.

The strict Italian divorce law of 1970 is hardly a return to the legal state of affairs that prevailed in Roman times. But it does seem to be an effort to conform the law to behavior and to bring *de facto* situations within the law.

Just as *The Tinker's Wedding* raises some interesting questions about legal and social institutions, this brief history (whose development must await Chapter 7) raises a number of interesting questions about the reciprocal interaction of law, behavior, and ideas. How did the ideas of indissolubility and ceremonial marriage become established in canon law in the first place? How did canon law succeed in securing, to the extent that it did, general acceptance, if not general practice, of these ideas? If the ideal of indissolubility thus enshrined in religious and secular law was out of correspondence with actual Italian marriage behavior, why was it so difficult to secure the acceptance of the new legal principle of limited dissolubility? Is there any reason why the ideal enshrined by the law should conform to whatever form or forms of behavior are widespread in society? Or, to the contrary, does the State or society have an interest perhaps in maintaining legal symbolism which does *not* correspond to reality? Do individuals have an interest in the maintenance of such symbolism? What is the relationship of politics and ideas to family law and behavior, and vice versa? At the end of this book a few notes toward the answers to these questions are made. At this point the questions are posed, in the context of the Italian developments, just to start a train of thought which will be picked up again and again in the succeeding chapters.

III. Method and Plan of Presentation

One thing will grow plain when compared with another: and blind night shall not obliterate the path for thee, before thou hast thoroughly scanned the ultimate things of nature; so much will things throw light on things.

Lucretius, *De Rerum Natura*, I.
1115–1118. (Translation by
George Santayana).[35]

It is the intention of this book to take advantage of the opportunity for comparative analysis offered by the present period of legal, social and ideological change, albeit with full awareness of the hazards of trying to analyze change while the midst of it, and the danger of being misled into seeing as trends what may be merely fashions of the moment. A safe way of proceeding might be to concentrate on those movements which are already advanced enough to have given rise to clearly discernible patterns and which have already transformed much of the law of England, France, the United States and West Germany, such as the modernization of the divorce laws and the implementation of the principle of sex equality. But the course to be pursued here is a riskier one. While the well-known, sweeping changes wrought by the acceptance of the ideas of no-fault divorce and equal rights have been occupying the center of the stage, hundreds of little changes, involving every aspect of the way the legal system affects the family, have been taking place in the statutes and judicial decisions of all these countries Underneath all, hard to measure and even harder to compare with the past, are of course the never-ending processes of gradual change in marriage behavior; and, still more gradual, change in family behavior; and the fluctuations in the way people think about marriage and the family. In spite of the dangers and difficulties involved, this book will attempt to take a close look at this mass of seemingly discrete phenomena, these small changes perhaps unimportant in and of themselves, to see whether changes in the molecules of the system may not be producing structural changes with far-reaching consequences.

Thus, Chapters 2 through 6 of this book are concerned with a description of this process of molecular change in the four countries whose law will be the principal subject of analysis, with references where appropriate to certain developments in other West European countries. These chapters deal first with legal and social changes affecting family or family-like relationships between individuals; then with changes in the legal relationships among individuals and families and organs of the State. Then, in Chapter 7, the current period of change is viewed in the context of what has gone before. That is, present legal developments are related to the whole process of juridification of marriage. Once this relationship is made clear, certain distinctive features of the present relationship of the State to the family stand out. Finally, in Chapter 7, we return to the questions which have been posed at the outset, in the belief that the study here conducted, while it cannot answer them, can contribute some ideas toward the solution of those puzzles of law and behavior which they express.

This method or presentation corresponds to the way in which the idea for this book took shape. During eight years of collaboration with Professor Max Rheinstein of the University of Chicago Law School, first on a book concerning the law of succession, then on a chapter of the International Encyclopedia of Comparative Law concerning the property and personal relationships of those persons whom the various legal systems consider to be married to one another, the author was immersed in the minutiae of those legal changes which, in the 1970s, have transformed legal patterns which were centuries old. Out of this process of immersion in detail came the conviction that comparative and historical analysis throws into relief certain trends which are not readily perceptible when current developments in one system alone are examined. The conviction came, further, that the transformation of family law is related to the transformation of the nature of property and forms of wealth and to the "statization", if it may be so called, of family functions, in ways to which attention has not yet been sufficiently drawn. Finally, as the title of this book indicates, it is believed that, overall, the process has already resulted in a change of the relationship of the State to the family that in future times will be seen as a turning point of major significance.

Obviously, it is not possible to make an exhaustive catalog of all legal changes affecting the family in the past twenty, or even in the past two, years in one country, let alone four. Some selection must be made. Thus, I have gathered here those developments which seem to be the most striking and suggestive, both those which are of the *lex lata*, the existing law, and those which are of the *lex ferenda*, the law which may or may not be in the making. In the latter group are included not only the principal law reform proposals but the currents coming from the learned writing. So far as the *lex lata* is concerned, the inquiry does not neglect the more highly visible trends, but through examination of surrounding less well-known changes, it presents such phenomena as the change in divorce laws, the elimination of legal distinctions between legitimate and illegitimate children, and the thrust toward sex equality in a new light. While the central concern of this book is the changing relationship of the State to the family, the most significant aspects of this change appear in connection with marriage. Therefore, legal developments affecting marriage are the principal topics treated here.

IV. Uses and Misuses of Comparative Law

I have borrowed this title from Professor Otto Kahn-Freund,[36] first, to call attention to some of the peculiar difficulties which are involved in making comparisons among legal systems, particularly among family law systems, and second, to point out why in spite of these difficulties the comparison is worth making.

In any comparative legal study, the hazards can be summed up in one word: context. To understand a legal rule in any system, one must have some understanding of its social and economic background and its practical consequences in operation.[37] Thus, no matter how carefully limited the scope of a project may be, one runs the risk of missing real functional similarities and differences unless one compares not only the rules themselves, but their social context and the manner in which they actually operate within their surrounding legal systems.[38] To what extent, for example, do various procedural devices make a particular substantive legal rule difficult to apply, or extend its application beyond those cases which the wording of the rule itself suggests?[39] To what extent do general social norms make it practically difficult for a clearly expressed legal sanction to be applied?

In addition to these difficulties at the practical level, there is always the more complex problem of determining the proper subjects for comparison. Social problems and conditions within a system are hard to identify, and too hastily "naming" a condition may distort reality or produce the illusion that a problem has been solved.[40] It may be that the social and economic contexts of a particular problem are not really comparable, raising questions about the validity of comparisons or the utility of models from one system for another. Also, the policy aims of the systems one is attempting to compare may be different.

All of these problems can be aggravated when the field of legal comparison involves family law, rather than, let us say, commercial law. But comparison is both feasible and desirable in the four countries dealt with here. Despite some differences, they are at broadly comparable stages of social and economic development. They are variants of the same culture. Basically their family law is responding to the same needs and problems. What differences there are to a considerable extent are the results and appearances of somewhat different legal techniques and somewhat different constellations of political forces. Furthermore, differences among the marriage and divorce laws of the four countries have been steadily reduced during the last two decades.

Kahn-Freund lists a number of factors which show the diminishing strength of obstacles to family law comparison in developed countries:[41] gradual cultural assimilation as exemplified by the fact, for example, that people in London, Munich, New York and Paris read the same kind of newspapers and weekly news magazines, watch similar (or the same) television programs and worship the same pop heroes; gradual economic assimilation in the sense that people in developed countries earn their living in ways almost indistinguishable from one country to another and that their manner of spending their earnings follows similar patterns owing to the evolution of trade, mass production and advertising; the ease with which people move from place to place; and the emergence of similar legal problems with respect to employment and housing. One might add to this list the apparently declining influence of formal religion, the apparent increase in family disorganization and the fact that, in the four countries with which we are primarily concerned here, the labor force participation rates of women are within a few percentage points of each other, symbolic of the change in sex roles and in family structure that is taking place.

Obviously the ease and utility of comparisons are increased, the more closely these various environmental factors resemble each other in the countries to be compared. Thus a comparison among the four countries to be treated here is easier in some ways than a comparison of any one of them would be with a country where political factors are sharply different, either where the political influence of organized Catholicism has been as great as in Ireland, Italy, Portugal, and Spain,[42] or where the system of family law has been influenced by the thought of August Bebel, Friedrich Engels and V.I. Lenin. However, the experience of Sweden poses a tantalizing problem. Its version of socialism, its objective social and cultural conditions, are sufficiently different from those of the four countries here considered to render us cautious about treating legal developments there as portents of the future. Yet the conditions are close enough that it is impossible not to see their evolution as one likely direction which events in England, France, the United States, or West Germany might take. Thus, Swedish law is frequently referred to throughout this book.

In the case of England, France, the United States and West Germany, among the factors which simultaneously facilitate comparison and render it increasingly useful, is the remarkable degree to which the family law of all these systems has become open to foreign influences. This is more true in West Germany and England than in France and the United States, but in all four countries, as we shall see, legislatures and law revision commissions have scanned foreign law in the effort to adjust their own law to social change which they perceive as being shared by other countries. Also, each of the legal systems in question has generated a vast amount of case and statutory law and learned writing on the subjects here considered, so that legal and social science materials are readily accessible. Finally, not only has there been a certain amount of comparative study and exchange of ideas among these countries, but there has also been, as we shall see, a quite remarkable coincidence of similar legal developments produced at about the same time in the various systems apparently independently of each other.

Thus the chances seem good for being able to make a meaningful comparative analysis of the American, English, French, and West German family law developments. But the very familiarity of these developments itself can pose an obstacle. As Margaret Mead has pointed out,[43] the closer cultural behavior is to that of that observer, the harder it is to discern. To the extent that it is unquestioned and below the surface of consciousness, it is of course, unassailable by analysis. One answer to this problem is that an aspiration of comparative analysis, and sometimes its great virtue, is to bring to the conscious level much that would otherwise remain hidden or disguised.

It has been necessary to set forth these methodological considerations in a rather abstract fashion at the outset. Such discussion may mean little at this point to readers other than those who belong to the group which Engels rather scornfully referred to as "the comparative jurists".[44] But by the end of this book these considerations will have acquired concrete meaning. And perhaps by that time, any reader who is not a comparative jurist will have become one. After all, it is a group which has included Aristotle, Montesquieu and Max Weber. In this spirit, then, an adventure in comparative legal study should be regarded, as John Hazard puts it, as "an awakening of thought".[45]

NOTES

[1] *Weber* 35. So far as family law is concerned, this process is described at some length in Chapter 7 *infra*.

[2] *König* 21.

[3] E.g., the legal symbolism of the husband–wife relationship in England, France, the United States and West Germany discussed in *Glendon, Family Power & Authority*.

[4] "The beginning of family formation may be either marriage or parenthood. It should not be concluded from the fact that sexual intercourse is a prerequisite for pregnancy that all peoples regard marriage or the establishing of a man–woman relationship as the first step in family formation.... [I]n the extreme case marriage is viewed as irrelevant to family formation." *Winch* 1.

[5] *König* 38, 40.

[6] *Id*. at 28.

[7] *Id*. at 33.

[8] *Id*. at 21.

[9] *Id*. at 37.

[10] *Id*. at 39: "[M]an's ideas concerning the topic of love-and-marriage are more diverse and flexible than the structure of the family. While notions concerning love and marriage often change with the fashion, the family as a universal human institution, is not so easily changed."

[11] Let it not be thought however that it will always be easy to determine the content of this set. The legal system may define marriage by referring to the rules of some other system, as is described *infra* at p. 8. Or the legal system itself may recognize different types of marriage: "full" marriage, and some marriages which have fewer legal effects than full marriage, such as the morganatic marriage of royal and aristocratic European families, or the union of male and female slaves known in Roman law as *contubernium*. One might also view in this light the *union libre*, or "shadow institution" of legal marriage discussed in Chapter 3 herein to the extent that it has begun to draw to itself the attribution of some but not all the legal incidents of marriage.

[12] E.g., "Marriage may be defined as a culturally approved relationship of one man with one woman (monogamy), of one man with two or more women (polygyny), or of one woman and two or more men (polyandry), in which there is cultural endorsement of sexual intercourse between the marital partners of opposite sex and, generally the expectation that children will be born of the relationship." *Winch* 2.

[13] *König* at 39. American courts have sometimes made heroic efforts in trying to determine whether a legally recognized common law marriage (*infra* n. 14) has taken place: common law marriage held to exist after couple had spent a few nights together in a hotel, Madewell v. U.S., 84 F. Supp. 329 (E. D. Tenn. 1949); but not where man suddenly died shortly after the couple checked into hotel, Estate of Kieg, 140 P.2d 163 (Cal. App. 1939). The cases are from *Clark, HB*. 57.

[14] Note that the American institution of "common law marriage" belongs in the domain of Set A, because it is a form of legal marriage, recognized by some 13 American states to come into being when a man and woman agree to be husband and wife and "hold themselves out to the world" as married, and which, in legal theory at least, is binding until terminated by legal divorce. See in general, *Clark, HB*. 45–48. Here too belong those unions converted into legal marriages by such measures as Art. 133 of the Bolivian Constitution of 1946 which deems stable cohabitation for two years the equivalent of formal marriage. Similar provisions are frequent in Central and South American countries where the formal marriage requirement of the Council of

Trent was long not in effect and where informal marriage still is taken for granted and accepted in what Oscar Lewis has called the "culture of poverty". See generally, Arraros, Concubinage in Latin America, 3 J. Fam. L. 330 (1963).

[15] As Rheinstein has pointed out, in the medieval world "law" (in the Weberian but not the Austinian sense) was not equivalent to the norm system sanctioned by the State because the State was only one of several political organizations, continuously vying with each other for jurisdiction over various aspects of social life as well as for political power. *Rheinstein, Encyc. Intro.* par. 7. See Chapter 7 *infra*.

[16] *Rheinstein, Encyc. Intro.* par. 10.

[17] Thereby giving rise to exceedingly complex conflict of laws and jurisdictional problems when persons of different religions, groups or nationalities are involved, or when the status of persons married or divorced abroad must be determined under local law.

[18] *Sundberg, Nordic Law* 40, commenting on the fact that the directives given by the Swedish Minister of Justice for the reform of family law specify that future legislation should be drafted so as not to favor in any way the institution of marriage as compared with other forms of cohabitation.

[19] First published in 1907. All references hereafter are to the edition of *The Tinker's Wedding* in The Complete Plays of John M. Synge 180–209 (1960), reprinted with permission of Random House, Inc.

[20] *König* at 40–41.

[21] See Chapter 7 *infra* at p. 310.

[22] Canon 1015(3). *Bouscaren & Ellis* 467.

[23] Canon 1098. *Bouscaren & Ellis* 590–591.

[24] *de Reeper*, The History and Application of Canon 1098, 14 Jurist 169 (1954).

[25] *Rheinstein, Encyc. Intro.* 12–13.

[26] Note, in applying the type of analysis suggested by the preceding section, that the classification of children born outside legal marriage as "illegitimate" is a purely legal construct. This definition of illegitimacy depends on the content of Set A of legal marriages, that is, upon the definition of legal marriage. A sociologist's definition of legitimacy has to take into consideration other norms as well as legal ones. Note too that the legal category of "illegitimacy" does not exactly coincide with the set of children who are *not* living with two parents in families, any more than the set of "legitimate" children exactly coincides wtih the set of those who *are* living with two parents in families.

[27] "Here, [in family law] if anywhere, the law must be seen as the outcome of social forces and as a force which in turn impinges on people in society, on their habits and their convictions." Kahn–Freund, quoted by Gough in Book Review, 37 Mod. L. Rev. 118 (1974).

[28] Marriage Stability, Divorce and the Law (1971).

[29] *Carbonnier, 2 Droit Civil 79.*

[30] For a good short description of Italian marriage up to the 1970 reform, see W. Flieg, Die Ehescheidung im italienischen Recht 19–38 (1975).

[31] *Jolowicz* 113.

[32] *Id.* at 245.

[33] *Rheinstein, M.S.D.L.* 16.

[34] In this paragraph I follow the account of Rheinstein in Chapters 1 and 7 of *M.S.D.L.*

[35] G. Santayana, Three Philosophical Poets 32–33 (1953; orig. publ. 1910).

[36] *Kahn-Freund* 1.

[37] Drobnig, Methods of Sociological Research in Comparative Law, RabelsZ 35 (1971) 496, 498.

[38] See in general, Ault and Glendon, The Importance of Comparative Law in Legal Education, in Law in the United States of America in Social and Technological Revolution 67 (Hazard and Wagner eds. 1974).

[39] The work of Rudolf Schlesinger has, perhaps more than any other, made all students of comparative law aware of the importance of procedure for any real understanding of how substantive rules operate. See R. Schlesinger, Comparative Law. Cases–Text–Materials (3d ed. 1970).

[40] See Ault and Glendon, *supra* n. 38 at 76.

[41] *Kahn-Freund* 8–10.

[42] It is, however, an index of the profundity of the current changes affecting the modern family, that in May 1975 both Italy and Spain enacted complete revisions of their family law, substituting the *Leitbild* of equality for the formerly pervasive provisions enshrining male predominance. The Italian and Spanish changes are in some ways more striking than those of England, France, the United States and West Germany, considering the differences between the new law and the old. See Jayme, Zum neuen italienischen Familienrecht, insbesondere zum Ehetrennungsrecht, FamRZ 1975, 463; and Jayme, Zur spanischen Familienrechtsreform vom 2. Mai 1975 und ihren Auswirkungen auf den deutsch–spanischen Rechtsverkehr, FamRZ 1976, 185. Another sign of the diminishing obstacles to intra-European family law comparison is that a major item on the 1976 agenda of the 10th Conference of the European Ministers of Justice was the harmonization of family law among the member States of the Council of Europe. Note, 126 New L. J. 631 (1976).

[43] M. Mead, Culture and Commitment 29 (1970).

[44] F. Engels, The Origin of the Family, Private Property and the State 79, 85 (Leacock ed. 1972; orig. publ. 1882).

[45] Hazard, Area Studies and Comparison of Law; The Experience with Eastern Europe, 19 Am. J. Comp. Law 645,653 (1971).

FORMATION OF LEGAL MARRIAGE

> Much of what I...shall have to relate, may perhaps, I
> am aware, seem petty trifles to record.... Still it will
> not be useless to study those at first sight trifling
> events out of which the movements of vast changes
> often take their rise.
>
> Tacitus, *Annals* 4.32.

I. Introduction

In none of the four countries whose law is examined in this book, has there
been any single major change in recent years in the rules of positive law
governing the formation of the legal institution of marriage. In contrast to
other areas of family law (such as those dealing with divorce or children born
outside legal marriage), the law concerning an individual's eligibility to enter
the married state, the permissible range of choice of spouses, and the preliminaries and procedures required to conclude a legally valid marriage, has
remained stable. What change there has been in the statutory law of England,
France, West Germany and the states of the United States has involved
mostly adjustment of age and parental consent requirements, or waiting
periods, or administrative matters.

But viewed in their historical context, these apparently trifling changes are
the end of a long chain of events, starting around 1800, which has gradually
freed individuals from constraints on their ability to marry or on their choice
of marriage partner.[1] Strict parental and family consent requirements
designed to give families control over the admission of new members had
been established in numerous European laws in the mid-16th century and
were to be found in the Prussian General Code of 1794 and the French Civil
Code of 1804. During the 19th century, these consent requirements began to
be relaxed. Certain other constraints on marriage which had been established,
not in the interest of family authority, but according to various conceptions
of the public interest, began to disappear too. These latter constraints had
sometimes taken the form of legislation directed against marriages of

paupers. Other such laws had sought to protect the financial independence and social respectability of army officers and public officials by requiring that they obtain official permission to marry. Still another version of the public interest appeared in the 20th century, particularly in the United States, where many states adopted laws directed against the marriages of persons with epilepsy, tuberculosis, alcoholism, or venereal disease.[2] Today, little is left of the American eugenics and other health laws except the requirement, in many states, of a pre-marital examination for venereal disease.[3] The 20th century eugenic marriage legislation of National Socialist Germany which tried to weed out those deemed racially, physically or mentally unfit for marriage has disappeared without a trace.[4]

In all respects, the development of marriage law has been one of small steps. But in recent years the difference between the extensive regulation of marriage formation which was once taken as self-evident and the minimal controls which exist today has become so great that the idea of a basic individual right to marry has emerged.

If, behind and beyond the various minor changes taking place today, one looks to constitutional pronouncements, to the scholarly writing, and to the law reform proposals put forth in France, the United States and West Germany, it is clear that a banner has been raised over the slowly shifting minutiae of their marriage law. The banner is one of the gaily-colored pennants of the pursuit of happiness, and the words inscribed on it are "Freedom to Marry" and "Marriage – A Basic Human Right". Thus, the changes, though minute, have been given a certain direction and impetus in those countries. In England, the law seems to be subject to the same influences as elsewhere, but these influences so far have not been sloganized.

This Chapter will examine the current evolution of American, English, French and West German law concerning the formation of legal marriage. Since the object of our study is to try to discern the relationship of the State to the family as revealed through the law, the selection and organization of the material in this Chapter does not follow the conventional pattern of legal treatises where the law of marriage formation is usually presented either in conjunction with, or with a view toward resolving, questions regarding the validity of a marriage. Here, in order to see more clearly how recent changes in the law reveal changes in the relationship of the State to the family, we will consider first those aspects of marriage formation law which pertain to one's ability to enter legal marriage: (who may get married); second, the law relating to the choice and number of spouses: (who may marry whom); third, compulsory pre-marital procedures; fourth, compulsory formalities for the actual conclusion of marriage; and finally, the emergence of legal expressions of the ideology of freedom to marry.

Reference will be made here to the sanctions for non-observance of these legal norms only insofar as necessary to give an indication of the weight of the policy which a particular norm represents. Thus, in the following discussion of "state-imposed limitations" and "compulsory procedures", attention is meant to be drawn primarily to the simple fact that certain marriage prohibitions, conditions and rites have been cast as legal rules, and that, in some cases, these rules or their sanctions have recently changed. The violation of a given norm may prevent a legal marriage from coming into existence at all (as seems so far to be the case with same-sex marriages in all four countries). It may make the marriage voidable upon the application of one of the parties, or even occasionally upon the application of certain other persons, (as is sometimes the case with the marriage of under-age persons). It may entail criminal sanctions as well as the voidability of the marriage (as is often the case with bigamy or incest).

Without affecting the validity of the marriage, it may entail penal sanctions for those who knowingly violate the norm (as is sometimes the case when an unauthorized official celebrates the marriage) and finally, it may entail no legal sanctions for the parties at all (as where a woman in France or Germany marries before expiration of a waiting period between the termination of her prior marriage and her entry into a new one). Where the sanction for non-observance of a norm is the voidability of the marriage, this may be absolute or relative. That is, certain marriages in violation of legal norms may be declared null simply upon proof that the norm was violated, and the decree of nullity will operate retroactively. Others are valid until voided, and will usually be declared null only if certain conditions other than violation of the norm are present: the suit must be brought by the proper party, within a specified period of time, and no events curing the defect must have intervened.

II. State-Imposed Limitations on an Individual's Ability to enter the Legally Married State: Who may Marry

A. Generally

One can say in general that all of the legal systems here examined carefully avoid imposing conditions concerning an individual's personal characteristics which would tend to rule out completely the possibility of marriage for

certain people. Those legal provisions which do limit a person's legal eligibility to enter marriage tend not to do so definitively. Rather, they prescribe
that a certain age must be reached, a preliminary consent must be obtained, a
waiting period observed, or the condition which has prevented the person
from marrying must be cured.

Thus, various mental conditions which are or can be permanent do not in
principle prevent a person so afflicted from marrying. All four systems of
marriage law are based on the premise that marriage is a consensual union.
Consequently, a consent which is defective because of mental disease or
deficiency affects the validity of the marriage.[5] But the provisions governing
the matter are everywhere characterized by their leniency and their tendency
to promote the validity of the marriage. In the first place, the mental capacity
required for marriage is minimal, often described as less than that required for
the transaction of business.[6] Second, if a marriage is to be attacked for want of
consent, it must be proved that the ability to consent was lacking at the very
time the marriage was celebrated.[7] Proof of the mental condition at an earlier
or later time will not in itself suffice. Finally, even if defective consent at the
time of marriage can be proved, the parties who are permitted to avoid the
marriage and the time within which they must act are limited.[8] In the United
States, the draftsmen of the Uniform Marriage and Divorce Act concluded
that the premarital medical examination widely required by state law did not
need to be preserved, although they did include an optional section for states
choosing to keep the requirement.[9] Recently, it has been suggested that
restrictions on marriage based on physical[10] or mental capacity are questionable as a matter of American constitutional law.[11] In France, where eugenic
marriage legislation did not find a reception, it has been held in conflict of law
cases that French public policy is offended by foreign laws which make
persons afflicted with various illnesses ineligible to marry.[12] The Swedish
legislature, acting on recommendations of the Minister of Justice and his
Committee for Family Law Reform to the effect that epilepsy, mental illness
and venereal disease should no longer be bars to marriage, recently abolished
all impediments to marriage except existing marriage and close blood relationship.[13]

A few laws and administrative regulations remain which require persons
holding certain public positions to obtain official permission to marry. These
are relics from the time when political, as well as family, control over certain
marriages was legally reinforced.[14] Most regulation of remarriage is also
anachronistic and dying out. However, in France and West Germany, a
woman is still prohibited from marrying within a time, roughly corresponding in length to the gestation period, dating from the dissolution of her

previous marriage by death, divorce or annulment, unless she has meanwhile given birth.[15] This rule, carried along from the Prussian General Code of 1794 and the French Civil Code of 1804, was supposed to prevent "confusion of paternity" arising from the interplay of legal presumptions.[16] In both France and West Germany, the prohibition is now deprived of most of its force by a liberal policy of dispensation and by the fact that a marriage contracted in violation of the prohibition is valid.[17] But, curiously, neither the French Divorce Law of 1975 nor the German Marriage and Family Law Reform of 1976 has eliminated the provision despite the fact that it is an anachronism and a violation of the principle of equality of the sexes.

In the United States, the Uniform Marriage and Divorce Act[18] contains no restrictions on remarriage such as those still to be found in the laws of several states which impose a delay before the "guilty" party can remarry, or a waiting period before the divorce decree becomes "final".[19] But a more modern type of state interest in regulation of remarriage can be seen in a Wisconsin law which requires a person legally obliged to support children of a previous marriage or a prior spouse to obtain judicial permission to re-marry.[20] Quite apart from the question of its constitutionality,[21] the Wiscon-sin attempt to control remarriage is not likely to have much impact. Regard-less of their views on the underlying policy, the various American states have shown little inclination to adopt laws aimed at making marriage more difficult. The ease of evasion by marrying in another state practically guaran-tees the ineffectiveness of such "reforms".

An exception to the general trend of minimal or reduced State involvement in the question of who may marry[22] exists regarding the age at which one may marry. State regulation of this subject remains extensive but, as the following subsection shows, the basis of regulation has shifted from the reinforcement of family participation in, (and sometimes control of,) the marriage decision to social concern about the risks supposedly involved in youthful marriages. The family interests once protected by the law primarily involved the family's own economic interest in the choice of spouse. Current regulations are primarily directed toward the welfare of the young persons themselves and any offspring they may have, in view of the high divorce rates generally reported for early marriages.[23] In spite of these data, however, England, France and West Germany and the American Uniform Act have all within the past few years set 18 years as the age of marriage without consent for both men and women. For the most part this represents a *lowering* of the age, although in some places it has meant raising the age for women. But even this modern regulation of the age of marriage is more an expression of what the legislature, and possibly society at large, thinks is proper, than an actual impediment to early marriage. This is so because most of the laws allow for exceptions and the sanctions for their violation are limited.

Inasmuch as regulation of the age of marriage is the only area of the law pertaining to an individual's ability to marry which has undergone much change in recent years, it is worthwhile to take a close look at the current evolution.

B. Age of Marriage

1. France

In the original scheme of the French Civil Code of 1804 the consent of the parents to a marriage had to be obtained, on pain of nullity, by women up to age 21 and by men up to age 25.[24] Even after the parties had passed the ages at which consent was *required*, they were legally obliged to *solicit* the consent of their parents through formal requests known as *"actes respectueux"*.[25] Three such requests had to be made by men under 30 and women under 25, and even older men and women still had to make one such request. After each request, a month had to pass to await an answer. So, in the case where three requests were required, the ceremony could be held up for three months – time for the "infant" to reflect, to be subjected to family pressure, and perhaps to abandon his or her plans. It is said that this system was taken over by the Civil Code from the pre-revolutionary law because it seemed necessary for families to have some control over a situation (marriage) which created responsibilities on the part of the family of origin of each spouse and which potentially involved the dispersal of family wealth. The degree to which the extended family could be implicated in any given marriage decision can still be seen in the complicated provisions governing consent where a parent or close relative is not available.[26]

In the early part of the 20th century, much of this legal reinforcement of family control was dropped.[27] The age at which a person could marry without consent was lowered to 21 for both spouses in 1907. The entire system of legal parental control of marriages of those over 21 disappeared in 1933 with the abolition of the system of the *"actes respectueux"*. For those under 21, consents became much easier to obtain in 1927 when the Civil Code was amended to provide that in case of disagreement between mother and father the division of opinion would be equivalent to consent. Previously the father's refusal would block the marriage even if the mother had consented.

As of 1974, the age of majority and thus the age at which one can marry without first obtaining parental consent was reduced from 21 to 18.[28] The ages of legal capacity to marry *with* the requisite consents are 15 for the female partner, and 18 for the male partner.[29]

The age of capacity to marry with consent is thought to be related to the physiological aptitude for marriage.[30] Even the minimum age requirements of 15 and 18 can be dispensed with "for serious reasons" by the Procureur of the Republic for the place where the marriage is to be celebrated.[31] A sufficient reason is usually the pregnancy of the female partner.[32] Two recent changes have simplified the procedure for seeking such dispensations, once available only from the Head of State. In 1968, the fee was lowered,[33] and in 1970, the power to dispense was transferred from the President of the Republic to the local *procureurs,* statistics having shown that the procedure was in fact no longer exceptional.[34]

Although there has been a steady relaxation in the law governing parental consent, French law on this point remains the most complicated of the four countries here examined. It seems likely there will be still further relaxation. At present, if both parents refuse permission to the marriage, a minor has no recourse. The view has been expressed that in such circumstances the minor ought to be allowed to seek permission from a court, as he can do in England, West Germany and in most of the United States.[35] The French courts, which at present have no power to grant dispensations in such cases, have shown their disapproval of certain instances of parental withholding or revoking of consent (at least when the marriage age was 21) by awarding damages against the parent for "abuse of right".[36]

A survival from the scheme of 1804 which seems unlikely to last much longer is the system of "oppositions" to marriage.[37] The opposition is a formal legal procedure by which certain persons are permitted to notify the official who is to celebrate the marriage that a legal obstacle to the marriage exists. The official so notified cannot proceed until the opposition has been lifted by a court order. Thus, even an unfounded claim can be a last resort for parents who feel that time is on their side. The system has largely fallen into disuse (an average of five oppositions per year are filed in the Department of the Seine) and the Commission for the Reform of the Civil Code has proposed limiting the right to file such a document to the *ministère public.*[38]

Elaborate as all these rules concerning age of marriage are, the sanctions for marriages entered in violation of them are not severe. A marriage of a woman under 15 or a man under 18 is valid until declared null by a court. The defect in such a marriage can be cured by the attainment of majority by the under-age party or by the pregnancy of the female partner.[39] A marriage in violation of the consent provisions can be avoided only upon the suit of the parties or the person whose consent was required, within one year from the attainment of the age of majority by the under-age party or parties, or within one year of the discovery of the marriage by the person whose consent was required.[40]

2. *West Germany*

The pattern of evolution of German law on marriage age is most clearly seen if it is traced back beyond the German Civil Code of 1896 to that one of its antecedents which has been termed the first modern code, the Prussian General Code of 1794.[41] This Code had in common with the nearly contemporaneous Code Napoleon that its idea of enlightenment in the area of freedom to marry was that parents should not be permitted to impose the family's choice of spouse upon their child.[42] However, like the French code, the Prussian Code contained an elaborate system of rules obliging a child to get parental or family permission to marry the person of his or her *own* choice.

It was nearly a century later that the German Civil Code began to be prepared for a unified Germany. By this time social and economic changes had already diminished the possible influence which most parents could in fact exert on their children's choice of spouse,[43] and also the interest which the older generation had in maintaining the legal structures appropriate to an earlier mode of social organization.[44] This erosion was already evident in an 1875 law which eliminated the requirement of family consents to marriage in the case of a daughter over 24 and a son over 25.[45]

Nevertheless, the second draft version of the German Civil Code of 1896 retained the requirement of consent for both sons and daughters up to age 25, even though the age of majority for other purposes was set at 21. The consent requirement was expressly based, not on the duty of the parents as custodians to watch over the interests of their children, but on the duty of the children to observe filial respect and piety, or in other words, as Dörner has put it, upon the family and personal interests of the parents.[46] The debate on this draft in the Reichstag resulted in the assimilation of capacity to marry to legal majority for men, and in establishing the age of capacity to marry at 16 for women. The arguments which carried the day were not those based on the theoretical inconsistency of having two different ages of capacity, but those based on the effects of social and economic change. It was pointed out that the pattern of economic relationships of a great part of the population was not one of dependence of children on their parents, but one in which children of 21 and even younger were on their own, often contributing to the subsistence of the family and thus in a position to found a family themselves.[47] It was also argued that the prolongation of parental authority was irreconcilable with the modern ideal of marriage for love, irrespective of the wealth and social position of the partners.[48] Thus, it has been pointed out that the second draft and the Code provisions as eventually adopted embodied two different conceptions of social reality. The draft manifested a view of the world in which the marriage of a child has significance for the property relationships and family interests of the families of origin and in which these interests can be protected by economic sanctions such as withdrawal of support or disinheritance.[49] The Civil Code itself, however, reflected the actual decline of economically fostered parental control and the interests of wide groups of the population where economic dependence did not continue beyond majority and where substantial family property did not pass from generation to generation.[50]

The family law of the National Socialist period brought a lowering of the age of majority for men to 18 for marriage purposes.[51] But the age for men was changed back to 21 by the Marriage Law of the Allied Control Council of 1946, which remained in effect until 1974.

The age of legal majority was changed in West Germany in 1974, the same year it was changed in France, to make both men and women legally free to marry without parental consent at 18.[52] Previously, as we have seen, the age was higher (21) for men, and lower (16) for women.[53] Under the 1974 law, a minor requires the consent of his legal representative (normally both parents) in order to marry below the age of 18.[54] If the consent of the legal representative is withheld without substantial reason the minor may request a dispensation from the guardianship court.[55] But dispensation of one party from the basic requirement of having reached majority is available only if the other party to the prospective marriage has reached majority, and the party seeking dispensation has reached the age of 16.[56] This, too, represents a change from the prior law under which a man could marry with dispensation from the age requirements only if he had reached 18, while dispensation was available to the female partner even if she was under 16.[57]

With respect to the raising of both the age of marriage and consent for the female partner, the 1974 reform was in part motivated by concern that she should not impair her own personal development through premature marriage.[58] As in France, dispensation from the age requirements has been given commonly for the reason that a child is expected, but there is growing uneasiness about invoking marriage as the automatic solution to this problem.[59] In view of the facts that early marriages in West Germany, as elsewhere, are especially prone to end in divorce; that the children of divorce can be as disadvantaged as illegitimate children; and that the personal development and education of the minor spouse may be impaired by the marriage, it has been said that the court should try to determine in each case whether the marriage is desirable, after a careful balance of the interests of the minor spouse and the interests of the expected child.[60]

The focus on the interests of the minor is evident in the legal treatment of parental consent, as well as the issue of whether a court should dispense with the age or consent requirements. Unlike in France, the consent of both parents is in principle required in West Germany for the marriage of a minor.[61] But the refusal of one or both parents can be appealed to the guardianship court which then decides whether the consent was withheld in the best interests of the child.

3. England

The chief characteristic of English law concerning age of marriage and age of consent, which has constantly differentiated it from the French and German modes of regulation, is not any particular provision, but its past and present restraint in dealing with the whole question. In the past, English law had no such elaborate system of family control of or participation in the marriage decision as did the Prussian General Code and the French Civil Code. Currently, while law reformers are aware of the problems of youthful marriages, they seem presently inclined to doubt that law is an effective agent for reducing them.

The seeming indifference of English law to matters which were viewed elsewhere as crucial is in part due to the lack of codification in England and its practical case-by-case approach to legal problems. Montesquieu noted the divergence of the English situation from that with which he was familiar in 18th century France:

In England the law is frequently abused by the daughters marrying according to their own fancy without consulting their parents. This custom is, I am apt to imagine, more tolerated there than anywhere else from a consideration that as the laws have not established a monastic celibacy, the daughters have no other state to choose but that of marriage, and this they cannot refuse. In France, on the other hand, young women have always the resource of celibacy.[62]

Until the middle of the 18th century, a valid marriage could be contracted in England by an informal present exchange of consents. But by then it had long been customary for marriages to be celebrated in church and for the church authorities to require the consent of parents of parties under 21.[63] These customs became legal requirements in 1753 when Lord Hardwicke's Act was passed, partly in response to the concerns of parents of daughters.

The common law rule that a wife's personal property vested in her husband immediately upon marriage made such families vulnerable to valid informal marriages, particularly as personal property had begun to rival and replace real property as a source of wealth and power.

Lord Hardwicke's Act was not completely effective in putting a stop to marriages without parental consent. Many couples evaded it simply by marrying in Scotland. [64] However, Engels undoubtedly had a point when he observed, commenting on the relative leniency of English marriage law, that there is more than one way to influence a child's marriage decision: in England, although a child could marry without parental consent, his parents were legally free to disinherit him; in France and Germany on the other hand, where parental consent was required, children could not, in principle, be disinherited. [65] So long as English property law permitted and even facilitated indirect control of the marriage decision by such devices as the strict family settlement, it was unnecessary to establish direct legal control through the marriage law itself.

In present-day England, the age of capacity to marry is 16 for both sexes. Consent of both parents is required for persons between 16 and 18. [66] Persons over 18 can marry without restriction.

With respect to the age of capacity, it was only in 1929 that one had to have reached the age of 16. Previously, the ages of capacity were fixed, in accordance with Roman law tradition, at 14 for a boy and 12 for a girl. The reason for the change in 1929 seems to have had little to do either with issues of parental authority or with social concern over youthful marriages. Rather it seems to have been due in part to the fact that Great Britain was participating at the time in a League of Nations effort to outlaw child marriage in India and other oriental countries. England prudently changed its own law so that its moral authority would not be impaired in the event someone should think to examine British law on such matters. [67] Recent suggestions to raise the age still higher in view of the increased chance of an early marriage ending in divorce have not met with much enthusiasm, it being said that the raising of the age to, say, 17, would be a hopeless attempt to swim against the biological tide, that many young people are mature and capable at 16, and, finally, that the public demand for change is not strong. [68] There is at present no dispensation available from the minimum age requirement.

As to the age of consent, it was lowered from 21 to 18 in 1969 when the age of majority generally was set at 18. [69] But the consent provision in English law is not backed up by provisions making the marriage contracted without parental consent voidable. The consent requirement is purely directory. If the couple succeeds in having a marriage ceremony performed without it the marriage is valid.[70] If consent of the parents is sought and one or both parents refuse to give it, the refusal can be reviewed by a court which will dispense with the requirement of consent if the denial is found to have been unreasonable.[71]

There is sentiment in the learned writing to the effect that the case for even this relatively limited retention of a requirement for parental consent is weak.[72] In neighboring Scotland the absence of a consent requirement seems to have produced no ill effects.[73] It has been urged that positive ill effects are apt to result from the requirement of consent, in that parental opposition may strengthen a young couple's determination to enter an ill-advised marriage, or may even encourage pregnancy as a means of extracting consent.[74] The Latey Committee, however, rejected the various arguments for change on the basis that there was little public sentiment for change and that in any event "law is useless as a strengthener of family ties".[75] The Committee's attitude has been summarized as amounting to an acknowledgment that "...the effective factor is the state of the parent–child relationship, not the legal prohibition".[76] Thus one might say the English law, both past and present, has been consistent in leaving the age of marriage primarily to be regulated otherwise than by legal norms.

4. United States

Like English law, American law developed without an elaborate legal framework for direct family participation in or control of the marriage decision. But in recent years the laws of the various states have not been characterized by quite the same degree of *laissez-faire* as has the law of England. The Uniform Marriage and Divorce Act of 1970 established for both parties the age of marital capacity at 16 and the age of marriage without consent at 18. The Act was criticized by the Family Law Section of the American Bar Association as conflicting with "the overwhelming judgment of state legislatures".[77] This criticism was well-founded in the sense that in 1968 the age of capacity was set at 18 for males and 16 for females in 32 states, and the age of marriage without consent at 21 and 18 in 31 states.[78] But most of these laws were old. The wave of change was already in the direction chosen by the draftsmen of the Uniform Act, who were concerned not to stir up unneccessary controversy. Moreover, the equalization of the age for males and females in the Uniform Act was prudent in order to eliminate the likelihood that a difference would eventually be attacked as an unconstitutional sex-based classification.[79]

American studies of the high incidence of failure of marriages involving youthful partners,[80] have been the primary factor influencing the setting and retention of parental and judicial consent requirements and of the age thresholds in the various states.[81] A few states have even gone so far as to require premarital counselling before any couple, one of whom is under 18, will be allowed to marry, even where parental consent has been obtained.[82] In California a law of this sort was passed in 1970 as a reaction to the fact that teenage marriages have figured in 40% of the divorces in that state.[83] But in practice it has turned out that counselling is often perfunctory and that judges seldom refuse permission to marry.[84]

The path chosen by the draftsmen of the Uniform Act seems to reflect agreement with the English judgment that any attempt to make marriage more difficult for young people would be ineffective and perhaps even counter-productive. That the concern of the Uniform Act in its age provisions is primarily for the young partners themselves appears from the facts that a marriage contracted in violation of the age provisions is valid until decreed null and that the conditions under which nullity can be decreed are strictly limited.[85]

III. State-Imposed Limitations on Number and Choice of Spouses: *Who may Marry Whom*

A. Generally

The right to choose one's spouse is complementary to the right of an individual to enter the married state. But long before either of these ideas was cast as involving a basic right, legal restrictions on the field of possible spouses available to any given person were diminishing. Presently in England, France, West Germany and the United States, the only such restrictions which are framed as absolute prohibitions are those based on kinship and currently existing marriage. Even in these two areas we will see that the prohibitions have become in fact less absolute than is generally believed. With respect to kinship restrictions, the circle of prohibited degrees of relationship is everywhere being drawn more narrowly, and restrictions based on affinity, that is, on the relationships which come into being through marriage, are disappearing. While simultaneous marriage to more than one person remains formally forbidden, such marriages in fact produce legal consequences ever more closely resembling those of any other marriage.

Marriage between persons of the same sex, while not expressly made the subject of a marriage prohibition in the four countries, is still generally considered to be forbidden and invalid by implication because the marriage laws speak in terms of a man and a woman.[86] This certainly seems to be the case in England, France and West Germany. In France, in 1960, two women who used a man's birth certificate in order to marry, were arrested and sent to prison.[87] In 1975 an individual who had undergone a sex-change operation was refused the right to have the designation of his sex changed from masculine to feminine on his birth certificate, the court saying that mere "corporeal modifications", while they may have the effect of eliminating most of a person's original sex, do not thereby confer upon him a new sex.[88] In the United States, where the question recently has been the subject of litigation, the cases so far have held that persons of the same sex cannot marry.[89] But in 1975 there were reports that marriage licenses had been issued to homosexual couples in the United States and that a number of such "marriages" had been performed.[90] Whether any legal consequences (for tax or inheritance purposes for example) will follow from these unions is another question.[91] As to these consequences, however, there appears to be a division of opinion among homosexuals, some persons declaring that their reason for marriage is to acquire benefits accorded to other married couples, others rejecting the idea of imitating or adopting the bourgeois ideas of heterosexual society.[92]

In all four countries, restrictions other than those on simultaneous marriages, homosexual marriage and marriage between close relatives, either are only directory (that is, they do not affect the validity of the marriage concluded in spite of them), or a dispensation from their application is available. Of this latter type, for example, was the former prohibition in the German Marriage Law against marriage between a spouse divorced for adultery and the person with whom the adultery was committed.[93] A marriage entered in violation of the provision was invalid, but the prohibition was long of little practical consequence because dispensations were freely granted.[94] In 1976 it was repealed by the Reform Law as a logical consequence of the elimination of the fault principle.[95] A similar prohibition in France was repealed in 1904.[96]

In all four countries the conventional wisdom is that the law in general, just as it has been solicitous of the individual's ability to marry, has become increasingly watchful to protect his freedom of choice of spouses, even to the point of guarding this freedom from those kinds of private pressure occasionally sought to be exerted through conditions in gifts and wills.[97] But we must be careful to recall that it is one's *legal* freedom to marry and to choose a spouse which is thus described. In fact, the choice of a spouse is probably much less free than generally supposed, being heavily influenced, if not determined, by social factors.[98] It is also commonly said that the only absolute marriage prohibitions in these countries are those of polygamy and incest.[99] (Same sex marriage is not usually conceptualized as the subject of a marriage prohibition, but rather as being outside the scope of marriage altogether). The following sections of this subchapter will inquire into whether and in what sense it is correct to say, in view of recent changes, that even polygamous or incestuous marriages are absolutely prohibited.

B. Polygamy

At first sight it seems fully justified to state that in England, France, the United States and West Germany there is an absolute prohibition of simultaneous marriage to more than one person. In each country, the laws provide that no one may enter a marriage, prior to the dissolution of a previous marriage,[100] and, except in certain American states, that the act of entering such a marriage is criminal.[101] No dispensations are allowed.

It is important to notice, however, that this one-marriage-at-a-time rule behind which the legal systems of the West have seemingly thrown so much weight is not what a social scientist would call a general prohibition of polygamy. Polygamy, which is the most common form of marriage in past and present human society, can be simultaneous (in which more than one spouse is simultaneously present), or successive (in which the spouses are married one after the other).[102] It is of course only simultaneous polygamy which is prohibited by the laws with which we are here concerned. They do not at all affect successive polygamy which is so popular in Western industrialized societies that, as we shall see, especially in Chapters 5 and 6, the law is fast changing to adapt to it.

The legal systems here in question however tend for the most part to reserve the use of the word "polygamy" for that kind of polygamy which is not very popular in the West. Nowhere is the difference between viewing polygamy as a legal phenomenon and as a social phenomenon more clearly illustrated than in the majority and dissenting opinions in a United States Supreme Court case. The case involved the question of whether members of a sect of polygynous heretical Mormons travelling with their wives violated a federal statute making it a crime to transport a woman across state lines "for the purpose of prostitution or debauchery, or for any other immoral purpose".[103] Mr. Justice Douglas, writing for the majority, upheld the convictions of the Mormons saying, "The establishment or maintenance of polygamous households is a notorious example of promiscuity.... These polygamous practices have long been branded as immoral in the law....

[T]hey are in the same genus as the other immoral practices covered by the Act."[104] Mr. Justice Murphy, dissenting, did not agree that the conduct was comparable to prostitution and commercialized vice. After pointing out that the practice involved in the case was, properly speaking, not polygamy but polygyny, he said "[W]e are dealing here with...one of the basic forms of marriage.... [It] is basically a cultural institution...." The fact that it is condemned by the dominant culture "...does not alter that fact that polygyny is a form of marriage built upon a set of social and moral principles".[105]

Since 1946, when this opinion was written, there are signs that the degree of our Western disapproval of the type of polygamy we do not practice has diminished, even as our practice of the kind we favor has increased. It is true that the marriage prohibition still stands, but the sanctions for simultaneous polygamy have begun to be softened in three ways.

In the first place, the legal effects of a marriage entered in violation of the prohibition are beginning to approach the legal consequences of any other marriage. For example, the children of such a union can be legitimate.[106] If proceedings are brought to declare the marriage void, support or other economic measures may in certain cases be ordered as after a divorce.[107] Second, the attitude of the State toward such marriages as expressed through the criminal law seems to be growing less harsh. The criminal law is very seldom enforced against bigamists in the United States, and in some American states, bigamy has ceased to be a crime altogether.[108] In West Germany and Sweden, it may be punishable by a fine.[109] Finally, in conflict of laws cases, foreign simultaneously polygamous marriages are increasingly recognized, perhaps indicating a diminution of the strength of local public policy against them.[110]

As for the proliferation of successive polygamy among us, the ways in which the law has changed to accomodate the practice will be described in Chapters 5 on divorce and 6 on the consequences of divorce. Here it may merely be pointed out that the experience of other parts of the world with simultaneous polygyny (by far more common than polyandry) may be instructive as to the limits of our practices as well as theirs. Simultaneous polygyny has always been self-limiting owing to the necessity to keep within control the tensions in society that a shortage of women can create, and to the economic limits on the number of wives one man can support.[111] The applicability of the second point to the Western situation hardly needs demonstration. As Chapter 6 will show, all the legal systems here considered are currently wrestling with the question of whether responsibility for successive spouses belongs to their one-time marriage partners or to society at large, not to mention the problems of children produced in the course of successive unions. Montesquieu, in maintaining that "a plurality of wives greatly depends on the means of supporting them", pointed out that this does not necessarily mean that a man with multiple wives has to be richer than others, provided that he lives in a clime where it costs little to maintain wife and children.[112] Interestingly enough, the countries which Montesquieu thought favored by nature are now moving toward the abolition of simultaneous polygamy.[113] It may be that the modern climates favoring polygamy are those of the affluent welfare states of the industrialized part of the world.

C. Incest

As with polygamy, when discussing incest it is important to distinguish between legal and social conceptions. The legal systems are concerned with *marriage* prohibitions based on kinship or affinity. These may or may not coincide with what has been called the incest taboo, which pertains to *mating*.

All of the legal systems here examined have in common the fact that their lists of marriage prohibitions based on kinship were once quite extensive[114] but today have gradually been reduced. Of the remaining prohibitions, some are absolute, and others are within a zone of tolerance, in the sense that they can be officially dispensed or that marriages entered in violation of them are not invalid.

In all four countries marriage in the direct line of ascent or descent, and between siblings of full or half blood, whether the relationship is legitimate or illegitimate, is within the zone of absolute prohibition. Beyond this circle of unanimity, there are minor variations among the countries. That this circle does not constitute an irreducible minimum for Western countries is indicated by the fact that Swedish law was recently changed to provide that the marriage prohibition between half-brother and sister can be dispensed.[115] The four systems all started out with prohibitions based on the extensive network of canon law impediments. But each has developed its own peculiarities.

In France, in addition to the core relationships listed above, marriage is absolutely prohibited between ascendants and descendants related by adoption, or by affinity, if the person through whom the affinity was created is living.[116] Thus, for example, the father of a divorced son can not marry his former daughter-in-law so long as the son in living. Since the Code of 1804, dispensations have been made available in the following cases: marriage between adoptive brother and sister; marriage between aunt and nephew or uncle and niece; marriage between persons related by affinity in the direct line if the person creating the link is deceased; and marriage between brother- and sister-in-law if the marriage creating the alliance is dissolved by divorce.[117] In this last case, if the marriage creating the alliance has been terminated by death, no dispensation has been necessary since 1938.[118] In all these cases, it has been said that "it is no secret that dispensations are freely given".[119] With regard to the actual demand for dispensations, French studies in 1948 and 1954 showed that uncle–niece marriages were uncommon and becoming increasingly rare.[120] When they did occur they were usually regularizations of existing cohabitations. Marriages between cousins (which are not legally restricted in France) were found to be frequent only in psychologically or geographically isolated places, such as the poor sections of large cities or island or mountain regions. The studies found that in some cases intra-family marriage was apparently used by families to prevent division and dispersion of family property.

In Germany, there are no absolute prohibitions outside those mentioned above as being common to the four systems.[121] Dispensation is available and its denial is the exception rather than the rule in the case of marriages between persons related by affinity (including step-parents and step-children) in the direct line. Marriages between adoptive parents and children are valid even if entered into in violation of the laws purporting to forbid them. Affinity in the collateral line is no longer an impediment of any kind. The abolition of the prohibition concerning affinity in the direct line is presently under consideration. A prohibition of marriage between persons, one of whom has had a sexual relationship with a relative of the other, was declared unconstitutional in 1973.[122]

In the United States, the scheme of the Uniform Marriage and Divorce Acts adds to the prohibitions listed above as common to all four countries, marriages between ascendants and descendants or between siblings related by adoption; and marriages between aunt and nephew or uncle and niece with a special exception as to these for "the established customs of aboriginal cultures".[123] The Act does not prohibit first cousin marriages which are however prohibited in about half of American states.[124] Prohibitions based on affinity and remote consanguinity have been gradually dropping out of state law, do not appear in the Uniform Act, and are in any event of doubtful constitutionality.[125]

Absolute prohibitions which exist in England, in addition to the core prohibitions mentioned above, are: marriages between allies (including step-parents and step-children) in the direct line; marriages between adoptive parents and children or adopted siblings; and marriages between aunt and nephew or uncle and niece.[126] No dispensations from any of these prohibitions are available and the prohibitions continue even after the death of the person creating the prohibited relationship.[127] Thus, for example, a man could not, as in France, marry a woman who had been married to his deceased son. Most English affinity prohibitions were dropped in a series of reforms beginning in 1907.

There is no ready explanation of the basis for current legal regulation of marriages between persons related in various ways. The French writer Carbonnier calls the remaining absolute prohibitions common to all four countries the "zone of horror".[128] But clearly this is not the Swedish perception. Freud's argument that the rigorous prohibition of certain relationships in law and custom establishes that these relationships cannot be naturally abhorrent, – else there would be no need for prohibition[129] – has widely influenced legal discussions of the matter. The views of Lévi-Strauss and others that rules about incest are not so much prohibitions as rules linked to structural exchange processes which promote marriage outside a defined group[130] have also tended to dispel the "horror theory" from legal thought. Many writers reject also any idea that the legal prohibitions are eugenic in origin.[131] The theory that certain relationships have been socially and legally discouraged because of their potentially disruptive effect within a single household has found more acceptance, especially as helping to explain why the affinity prohibition has largely dropped out.[132] Where successive polygamy is widely practiced and it is common for half-brothers and sisters to be raised in different households, the prohibition against marriage by half-siblings may in time weaken too, as it already has in Sweden.

Even with respect to the present minimum core of absolute prohibitions, the marriage law alone does not give a complete picture of the attitudes towards incest expressed through the medium of law. In all four countries, the sexual relationships which are the subject of absolute marriage prohibitions are also typically the subject of criminal prohibitions. On the one hand, this fact would seem to indicate the strength of the policy against certain types of relationship. On the other hand, there are signs of a movement either to decriminalize this behavior or at least to drastically reduce the penalties applied to it.[133]

In England[134] and most American states sexual relations between members of the core family are still classified as the crime of incest. Respectable opinion in these countries, however, has advocated an approach similar to that of France, eliminating the crime of incest as such and classifying as offenses only those sexual relations between relatives which involve a minor and a person who by virtue of his position with respect to the minor, is presumably in a position to abuse his or her authority.[135] Since non-relatives are punishable under this classification, the law must be regarded not as primarily an incest prohibition but as a law for the protection of minors. It has been suggested in England, where incest was made a statutory crime only in 1908, that the crime should be deleted from the statutes and prosecutions should take place only where the circumstances would justify a charge of sexual assault, while other cases could be dealt with by the legal power to remove children from their parents.[136] West Germany recently has revamped its criminal law pertaining to sexual relations between relatives. The title of the offense has been changed from Incest (*Blutschande*: literally, "shaming of the blood") to Sexual Relations between Relatives. The penalties have been changed to make it possible to punish the offense simply with a fine rather than with imprisonment. Brother and sister under age 18 have been exempted from the application of the section.[137] The view that incest should be subsumed under the concept of protection of minors as in France has been advocated in West Germany.[138] In 1976, the Swedish government was considering the recommendation of a Committee appointed by the Minister of Justice that criminal penalties for incest between parent and child or brother and sister be abolished.[139]

To complete the picture, it must be pointed out that incestuous marriages, like polygamous marriages, even where void, produce many of the same legal effects as any other marriage.[140] Thus, it seems that so far as the law is concerned, its attitude is something like that expressed by Mrs. Waters in the film version of Fielding's *Tom Jones*. When told that she had slept with her own son, Mrs. Waters' face first expressed all the horror that society commonly associates with incest. A few seconds later, however, after having thought the matter over, she shrugged her shoulders and went on about her business.

The fact that the content of the marriage prohibitions and the regulation of sexual relationships between related persons in Western societies seems to be gradually changing should not be too surprising. While the incest taboo has often been said to be universal, this must be understood as meaning that some sort of prohibition on mating is universal, not that a particular set of relationships is universally tabooed.[141] As Lévi-Strauss has pointed out, the content of the taboo is connected with terminology, and is dependent on what relationships a particular culture is linguistically capable of describing, since a society cannot prohibit what it cannot name or classify.[142] Some recent support has even been given to Engels' assertion, long thought to be erroneous, that some societies exist which have no incest taboo at all.[143] In any event, the content of the taboo, if one does indeed exist, has changed with the changing structure of societies,[144] and in the present period of intense social change affecting the family it is not unthinkable that it should change within

Western societies, or even that Western legal systems should content themselves with leaving such behavior increasingly to be regulated by norms other than legal ones, that is, by the taboo. This, essentially, is what the Swedish Minister of Justice's Committee has recommended.

IV. Compulsory Pre-Marital Procedures

For a long time, nullity was the only sanction available as a practical matter for marriages which political or ecclesiastical authorities desired for one reason or another to prevent.[145] So long as valid marriages could still be concluded informally, there was only the crude technique of avoiding the marriage so entered or the still cruder technique of punishment to back up whatever marriage policies were sought to be implemented. As the machinery of public adminstration became more efficient in England, France and Germany, however, it became possible to implement marriage policies through the requirement of a public ceremony, preceded by publicity and eventually by the issuance of a license. These methods of enforcing the marriage laws of modern states are less effective in the United States than elsewhere because of the lack of a nationwide system of registration of civil status there and the continuing possibility of concluding a valid informal marriage in several American states.

For our purposes, the preliminaries required by modern states before a marriage can take place are revealing as indications of the degree to which the State is actively involved in regulation of marriage formation, as opposed to contenting itself with the promulgation of rules which describe ideal behavior in the area but which have no real sanctions. Thus, to the extent that the various rules regarding marriage preliminaries are not contrived to identify problem cases, and to prevent persons from marrying in violation of the rules concerning who may marry whom, they indicate the measure to which in a given country the various marriage restrictions are merely statements of a certain idea of the way things ought to be.

We will be less concerned here with the modern law of nullity, which tells us how effective a marriage entered in violation of the legal rules will be. Nullity has ceased to be a major technique for control of marriage formation and is now primarily remedial in function, except perhaps in the United States where an invalid marriage can be collaterally attacked. But where the system of licensing and registration of civil status is as efficient as it is in France or West Germany, the law of nullity ceases to be itself a significant mode of regulation. It is concerned with problems which are, for our purposes, secondary, that is with the effects to be given to a marriage entered in spite of attempts to prevent it.

Compulsory marriage preliminaries, on the other hand, not only give us a good idea of the weight behind various marriage policies in a legal system, but provide another kind of clue to the nature of the relation of the State to the family. They furnish a convenient occasion for society to enforce certain policies by conditioning the celebration of marriage upon the happening of whatever event the legislature has deemed important. Thus, for example, individuals may be required to have a medical examination before they may marry, or, as a supposed deterrent to hasty marriages, a specified period of time must elapse between the declaration of intention to marry and the marriage itself. In a growing number of American states, the state has taken the occasion of the application for a marriage license to require the licensing official to dispense birth control information. As we saw in subsection II above, certain American states have also taken this occasion to require premarital counselling for under-age couples. Let us consider in detail the patterns of compulsory premarital regulation in each of the four countries.

A. England

The law of marriage preliminaries in England is complicated because four separate alternative sets of premarital procedures, two civil and two ecclesiastical, are generally available to marrying couples, not to mention extraordinary civil and ecclesiastical procedures which are available in certain emergencies. The apparent complexity of the system however masks the fact that the system as a whole exercises little control over the formation of marriage and that the English state takes little advantage of the occasion of marriage to promote any particular social policies. The four sets of ordinary marriage preliminaries can be briefly described as follows:

1. Civil Marriage Preliminaries

a. Superintendent Registrar's Certificate[146]

To obtain this certificate of permission to marry, the parties must notify the Superintendent Registrar for the district where each has resided for at least seven days of their intention to marry and must solemnly declare that the residence requirement is satisfied, that any required consents have been obtained, and that there are believed to be no impediments to the marriage. This notice is then entered in a marriage notice book which is conspicuously displayed in the Superintendent Registrar's office and open to public inspection. After the notice has been displayed for 21 days, the Superintendent Registrar's certificate, which is the authorization to marry, is issued. The marriage can then take place at any time within three months of the issuance of the certificate. About one half of all civil marriages in England are pursuant to this procedure.

b. Superintendent Registrar's Certificate and License[147]

This procedure, also known as Special License, is faster than the foregoing one, involving practically no publicity and only a one-day wait between the giving of notice and the marriage. Although intended to be exceptional, it has come to be used in about half of all English civil marriages. Apart from the fact that it costs £5 more, it differs from the foregoing procedure mainly in that the notice, while entered on the marriage notice book and open to inspection by the public, is not displayed, and in that the marriage can take place upon the expiration of one whole day after the day of giving notice. Thus if notice is given on a Monday, the marriage can take place on Wednesday.

2. Ecclesiastical Marriage Preliminaries

a. Banns[148]

This procedure, which is followed in 94% of Church of England weddings, requires written notice of intention to marry, stating the full names of the parties, their places of residence and how long they have lived there. No declaration concerning capacity to marry or consents is required. Seven days after such notice is given, the banns of marriage are published. That is, the proposed marriage is entered in a church register and is announced publicly at church services on three successive Sundays preceding the solemnization of the marriage. Thus the total waiting time between notice and marriage is apt to be between three and four weeks.

b. Common License[149]

This procedure is analogous to the civil marriage by Special License, involving virtually no publicity, no waiting period and no opportunity for objections to the marriage to be raised. But unlike its expedited civil analogue, it can be used only if special permission is obtained. In fact, it is seldom used.

The most striking characteristic of the English scheme as a whole is its lack of compulsion. There is no requirement of any medical test; no procedure for documentary proof or even for checking up on the truth of declarations made in the notice to marry; and the publicity provisions have been described as "largely nugatory".[150]

Some of these characteristics of the system have been seen in England as defects. There seems to be little enthusiasm for medical tests or longer waiting periods, but a Law Commission study in 1973 has recommended a uniform system in which all persons intending to marry would have to give notice in a single prescribed form, and to produce birth certificates, evidence of identity, and evidence of the termination of any prior marriage.[151] It has also been suggested that the Registrar should have more duties in connection with verifying the information submitted to him. In this area, however, England is struggling with a conflict familiar to Americans as well. Observing that endorsement of birth certificates with a note of marriages and their termination would help avoid bigamy, Cretney has stated that, "What is really needed is a National Register of Civil Status.... Anything less is an unsatifactory compromise." But at the same time he has recognized that even the idea of a national record keeping system is "anathema to many."[152]

B. France

In contrast to the English system, the uniform preliminaries required prior to the compulsory civil marriage of French law present a pattern of real "juridification", mostly directed at backing up the French legal requirements concerning eligibility to marry and choice of spouse described in preceding sections.

The first step required of a French couple who intend to marry is the production of a medical certificate, not more than two months old, certifying that each has been "examined with a view toward marriage".[153] Unlike some American state laws which permit a marriage license to be refused if the certificate reveals the existence of certain conditions,[154] French law seeks only to assure that each person is well informed about his or her own physical condition before he or she marries. The results of the examination do not appear on the certificate, which says only that the examination took place. The results are made known only to the person examined, not to the future spouse or to any public official. Thus, the results of the medical examination cannot in any way be an impediment to marriage. But to make sure that the examination takes place, it is tied to the next required step in marriage preliminaries, publication, which cannot take place until the certificates have been filed. Even this relatively lenient medical certificate requirement was disapproved by the French Civil Code Reform Commission, perhaps because of its origin in a Vichy law.[155]

After the medical certificates have been filed, publication of the marriage must take place for a period of at least 10 days before the marriage, in the fashion prescribed by the Civil Code :

Before the celebration of the marriage, a notice of the intended marriage must be posted at the door of the city hall (*mairie*) of the commune where the marriage is to be celebrated, and of the place of the domicile or residence of the future spouses. The notice is to contain the first names, surnames, occupations, domiciles and residences of the parties, and the place where the marriage is to be celebrated. [156]

This procedure, which is a secular version of the banns of marriage, is supposed to give the relevant community the opportunity to call attention to any impediments to the marriage either through simple notice to public officials, or through formal oppositions [157] in cases where these are permitted. Dispensations from the requirement of the waiting period or from the publication itself can be granted by the local *procureur* for "serious reasons", which in the former case are apt to be the imminent birth of a child, and in the latter that the marriage is the regularization of a union which has long passed in the community for a legal marriage. [158]

Finally, before the marriage itself can be celebrated, the birth certificates of the parties must be sent to the official who will celebrate the marriage. [159] The certificates, which must not be more than three months old, contain entries on their margin of any marriages previously entered by the parties, and the names of former spouses. This may, in certain cases, make the production of more certificates necessary before the marriage can be celebrated. If the birth certificate cannot be obtained, the information it would have contained must be established by at least three witnesses. Additional procedures are required if a prospective spouse is not of French nationality. It has been said that the French premarital formalities are so formidable that they "...have often had the effect of frightening poor ill-educated people from entering upon a marriage and so of fostering 'free unions'". [160] It has also been observed that some aspects of this system of premarital formalities, such as publication at the door of the *mairie,* are archaic and that the system of oppositions is practically unused. However, the Code Reform Commission recommended the retention of the system as it stands and there seems to be no serious support for change. [161]

C. West Germany

Like the French system, the West German law governing marriage pre-liminaries is characterized by requirements designed effectively to bring to light any impediments to the marriage before the compulsory civil ceremony takes place. Like the French system, it is aided in doing this by a system of registration of civil status which is more comprehensive than in England or the United States. In West Germany, the first step which must be taken by persons intending to marry is the production of their birth certificates, or authenticated entries or extracts from the Family Book[162] and any necessary consents from parents or guardians.[163] Furthermore, the Registrar of Civil Status (*Standesbeamte*) is obliged to satisfy himself before the marriage as to whether there is any marriage impediment and to require further documentary proof where necessary, as when one of the parties is not of German nationality.[164] Only if the Registrar has accepted the documentary evidence, can the parties proceed to the next required step which is the posting of public notice at a designated place for one week prior to the marriage.[165] It has been argued that this notice, which can be dispensed with by the Registrar, serves its purpose of bringing unknown impediments to light only in small communities, and its abolition is under consideration.[166] Others have argued that it should be retained, however, on the ground that even though it may be useless in bringing impediments to light, it does serve the purpose of assuring a minimal period of reflection and preparation.[167]

In the case of the marriage of anyone who is the guardian of a minor child, or of certain other individuals who are under fiduciary obligations, West German law takes the occasion of marriage to require a certificate attesting that the person wishing to marry has fulfilled his legal duties to the person to whom he is obligated, or that such duties do not exist.[168] A marriage entered in violation of this provision is valid, but it may result in the loss of the violator's control over the property of the person for whom he is responsible.[169]

At present, West German law requires no medical examination, but suggestions for reform have included a recommendation for a confidential certificate of the French type which would leave the freedom to marry unaffected.[170] It has also been suggested that German marriage preliminaries ought to include the dispensation of information about the legal effects of marriage on property, a subject about which persons entering marriage are often ignorant but which may profoundly affect their lives.[171]

D. *United States*

The presentation of American marriage preliminaries and American marriage formation law in general involves two unique problems. In the first place, there is no "American" law of marriage formation, except insofar as recent federal constitutional pronouncements have affected the states,[172] but rather a group of state laws exhibiting great variety. Second, as an aspect of this variety, certain states recognize a form of legal marriage, the so-called "common law marriage", which involves no preliminaries and no formalities. As to the first problem, here as elsewhere in this book, the principal patterns and the most significant deviations from these patterns will be presented. As to the second problem, it merely needs to be remembered that the discussion here pertains to formal marriage. The institution of common law marriage will be discussed below in connection with the formalities (or lack thereof) required by each system for the solemnization of marriage, and again in Chapter 3.

All states and the Uniform Act require a license before formal marriage and the majority of states (but not all) impose a waiting period (usually three days as in the UMDA) between the application for the license and its issuance.[173] The licensing statutes usually require that the parties state under oath their names, ages, any relationship between them, whether they have been previously married, and if so how their marriages were terminated. If the statements of the parties do not reveal any irregularities, the license is issued.[174] The licensing official need not make any investigation on his own. The Uniform Marriage and Divorce Act has followed this pattern. It does not require documentary evidence of eligibility to marry. In fact it rejected the suggestion of the Family Law Section of the American Bar Association that, in line with the practice of some states, a copy of any divorce decree should be required in addition to the simple declaration of the parties regarding previous marriages. It continues the basic system of the law of the states which, like English law, takes the information on the license application at face value. In the United States there is no system of publicity of the intended marriage and the marriage itself can take place as soon as the license is issued. Many states require a physician's certificate stating that each party is free from venereal disease before a marriage license will issue, but the requirement is easily evaded by marrying in another state and a marriage contracted in violation of the requirement is not invalid.[176] As we have seen, the draftsmen of the UMDA concluded that a pre-marital medical examination was unnecessary.[177]

It is critical to the understanding of this scheme of regulation to be aware of the fact that nearly every aspect of a particular state's plan of regulation can be avoided simply by going to another state whose law does not happen to include that aspect. There has been a great deal of sentiment in the United States that a longer waiting period would be desirable, but the ease of evasion of this or any other change making marriage more difficult has discouraged any reforms along these lines. Thus, compulsory counselling, waiting periods, restraints on remarriage and consent requirements are being rejected or abandoned by the states at least as much out of despair as on principle or under the influence of recent constitutional doctrines. Only licensing itself seems likely to be retained. One authority's concern that it is even questionable whether the state can "license" a basic civil right, has not found any serious reception so far.[178]

Thus, American law as a whole is as lax as the English with respect to finding out whether marriage impediments exist. As does England, the United States lacks any system of registration of status which in itself would provide checks on bigamous marriages. Unlike the English system however, American law has begun to manifest new and distinctively modern types of state interest in its law concerning marriage preliminaries. For example, an increasing number of states have recently passed laws requiring that birth control information be dispensed to all applicants for marriage licenses.[179] Another type of interest is manifested in requests on license application forms for information which is not concerned with revealing impediments to the marriage but rather with the gathering of data to be used for the study of family life. This type of innovation poses a problem for reformers, torn between the wish to protect privacy and the desire to make better laws. Finally, although the Uniform Act, in the words of its draftsmen, "greatly simplified premarital regulation", and generally follows a policy of minimal regulation, it does include the social security numbers of the parties as items of required information on the marriage license application.[180] On the surface, this is a seemingly unimportant item, but it assumes significance when we come to consider the economic consequences of marriage dissolution in Chapter 6. It was inserted in the Uniform Act, over the objections of commissioners concerned about governmental data gathering, for the purpose of laying the groundwork in the marriage license for the day when the bridegroom, now a deserting husband and father, must be located for the purpose of enforcing support obligations. The social security number is fast becoming the basis of a national system of identification in the United States. Pressures to institute such a system are quite strong, and the counter-pressures are equally strong.[181] However, any change from the present system in which an American can freely drop or assume an identity will of course have important repercussions for marriage and divorce law.

V. Compulsory Formalities for the Conclusion of Marriage

While the laws concerning marriage preliminaries are indicators of the degree to which various marriage restrictions are in fact policed, the laws establishing certain formalities for the actual celebration of the marriage are revealing of two entirely different aspects of state involvement in marriage regulation: (1) the extent to which marriage rituals, usually religious or customary in origin, have been juridified and made uniform for all groups of the population, and (2) the ideology of marriage being communicated by the legal system. The laws concerning registration of the marriage once it has been celebrated obviously bear an important relationship to the structure and effectiveness of the official record-keeping methods, which in turn aid in enforcing the system of marriage impediments. So far as the required formalities for the celebration of marriage are concerned, the systems of France and West Germany, where the only method of forming a valid marriage is a compulsory civil ceremony, must be examined separately from those of England and the states of the United States, where very different examples of what one might call pluralistic systems are in force.

A. Pluralism: England and the United States

1. England

a. Celebration

Until 1753 marriages could be concluded in England by a simple exchange of consents with no other ceremony.[182] Lord Hardwicke's Act that year changed this by making an ecclesiastical ceremony in the Church of England, with publication of banns and registration of the marriage, compulsory for all persons except members of the Royal Family, Quakers, and Jews.[183] Thus, under this scheme, protestant dissenters and Catholics had to marry by the Anglican rite or not at all. When partial secularization of marriage came to England in 1836 it came not in the form of the compulsory civil ceremony for everyone as in France and Germany, but in a law permitting two parallel marriage systems, those of religious and civil law, to exist side by side.[184] The main lines of the system laid down in 1836 still exist today. English couples may marry according to the rites of the Church of England (as did 160,059 couples in 1971); or civilly (as did 167,101 couples in 1971); or according to the rites of any non-Anglican religion.[185] Quakers and Jews continue to form a separate category. Thus, to discover what aspects of marriage ritual are legally required in England, one must examine not one but four separate systems:

(1) Civil Marriage[186]

This form of marriage is the most common type in England at the present time. The parties marry in the office of the Superintendent Registrar, between 8 a.m. and 6 p.m., with open doors, in the presence of a Superintendent Registrar who acts as celebrant and a Registrar who attends to the formalities of registration. The ceremony itself consists of the exchange of consents in the prescribed form: "I call upon these persons here present to witness that I, AB, do take thee, CD, to be my lawful wedded wife (husband)." The parties are also required to declare that they know of no impediment to the marriage. It is apparently the custom, though not required by law, for the Registrars to make the following statement:

It is my duty to remind you of the solemn and binding character of the vows you are about to take. Marriage, according to the law of this country, is the union of one man with one woman, voluntarily entered into for life to the exclusion of all others.

Cretney has described the total effect as "bureaucratic" and lacking in solemnity, and the physical surroundings of the Registry offices as "depressing".

(2) Anglican Marriage[187]

These marriages are nearly as common as civil marriage in England. The law leaves the details of the ceremony to the Church of England, providing only that there must be two witnesses and that the marriage rite must be that of the Book of Common Prayer or any other currently authorized ritual.

(3) Non-Anglican Religious Marriage[188]

The form of the ceremony is largely left to the parties and the church authorities, but certain aspects of procedure and ritual are legally required. The marriage must be celebrated by an "authorized person" in a "registered building". These requirements are administered so as to assure that the non–Anglican religious ceremony is in fact a religious ceremony of some sort and not a secular "marriage mill" in competition with the Registry office. The ceremony itself must take place between 8 a.m. and 6 p.m. with open doors in the presence of two or more witnesses and a registrar or "authorized person". At some point in the ceremony the parties must state: "I do solemnly declare that I know not of any lawful impediment why I, AB, may not be joined in matrimony to CD."

(4) Quaker and Jewish Marriages[189]

Since Lord Hardwicke's Act, these marriages have been in a special category. They need not be celebrated in a "registered building" nor by an "authorized person" and the form of the ceremony is left entirely to the religious rules of these groups.

The pluralistic system just described has been criticized in England. It has been said that the proliferation of procedures for preliminaries as well as for celebration of marriages is understood neither by the public nor by the persons who must administer the system.[190] The major objection is that it is not entirely clear what effect certain procedural irregularities will have on the validity of the marriage.[191] Owing to the general laxity concerning the form for the ceremony, it has been thought that the parties may sometimes not even fully understand that a marriage (as opposed to licensing, for example) is taking place.[192] A joint working party of the Law Commission and the Registrar General's office suggested that the intoduction of the compulsory civil ceremony as the only legally permissible way to form a marriage would be the simplest and most effective means of solving these problems.[193] Concluding, however, that such a reform would be strongly resisted by the churches and the general public, the Law Commission in its 1973 report on the Solemnization of Marriages recommended that the present pluralist system be retained but that safeguards be added through the introduction of uniform preliminaries and more standard elements.[194]

b. Registration

The Marriage Act of 1836, together with the Births and Deaths Registration Act passed immediately after it, brought into existence the Superintendent Registrars of births, deaths, and marriages.[195] Today all marriages, however concluded, must be registered in their offices. The public record of marriages serves to provide records necessary for the parties' own proof of their status for tax or social security purposes, and for the assembly of vital statistics. However, it is not centralized or cross-indexed with other types of records so as to provide an effective system which would enable third parties or the government to obtain information about any given individual's civil status.

2. United States

The version of pluralism in effect in the United States differs from the English version in two important respects. First, as already noted, American law is unique among that of the four countries here examined in that a legally valid marriage can be formed in 13 states with no formalities whatever. Second, American law differs from the English in that its version of the parallel civil and religious methods for concluding marriages does not accord the same degree of deference to religious law and does not reserve the privilege of concluding a marriage outside the office of a public official to those persons who wish to be married in a religious ceremony. In short, the American system as a whole is characterized by a higher degree of informality than the other systems and by the smallest degree of compulsory ritual.

a. Informal Legal Marriage

As in England until 1753 and in Scotland until 1940, couples in 13 American states can form a legal marriage simply by agreeing to be husband and wife and holding themselves out as such.[196] Obviously where such "common law" marriages are recognized, there are no compulsory preliminaries or formalities pertaining to them.

b. Formal Legal Marriage

In most American states, however, the very existence of statutes regulating marriage preliminaries and the conclusion and registration of marriage has been interpreted to exclude the possibility of forming a legal marriage informally. But as to the conclusion of marriage, regulation is kept at a minimum. A wide variety of civil and religious officials are authorized to perform marriages. Most states require witnesses, but do not impose any particular form of ceremony.[197] Every state has provision for recording of marriage certificates, but even this record can be kept confidential in some instances.[198] Certain states which do not recognize common law marriage do recognize a type of legal marriage arising from the registration of a written declaration that a marriage exists.[199] Even the minimal existing regulation is now thought to be of questionable constitutionality.[200] One authority has recommended an outright shift to marriage recording or registration laws.[201] However, it is not too much of an exaggeration to say that the present legal regulation of marriage in the United States is already basically just a matter of licensing and registration.[202] This appears clearly in the Uniform Marriage and Divorce Act which does not innovate in this area but simply embodies well-established features of state law. The Act has a "solemnization and registration" provision whose accompanying comment explains that the provision was "designed to take account of the increasing tendency of marrying couples to want a personalized ceremony, without traditional church, religious *or civil* trappings".[203] According to the draftsmen, the provision "authorizes one of the parties to such a [personalized] marriage ceremony to complete the marriage certificate form and forward it to the appropriate official for registration".[204] While it is true, as the draftsmen say, that there is some tendency of marrying couples in the United States to want a personalized informal exchange of consents, this tendency is balanced by an attachment in other sectors of society to marriage rituals which are as elaborate as ever.

What the Act really seems to be trying to do is respond to the fact that there are many different marriage ideas and practices in American society. It establishes a procedure which can be whatever the parties want it to be, a $10,000 ritual or simple registration of the fact of exchange of consents. The Uniform Act is really just a marriage registration law. Whether or not many couples will take advantage of this option which the Act offers to dispense with a ceremony is, however, the wrong question to ask here. It is highly unlikely, even if this feature of the act were well publicized, that there would be a "rush to the register". The important fact here is not the tendency, identified by the draftsmen, to want to dispense with religious and civil trappings, but rather the tendency to dispense with formal legal marriage altogether. The registration option of the UMDA will not win back or win over many of those who for one reason or another have decided to dispense with the legal institution of marriage. The spread of informal, *de facto* marriage among diverse social groups and its important, although largely unremarked, effect on enacted law will be discussed in Chapter 3 of this book.

In leaving this subject, let us note that in contrast to France and West Germany, the registration systems of the various American states operate as in England, to make records available to the parties and to permit the accumulation of vital statistics, but are not so organized as to provide the basis for a reliable check on the identity or marital status of any particular individual by public officials or third parties.

B. Compulsory Civil Ceremony: France and West Germany

1. France

a. Celebration

It was from France that the compulsory civil marriage ceremony spread to other parts of the world as a different reaction to the ecclesiastical monopoly of marriage formation from that which took place in England.[205] The Civil Code of 1804, inspired in this respect by French revolutionary legislation, made marriage a completely secular institution. It denied all legal effect to religious celebration of marriages. Today, the practice of having two marriage ceremonies (the civil one required by law to precede any religious one) is still followed by a great many French couples.[206]

Although completely secularized, French law of marriage formation requires more elements of ritual than any of the other systems here examined. In fact the secular ritual is quite comparable to a religious ceremony. The marriage must be celebrated by the *officier de l'état civil* (often the *maire*) of the commune.[207] The celebrant of the marriage must formally ask the future spouses (and, if they are minors, their ascendants who are present and who authorize the marriage) to declare whether a marriage contract has been made, and if so the date of the contract as well as the name and place of residence of the notary who has kept the contract.[208] As part of the ceremony the celebrant must read to the future spouses certain articles of the French Civil Code.[209] This is what he reads:

Spouses mutually owe each other fidelity, support and assistance. The spouses together assure the material and moral direction of the family. They provide for the upbringing of the children and prepare for their future. If the matrimonial agreement does not regulate the contribution of the spouses to the expenses of the marriage, they contribute to them in proportion to their respective abilities. The spouses are mutually bound to a community of life.

These provisions are taken from that part of the Code which sets out certain rules which apply to all marriages and which cannot be varied by contract. Their symbolic as well as legal character is apparent, as is the fact that the compulsory code reading at the marriage ceremony is a way in which a certain ideology of marriage is transmitted. The ideology currently enshrined in the Code is not, however, the one which has always been there.[210] Thus, while a couple today hears that they direct the family together, prior to 1970 they would have heard that "The husband is the head of the family." Prior to 1938, they would have heard the original language of the Code Napoleon: "The husband owes protection to his wife, the wife obedience to her husband." After the Code reading, the celebrant receives from the parties, one after the other, the declaration that they take each other for husband and wife. He then pronounces "in the name of the law" that they are united in marriage, and draws up the marriage certificate on the spot.[211]

This ritual, an elaborate one compared to that required by the other legal systems here examined, has been criticized in much the same way as has the British civil ceremony for having become "banal" and "bureaucratized".[212] However, even through the criticism, one can see that much importance is attached to the ceremony:

Even though secularized, marriage has a sort of religious gravity which is peculiar to it and which separates it from the free union – a gravity based on the idea that man's binding himself until death is an aspect of his intimation of mortality and his struggle against the ephemeral nature of his existence.... As for the minority who marry only civilly, it is difficult to reconstruct their ethical notions, but no matter how little of the sublime there is in the civil rites...with which they content themselves, it is likely that they attribute to marriage at least that sacred value which popular morality accords to any exchange of promises.[213]

The soundness of such ideas is not in question here. It is the tone which tells. Marriage formation law seems to partake in France of the nature of what the American sociologist Robert Bellah calls "civil religion".[214]

b. Registration

Unlike England and the United States, France has a system of marriage registration which, together with a national identity system, permits verification of statements made by individuals concerning their civil status and facilitates the policing of the system of marriage impediments. Not only is the marriage certificate itself recorded, but, as seen above, a note of the marriage is entered on the margin of an individual's birth certificate. This is but an aspect of that system, which France gave to the rest of the world, of complete registration under state control of those events such as births, deaths, marriages, and divorces which affect a citizen's legal status.[215] As the examples of England and the United States demonstrate, the system which was established, elaborated and perfected in France, and imitated all over the world, has not been implemented everywhere with such thoroughness as in its home country. Nor has thoroughness in these matters been seen everywhere as desirable.

2. West Germany

a. Celebration

The system of compulsory civil marriage was introduced in all of Germany in 1875, and continued in the German Civil Code of 1896 as well as in the present Marriage Law.[216] As in France, the civil ceremony must precede any religious ceremony, and the practice of the double ceremony is common.[217] The German version, however, has fewer aspects of obligatory ritual than the French and the whole idea of compulsory civil marriage is presently controversial in West Germany.[218]

The current Marriage Law provides that a marriage does not come into being unless concluded before a public official (usually the *Standesbeamte*).[219] As to required aspects of ritual, German law is content with specifying that there should be two witnesses and that the registrar should ask each of the future spouses whether they wish to enter marriage with the other.[220] After they have assented, the registrar is to pronounce "in the name of the law" that they are from then on legally bound spouses, and to enter the marriage in the "Family Book".[221] The Reform Law of 1976 added that the spouses must be asked at the time of the ceremony whether they wish to make a stipulation concerning the name they will bear in the future.[222] German law also specifies, with unintended irony, that the ceremony "shall be appropriate to the significance of marriage" and that it shall be conducted in solemn fashion.[223]

It has been contended that the obligatory civil marriage is unconstitutional as a violation of Article 4 of the German Constitution (which guarantees freedom of religion) and that therefore the option of concluding a marriage by religious ceremony should be made available.[224] However, this argument has been met by the contention that the complete separation of Church and State in the present marriage formation law satisfies the Constitution.[225] In any event, the Marriage and Family Reform Law of 1976 left the matter untouched.

b. Registration

In West Germany registration of civil status is not centralized. As in France, however, it is, together with a national system of identification, organized in such a way as to permit effective verification of vital information about spouses. Registrars of civil status are required by law to keep a marriage book, a family book, a birth book and a death book.[226] It is the family book which collects and coordinates records of changes in civil status, of deaths, births, marriages, marriage terminations by divorce or annulment, and remarriages, in order to facilitate inquiry into all aspects of a person's current status.[227]

C. Swedish Comparison

In Sweden, as in England, civil marriage was made an alternative to religious marriage, rather than a compulsory procedure. As in England, too, marriages in Sweden must be concluded before a religious or civil authority, not informally. But certain features of Swedish regulation of the conclusion of marriage set it apart from the other systems we have described here as pluralistic.

In the first place, both the optional civil ceremony and the secular version of the Tridentine decree abolishing informal marriage appeared late in Sweden. Civil marriage was made available for marriages between Christians and Jews in 1863, but did not become an option in other situations until 1908.[228] The Swedish law providing that civil or religious celebration is the only means of concluding a valid marriage did not appear until 1915.[229]

The most interesting feature of the 1915 legislation on Conclusion and Dissolution of Marriage, however, is the introduction of a new idea about marriage itself. The 1915 law prescribed the following formula to be read by the pastor or secular official by whom the marriage is preformed: "The end of marriage is the welfare of the individuals who desire to enter matrimony. Do you AB take CD as your wife for better or for worse? Do you CD take AB as your husband for better or for worse?"[230]

This allusion to individual welfare may have been in furtherance of the purposes which Folke Schmidt ascribes to the early 20th century Swedish marriage legislation: the liberation of marriage from its religious foundations and the liberation of wives from dependence on their husbands.[231] Subsequent developments have gone beyond this, however. In 1969, the government's Committee for the Reform of Family Law recommended that the civil or ecclesiastical ceremony become a purely voluntary occasion and that marriage be initiated by simple registration.[232] This proposal having failed, the Committee recommended in 1972 that official recognition of religious marriage be eliminated, and that marriage be concluded by a formal declaration to the Population Registration authorities.[233] Three poets were commissioned to the draft the text of the declaration. However, the comprehensive revision of Swedish Family Law which took place in 1973 did not adopt these proposals.[234] Instead, it made another change, just as profound on the ideological level. The 1973 reform, effective in 1974, gives couples the option to request the official performing a civil marriage to omit from the ceremony the exchange of vows for life.[235]

VI. The Ideologizing of Freedom to Marry

In one sense one can say that the evolution of English, French, German and American marriage formation law has long been marked by currents favorable to the right to marry and to freely choose one's spouse. As the discussion of each aspect of marriage regulation has shown, nearly all elements of political, ecclesiastical or family control over the marriage decision have disappeared from the law of marriage formation in all four countries in a long, slow, process of change. Social and economic changes constantly propelled the law in the direction of freedom to marry, but the legal changes took place without any particular reference to the idea of a fundamental human right to marry.

At the present time, no "right to marry" is to be found expressly stated in the Constitutions of France, West Germany or the United States, or in any law of England, although some international conventions and declarations in which these nations have participated do recognize a right to marry.[236] Yet, beginning in the 1960s in France, West Germany and the United States, courts at the highest level, dealing with the few remaining restrictions on an individual's freedom to marry or to choose one's spouse, began to articulate the issues as involving a fundamental human right. In England, the evolution of the law proceeds along much the same lines as in the other three countries but without ideological discussion.[237]

The pronouncements of the French Court of Cassation, the German Constitutional Court and the United States Supreme Court, together with their reception in the learned writing in each country, crown the developments recounted here, and at the same time create a new atmosphere for the further development of the law of marriage formation. In each country that atmosphere is somewhat different.

A. France

The evolution of the law of marriage formation in the direction of increased freedom to marry and to choose one's spouse can be seen more clearly in the changes that have occurred in the French Civil Code of 1804 than in the law of England, Germany and the United States. A similar evolution has taken place in the two latter countries, but in England and the United States it has been less visible, being concealed in piecemeal case-law and statutory reforms, rather than emblazoned upon a national monument, as one may well characterize the French Civil Code. In Germany, marriage law was codified, but by the time the Civil Code was prepared for the politically unified nation, many of the ideas which had produced transforming changes in the French Civil Code were already accepted and thus formed the basis of the German Civil Code which went into effect in 1900.

In present day France, it has been asserted that, "An affirmation of the liberty of man in the formation...of the matrimonial bond is the essence of the French message for the social order", and, "The history of our marriage law for fifty years is the history of a continuous liberation."[238] The roots of this message have been traced back to the emphasis on individual liberty in the French Declaration of the Rights of Man of 1789.[239] But a right to marry did not spring directly from the French Revolution. Indeed, the Code Napoleon of 1804 retained the individualistic property notions of the French Revolution more than the revolutionary ideas of individual liberty. The family law of the Code remained in general marked with the tie between blood and soil and imprinted with the traditional conceptions of the pre-revolutionary law. Its provisions reinforced hierarchy in the family and the strength of family ties. But because social change had already begun to affect the organization of family life,[240] the family law of the Code was in some ways already out of date in 1804. This fact was not altogether unrecognized by the draftsmen.[241] However, the speed with which the Code had to be drafted under pressure

from the First Consul meant that many of its provisions were simply taken
over from pre-existing law, particularly from the Custom of Paris.[242]

As the evolution of French marriage formation law shows, the original
scheme of the Code (in which the marriage of a member of a family group
was treated as very much the affair of the group which the marriage
was destined to perpetuate) has given way to a scheme in which marriage
is treated primarily as an individual affair. This growing individualiza-
tion of French family law has occurred simultaneously with the decline
of individualism in French property law. The two movements are doubt-
less connected, in the sense that the increased distribution of both
wealth and the burden of economic calamities has made individualism in
family law possible. As one French writer has put it, "when this role of
assuring security is transferred from the family to the state, the social bond
becomes stronger but, proportionately, the family bonds relax and we tend to
approach the ideal to which the men of 1789 aspired: every individual would
have a direct relationship with the state, without 'intermediaries' ".[243] As we
have seen, French law has in fact come to protect individual marriage choice
against interference from family ties and family hierarchy, but it still, to a
greater degree even than the other three systems, bears traces of an older
order.

It was not until 1968 that the diverse transforming trends were brought
together in an idea of a "right to marry" by the highest French Court for
private law matters, the Court of Cassation.[244] The ground for this decision
was probably prepared by a 1963 Paris Court of Appeals decision in which
the right was first articulated judicially in France and where it received what is
thus far its fullest expression by a French court.[245] The 1963 case was a suit by
an Air France stewardess seeking damages from the company for wrongful
breach of her employment contract. The company's defense was a clause in
the employment contract which purported to give the employer the right to
terminate the contract upon the marriage of the employee. The employee had
good grounds in both contract law and labor law for resisting this defense,
and the court did in fact rest its decision for the employee in part upon these
grounds. So it is all the more remarkable that the court went on to say that even
if the clause in the contract could survive the objections made to it as a matter
of contract and labour law, it should be held void as a matter of public policy.
The court said,

[T]he right to marry is an individual right *d'ordre public*[246] which cannot be limited
or alienated;...as a result in the area of contractual relationships...the freedom to marry
should in principle be safeguarded and in the absence of obvious and imperative

reasons, a no-marriage clause should be declared void as infringing a fundamental personal right.[247]

The court further remarked that such a restriction on marriage, because of its tendency to encourage the formation of illegitimate unions (not forbidden by the employment contract), constituted an infringement of good morals.[248]

The case was noted at once as a landmark.[249] But in 1964 the Court of Cassation, in a case dealing with a similar clause, never reached the question whether a fundamental right was involved.[250] Then in 1968, again in the context of ruling on the validity of a no-marriage clause in an employment contract, the Court of Cassation broke new ground by striking down the clause as an unreasonable restriction of the "right to marry and the right to work".[251] Finally, in a 1975 case, once more in the employment context, the Court of Cassation affirmed that the freedom to marry was a principle *d'ordre public.*[252]

B. West Germany

The German Civil Code of 1896 is nearly a century younger than the French Civil Code. In contrast to the French Code, it was the product of years of careful drafting, public scrutiny of drafts, and extensive revision. It never contained such vestiges from earlier times as the French Code's requirement of a formal request by even an emancipated adult son or daughter for parental permission to marry, or the elaborate system of formal family "oppositions" to marriages.[253] But it is nevertheless fair to say that the family law in this turn of the century code, which went into effect on 1 January 1900, emphasized the cohesion and hierarchical organization of the family unit more than the independent individuality of the persons composing that unit.[254] As in France, a number of adjustments in German family law have occurred within the past 50 years, and especially within the period following the end of World War II.[255]

In West Germany, the idea of a fundamental right or freedom to marry seems to have been first expressed judicially by the Federal Supreme Administrative Court (*Bundesverwaltungsgericht*) in 1962,[256] and then taken up by the Federal Constitutional Court (*Bundesverfassungsgericht*) where it was announced first in 1970, and then, emphatically, in 1971.[257]

Like the French cases discussed above, the 1962 West German case arose in the employment context. Here, however, the employer was the State and the plaintiff was a police official who had married without securing the advance permission he was required to seek under administrative regulations.[258] The

Supreme Administrative Court did not invalidate the requirement of permission, but it did hold that the refusal of permission to marry was an infringement of Article 6 line 1 of the Constitution of 1949, under the particular circumstances of this case where it appeared that a child had already been conceived. The court went on to protect the official's job by holding that his marriage in defiance of regulations was not a "gross violation" of his official duties.

The constitutional article referred to says nothing about a right to marry. It simply reads that: "Marriage and the family enjoy the special protection of the state."[259] However, the view that the constitutionally protected institution of marriage rests "upon the free decision of husband and wife" was expressed by the Constitutional Court in 1970.[260] Then, in 1971, the Constitutional Court addressed the issue more fully in a case involving the question whether a Spaniard, wanting to marry a German woman divorced in Germany from a German husband, had sufficiently complied with the statutory requirement that a foreigner must produce documentary evidence of his capacity (under the law of the state of which he is a national) to marry, given that his future wife's divorce would not be recognized in Spain.[261] Holding that the denial of permission to marry in these circumstances was in violation of the Constitution, the court said that Article 6 line 1 guarantees even to a foreigner the "freedom to marry" (Eheschliessungsfreiheit) with a spouse of his own choice.

Neither the judicial decisions nor the constitutional provision they rely upon are unqualified. Article 6 line 1 is certainly ambiguous so far as marriage formation is concerned. Far from creating an unbounded freedom to marry, the fact that it places marriage and family under the special protection of the State arguably supports marriage impediments to the extent that they are accepted as "protective".[262] Likewise, Article 12 of the European Convention on Human Rights, often cited in West German discussions, seems primarily intended to prevent discrimination against persons or groups of persons in marriage, and expressly refers to the laws of the individual states: "Men and women of marriageable age have the right to marry and to found a family, according to the national laws governing the exercise of this right."[263]

Consequently, in West Germany as in France, it is uncertain what practical consequences will flow from the new "right to marry". It has been argued recently in West Germany that Article 6 of the Constitution, together with Article 4 guaranteeing freedom of thought and religion, mean that certain aspects of the marriage formation law are constitutionally required. Some think that the introduction of optional religious celebration of marriage is required by religious freedom. Others think religious freedom requires the continuation of the compulsory civil ceremony.[264] One writer counsels against framing such issues as constitutional questions, contending that, judging by experience, the "...persuasive power of such reasoning is small, and the arguments lead rather to an aggravation of existing differences".[265] From this point of view, the approach which England has so far taken to the legal issues of marriage formation – practical, functional, without sloganizing the issues – has much to recommend it.

C. United States

Articulation of "the freedom to marry" by the United States Supreme Court came in 1967, in one of the many cases raising issues of racial discrimination which reached the Court in the 1960s. As in France and Germany, the decision by the highest court had been foreshadowed by decisions of lower (in this case, state) courts.[266] The case, which, as fate would have it, was called *Loving v. Virginia*,[267] involved a Virginia statute prohibiting inter-racial marriages. In a unanimous opinion written by the late Chief Justice Warren, the Court struck down the Virginia statute (and by implication the 15 other state miscegenation statutes then existing) as violative of the Equal Protection and Due Process clauses of the 14th amendment to the United States Constitution.[268] In holding that the statute deprived the Lovings of liberty without due process of law the Court said: "The freedom to marry has long been recognized as one of the vital personal rights essential to the orderly pursuit of happiness by free men", and "Marriage is one of the 'basic civil rights of man', fundamental to our very existence and survival....Under our Constitution, the freedom to marry, or not marry, a person of another race resides with the individual and cannot be infringed by the State."[269]

But for this language, which like that of the French and West German courts went beyond what the decision of the case actually required, *Loving v. Virginia* would have been an unremarkable application of the Equal Protection Clause of the 14th amendment to the United States Constitution, a part of the process of granting full equality to members of minority groups. But with this language, the case is now widely understood to call into question much state regulation of marriage.[270]

In contrast with England, France, and West Germany, marriage formation in America (as well as its effects and dissolution) is governed, as already pointed out, not by national law, but by the laws of the several states. Thus, *Loving* has a special significance in the American federal system because, in view of the legal supremacy of the federal Constitution, it potentially sub-

jects to federal re-examination and evaluation much state statutory and case
law which had previously been taken for granted.

Actually, as we have seen, the American state law of marriage formation
already had been developing in broadly similar fashion to that of England,
France and Germany. It too was gradually dropping anachronistic provisions. One leading American family law scholar, a former law school dean
who became a member of the United States Congress, sees the *Loving*
decision as giving constitutional status to a pre-existing "profound consensus" in the United States that the state and the law should say "as little as
possible about who should marry whom".[271] Without doubt, however, the
Loving decision will affect the further development of state law. Its influence
is apparent in the provisions of the Uniform Marriage and Divorce Act.

VII. Summary

The examination of marriage formation law in this chapter is far from
demonstrating in itself that the posture of the State with respect to the family
is radically changing in the four countries whose law we have just surveyed.
And yet the foregoing examination is an important part of the case to be
made. Thus far, there are two important points to be made: state involvement
in the questions of who can marry, who marries whom, and how they do it, is
diminishing; modern forms of state involvement in some aspects of marriage
formation which affect society in general are increasing. The strength of the
trends is not the same in all four countries. The reasons why it is believed that
the foregoing survey supports these contentions will be briefly summarized.

As to the diminution of State interest in who marries whom, the marriage
restrictions in all four countries are primarily statements of what ought to be.
In England and the United States, especially in the latter, the marriage
impediments lack teeth. There seems to be no really effective way of preventing anyone who is determined to do so from evading them. In addition, as we
have seen, the number of restrictions is everywhere being reduced to those
involving age, simultaneous polygamy and marriages among members of
the core family. Even these restrictions are not so absolute as they appear.

So far as the manner in which marriages are concluded is concerned, at
present only France exhibits much interest in this matter. In the United
States, where the state systems are scarcely distinguishable from simple
marriage registration, this tendency has been enshrined in the Uniform Act.
It is interesting that in the three countries where it can be said that some
marriage ritual is compulsory, dissatisfaction with the rituals has been regis-

tered but in the end there is no move toward change. England has eyed the compulsory civil ceremony, West Germany has studied the pluralist compromise, and France has recognized that much of its system is anachronistic, but their reluctance to alter long-standing laws can best be explained by the fact that these laws have become part of the mores and have acquired a "feeling of oughtness". [272]

The UMDA draftsmen have stated that premarital regulation has been reduced to a minimum and that, as to this minimum, "substantial compliance" is enough. [273] In general, it should be added that while there has been little change overall, the existing laws governing marriage formation are old laws, and that what change has taken place, has occurred along the lines here indicated. The marriage laws of all four countries have undoubtedly been, and will continue to be, affected by their new approach to divorce law. Some will reason that once having furnished free exit from marriage, there is less reason to carefully guard the entrance. There is virtually no legal response to the cry from some quarters that marriage ought to be made more difficult, and what movement there is seems clearly in the direction of reducing impediments and formalities, as well as to mitigate the consequences of disregarding them. In the United States, all of these trends are reinforced by the tendency of the law to respond to diversity by becoming "neutral".

As for the increase in peculiarly modern forms of state interest, one can point to the use of the occasion of marriage to communicate certain types of information to the prospective spouses – whether it be the message of equality, as in France; or information about birth control as in many American states. Social interest in record keeping and data gathering is also apparent, especially in the American system where it was not built in as it was in France and Germany. Sometimes the purpose of information gathering is in pursuit of the vague and benign aim of studying and helping "the family". Sometimes it is for a more definite purpose, as is the case with the requirement of the social security number to facilitate enforcement of family support obligations in the United States.

Finally, and most importantly, if we may look ahead to what has happened to the legal institution of marriage itself as described in Chapters 3 through 6, the various regulations concerning entry into the institution will be put in a whole new light. The ensemble of apparently trifling changes in the manner in which the legal institution of marriage is formed is itself one small but essential aspect of the revolution which is taking place in the way the Western State interacts with the family in the late twentieth century. As Chapters 3 and 4 will show, it is becoming increasingly difficult to distinguish the married state from the unmarried state or from the situation of persons who live in what we have described in Chapter 1 as *de facto* marriages. In this light then, the ideologizing of the freedom to marry has appeared on the scene, just at the moment when legal marriage is ceasing to have much significance. As marriage impediments and formalities fall away, those exercising the "right to marry" may find that life on the other side of the door they have tried so hard to open is not much different from life outside "legal" marriage. In passing through the door, however, they may encounter an unlooked-for intimacy with the State. Long before it gets to the point where their photographs and fingerprints are taken and a package of contraceptives is pressed into their hands as they cross the threshold, many couples may decide that the "freedom to marry" is not worth pursuing.

If, as will be argued in the following chapters, legal marriage is being drained of much of its content, the remaining formalities of legal marriage described in this chapter begin to appear as juridified versions of marriage rites, a class of social phenomena practically universal in human societies and, as mating rituals, common even among animals.[274] In societies where marriage has not been extensively juridified, it has nevertheless typically been accompanied by ritual. One may think of the Roman gifts of fire and water, Michael's capture of Sarah in Chapter One, or the marriage palaces of the Soviet Union. It is doubtful whether debasement or disappearance of those rites petrified in law will much affect such a persistent aspect of human behavior. Thus the description of legal developments in this chapter is in no way meant to dispute the underlying assumption of Yeats' question, "How but in custom and ceremony are innocence and beauty born?"

NOTES

[1] The process of legal and social change which transformed French and German family law from the time of the Prussian General Code of 1794 and the French Civil Code of 1804 to the present is well described in the valuable book by H. Dörner, Industrialisierung und Familienrecht (1974). For the larger context, that of legal developments generally in this period, see F. Wieacker, Privatrechtsgeschichte der Neuzeit 348–586 (2d ed. 1967). For a description of how legal regulation of marriage came to be established in the West in the first place, how it expanded and how it is presently contracting, see Chapter 7 *infra* of this book.

[2] I. C. Vernier, American Family Laws §43 (1931); Note, 53 Harv. L. Rev. 309 (1939).

[3] *Clark HB* 86–87

[4] See generally, Schoch, Divorce Law and Practice under National Socialism in Germany, 28 Iowa L. Rev. 225 (1943); also, Loewenstein, Law in the Third Reich, 45 Yale L. J. 779, 797 (1936).

[5] England: *Cretney* 22; France: French C.C. art. 146: "There is no marriage where there is no consent"; United States: *Clark HB* 95; West Germany: *Beitzke* 292.

[6] *Cretney* 22; *Carbonnier, 2 Droit Civil* 40; *Clark HB* 96. But the consent of a conservator or guardian may be required for certain individuals, *Beitzke* 292; *Carbonnier, 2 Droit Civil* 34, 40.

[7] *Cretney* 22; *Carbonnier, 2 Droit Civil* 34–35; *Clark HB* 99; *Beitzke* 292.

[8] *Cretney* 58–60; *Carbonnier, 2 Droit Civil* 34–35; *Beitzke* 292; *Clark HB* 97–98; UMDA §208 (1).

[9] UMDA §203 and Comment thereto.
The Uniform Marriage and Divorce Act (UMDA) was recommended in 1970 by the National Conference of Commissioners on Uniform State Laws, with the approval of the American Bar Association, as a model for adoption in all states. The provisions of UMDA are the focal point of the discussion of American law in this chapter because they are typical of the type of change which has already taken place in the various states as they have modernized their marriage law, and because they are likely to be influential as a model for states revising their marriage law in the future.

[10] Only a few American states still have marriage impediments based on physical conditions such as epilepsy or venereal disease. *Clark HB* 86–87. In England at one time impotence was treated as an impediment to marriage. *Cretney* 57–58. The trend now is to treat such conditions as impotence or communicable venereal disease as grounds for avoiding the marriage, if they are unknown to the other party at the time of marriage and if they are raised within a reasonable period of time after the marriage.

[11] *Drinan* 51; *Foster* 64.

[12] See §VI *infra* for a discussion of the American Constitutional trends.

[13] Note, *Current Legal Developments, Sweden,* 19 Int. & Comp. L.Q. 164 (1970); Note, *Family Law – Sweden,* 22 Int. & Comp. L. Q. 182 (1973); Note, *Family Law – Sweden (follow-up),* 22 Int. & Comp. L. Q. 766 (1973).

[14] *Dörner* 136. In England, under the Royal Marriages Act of 1772, 12 Geo. 3 c.11, the consent of the Sovereign is required for the marriage of descendants of George II. But the Act exempts the issue of princesses who have married into foreign families, so it seems that there are few if any members of the royal family to whom the Act still applies. *Cretney* 50. In France, certain military personnel, foreign service officers and members of the diplomatic corps must still obtain consents to their marriages (French C.C. art. 164*ff.*), but marriages entered without these consents are valid, although the persons who enter them may be subject to various penalties. Most military authorizations were abolished by a law passed in 1972. *Bénabent* 449.

[15] French C.C. art. 228, 296; German EheG §8.

[16] *Beitzke* 40, 41; *Carbonnier, 2 Droit Civil* 51.

[17] *Ibid.*

[18] See Note 9 *supra.*

[19] In 1968, 22 states were said to have had such restrictions. *Foster* 66.

[20] Wis. Stat. Ann. §245.10 (Supp. 1975).

[21] It was held unconstitutional by a three-judge court in *Redhail v. Zablocki*, 418 F. Supp. 1061 (D.Wis.1976).

[22] It is worth noticing in this subchapter on the ability to marry, that in French and German law even marriage with deceased persons has been allowed. "Posthumous marriages" are still permitted in France by permission of the Head of State in cases where the intent to marry has been established by public notice or the drafting of a marriage contract and one of the parties has died before the ceremony could take place. (French C.C. art. 171.) No legal effects attach to such a marriage other than the legitimization of children. In Germany, a 1943 decree which permitted similar marriages has been repealed. *Beitzke* 29.

[23] *Beitzke* 291; *Cretney* 18; Weiss & Collada, Judicial Consent to Marry, 3 Fam. L. Q. 288, 288–289 (1969).

[24] *Bénabent* 449

[25] *Carbonnier, 2 Droit Civil* 43–44.

[26] French C.C. arts. 149–160 spell out in detail the formalities and procedures to follow if parents or other relatives are dead, or incapable of consenting, or cannot be found, or where the child is adopted or illegitimate.

[27] Described in *Carbonnier, 2 Droit Civil* 43–44.

[28] Law no. 74–631 of 5 July 1974 (J.O. 7 July p. 7099). French C.C. arts. 148, 388, 488.

[29] French C.C. art. 144.

[30] *Carbonnier, 2 Droit Civil* 31–32.

[31] French C.C. art. 145.

[32] *Carbonnier, 2 Droit Civil* 32.

[33] *Bénabent* 447.

[34] Art. 145 of the Civil Code as modified by Law no. 70–1266 of 23 Dec. 1970.

[35] *Bénabent* 451.

[36] *Ibid.*

[37] French C.C. arts. 172–179.

[38] *Carbonnier, 2 Droit Civil* 60.

[39] French C.C. art. 185.

[40] French C.C. arts. 182, 183.

[41] The *Allgemeines Landrecht für die Preussischen Staaten* (ALR) was inspired by Frederick II of Prussia, and became law in 1794, four years after his death. *Rheinstein, M.S.D.L.* 25.

[42] *Dörner* 38; cf. *Carbonnier, 2 Droit Civil* 45.

[43] *König* par. 34.

[44] *Dörner* 94.

[45] *Id.* at 95.

[46] *Ibid.*

[47] *Id.* at 96.

[48] *Ibid.*

[49] *Ibid.*

[50] *Ibid.*

[51] Grossdeutsches Ehegesetz of 6 July 1938, RGB1. 1.807 S1.

[52] Law of 31 July 1974, effective 1 January 1975, BGB1. 1713, amending *inter alia* EheG §1.

[53] *Beitzke* 291.

[54] Where the legal representative does not have the care of the person of the minor or where there is another custodian besides him, the consent of the custodian is also required by EheG §3. *Beitzke* 292.

[55] EheG §3.

[56] EheG §1.

[57] *Beitzke* 291.

[58] *Ibid.*

[59] *Ibid.*

[60] *Ibid.*

[61] *Beitzke* 293.

[62] Montesquieu, Spirit of the Laws, Book XXIII. Ch. 8 (1748).

[63] *Bromley* 27.

[64] *Bromley* 28.

[65] Engels, The Origin of the Family, Private Property and the State 136 (Leacock ed. 1972; orig. publ. 1882).

[66] Marriage Act 1949, 12, 13 & 14 Geo. 6 c. 76, s. 2, 3, as amended. If the parents are not alive, or are unavailable for other reasons, detailed statutory provisions govern the steps to be taken to obtain authorization to marry. Marriage Act 1949, s. 3(1), 2nd Sched.

[67] *Cretney* 16.

[68] *Id.* at 19.

[69] Marriage Act 1949 s. 2(1), as amended by the Family Law Reform Act 1969. *Bromley* 30.

[70] Marriage Act 1949 s. 48.

[71] Marriage Act 1949 s. 3(1) provisos (a) and (b).

[72] *Cretney* 55.

[73] *Cretney* 53.

[74] *Ibid.*

[75] Report of the Committee on the Age of Majority (Latey Report) par. 106 (1967), quoted by *Cretney* 54.

[76] *Cretney* 54.

[77] UMDA s. 203 (1). An optional subsection permits marriage of persons below the age of 16 with both parental and judicial consent. Report on the Uniform Marriage and Divorce Act of the Joint Meeting between the Representatives of the Section of Family Law and the National Conference of Commissioners on Uniform State Laws, 5 Fam. L. Q. 125, 135 (1971).

[78] *Foster* 72.

[79] In Stanton v. Stanton, 421 U.S. 7 (1975), a statute specifying a greater age of majority for males than for females was held unconstitutional, in the context of child support, as a denial of equal protection.

[80] *Foster* 73.

[81] Weiss and Collada, *supra* n. 23 at 289.

[82] *See* Cal. Civil Code §4101(b) (West Supp. 1976); Ohio Rev. Code Ann. §3101.05 (Supp. 1975); Utah Code Ann. §§30–1–30, 30–1–33 (Supp. 1975).

[83] New York Times, Aug. 6, 1975, at 24.

[84] *Ibid.*

[85] UMDA s. 208 and Comment thereto.

[86] *Beitzke* 43 (Marriage between persons of the same sex is *Nichtehe,* that is, no marriage comes into existence); *Carbonnier, 2 Droit Civil* 31; UMDA §201 and Comment thereto; *Cretney* 17 ("The fact that behavior is not so offensive as to call for criminal sanctions does not mean that society should provide an institutional framework for it.")

[87] M. Amos and F. Walton, Introduction to French Law 66 (3d ed. 1967).

[88] Cour d'appel de Limoges, 4 June 1975, D.S. 1975. Som. 121. See also Cass. civ., 16 Dec. 1975 (2 cases), D.S. 1976, 397. Note Lindon.

[89] Baker v. Nelson, 191 N.W.2d 185 (Minn. 1971), *appeal dismissed* 409 U.S. 810 (1972); Jones v. Hallahan, 501 S.W.2d 588 (Ky. App. 1973).

[90] New York Times, April 27, 1975.

[91] Comment, *The Legality of Homosexual Marriage*, 82 Yale L. J. 573 (1973).

[92] D. Teal, The Gay Militants 291 (1971).

[93] EheG, former s. 6.

[94] *Beitzke* 40.

[95] 1. EheRG 1976 art. 3.

[96] *Bénabent* 463.

[97] In all four countries such private restrictions are upheld to a limited extent if "reasonable", and if they do not absolutely preclude or require marriage. But they are not favored and the tendency everywhere is to construe them strictly.

[98] *König* pars. 60, 80, 83.; Girard, Le choix du conjoint, une enquête de sociologie en France (1964); *Carbonnier, 2 Droit Civil* 58; Kerckhoff, Patterns of Homogamy in Mate Selection, Catton and Smircich, Propinquity in Mate Selection Reassessed, and Winch, Need Complementarity Reassessed, in Sociology of the Family 162–215 (Anderson ed. 1971). An economic analysis has been attempted in Becker, A Theory of Marriage, 81 J. Pol. Ec. 813 (1973).

[99] UMDA §207 Comment ("The Act eliminates most of the traditional marriage prohibitions and, consistent with the national trend, eliminates all affinity prohibitions. Only bigamous and incestuous marriages are prohibited".); *Beitzke* 37 ("The existing law follows a modern tendency to diminish marriage prohibitions where feasible.... According to the Marriage Law, only the prohibitions based on relationship or currently existing marriage are absolute prohibitions."); *Bénabent* 462.

[100] French C.C. art. 147; England, Matrimonial Causes Act 1973, s. 11(6); West Germany, EheG §5; UMDA §207.

[101] French Penal C. art. 340; England, Offenses Against the Person Act 1861, 24 & 25 Vict. c. 100, s. 57; West Germany, StGB §171; United States: *Clark HB* 61–62.

[102] G. Murdock, Social Structure 24 (1949); *König* par. 65.

[103] United States v. Cleveland, 329 U.S. 14 (1946). The Church of Jesus Christ of Latter Day Saints (Mormons) officially abolished simultaneous polygyny in 1890. The practice was continued however by certain Mormons who doubted the authenticity of the direct revelation from God on which its abolition was based.

[104] 329 U.S. 14 at 19.

[105] *Id.* at 26.

[106] In West Germany and several of the United States, a child of a void or voidable marriage is deemed legitimate regardless of the good or bad faith of one or both of the spouses in contracting the marriage. In England and in some American states children of void marriages are deemed legitimate if at least one of the parties to the marriage reasonably believed the marriage was valid. France and some American states, however, still place "adulterine and incestuous bastards" in a different class from ordinary bastards. See generally, *Krause, Int. Encyc.* par. 39–44, and 51.

[107] England, *Cretney* 9, 56, *Bromley* 49; West Germany, *Beitzke* 43, and I. E. Cohn, Manual of German Law 225 (2d ed. 1968); United States: UMDA, Prefatory Note p. 4 and §207, 209; France, *Carbonnier, 2 Droit Civil* 111–113.

[108] *Clark CB* 88. Bigamy is no longer a crime in Alaska and Minnesota.

[109] Germany: StGB s. 171 (confinement up to three years or a fine); see also *Sundberg, Marriage or No Marriage* 231. Under the French Penal Code art. 340, the penalty for bigamy is 6 months to three years confinement and a fine of 500 to 20,000 Old Francs.

[110] *Cretney* 9; *Bromley* 24; BVerwG, 18 July 1974, noted by Jayme, FamRZ 1975, 338–341; cf. Cour d'appel de Lyon, 21 May 1974, D.S. 1975. Jur. 9, noted by Guiho. UMDA §210 codifies the principle that marriages valid by the laws of the state where contracted are valid everywhere, and expressly fails to incorporate the traditional exception for those marriages which contravene some strong public policy of the jurisdiction. In England, the Matrimonial Proceedings (Polygamous Marriages) Act 1972, c. 38, made polygamous marriages justiciable in English courts for the first time. Re-enacted as s. 47 of the Matrimonial Causes Act 1973, c. 18, it nullified the long-standing rule of English law denying either party to a polygamous marriage the right to seek the adjudication of disputes or remedies offered by English courts in matrimonial cases.

[111] *König* par. 65; L. Mair, Marriage 153 (1971).

[112] Montesquieu, Spirit of the Laws, Book XVI. Ch. 3 (1748).

[113] Mair, *supra* n. 111 at 204; *Kahn-Freund* 10; Opoku, Reform of Marriage and Divorce Laws in Francophone West Africa, 7 Ghana L. J. 107, 111–113 (1970).

[114] The extensive lists came from the canon law prohibitions which once reached to the seventh degree of kinship by civil law computation. "Marriage", Encyclopedia Brittanica 755 (11th ed. 1911). See Ch. 7 *infra* at 312–313.

[115] Note, *Family Law – Sweden*, 22 Int. & Camp. L. Q. 182 (1973); Note, *Family Law – Sweden (follow-up)*, 22 Int. & Comp. L. Q. 766 (1973).

[116] French C.C. arts. 161–164; *Bénabent* 462.

[117] *Bénabent* 462.

[118] *Ibid.*

[119] *Ibid.*

[120] Described in *Carbonnier, 2 Droit Civil* 60.

[121] EheG s. 4; *Beitzke* 37–38.

[122] NJW 1974, 545.

[123] UMDA §207. The exception for aboriginal cultures has the curious effect of permitting uncle–niece marriages among American Indians but not among Jews, although such marriages are accepted in Jewish religious law.

[124] *Foster* 61.

[125] *Drinan* 51; *Foster* 61–63.

[126] Marriage Act 1949, Sched. 1, as amended. By case law these prohibited degrees include illegitimate and half-blood relationships. Marriage is also prohibited between an adopted person and those who adopt him, but not between the adopted person and any other relatives by adoption. Adoption Act 1958, 7 & 8 Eliz. 2 c. 5, s. 13(3).

[127] *Bromley* 26.

[128] *Carbonnier, 2 Droit Civil* 52.

[129] S. Freud, General Introduction to Psychoanalysis, 21st Lecture (1917).

[130] Mair, *supra* n. 111 at 20–21. Maisch, Incest, 48–49 (1972). Cf. St. Augustine, The City of God XV.16: when an abundant population made it possible, it was right that men should choose for wives women who were not already their sisters "so as to bind together by family love a larger number of people".

[131] E.g. *Beitzke* 37; *Cretney* 12–13.

[132] E.g. *Carbonnier, 2 Droit Civil* 52; *Cretney* 13.

[133] Reduction of penalties has been the approach of the Model Penal Code in the United States: American Law Institute, Model Penal Code §230.2 (Proposed Official Draft 1962); as well as that of West Germany, *infra* at n. 137.

[134] Sexual Offenses Act 1956, 4 & 5 Eliz. 2 c. 69, s. 10 and 11.

[135] French Penal C. art. 331.

[136] West, Thoughts on Sex Law Reform, in Crime, Criminology and Public Policy 481 (Hood ed. 1974).

[137] StGB s. 173; Schönke-Schröder, Strafgesetzbuch Kommentar 1011–1013, 1016 (1974).

[138] Maisch, *supra* n. 130 at 75, 86.

[139] The New York Times, March 7, 1976, at 7 E, cols. 3–4.

[140] *Beitzke* 43; *Cretney* 56; Cohn, *supra* n. 107 at 225; UMDA §207, 209; *Carbonnier, 2 Droit Civil* 111–113; and see text at n. 107 *supra*.

[141] *König* par. 24, 47.

[142] C. Lévi-Strauss, Elementary Structures of Kinship 12–25 (1969; orig. publ. 1949).

[143] Studies cited in Maisch, *supra* n. 130 at 35.

[144] *König* par. 47.

[145] See ch. 7 *infra*.

[146] *Bromley* 47–48; *Cretney* 35–36.

[147] *Bromley* 38–39; *Cretney* 36.

[148] *Bromley* 33–35; *Cretney* 37–39.

[149] *Bromley* 32–33; *Cretney* 39–40.

[150] *Cretney* 47.
[151] Law Commission Report No. 53, Annex par. 39–41.
[152] *Cretney* 48–49.
[153] French C.C. art. 63.
[154] *Infra* §IV.D.
[155] *Carbonnier, 2 Droit Civil* 34.
[156] French C.C. art. 63, 64, 166.
[157] *Supra* §II.B.1.
[158] French C.C. art. 169; *Carbonnier* 51.
[159] French C.C. art. 70, 71.
[160] Amos & Walton, *supra* n. 87 at 62.
[161] *Carbonnier, 2 Droit Civil* 60.
[162] *Infra* §V.B.2.b.
[163] PStG s. 5; *Beitzke* 27.
[164] *Beitzke* 27.
[165] EheG s. 12; PStG s. 12; PStG s. 3.
[166] *Beitzke* 28.
[167] *Neuhaus* 61.
[168] EheG s. 9.
[169] *Beitzke* 42.
[170] *Neuhaus* 62.
[171] *Ibid.*
[172] See *infra* §VI.
[173] *Clark HB* 38; UMDA §204; the waiting period requirement has recently been repealed in New Mexico, N.M. Stat. Ann. §57–1–11.1 (1969), repealed 1973 (Supp. 1975); and North Carolina, N.C. Gen. Stat. §51–8.1 (1966), repealed 1967 (Supp. 1975).
[174] *Clark* 37.
[175] Report, *supra* n. 77 at 145.
[176] *Clark* 86.
[177] *Supra* n. 9.
[178] *Drinan* 54.
[179] Georgia, Hawaii, Kentucky, Maryland, Michigan, New Hampshire, South Carolina.
[180] UMDA §202 (1).
[181] The ease with which one can establish a new identity, together with a complete set of papers including birth certificate, driver's license, social security number and passport is described step-by-step in a front page article in the Wall Street Journal of 8 January 1976, together with a report on the work of a federal task force established to devise ways to make it harder to acquire personal documents. The article also presents the position taken by the American Civil Liberties Union in opposition to any national identification system. A proposal for a comprehensive and computerized system of marriage registration was put forward by U.S. Congressman, then Dean, Robert F. Drinan, S.J., in *Drinan* 54.
[182] *Infra* Ch. 7.
[183] Marriage Act 1753, 26 Geo. 2 c. 33 (Lord Hardwicke's Act.)
[184] Marriage Act 1836, 6 & 7 Will. 4 c. 85; *Cretney* 34.
[185] *Cretney* 36, 37.
[186] *Id.* at 41, 49.
[187] *Id.* at 44.
[188] *Id.* at 41–43.
[189] *Id.* at 44–45.
[190] Working Paper of the Law Commission No. 35, par. 5.
[191] *Cretney* 46.
[192] *Id.* at 49.
[193] Working Paper of the Law Commission No. 35, par. 70.

[194] Law Commission Report No. 53, par. 21–2.

[195] *Cretney* 34.

[196] *Infra* Ch. 3 at 81.

[197] Several states expressly provide that no particular form of ceremony is required except that the parties must declare that they take each other as husband and wife. *Clark* 39.

[198] Cal. Civ. Code §4213 (1970), *as amended*, (Supp. 1975).

[199] Cal. Civ. Code §4213 (West 1970), *as amended,* (Supp. 1975); Mont. Rev. Codes Ann. §48–130 (1947), *as amended*, (Supp. 1975); Tex. Fam. Code §1.94 (1975).

[200] See §VI *infra*.

[201] *Drinan* 54.

[202] "Because of the absence of standards in this area, it would appear that it would be more appropriate to call the procedure for securing a 'license' to marry a mere recording or a registration of a marriage." *Drinan* 50.

[203] Emphasis added. UMDA §206 and Comment thereto.

[204] *Ibid.*

[205] *Carbonnier, 2 Droit Civil* 15, 18, See Ch. 7 *infra* at 315.

[206] *Carbonnier, Flexible Droit* 137. In Paris, in 1973, 7,140 of 16,492 civil marriages were followed by a Roman Catholic ceremony, Le mariage à la trâine, Le Nouvel Observateur, 2 Feb. 1976, at 32, 33.

[207] French C.C. arts. 74, 75, 165.

[208] French C.C. art. 75. See Ch. 4 *infra* at 170–171.

[209] *Ibid.*

[210] The evolution from hierarchy to equality is described in *Glendon, Family Power & Authority* 4–7.

[211] French C.C. art. 75.

[212] *Carbonnier, 2 Droit Civil* 59, 61.

[213] *Carbonnier, Flexible Droit* 137.

[214] R. Bellah, Beyond Belief. Essays on Religion in a Post-Traditional World 168 (1970).

[215] *Rheinstein, M.S.D.L.* 198, 204.

[216] H. F. Thomas, Formlose Ehen 95 (1973).

[217] *Beitzke* 26; PStG s. 67.

[218] *Beitzke* 26.

[219] EheG s.11.

[220] EheG s. 13.

[221] EheG s. 14.

[222] EheG new s. 13 A. See Ch. 4 *infra* at 131–134.

[223] PStG s. 8.

[224] *Beitzke* 26; *Neuhaus* 60.

[225] *Beitzke* 26.

[226] PStG s. 1.

[227] PStG s. 2., 12 *et seq.*

[228] *Schmidt (1971)* 196.

[229] *Id.* at 204.

[230] *Rheinstein, M.S.D.L.* 127.

[231] *Schmidt (1971)* 197.

[232] Note, *Current Legal Developments, Sweden*, 19 Int. & Comp. L. Q. 164 (1970); Note, *Family Law – Sweden (follow-up)*, 22 Int. & Comp. L. Q. 766 (1973).

[233] SOU 1972: 41. I am indebted to Professor Jacob Sundberg of the University of Stockholm Law Faculty for information on this aspect of Swedish law and citations therefor.

[234] According to Professor Sundberg, the government-owned Swedish radio station, under the impression that the proposals had been adopted, has produced some public confusion about the matter by broadcasting programs containing the three poetic texts.

[235] New §3a added by KK 1973 No. 694, to KK 20 Nov. 1964.

236 Universal Declaration of Human Rights, adopted by the General Assembly of the United Nations on 10 December 1948 (Art. 16–1: "Men and Women of full age, without any limitation due to race, nationality or religion, have the right to marry and to found a family."); International Covenant on Civil and Political Rights, adopted by the General Assembly of the United Nations on 16 December 1966, Art, 23–2; European Convention for the Protection of Human Rights and Fundamental Freedoms, signed in Rome on 4 November 1950, Art. 12.

237 The method of the Law Commission in its Report on Solemnisation of Marriage in England and Wales, Law Commission No. 53. is to proceed issue by issue, taking account of available evidence of behavior and opinion, as well as of arguments for and against any proposed change in the law.

238 Carbonnier, Terre et ciel dans le droit français du marriage, Études Ripert 328 and 327 (1950).

239 *Bénabent* 440.

240 *Dörner* 119*ff*.

241 *4 Mazeaud* 109–110.

242 *Ibid*.

243 *Bénabent* 443.

244 Cass. Civ. Soc. 7 Feb. 1968, D.S. 1968. Jur. 429.

245 Cour d'appel de Paris, 30 Apr. 1963, D. 1963 Jur. 428. "Full expression" by a French court is however a matter of a few lines, in contrast to the rambling discourse one often finds in English or American judicial opinions. The classic work comparing the cryptic French style and its history with the German and common law styles is J. Dawson, The Oracles of the Law (1968).

246 This characterization is significant. The concept of public order (*ordre public*) is an important one in French law. A great body of legal writing and case law has grown up in the effort to give content to Art. 6 of the Civil Code which provides that, "One may not derogate by private agreement from laws based on public order (*ordre public*) and considerations of morality (*bonnes moeurs*)."

247 Cour d'appel de Paris, 30 Apr. 1963. D. 1963. Jur. 428–429.

248 *Id.* at 429.

249 A. Rouast, note to D. 1963. Jur. 429–430.

250 Cass. Soc. 27 Apr. 1964, D.S. 1965. Jur. 213.

251 Cass. Soc. 7 Feb. 1968, 429.

252 Cass. Ch. mixte, 17 Oct. 1975, D.S. 1976. Jur. 511.

253 *Supra* at 30.

254 This is amply demonstrated in the survey by Markovits, Marriage and the State: A Comparative Look at East and West German Family Law, 24 Stan. L. Rev. 116 (1971).

255 Most of the marriage provisions of the Civil Code were removed from the Code and extensively modified by the National Socialist Marriage Law for Greater Germany (Grossdeutsches Ehegesetz) of 6 July 1938, RGB1. I. 807. The 1938 law was modified and re-enacted by the Allied Control Council, Control Council Law No. 16 of 20 February 1946, 1946 KRAB1. 77 (cited herein as EheG). The 1976 Marriage and Family Reform law brought major changes to the law governing divorce and its consequences, but marriage formation in West Germany is still basically governed by the Control Council Law. The history of the 1946 law is discussed in *Rheinstein, Family and Succession* 27, 46.

256 BVerwG, FamRZ 1962, 303.

257 BVerfG, NJW 1971, 1509.

258 BVerwG, FamRZ 1962, 303. See *supra* at 27.

259 *Grundgesetz* (Basic Law) of 1949, Art. 6, I.

260 BVerfG 29, 166 (1970).

261 BVerfG, NJW 1971, 1509. See Stöcker, Der internationale Ordre Public im Familien-und Familienerbrecht, Rabelsz 38 (1974) 79–127.

262 *Beitzke* 36.

[263] European Convention for the Protection of Human Rights and Fundamental Freedoms, *supra* n. 236.

[264] *Neuhaus* 60.

[265] *Ibid.*

[266] Most important of those was Perez v. Lippold, 198 P.2d 17 (Cal. 1948).

[267] 388 U.S. 1 (1967).

[268] Section 1 of the 14th amendment, added to the U.S. Constitution in 1868, provides: "All persons born or naturalized in the United States, and subject to the jurisdiction thereof, are citizens of the United States and of the State wherein they reside. No State shall make or enforce any law which shall abridge the privileges or immunities of citizens of the United States; nor shall any State deprive any person of life, liberty, or property, without due process of law; nor deny to any person within its jurisdiction the equal protection of the laws."

[269] Loving v. Virginia, 388 U.S. 1, 12 (1967). The interior quote is from Skinner v. Oklahoma, 316 U.S. 535, 541 (1942), which held unconstitutional a law providing for the compulsory sterilization of habitual criminals.

[270] *Drinan* 48–57; *Foster* 51–80.

[271] *Drinan* 49.

[272] *Weber* 3.

[273] UMDA Prefatory Note p. 4; Comment to §201.

[274] *König* par. 23; Mair, *supra* n. 111 at 100–103.

MARRIAGE-LIKE INSTITUTIONS

Boire, manger, coucher ensemble
Est mariage, ce me semble.
Old French proverb[1]

I. Introduction

Whatever we can piece together thus far about the posture of the State with respect to marriage as expressed through the law of marriage formation is inconclusive. By moving to an entirely different observation post, however, we can learn a good deal about legal marriage. In this Chapter, we will approach legal marriage by looking at its shadow institution. Although informal marriages still largely remain in what the French legal sociologist Jean Carbonnier calls the domain of "non-law", their existence both affects the legal institution of marriage and creates its own body of law. The latter has grown in size and importance as the phenomenon of cohabitation, or *de facto*, or informal marriage has become more and more widespread and accepted among diverse social groups. In fact, it is only when developments in the areas of formal and informal marriage are compared, that the full significance of the developments in either emerges. Thus, to further our understanding of the law of marriage, it is helpful to consider to what extent social conduct is changing existing legal structures, to what extent it is bringing new legal forms into existence, and finally, to what extent it is simply draining the old legal forms of their content.

This Chapter will therefore be concerned with the legal treatment of those heterosexual unions which are entered with some idea of duration and in which the couple hold themselves out to the relevant community as in some way belonging together, but which are not recognized by the legal system as "marriages" (in other words, with that behavior which was described in Chapter 1 as belonging to that part of Set B which does not intersect with Set A)[2] This working definition is artificial, just as is any legal classification, in the sense that the manifold reality of human mating behavior does not arrange itself neatly into categories. However the definition is not meant to describe mating behavior. Rather it is to serve as an aid in discovering how legal systems are being affected by the presence of behavior which imitates legal marriage. As will be shown in this Chapter, these shadow–marriages have forced themselves upon the legal systems, especially in France and the United States, in a burst of litigation which cannot help but change the structure of legal marriage in those systems.

Within the shadow–institution of legal marriage, as within legal marriage itself, there are many mansions. Traditionally, many marriage–like situations have involved partners who are not legally eligible to marry, usually because one or both of them has a previous legal marriage which is dissolved in fact but not in law. Indeed, one of the reasons why restraints on marriage and remarriage have been reduced in the newer laws, and why divorce laws have been liberalized, is that even if older marriage and divorce laws could be maintained on the books, this would only increase the number of *de facto* unions. Another large proportion of informal unions is accounted for by persons who, like the Tinkers Michael and Sarah, are members of what Rheinstein has called "groups neglected by the law" – those subcultures of the poor, or of racial and ethnic minorities for whom the structures of traditional marriage and divorce law have sometimes been irrelevant and with whom the framers of such laws were rarely concerned – groups ignoring and ignored by traditional family law.[3] Here one might think, not only of Michael and Sarah, but of the Italian, Turkish, Yugoslavian and North African migrant workers in Europe (and the "white widows" they have left behind in their own countries); and of the economically disadvantaged "poor white", Afro-American, Indian, and Puerto Rican populations of the United States.[4]

Apart from these two groups, (one consisting of many persons who would marry if they were legally able to do so, and the other including many for whom marriage is a cultural rather than a legal concept) there has been a small group which has avoided marriage on ideological grounds. In this group the legal marriage bond is seen as an unacceptable infringement of individual liberty, or as incompatible with the dignity of a mutual ethical commitment.

Today, however, informal marriage is becoming increasingly common among other social groups and, perhaps more significant, increasingly accepted. The two facts interact. The more persons in a particular group "live together", the more it is accepted. The more acceptance this alternative to formal marriage gains, the more people employ it. But while the free union has gained acceptability in certain sectors of society, it has been remarked that, in France and West Germany at least, it has lost ground among groups who see legal marriage as a symbol of bourgeois respectability, and bourgeois respectability as a desirable goal.[5] Alongside the groups who have traditionally been involved in informal marriages are now many who cohabit, rather than marry, for economic reasons. These include persons for whom legal marriage would involve the loss of pensions, alimony or other benefits terminable or reducible upon legal marriage;[6] and in the United States, as formerly in Sweden, some who do not marry because of unfavorable tax rates for certain categories of married taxpayers.[7] The practice of informal marriage thus seems to be becoming more widespread among diverse social groups[8] whose motivation ranges from the purely economic as in the case of many elderly people; to inability to enter a legal marriage, or unwillingness to be subject to the legal effects of marriage; to a desire for a "trial marriage"; or to a lack of concern with the legal institution. This lack of concern is nothing new among groups which have been accustomed to form and dissolve marriages (in the social sense) without coming into contact with legal institutions. Among them, it is but an aspect of the irrelevance of traditional family law, property-oriented and organized around the ideals of dominant groups, to the lives of some of the other groups in the population. Significantly however, lack of concern with marriage law has been growing (in varying degrees in the various countries) among many who are definitely not outside the mainstream of their own societies and who until recently accepted unquestioningly the traditional structures of the enacted law, but who now find on balance that the enacted law has no advantages to offer over informal arrangements. Others simply wish to *épater la bourgeoisie* but, unfortunately for them, the bourgeoisie itself has started to practice cohabitation.

It is beyond doubt that for most persons marriage still means religious or civil formalities and official registration of their status. But it is equally clear that the phenomenon of informal marriage has become widespread. It is a phenomenon which is hard to measure or to compare with behavior in the past. Nonetheless, some evidence is available that, in the countries with which we are here concerned, an increasing amount of marriage behavior is taking place outside the framework of formal legal marriage.[9] Indeed, according to a recent article by a Soviet sociologist remarking on the "relatively recent phenomenon" of "large-scale avoidance of marriage",[10] the phenomenon is not confined to the Western countries dealt with here.

Still, one must be careful not to exaggerate. Informal unions have always existed wherever official marriage law has been irrelevant to certain groups within the population, or where the restrictions on entering and leaving formal marriage have made it impossible or difficult for certain people to marry legally. What seems to be new, so far as behavior is concerned, is the synergism through which cohabitation as an alternative to legal marriage is spreading to groups among whom it was previously uncommon. Some facts are readily observable. For example, open cohabitation has become a significant fact of life in sectors of society where before, if it existed at all, it was concealed. Concealment has sociological significance because it deprives cohabition of one of the elements of that type of conduct which sociologists would call "marriage" – attestation to the relevant community.[11]

Further light can be thrown on the outlines of the shadow institution by looking at the figures which are available concerning the legal institution. Much of the current thinking about marriage behavior may need to be re-examined in the wake of the most recent reports on the marriage rate. It has become commonplace to point out that while ever-increasing numbers of people are dissolving their marriages in their grim and relentless pursuit of happiness and personal fulfillment, most divorced persons pay marriage the compliment of trying again.[12] In fact, remarriage has been as much a part of what Rheinstein has called the eudemonistic ideal as has divorce.[13] But while the marriage rate has held fairly steady in England in the past ten years, it has been declining in West Germany during the same period, and has just begun to decline in France.[14] In the United States, the total number of marriages and the marriage rate suddenly dropped in 1974, the first significant decline since the end of World War II.[15] These statistics cannot be conclusive on the extent and duration of changes in the institution of legal marriage. They are just pieces of information which, when put together with others, may bring into clearer focus what is actually happening in the various societies and legal systems.

Another piece of the puzzle may be found in the positive law itself. There are a number of current legal developments which are particularly striking. In one sense cohabitation has always had legal effects and there has always been a body of cohabitation law in the countries treated here. One legal response to cohabitation in the past has been to pretend it is something else and then attribute to it the desired legal incidents. Thus, what in effect were cohabitation cases in the past have often been disguised as cases involving betrothals, presumptively legal marriages, implied agreements to pay for services, etc. Because informal marriage exists in every society, every legal system has had to provide some ways to deal with the problems it generates. Professor Walter Weyrauch has convincingly demonstrated that this is the correct way to view not only the American institution of "common law marriage", but also the myriad devices of the law of proof and presumptions which are the functional equivalent of common law marriage in those American states (and, one might add, European countries) which do not recognize it.[16]

So the interesting question now becomes whether the increase in, and increased visibility and respectability of, informal marriage will bring about a casting-off of these legal fictions and the direct attribution of economic consequences based on *de facto* dependency. As we shall see in Chapter 6 the answer in public law is definitely yes. It has already been largely accomplished. In the area of private law, so far, the distinction between formal and informal marriage has been maintained in the sense that even in Sweden it has been explicitly reaffirmed while the process of minimizing its importance continues with vigor.[17] But this Chapter describes a number of indications that the distinction itself is in many ways being eroded to the point where it may only consist in the rites described in Chapter 2 on marriage formation and the reverse rites described in Chapter 5 on marriage dissolution.

In what ways is the phenomenon of cohabitation affecting the law? In the first place, it is affecting the law by claiming its attention. We will see that in France and the United States there has been a remarkable increase of litigation in which this form of social conduct is explicitly involved. No doubt the increase in litigation arises not only from the increase in cohabitation but also from the disappearance of reluctance to publicize it. Many of these cases provide evidence of increasingly tolerant judicial attitudes toward alternatives to formal legal marriage. In Sweden, and to some extent in the United Kingdom, the legislature too has accommodated informal marriage in private law matters.

Second, changes in the illegitimacy law of England, France, the United States, and West Germany have in less than 10 years gone far toward depriving formal marriage of one of its traditionally most important effects, that of distinguishing the legitimate family from all others. This transformation is part of a world-wide pattern of approximating the status of the child born outside marriage to that of the child born within marriage. In addition, all four countries have made changes which facilitate the establishment of paternity, without which newly acquired legal rights against a father would be meaningless. Also pertinent is the fact that formal marriage is being drained of some of its content by the increasing number, and social acceptance, of births outside legal marriage.

Another legal development concerns the relations between the partners to informal unions. Just as every society with which we are here concerned has always known informal marriages, so each legal system has had to deal one way or another with the practical economic and child-related problems generated by such unions – problems not unlike those generated by legal marriages. In France and the United States, and to some extent in England, a body of "new" cohabitation law is being formed as courts and legislatures are showing more receptiveness to increasing (or at least increasingly visible) legal claims based on marriage-like unions. One change from the way in which *de facto* unions were treated in the recent past is that there is now little evidence that relief is being denied on punitive or moralistic grounds.

There seem to be two different patterns or phases of the new legal treatment of cohabitation. One, which could be called the French pattern, so far seems to have moved toward attributing more and more legal consequences to cohabitation so that it resembles legal marriage, which in France (as we shall see in Chapter 4) still involves relatively more legal consequences than it does in Sweden or the United States. The Swedish pattern is quite different. There, legal consequences are attributed to cohabitation in a conscious effort to eliminate discrimination against unmarried cohabitation. However, legal marriage itself is losing so many of its legal attributes that the situation is more accurately described as an assimilation of legal marriage to cohabitation at a new, low, level of regulation, than *vice versa*. The fifty states of the United States, where the law is in flux on these matters, provide examples of both the French and the Swedish approach as well as of the traditional approaches of punishing irregular conduct where it is identified as such or pretending that it is legal marriage and treating it accordingly. In West Germany, no "new" cohabitation law seems to be developing so far. *De facto* spouses seeking adjustment of their economic affairs upon termination of their relations must, if they can, fit their situation into traditional legal rubrics.[18] In England, however, a body of "new" cohabitation law is rapidly developing in response to practical problems arising between unmarried couples.

Increased official tolerance of, or at least indifference to, sexual relations other than those within the framework of legal marriage is expressed through recent changes in criminal law tending to treat sexual acts in private between consenting adults as outside the concern of the legal system,[19] and in the disappearance of adultery as a ground for divorce or as a ground for legal action against a third party who disturbs the legal marriage relationship. A recent American immigration case has even redefined "adultery", saying that a married foreign national's cohabitation with a woman was not adultery within the meaning of the Immigration and Nationality Act since he lived with the woman *only* while his wife was living in another country and he stopped doing so as soon as his wife arrived in the United States.[20] So, even where *de facto* unions are not legally approved and protected, they are not necessarily illegal, and are becoming increasingly exempt from official disapproval.

Finally, the new illegitimacy law, together with the apparatus of the welfare state, goes far to diminish the importance of the distinction between informal and formal marriage for those great numbers of citizens who consume what they earn and are thus not concerned with private law rules concerning distribution of family property.

To this point, all we have noted is that informal marriage is a type of social conduct which involves a small but significant number of people and that, as a social phenomenon, it has claimed the attention of the various legal systems. All this is pertinent to one branch of our inquiry – that concerning the extent to which social conduct has ceased to be oriented to the system of enacted law. If, in a sense, the legal order exists only to the extent that social conduct is oriented to it,[21] the phenomenon of informal marriage, to the extent that *it* exists, diminishes the significance of enacted norms. But since couples in the countries whose law we are examining are hardly engaged in a mass exodus from formal marriage into free unions, this should leave a considerable quantity of good old wine in the good old bottle of formal marriage. There is a leak, but it is small.

But it is equally important for us to know whether and how informal marriage has changed the law. Why should the practices of this minority have an effect on enacted law? In discussing the emergence and development of new legal norms, Max Weber discusses the influence of changes in the external conditions of social and economic life and asserts that alone they are not enough. "The really decisive element has always been a new line of conduct which then results either in a change of the meaning of the existing rules of law or in the creation of new rules of law."[22] Weber discusses various ways in which change comes about, including the survival of forms of conduct best adapted to serve the economic and social interests of parties involved, but then states,

More frequent, however, is the injection of a new content into communal actions and rational associations as a result of individual invention and its subsequent spread through imitation and selection.... The parties to the new arrangements are frequently unconcerned about the fact that their respective positions are insecure in the sense of being legally unenforceable. They regard legal enforceability by the state as either unnecessary or as self-evident; even more frequently do they simply rely upon the self-interest or the loyalty of their partners combined with the weight of convention.[23]

It is really too soon to say whether the spread of informal marriage will turn out to be a new line of conduct which will bring forth new legal norms, although Weber's words, dealing with examples from altogether different areas of law, seem oddly pertinent. This Chapter will in any case demonstrate some new ways in which the social institution is making itself felt.

We will do this first by examining the "new" cohabitation law, in those countries where it has become overt and visible – England, France and the United States – with references where appropriate to West German trends. France will be considered first because there the *union libre* has long been openly, if not favorably, dealt with by the legal system, and it is thus possible to see most clearly the transition from "old" law to "new". We will then review the varied responses of the American states and England. Then we will turn to the law of Sweden which is included in this chapter because it represents *a* natural progression although not *the* necessary outcome of certain tendencies already present in English, French and American law. Finally, the dramatic post-1968 transformation of the legal position of children born outside legal marriages in all four countries will be reviewed briefly in order to fill out the picture of the extent to which informal marriage, in being juridified, is passing from the realm of non-law to the realm of law.

II. Unions Libres,[24] *Old and New*

The *union libre*, or free union, is a venerable institution in French law. Despite the fact that it is almost completely ignored by the Civil Code,[25] and only discreetly alluded to in other legislation, it has acquired enough of a legal existence through the case law to be described in the leading treatises as comparable to the Roman *concubinatus,* a kind of qualitatively inferior marriage with legal attributes.[26] The fact that a chapter on the *union libre* is a standard feature in French treatises on civil law[27] is itself a sign of its established character.

Despite constantly repeated statements that the *union libre* is becoming more widespread as a social phenomenon,[28] there is reason to believe that in France the change in the proportion of free unions to marriages is less dramatic than the change in the legal, and perhaps the social, attitude toward such unions.

Carbonnier expresses the opinion that such unions must have been as frequent in the Second Empire as at the present time, not only on the basis of evidence provided by French literature, but because of the absolute impossibility of divorce from 1816 to 1884[29] and the fact that adult children of any age had at least formally to request the opinion of their parents before marrying.[30]

By the early 1930s, free unions had drawn so many legal consequences to themselves that they were heralded as a new legal status.[31] But the further development and expansion of this trend was checked by a moralistic reaction which appeared in the Court of Cassation cases starting in 1937.[32] As to the status which the *union libre* had gained to that point and which it has maintained, the learned writers have been almost uniformly critical. While recognizing the practical necessity to solve certain problems in connection with the *union libre*, they have viewed the legal development of *de facto* marriage as undermining the institution of legal marriage.[33] In the 1970s the *union libre* is once again undergoing development as a legal institution. It is worthwhile tracing the outlines of the institution as it now exists to see in what manner it resembles legal marriage and in what way it remains an inferior status.

The major difference between legal marriage and a free union lies in what makes the free union "free": freedom to enter, freedom to exit. To the extent that formation and dissolution of legal marriage are becoming merely a matter of a rite and a reverse rite, the distinction is becoming a formal one only. Apart from entry and exit, a comparison must take into account the legal treatment of problems which arise upon termination of the relationship by separation or by death of one of the partners, and the legal position of children produced by such unions.

When a legal marriage in France is dissolved, the matrimonial property regime[34] is liquidated, and, in certain cases, one spouse may be required to pay support or compensation or both to the other.[35] When a *de facto* union breaks up, the French case law has had no trouble establishing a kind of matrimonial property system implied in law for those cases where the partners have acquired and mingled their property during their life in common.[36] The property so acquired is divided as if there had been a *de facto* partnership *(société de fait)* between the couple.[37] The principal difference between the *société de fait* which is said to exist in the *union libre* and the legal matrimonial property regime of community of acquests is that the former has to be proved while the latter comes into being upon the occasion of the marriage itself unless some other regime is chosen by contract.[38] But in both situations a partner who does not work outside the home can participate in the acquests made by the other partner. Besides the division of acquests through the device of the *société de fait*, there is the possibility of an action for compensation for services rendered if one partner has worked without pay in the business of the other.[39]

Just as one can see a kind of marital property system in the *société de fait*, so one can discern legal devices which operate to give *de facto* spouses a right of action similar to that available to legally married spouses through which damages resulting from the breakdown of the marriage may be awarded to the "innocent" spouse against the spouse who was "at fault".[40] Cases decided under general principles of French tort law have awarded damages to an abandoned mistress, reasoning that, although the breaking-off of a free union is not itself wrongful, the circumstances under which it occurs or even the circumstances under which the woman was induced to enter the liaison can be.[41] Agreements between *de facto* spouses for child custody upon dissolution of their relationship can be confirmed in the same way as similar agreements between legally married spouses upon divorce.[42]

The contours of the shadow institution have been filled out in various other ways. In statutes relating to pensions, leases and social security, the situation of a *de facto* widow has been likened to that of a legal widow.[43] Indeed, with respect to family allotments and payments under social insurance for a death in the family, the *de facto* spouse may be preferred to a legal wife who has been separated from the husband.[44] Through doctrines of apparent agency, a *de facto* spouse can bind the credit of the other in a manner resembling the domestic agency enshrined in the Civil Code.[45] Participation in free unions is of no concern to the criminal law even where adultery is involved, inasmuch as the crime of adultery was abolished in connection with the 1975 divorce reform legislation.[46] As a general matter, it is often said that the more a particular free union resembles marriage in stability and in the way the partners conduct themselves toward each other and the community at large, the more willing the courts have been, in one way or another, to give the union the effect of legal marriage.[47]

One of the most interesting developments in French law on the status of *de facto* marriages has concerned actions brought by a woman seeking damages for the wrongful death of the man with whom she was living and by whom she was being supported. A number of such actions were brought in the early 1930s, not so much, Dean Carbonnier thinks, because of an increase in free unions, as because of the increased propensity to make financial claims and to litigate rights among groups which formerly had had little access to the legal process.[48] At first damages were readily granted in these cases.[49] Indeed, one court went as far as to refuse damages to the legal wife and grant them to the woman who was actually living with the decedent,[50] while another awarded damages to two "concubines" of the same man, thus, in the shocked words of Professor H. Mazeaud, "legitimating polygamy and the *union libre* at the same time".[51] A reaction to this trend seemed to set in in a series of cases decided by the civil division of the Court of Cassation of 1937. These cases reconsidered the whole problem and announced the principle that a fatal accident to a *"concubin"* does not give rise to a cause of action by the survivor because her claim is not based on a "legitimate, legally protected interest", and because the harm she alleges is too difficult to measure, being based on a relationship which can be broken off at any moment.[52] The criminal division of the Court of Cassation, however, reacted in a different way, developing distinctions between stable and precarious unions, and between non-adulterous and adulterous unions, and continuing to award wrongful death damages to a woman who had lost her partner in a stable union uncomplicated by adultery.[53] Then, in 1970, a mixed panel of the Court of Cassation decided that a woman in a non-adulterous stable union could recover damages for the wrongful death of her partner without having to show any legal relationship between herself and the deceased.[54]

Summing up the state of the law on *unions libres* in 1971, Dean Carbonnier said, "This evolution of the law, as fragmentary and tentative as it is, has symptomatic significance: it permits the inference of an underlying change of attitude in bourgeois sectors of opinion."[55] This was the state of affairs until 1972 when, in the area of wrongful death, as well as in other aspects of the legal treatment of free unions, one can say that a new approach seems to have been inaugurated in French law. Three important legal developments in 1972 seem to bear out Carbonnier's observation and to indicate that the *union libre*, and with it the *de facto* family, may be entering a new phase of legal recognition. The first event was the law of 3 January 1972 establishing substantial legal equality between legitimate and illegitimate children. This law was seen in France, even more than similar reforms were elsewhere, as radically affecting the "legitimate" family. The other developments have come through court decisions on the legal effects of *unions libres*.

In 1972 the criminal division of the Court of Cassation, departing from all the post-1937 Court of Cassation decisions, awarded damages in a wrongful death case to a legally married woman who had been living in a free union with the decedent.[56] It is hard to imagine a case where a court could have been more tempted to depart from the previous line of decisions. The woman, physically handicapped and the mother of one child at the time she was abandoned by her husband, had been taken in by the decedent, had lived with him for 36 years and had had three children with him. The Court refused to consider the adulterous character of the liason a bar, relying on the technical ground that it was defendant's burden to prove that the former marriage still existed. Despite its appealing circumstances, the decision was described in an important periodical as "astonishing" and "dangerous", and was compared to a previous "lapse" of the Court of Cassation in which damages for emotional suffering had been awarded to the owner of a horse.[57] The reasons given for the author's criticism are revealing. Stating that everyone knows that the two main causes for entering free unions are the difficulty of getting a divorce and financial considerations such as the loss of a pension, the author argues that these unions should not be given legal effects because they present "formidable competition to marriage".[58] But of course it is just because *de facto* marriages have become so much a fact of life that the legal problems they generate must be dealt with and, as an inevitable by-product, that they come to acquire legal existence.

The last of the French wrongful death cases where the legal marriage of one party to a free union is legally relevant may have been decided. On 19 June 1975 the criminal division held that the defendant could not avoid liability even though the adulterous character of the plaintiff's liason was well-established. The court reasoned that the tort-feasor could not take advantage of the wrongful character of a situation "affecting the private life (*la vie privée*) of the opposing party...[and that] only the spouse of the victim had the legal right to [make it the basis of a complaint to the authorities of a lawsuit]".[59] Only a few days after this decision, the laws making adultery a crime in France were repealed.[60]

The apparent proliferation of informal unions inspired by the desire to avoid the termination of financial benefits has given rise to another legal development through which free unions are being equated with legal marriage. A 1972 lower court case which has been seen as an important development, involved the request by a Madame F. for an increase in alimony in view of the sudden success of her former husband, Monsieur B., an entertainer.[61] Monsieur B. however responded by claiming that she needed no increase because she was now living as husband and wife with a Monsieur V. Madame F. claimed, in the words of the court, that "the solace she receives from V. is not accompanied by any material advantage". The court permanently terminated alimony saying:

...[A]n innocent spouse who remarries loses the benefit of alimony (*la pension alimentaire*) by that fact alone...; the cohabitation of Madame F. and Monsieur V., consolidated by the birth of a child who bears the name of V. and who is raised by them together, has continued for more than 15 years and shows no sign of terminating in the near future;...the duration, the continuity and the stability of the reciprocal affective bonds, as well as the community of material interests which characterize this union, place the plaintiff in a situation equivalent to that of a woman who has remarried.[62]

M. Groslière, in his note accompanying the opinion in the Dalloz report, says that the "Parisian character" of the case should not obscure the general importance of the decision which derives from the fact that the Paris court "has in fact clearly assimilated the *union libre* to marriage and has taken pains to set forth all the elements which justify this equivalence".[63] M. Groslière finds it implicit in the case that the *union libre* produces the same effects as does legal marriage, including a duty of support between the partners, which renders alimony – the continuation of the duty of support from the former marriage – unnecessary.[64] The author of a 1975 article on the assimilation of the *union libre* to legal marriage also thinks that a duty of support between the partners to the union is part of the "crowning of the evolution by completely assimilating [the free union] to marriage".[65] Whether the juridification of *de facto* marriages will actually go this far in France remains to be seen. The technique of treating them as equivalent to formal marriage for purposes of cutting off benefits terminable upon legal remarriage has, significantly, been incorporated into the laws on pensions for widows of civil servants and military personnel, and into the 1976 French Divorce Law.[66] This development may, however, be no more than the result of a desire not to encourage free unions as an alternative to marriage and to prevent a *de facto* spouse from enjoying a superior financial position to a legal spouse. Apart from provoking speculation about whether *de facto* marriages now give rise to a duty of support, the 1972 alimony termination case has also prompted discussions concerning whether a divorced man's responsibilities for a new *de facto* family can be considered (in the same way that his remarriage would be), in terminating or reducing maintenance obligations to his ex-spouse. It has been argued that to deny consideration to this factor would serve only the "appearance of morality" because it would push people into legal remarriage simply in order to escape their alimony obligations![67]

The 1972 French legislation on the status of illegitimate children[68] has been perceived as having a profound effect on the relationship between the "legal family" and the *de facto* family. As mentioned, the Civil Code hardly recognized the existence of *de facto* unions. Beyond this, one can say the family law of the Civil Code so fully expressed a certain idea of the legal family that it was still possible for H. Mazeaud to say, in 1967, despite all the developments which we have described as having taken place before then, "There is no family in law but the legitimate family. No legal bonds exist between members of the so-called natural family."[69] It was possible to say this because although the case law had dealt with the practical problems of cohabitation – usually arising only on its termination by death or separation – the Code itself had enclosed the legal family, and only the legal family, in a network of provisions, both symbolic and sanctioned, designed to assure its cohesion, protection and continuation. The idea of the family enshrined in the Code and the system of law designed to strengthen it was, it has been said by University of Paris Professor Gobert, "brutally wiped out by the 1972 law regarding illegitimate children".[70] The real significance of the 1972 law in her view is that it involved "a complete rethinking of the idea of the protection of the family." "From now on the natural family is no longer neglected by the legislature and the legitimate family is no longer conceived of as a sanctuary".

"*De facto* relationships are from now on being taken into account by the law,...there is no longer a unitary conception of the family."[71]

Nevertheless, it seems to be distinctive of the French developments that the *union libre* has come to resemble legal marriage by drawing to itself many of the legal effects of marriage and by imitating others. Thus, it is possible to see the French situation as one in which the legitimate family prevails after all: "In appearance, it has certainly lost ground, but in fact it has imposed the matrimonial model on those who have declined to marry. No longer bothering to look down on its adversaries, it has transformed them in its own image."[72]

III. Informal Marriage American Style

In the United States the legal effects of informal marriages have traditionally been taken care of by legal devices which facilitate the pretense that an informal marriage was really a legal one. Chief among these is the presumption that when a couple has lived together, presenting the outward appearance of marriage, their union was initiated by a legal marriage.[73] This presumption is unavailable in France or West Germany, where, as we have seen in Chapter 2, documentary proof of marriage is readily available and required.[74] In a minority of states, a union presenting the outward appearance of marriage between persons who are legally eligible to marry each other is in fact a legal marriage by virtue of the doctrine of common law marriage.[75]

The change that has taken place within the past few years in the United States is that, socially and legally, informal marriage has increasingly ceased to be disguised as legal marriage. This would only be a change to the situation which has long prevailed in French law were it not for the fact that once out in the open the institution seems to be giving rise to a body of "new" cohabitation law.

It is estimated that 6 to 8 million Americans are involved in cohabitation arrangements.[76] Cohabitation has become a recurring subject in American popular songs and literature.[77] Its spread among diverse groups has been noticed and subjected to sociological inquiry.[78] It has found a place in the newest legal coursebooks,[79] the latest etiquette manuals,[80] and has even given rise to a couple of legal handbooks purporting to advise the partners how to conduct their unmarried life.[81] The writer of one of these handbooks asserts that Census Bureau figures show that the numbers of couples living together without marriage increased by over 700% from 1960 to 1970 (compared with only a 10% increase in the number of legally married couples).[82] Since the

Census Bureau had not set out to count such couples, there are obvious difficulties with trying to deduce these figures from what the Bureau did count.

But there is no mistaking the fact that informal unions as such have erupted into the legal system. For example, a number of recent child custody cases involve attempts to defeat the award of custody to, or to effect a change of custody from, parents who are in various forms of cohabitation arrangements. It is here, from trial judges who are on the front lines in marital and family matters, that one gets a view of how both life styles and judicial attitudes are changing. Thus, in an April 1975 New York case, a trial judge, refusing to change custody to the father from a mother who had been living with a man for three and a half years, said that such disputes must be determined "in the atmosphere of our current day thinking and mores", and noted that, "This past decade has seen many young couples cast aside traditional concepts and embark upon a lifestyle of their own, one of greater sexual freedom, a gratification of their own desires for a 'complete life'...."[83] Acknowledging the legal authorities which frown upon a mother's living with a "boyfriend", the court nevertheless held that "Residence together of an unmarried male and female without the benefit of a sermonized marriage is not per se evil nor one of immorality." What makes this case novel is not so much the result (many courts in the past would have left the child with the mother on the basis of the tender years of the child and a general disposition to favor maternal custody), but the change in tone. Courts reaching the same result have spoken disapprovingly of the mother's conduct. Other courts in similar circumstances have deprived the mother of the child.[84] The case is interesting not so much as a legal decision as because it constitutes in itself evidence of social change.

Perhaps even more indicative of changing times is a Minnesota case refusing to change custody from a cohabiting father. Noting that the case presents "...a question which is being raised with increasing frequency where custody of children is at issue", the court said it "does not believe it...necessary to either condemn or condone any relationship", and that "some informal relationships are very stable and can provide the emotional, psychological, and physical security necessary to raising children".[85] Ironically, custody had been voluntarily relinquished by the mother to the father in 1968 because of the mother's then–existing illicit relationship. Even so, the court refused in 1975 to return the children to the mother who was now in a stable legal marriage, saying that the father's "liason...appears to have a positive, rather than negative, effect on his boys".

Another situation in which informal marriage is increasingly demanding legal attention involves the recent spate of cases in which an ex-husband, paying alimony terminable upon his ex-wife's remarriage, claims alimony should cease because she is living in a marriage-like relationship. The cases go both ways and, again, their chief importance is not legal, but social.[86] They show another way in which changed marriage behavior in all social and economic classes is forcing itself upon the attention of the legal system. The problem has now become so commonplace that in many states it is being dealt with through clauses in divorce settlements. When a judge-made rule cuts off alimony because of informal remarriage, then the question becomes whether, as a "logical" consequence, a duty of support arises between the cohabitants. This very problem is now vexing the French.

Recent developments in the federal system, too, show how alternative life-styles are claiming the attention of the legal system and how in turn the legal system is working out new attitudes toward formal and informal marriage. The proliferation of communal group-living arrangements, especially on the East and West coasts, has provoked some municipalities to pass zoning laws designed to prevent persons unrelated by blood or marriage from living together in certain areas. The legal pattern which has begun to emerge, as the constitutionality of these and other statutes which deprive "irregular" households of benefits is tested, has an important bearing on the subject of this work because it may be establishing a zone of protection for the shadow institution of legal marriage, but not for other "irregular" living arrangements. In the 1974 case of *Village of Belle Terre v. Boraas* the Supreme Court upheld a zoning ordinance which permitted no more than two unrelated people to live together.[87] But it seems likely that the Supreme Court will not allow the line to be drawn at two. The previous year, in *United States Department of Agriculture v. Moreno*, the Court had found that the exclusion of households containing two or more unrelated persons from eligibility for a federal food stamp program violated the Constitution.[88] In 1975, a federal district court in New York ruled, in a case where a local law forbade two or more unrelated persons to reside together in a single family dwelling, that *Belle Terre* applies only to groups of more than two unrelated persons and that the principle of the *Moreno* case controlled the situation of cohabitation by an unmarried couple.[89]

The above developments show only how marriage-like situations have forced themselves upon the American legal system. Other trends indicate that marriage-like situations are drawing legal effects to themselves and creating a new body of law. Two recent developments in community property states are worthy of note in this connection. One concerns the rights of a *de facto* spouse upon a *de facto* divorce, or "splitting". The other concerns the rights of a surviving *de facto* spouse in the estate of her predeceased legally married partner. The cases arose in California and Washington.

California.   In 1973, a California intermediate appellate court was faced with a claim by a woman for a share of the property acquired with the earnings of the man with whom she had lived for eight years and with whom she had had four children.[90] Under California law, if the couple had been legally married, she would have been entitled to a half share of the community property. The same would have been true if she were a "putative spouse", i.e. not married but believing in good faith that she was. But the California Supreme Court had flatly held, in 1943, that a "meretricious spouse", a woman living with a man with no genuine belief that she is legally married, acquires no legal rights in his property by reason of the relationship, and, further, that no "equitable considerations" would be used by the court to adjust any resulting hardships.[91] In the face of this earlier holding by the highest court of the state, the California Court of Appeals held in *In re Marriage of Cary* that the 1943 decision had been superseded by the enactment in 1970 of a new Family Law Act in California (an act whose principal purpose was to establish no-fault divorce and which does not address itself to the meretricious relationship one way or the other).[92] Having thus "disposed" of the precedent, the court went on to hold that the relationship between the couple was so "familial" that it should have the same protection as legal and putative marriages, and divided the property acquired with the *de facto* husband's earnings equally. On the question of what sort of relationship would give rise to community property rights, the court said that there must be "an actual family relationship, with cohabitation and mutual recognition and assumption of the usual rights, duties and obligations attending marriage".[93] This bears a striking resemblance to the 1972 Paris case which set out the elements of the type of *union libre* which terminates alimony.[94]

In 1976, faced with a conflict among the appeals courts, the California Supreme Court declined to extend community property principles automatically to unmarried cohabitants.[95] However, stating that the judicial barriers to the "fulfillment of the reasonable expectations of the parties to a non–marital relationship" should be removed, it declared that the courts should enforce the understanding of such couples with regard to property.[96] If such understanding is not contained in an express agreement, the courts are to examine the conduct of the parties to determine whether it demonstrates an implied understanding to hold acquests as community property or in some other manner.

Washington.   In the 1972 Washington Supreme Court case of *In re Estate of*

Thornton, a woman who had been living with a man for 16 years prior to his death brought a claim against his estate for a share of the property accumulated in the cattle raising business in which she had aided him over that period.[97] She had lived in a "family relationship" with the decedent and they had had four children. The decedent had been legally married all this time to another woman who claimed a share of the estate as surviving spouse. The plaintiff's legal theory, adopted by the court, was that the circumstances and acts of the couple established an implied partnership between them even though there had been no express partnership agreement. This would be just another case where a legal fiction was contrived to deal with economic hardship resulting from a *de facto* but informal marriage, were it not for the fact that the Supreme Court of Washington took the occasion to discuss at length the question of whether a share of the "community property" on death could be claimed on the basis of the relationship of the parties alone. The court acknowledged that it had held in a 1948 case that such a relationship cannot give rise to community property rights and that property acquired by a man and woman in such circumstances will be presumed to belong to the person in whose name the legal title stands.[98] But the court said in *Thornton*, "We are dubious about the continuing validity of this legal presumption or fiction.... We have disclaimed, and continue to disclaim, any opinion or intended reflection on the moral status of a couple living in a meretricious relationship."[99] In 1976 the court hinted that it may begin to "apply community property laws by analogy" to determine the rights of parties to a "long-term, stable, nonmarital family relationship."[100]

Thus, both Washington and California have gone far toward assimilating the property consequences of legal and informal marriage in the areas both of dissolution and succession. These cases have attracted a great deal of attention.[101] They have even been heralded as the beginning of legal recognition of alternative life styles.[102] If they are more than sports, however, they are no more than recognition of *de facto* families in which the husband and wife have not concluded or have not been able to conclude a formal legal marriage. But as to these, the cases may be a recognition of the point made by the President of the Quebec Civil Code Revision Commission, Paul Crépeau, in a 1974 article in the Louisiana Law Review:

A modern Civil Code must also take into account the existence of couples who live as man and wife in a *de facto* conjugal union which may well be a very stable one. Should not the Civil Code take notice of such unions and provide basic rules for the protection both of the partners and of third parties in respect of alimentary claims and contributions to debts incurred for the benefit of the family unit? It might even be that a right of inheritance should be granted to the surviving partner when the union has been involuntarily dissolved by the death of the other. Such a right is perfectly conceivable in a system where the devolution of estates is fundamentally based on the theory of presumed affections.[103]

In the non-community property states of the United States, the Married Women's Separate Property Acts established a system at the turn of the twentieth century in which marriage, in principle, had no effect on the property rights of the spouses. In places where this system has been preserved in all its purity, without restraints on freedom of testation, such as Scotland, it is possible to say that there is practically no difference between married and unmarried persons so far as property rights are concerned.[104] However, in most American separate property states the courts have power to distribute married persons' property upon divorce in any manner that seems to the court equitable and just.[105] In these states, it will be interesting to see the extent to which the courts may begin to apply the same principles in dividing the property of unmarried couples as they customarily apply to married couples.

Certainly one type of legal response to widespread cohabitation can be to increase the economic incidents of such cohabitation. This form of response might be expected in France where formal legal marriage still entails many economic consequences *and* the difficulty of divorce has been a major reason why persons living together have not entered formal marriage. But this pattern does not fit the Washington and California situations. Both those states have, as we shall see in Chapters 4 and 5, gone far to decrease the economic effects of legal marriage[106] and to increase the availability of divorce.[107] Hence, if the developments in these states mean anything, further change is less likely to take place on the French model than it is on the Swedish model. In the latter, the approach is functional, intended to "solve practical problems arising from the cohabitation of a man and woman with family functions" regardless of whether a legal marriage has taken place.[108]

IV. England: A Cautious Accommodation

In England, as in France and the United States, writers have remarked upon the legal problems generated by "an increasing number of relationships of a certain kind between two persons".[109] The circumlocution is characteristic of the tentative and gingerly manner with which English law has begun to deal with these matters. In comparison with the French and American developments, the English cases at first hardly seem to justify the alarmed comment of one writer that "...the courts are well on the way to equating the legal rights of a regular mistress with those of a duly ringed and registered wife".[110]

Yet matters have progressed to the point where the author of a recent family law treatise can say confidently that the principle that marriage is an essential prerequisite to the creation of a legally recognized family unit is "now subject to many exceptions".[111]

So far, though, the exceptions have been limited in scope, and designed to provide for *de facto* dependents of an individual regardless of whether the dependency is based on a "legitimate" family relationship. The development of cohabitation law in England has been most marked with respect to the legal consequences of dissolution of a *de facto* union by the death of one of the partners. The single most striking development has undoubtedly been the adoption by Parliament in 1975 of new Family Provision on Death legislation under which, for the first time, a *de facto* spouse may claim reasonable maintenance out of the deceased partner's estate. The claim can only be made if the claimant was being wholly or partly maintained by the decedent before death. If so, and if the court finds that the claimant was not adequately provided for, it may allow the claim even though it necessitates overruling testamentary dispositions in favor of the "legal" family.[112] Responding to the inevitable criticisms that the act would reward immorality, the Solicitor-General pointed out that it was addressed to practical problems:

> Many of us who have practised in this area have come across tragic cases of a common-law wife who has devoted years to the deceased and, perhaps, helped him to build up a business and who then finds that she is deprived of any benefit or redress because she cannot produce a marriage certificate.[113]

In two articles which appeared in April 1976 Sebastian Poulter presented a point-by-point comparison of the legal position of a surviving *de facto* spouse with that of a surviving legal spouse in England.[114] He was able to demonstrate that while the legal spouse is in a clearly stronger position upon the death of her husband, an accumulating body of statutory and case law has drawn clusters of rights to *de facto* spouses which are functionally analogous to the rights of legal spouses in the death situation. Although the legal spouse alone is an intestate heir, English law, unlike West German law, places no obstacles in the way of providing for a *de facto* spouse by will.[115] Such a testamentary gift will not receive the special tax treatment accorded only to surviving spouses, and will of course be vulnerable to claims under the family provision legislation if relatives or other dependants of the deceased have not received adequate financial provision.

Poulter has traced in the case law the outlines of a system protecting an unmarried spouse's rights in the "matrimonial" home which does or can resemble the protection enjoyed by married people. Unlike in France, there is no wrongful death action available to an English *de facto* spouse, because *de facto* spouses are not listed in the Fatal Accidents Acts. However, it appears probable that this situation, which in England will require Parliamentary action, will change. In 1975, Graham, J., of the Court of Appeal, stated in the case of *K v. JMP Ltd.*:

If the Act of 1846 were being enacted for the first time today, it seems quite likely the [*de facto* spouse] might have been included and one may perhaps be pardoned for hoping that in due course Parliament will reconsider the scope of the Fatal Accidents Acts at least in this respect.[116]

Poulter thinks the stability of the relationship and the actual dependence of the surviving partner should be relevant factors if such claims are to be allowed. As to the problem which came up in France in the 1930s and shocked Professor H. Mazeaud, Poulter says:

Where the deceased left a widow as well as a mistress, both of whom had been dependent upon him, there seems no logical reason why both should not be entitled to succeed in their claim since at present both legitimate and illegitimate children are afforded the right to claim concurrently.[117]

The legal progress of *de facto* marriage has been marked so far in England by a series of responses to practical problems, which taken together form a considerable body of nascent cohabitation law. For example, the word "family" has been held to include a woman who had lived with the deceased, in deciding whether she was entitled to succeed to his rent-controlled lease under the Rent Acts.[118] Just as in the Parisian termination of alimony case and the American case of *In re Cary*,[119] the presence of children and the "family-like" mode of living were important factors in attributing legal consequences to the relationship. Similarly, Parliament has included a woman who lives with a wage earner "as his wife" and any children who are in fact provided for by the wage earner as "family" members within the meaning of the Family Income Supplements Act of 1970.[120] Under the intestate succession laws of England, when the estate of a decedent passes to the Crown for want of survivors, provision may be made as a matter of grace for any "dependents" of the decedent for whom he might reasonably have been expected to have made provision.[121] In much the same vein the courts will consider a man's "moral" obligation to a "mistress" in assessing his financial resources and existing obligations in order to determine how much he will have to pay his legal spouse in a divorce or separation proceeding.[122]

Against this background, two controversial 1975 *de facto* divorce cases awarding a "mistress" what amounts in effect to a share of the "matrimonial" home may be the beginning of an imitation of the legal effects of divorce. In the first case, the couple had lived as husband and wife and had had two children. When the union broke up, the woman was given a quarter share in the home which the man had bought and which they had fixed up together.[123] The majority and concurring opinions were based, respectively, on theories of constructive trust and implied agreement and were criticized as thinly veiled efforts to award the kind of relief which is available under the Matrimonial Proceedings and Property Act only to legally married spouses.[124] In the second case, it seems that the parties had never actually lived together, but that a man had bought a house for the use of a woman and the twin sons they had had together.[125] Later, when he asked her to vacate the premises, she was held to be entitled to £2000 for wrongful revocation of a "contractual license" to remain in the house so long as the twins were of school age. This case, too, was criticized as an attempt to provide matrimonial provision where there was no legal basis for doing so.[126] However, the case has also been seen as bearing important implications for the future in that the court provided for a "cast off mistress" in the same way it would have provided for a divorced wife.[127]

The tendency in English cases and discussions to characterize these informal situations as involving a "man" and his "mistress" may impede focusing on the marriage-like and family-like nature of many of these relationships. The terminology, drawing with it the stigma attaching to stereotyped ideas of the mistress situation, may color the legal treatment of all informal marriages. In this connection, it is significant that the French writers who most strongly disapprove of legal recognition of the *de facto* family use the word *"concubinage"* more than they do *"union libre"* to refer to all sorts of cohabitation, while others tend to reserve the former word for a sexual relationship which may involve economic dependency but does not involve marriage or family-like community of life.

It seems likely that informal marriage – whatever it is called – will gain further ground as a legal institution in England as it has in France and the United States. In connection with the 1975 Capital Transfer Tax Legislation which provided relief from tax on transfers between spouses, an amendment was proposed which would have accorded the same treatment to *de facto* spouses. The proponent of the amendment said, in introducing it, "Wedlock is not as highly valued these days as it once was. It would appear that a common law wife is excluded from these provisions and we do not see any reason why that should be so when the situation is a fairly normal part of the society in which we live."[128] The amendment was defeated, but the attempt is significant as an indication of how much is now open to discussion. The Chief Secretary to the Treasury, in opposing the amendment, acknowledged, "Of course it is true and I accept it that there will be many common law

wives...who will have lived with their partners for longer than some marriages."[129]

Professor Eekelaar has probably forecast the course future English
developments will take when he expressed his own view that courts should
step in to adjust practical, functional problems whenever parties to a relationship have been fulfilling roles equivalent to marital roles:

The argument here is not for the re-introduction of common law marriages and that *de
facto* relationships should be treated in all respects like legal marriages. It is that...there
is no reason for withholding the *adjustive jurisdiction* in those situations.[130]

V. Sweden: Where all Roads Lead?

It is the convergence and consummation of three distinct trends, each one
present to some degree in the other systems discussed here, which makes the
Swedish treatment of informal marriage distinctive. These three trends are
the emergence of informal marriage as a substantial social institution, its
development as a legal institution and the elimination from legal marriage of
many of the features which heretofore distinguished it from informal marriage.

In the first place, it seems that in Sweden living together (*sammanboende*) is a
recognized social status. People identify themselves as married, single or
sammanboende. A woman in this last status speaks of her "samba", as a legal
wife speaks of her husband. The social practice has roots in an intellectual
socialist rejection of formal marriage, and in the old rural custom of deferring
formal marriage but not cohabitation until a child is conceived.[131] It has now
become so widespread that it has taken its place beside legal marriage as an
accepted and socially approved form of behavior. The dramatic drop in legal
marriages from 61,000 in 1966 to 38,000 in 1972 has been explained by "the
spreading practice among young people to cohabit without formal contract
of marriage".[132] Further evidence of the *de facto* family taking its place beside
the legal family is the fact that, in 1969, 38% of all unwed Swedish mothers
were cohabiting with the father of their child.[133] Still other non-marital
children, it must be assumed, are in *de facto* families with new step-fathers.

In Sweden, legal reaction to changing social behavior has resulted in
attributing legal effects to cohabitation, eliminating many of the distinctive
features of legal marriage and merging the legal treatment of the practical
problems to which the two institutions give rise. This tendency can be seen
clearly in the 1969 Directives which were given by the Swedish Minister of
Justice to the governmental commission charged with the task of reforming

Swedish family law. The Minister advised that future legislation should be so drafted as not to favor in any way the institution of marriage as compared with other forms of cohabitation.[134] Legal marriage "should be a form of voluntary cohabitation between independent persons".[135] The object of the law should be to solve practical problems which arise "from the cohabitation of a man and a woman with family functions", and "not to give a privileged status to one form of cohabitation over others".[136] These same guiding notions have been expressed in the reports of Finnish government-supported committees on the Status of Women and the Reform of the Marriage Law.[137]

Many differences between marriage and other forms of cohabitation had been eliminated earlier in Sweden, "spurred", in Professor Sundberg's words, "by the disappearance of a positive interest in marriage as an institution as well as [by] the building of the social welfare state".[138] Thus, even before the 1973 legislation which implemented the 1969 directives, reforms of the status of illegitimate children had progressed to the point where they "...have certainly deprived parents of the idea that they are doing something for the benefit of their children when they marry".[139] Pension schemes, workmen's compensation and the welfare state had contributed to the decline in importance of inheritance and marital property. In order to discourage "tax divorces", the tax treatment of married and unmarried persons had been largely equalized. Adultery has not been a crime in Sweden since 1937.

In 1973, in keeping with the 1969 directives, additional distinctions were eliminated. The Directives had said that "[L]egislation should not under any circumstances force a person to continue to live under a marriage from which he wishe[s] to free himself."[140] The 1973 legislation made unilateral divorce on demand a reality.[141] As for alimony, which was already awarded in only 10% of divorces,[142] the Minister's suggestion that the starting point should be that there should be no alimony in principle[143] was followed.[144] The Minister had also stated that upon dissolution of a stable union the courts should have the same freedom to award custody of children as after a divorce and that the rules concerning the matrimonial home should apply by analogy.[145] These ideas were implemented in 1973 with the exception that unmarried couples cannot, as can married couples, be awarded mutual custody of their children upon separation.[146]

Legal marriage, then, seems to be stripped to the initial and terminal formalities, alimony in exceptional cases, succession, and the famed Swedish marital property regime of deferred community, which, while widely imitated elsewhere, has been described at home in the Swedish welfare state as the concern of persons with a "squirrel mentality".[147] The attribution of legal effects to informal marriage, on the other hand, has given birth to new legal problems, among them, how to define those unions from which legal consequences will flow and how to avoid "getting married" unknowingly. With respect to the first problem, the tax and social legislation give weight to the fact that the couple had children together. Otherwise it seems to be up to the courts to appreciate the nature of each situation.[148] As to involuntary "marriage", just as the Roman law at the time of the Twelve Tables evolved the solution of the *trinoctium*, Swedish law may be moving toward a solution based on whether a substantial break has occurred in the relationship.[149] But public policy favoring protection of *de facto* dependents will undoubtedly impose limits on individual freedom in this area.

VI. The Transformation of the Legal Status of Children born outside Legal Marriage[150]

The definition of "illegitimacy" within a given legal system is a function of the definition of "marriage". Both are legal categories imposed on the fluctuating variety of human mating and family behavior. With this in mind, it is not difficult to see that a legitimate child is not necessarily a child with a family and that an illegitimate child is not necessarily a child without one. Nor does the legal classification necessarily even indicate the degree of social acceptance a particular birth will be accorded. Goode has pointed out that where there is no property to inherit and none to protect by making certain that the proper families are united there is less concern attached to illegitimate birth.[151] Thus official statistics on illegitimate births shed little light on the actual social position of illegitimate children. As Goode points out, "[T]here will be little loss of honor if the community grants almost as much respect for non–marriage as for marriage."[152]

So far as traditional social distinctions are concerned, the position of an illegitimate child in a stable *de facto* family is comparable to that of a child in a stable legal family, while the position of an illegitimate child in a one–parent household is often not unlike that of legitimate children of divorced or separated parents. The position of illegitimate children in *de facto* families, to put it another way, is not "illegitimate" at all in the sense of Malinowski's Principle of Legitimacy[153] because such children have the all–important "sociological father".

Within the family, the position of a child living in a union which has not been formalized because of the difficulty of one parent's obtaining a divorce or because of the parents' lack of interest in formalities will not be much affected by the absence of ceremonial marriage. Within the society however, the child's position may be affected by cultural attitudes which can be quite variable. In the United States where there is a high correlation between illegitimacy and poverty,[154] attitudes vary from disapproval to indifference among the diverse groups and subgroups in the population.[155] In Sweden, on the other hand, where 20% of all births are outside legal marriage,[156] yet where 38% of illegitimate children live with their mother *and* father,[157] and where legal marriage has been declining,[158] the situation seems to be different. Studies undertaken in connection with divorce reform in England indicated that some 40% of "illegitimate" children there were in fact born into stable unions.[159] The break with the past which England, France, the United States and West Germany have made in their recent reforms departs from the notion that "legitimacy", understood as transmitted, ascribed, social status, can only derive from formal, legal marriage.

The impact of the recent legal developments affecting illegitimate children will thus be different according to the social circumstances of the child and according to the importance the society gives to transmission of ascribed status. Even the boldest efforts of the law cannot confer full equality upon an illegitimate child whose father is not or cannot be ascertained. But for children who are in *de facto* families recent legal developments go a long way toward obliterating the legal as well as the social disabilities previously attached to their status. It is especially with respect to these *de facto* situations that the new legal developments are most significant from the point of view of this work.

The reforms in the countries with which we are here concerned are clustered together chronologically: the United States Supreme Court decisions starting in 1968 (the same year the Soviet Union reformed its law on illegitimate children);[160] the English Family Law Reform Act of 1969;[161] the West German Law of 19 August 1969[162] (implementing the 1949 Constitution);[163] and the French Law of 3 January 1972.[164] They had been prefigured by the 1948 United Nations Declaration on Human Rights[165] and the 1967 General Principles of Equality and Non-Discrimination in Respect of Persons Born out of Wedlock of the UN Commission on Human Rights.[166] The gains made in recent national legislation in Europe have been consolidated in a proposed European Convention on the Legal Status of Children born out of Wedlock.[167]

We have already seen how the French Filiation Law of 1972, while moderate in comparison to those of many other countries,[168] has been seen as undermining the very institution of marriage.[169] It is true that the 1972 law accords increased importance to *de facto* relationships and decreased importance to legal marriage in ascertaining paternity and in ascribing legitimate status to a child. New Art. 340–4 provides that a continuous and steady relationship between the mother and alleged father establishes a *prima facie* case of paternity,[170] and legitimacy itself can be derived from a child's *"possession d'état"*, (treatment of him as a legitimate child regardless of the actual legal situation).[171] The significance of the new and expanded role of *possession d'état* has not been lost on the legal writers. Some view it as wholesome, realistic, and designed to assure a child his best chance of being secure in an intact family.[172] Others, uneasy about any legal recognition of the *de facto* family, disapprove this further blurring of the boundaries between law and non-law.[173]

In England, as late as in 1956, the Royal Commission on Marriage and Divorce had said:

So long as marriage is held to be the voluntary union for life of one man with one woman, that conception is wholly incompatible with the provision that one or the other of the parties can, during the subsistence of the marriage, beget by some other person children who may later be legitimated.... Any departure from that conception can only be made by ignoring the essential moral principle that a man cannot,during the subsistence of his marriage, beget lawful children by another woman. It is unthinkable that the state should lend its sanction to such a step, for it could not fail to result in a blurring of moral values in the public mind. A powerful deterrent to illicit relationships would be removed, with disastrous results for the status of marriage as at present understood.[174]

Only 13 years later the unthinkable became the law. The Family Law Reform Act of 1969 s. 14 gave illegitimate children equal inheritance rights with legitimate children from their parents.[175]

The West German Reform law of 1969 was passed to implement Article 6 of the 1949 Constitution which provides: "Illegitimate children shall be provided by legislation with the same opportunities for their physical and spiritual development and their position in society as are enjoyed by legitimate children."[176] The Reform Law repealed the basic illegitimacy provision of the Civil Code of 1896 which had read: "An illegitimate child and its father are not deemed to be related."[177] The reform law proceeds from the opposite starting point and accords the same legal consequences to the relationship between an illegitimate child and his father as to the legitimate relationship, in the absence of specific provisions to the contrary.[178]

It has frequently been pointed out that reforms in each of the four countries have stopped short of establishing complete equality between legitimate and illegitimate children, notably in the area of inheritance. In France and West Germany the rights of succession of the legitimate family are still preferred in the new legislation.[179] In the United States, the Supreme Court has upheld the constitutionality of intestate succession laws which postpone the rights of illegitimate children,[180] although not all states have chosen to retain such laws. In England, the illegitimate child's equal rights to inherit extend only to the parents and not to other relatives.[181] But to the extent that family property declines in importance and the welfare state becomes the first rather than the last resort in times of need, the importance of this exception to the general thrust toward equality diminishes. This is particularly true in the United States where illegitimacy is primarily an accompaniment of poverty.[182] In this connection it should be noted that in the four countries examined here public assistance is dispensed primarily on the basis of need and not family status.[183]

This chapter has been concerned with the effects of recent reforms on the *de facto* family, but it may be noted in passing that these reforms have, of course, improved the lot of many disadvantaged children who are not in *de facto* families. Indeed, insofar as the continuing process of equalization is tending to turn to the legal reinforcement of the tie between an illegitimate father and his child,[184] one may say that the trend is not only blurring the boundaries between legal marriage and *de facto* marriage, but also between the state of being married and the state of being unmarried. In both areas, as legal discrimination is removed there is reason to believe, as Rheinstein says, that "...removal of the legal discrimination may have educational effects and thus help to accelerate the end of a social discrimination which has its roots in conditions of the past rather than the present".[185]

I have attempted to trace in this Chapter, through examination of "cohabitation law", the emergence of a new legal institution which imitates legal marriage. If the events described here stood alone, they might be interpreted as an interesting but self-contained minor legal phenomenon, or as part of a process through which informal marriage is becoming as heavily regulated as legal marriage has been in the past, or at least a regulated second-class marriage.

But they do not stand alone. The legal effects of legal marriage have been changing as well, and it is to that process we must now turn. For if legal marriage is gradually losing its legal effects, then the events described here are certainly not self-contained, and may not be evidence so much of increasing legal consequences of cohabitation as they are of the gradual assimilation of the married to the unmarried state, and the relegation of both to regulation primarily by norms other than legal ones.

NOTES

¹ Quoted in *Ripert & Boulanger*, Par. 1254.

² Chapter 1 *supra* at 4–6.

³ *Rheinstein, Int. Encyc.* 12.

⁴ An excellent legal and social analysis of informal marriage in the United States with special attention to the groups involved in the practice prior to recent changes can be found in Weyrauch, Informal Marriage and Common Law Marriage, in Sexual Behavior and the Law 297 (Slovenko ed. 1965).

⁵ *Rheinstein, M.S.D.L.* 301; *Carbonnier, 2 Droit Civil* 194–195.

⁶ *1 Mazeaud* 42; Chabas, Le coeur de la cour de cassation, D.S. 1975. Chr. 41, 43.

⁷ As a reaction to "tax divorces", Swedish tax law was reformed to treat married and unmarried taxpayers the same in 1965, *Sundberg, Marriage or no Marriage* 231. Similiar reforms are being considered in the United States, *infra* at 178–179.

⁸ Sussman notes change between his own studies of alternative American family styles in 1972 and again in 1975, in that the laws have become more favorable than not to diverse living arrangements. As for behavior, he thinks there is presently a "critical mass" for change to varied family forms and marriage styles. Sussman, The Four F's of Variant Family Forms and Marriage Styles, 24 Fam. Coord. 563, 575–576 (1975).

⁹ Statements to this effect are found in: England: Morcom, When is a Spouse not a Spouse? 125 New L. J. 593 (1975); Gray, A New Lease of Life, 123 New L. J. 596 (1973); France: *Jeanmart* 18–30; *Saint-Cyr* 123; Le Mariage à la Traîne, Le Nouvel Observateur, 2 Feb. 1976, at 32–34. As to the United States, see Sussman, *supra* n. 8; and *infra* p. 91. In West Germany *Die Zeit* has reported a remarkable change in attitudes of young people toward informal cohabitation as evidenced by polls taken in 1967 and again in 1975. Of the 1967 group, only 24% of the young women and 48% of the young men said they "found nothing wrong" with a man and woman living together without marriage. Of the 1975 group, 85% of the young men and 92% of the young women "found nothing wrong" with this situation. Die Zeit, Apr. 30, 1976, POLITIK at 4 (International ed.).

¹⁰ Perevedentsev, The Family: Yesterday, Today and Tomorrow, 27 Curr. Dig. Sov. Press, No. 32, at 4 (1975). The cause most often cited for divorce in the Soviet Union is that the other spouse has started a new family, *Sundberg, Louvain Report.*

¹¹ Chapter 1, *supra* at 5.

¹² *König* 62–63; Report of the Commission on Population Growth and the American Future 103 (1972).

¹³ *Rheinstein, M.S.D.L.* 11.

¹⁴ Marriage Rates per 1000 population:

	1966	1967	1968	1969	1970	1971	1972	1973	1974
United Kingdom	8.0	8.0	8.4	8.2	8.5	8.3	8.6	8.1	—
France	6.9	7.0	7.1	7.6	7.8	7.9	8.1	7.7	7.6
West Germany	8.0	8.0	7.4	7.3	7.3	7.1	6.7	6.4	6.1

SOURCE: United Nations Department of Economic and Social Affairs, Demographic Yearbook 1970 (1971) and 1974 (1975); and *Beitzke* 30.

[15] United States

	1965	1970	1971	1972	1973	1974	1975
Rate	9.3	10.7	10.6	10.9	10.9	10.5	
Number	1,800,000	2,179,000	2,196,000	2,269,000	2,277,000	2,223,000	2,126,000

SOURCE: World Almanac and Book of Facts 1974, 1975 and 1976. The 1975 figure is an unofficial early Census Bureau report, which appeared in the New York Times, 21 May 1976, at 10, col. 2.

[16] Weyrauch, Informal and Formal Marriage – An Appraisal of Trends in Family Organization, 28 U. Chi. L. Rev. 88 (1960); Weyrauch, *supra* n. 4.

[17] Note, *Family Law – Sweden*, 22 Int'l & Comp. L. Q. 182 (1973).

[18] I am grateful to Professor Erik Jayme of the University of Munich Law Faculty for pointing out to me that a great many West German betrothal (*Verlöbnis*) cases in recent years have in fact involved the property affairs of cohabiting couples.

[19] Adultery is no longer a crime in England, France, West Germany and several American states. One might mention also the recent change in West German law concerning the offense formerly called *Kuppelei* (pandering), which has now been redefined and renamed so as to remove the threat of criminal liability for rooming house keepers or even parents who permit unmarried persons of opposite sex to stay together in the same house overnight. StGB §180. Schönke-Schröder, Strafgesetzbuch Kommentar 1016, 1044 (1974).

[20] Kim v. U.S. Immigration and Naturalization Service, 514 F. 2d 179 (D.C. Cir. 1975). Apparent accord: "Thou has committed/Fornication: But that was in another country/And besides, the wench is dead", from Marlowe's *The Famous Tragedy of the Rich Jew of Malta* (circa 1589), now well-known as the epigraph of T. S. Eliot's "Portrait of a Lady". But cf.: "What is of interest here is the paradox of a culture in which sexual infidelity has become extensive but is not taken lightly, and is a matter of great anxiety and concern." M. Lerner, American as a Civilization 595 (1957).

[21] Rheinstein, Introduction to *Weber* p. lxiv.

[22] *Weber* 68.

[23] *Ibid.*

[24] It has been said that *union libre* (free union) refers to a man and a woman who live together as husband and wife in the same household and is thus to be distinguished from *concubinage*, which designates a relationship between a man and woman with a certain stability but without a community of life. *Saint-Cyr*. But in fact the words *concubinage* and *union libre* are used interchangably by French courts and writers. The choice often seems to depend upon the attitude the declarant takes toward the behavior involved. See *infra* at 99.

[25] It is referred to only insofar as relations between the parties and their children are concerned. E.g. French C.C. art. 340–4.

[26] *Marty & Raynaud* 412; *Carbonnier, 2 Droit Civil* 187.

[27] *Carbonnier, 2 Droit Civil* 187; *Marty & Raynaud* 412; *1 Mazeaud* 37; *Ripert & Boulanger* 452.

[28] *Supra* n. 9.

[29] Chapter 5 *infra*.

[30] Carbonnier, Flexible Droit 139. See Chapter 2 *supra* at 29.

[31] Josserand, L'avenèment du concubinat, D.H. 1932, Chr. 45; Esmein, L'union libre, D.H. 1935, Chr. 49.

[32] E.g. Cass. Civ. 27 July 1937, D.H. 1938, 5; Cass. Civ. 10 Jan. 1963, D. 1963. Jur. 404.

[33] E.g. *Ripert & Boulanger* 452; *Marty & Raynaud* No. 371; but cf. *Bénabent* 445–446 who speaks of the *union libre* as "enriching" the field of choice for the individual among varying life styles.

[34] See Chapter 4 *infra* at 267.

[35] See Chapter 5 *infra* at 249.

[36] *Marty & Raynaud* 415–416.

[37] Representative cases are collected by *Marty & Raynaud* at 415, and by *Carbonnier*, at *2 Droit Civil* 197–198. In West Germany, a similar function is sometimes performed by the so-called *BGB-Gesellschaft* which takes its name from section 54 of the German Civil Code under which certain associations are legally treated as though they were partnerships.

[38] *Carbonnier, 2 Droit Civil* 190.

[39] *Ripert & Boulanger* 453.

[40] Under a provision added to the Civil Code by the 1941–1945 legislation, codifying a *jurisprudence constante,* a spouse who obtained a divorce could obtain damages for reparation of "the material or moral prejudice caused him by the dissolution of the marriage". French C.C., former Art. 301. The 1976 Divorce Reform law continued this possibility but limited its availability in new Art. 266 of the Civil Code. See Ch. 6 *infra.*

[41] Carbonnier, 2 Droit Civil 192–193; *Ripert & Boulanger* 453. A proposal for granting trial judges power to award damages for rupture of a free union anytime one partner is left in a state of need has been made by *Jeanmart* at 297.

[42] Trib. Paris, 13 Nov. 1959, D. 1960. Jur. 360.

[43] *Carbonnier* 191, 195; *Ripert & Boulanger* 454.

[44] *Marty & Raynaud* 370; *Jeanmart* 286.

[45] *Carbonnier, 2 Droit Civil* 190. Cf. French C.C. art. 220.

[46] Art. 17, Law of 11 July 1975.

[47] *Saint-Cyr.*

[48] *Carbonnier, 2 Droit Civil* 194.

[49] *Id.* at 191–192.

[50] Trib. Seine 12 Feb. 1931, D.H. 1931, 57.

[51] Paris App. 18 March 1932, D.H. 1932, 88; *1 Mazeaud* 51.

[52] *Supra* n. 32; *Carbonnier, 2 Droit Civil* 192; *1 Mazeaud* 52.

[53] *1 Mazeaud* 52.

[54] Cass. Ch. Mixte 27 Feb. 1970, D.S. 1970. Jur. 201, note R. Combaldieu.

[55] *Carbonnier, Flexible droit* 139.

[56] Cass. crim. 20 Apr. 1972, J.C.P. 1972.II.17278, note Vidal; D.S. 1972. Somm. 129.

[57] Chabas, *supra* n. 6.

[58] *Id.* at 212.

[59] Reported in Durry, Rev.trim.dr.civ. 1975, 709–710.

[60] *Supra* n. 46.

[61] Trib. Paris, 24 Nov. 1972, D.S. 1973. Jur. 414, note Groslierè.

[62] *Ibid.*

[63] *Ibid.*

[64] *Ibid.*

[65] *Saint-Cyr* 126.

[66] French C.C. new art. 283; as to pensions see *Saint-Cyr* 126–127.

[67] *Id.* at 128.

[68] *Infra* n. 164.

[69] *1 Mazeaud* 39.

[70] Gobert, La protection de la famille en droit civil 1–2 (unpublished monograph of the Société de legislation comparée, 1973).

[71] *Id.* at 16, 22, 23.

[72] Scapel, Que reste-t-il de la "paix des familles" apres la réforme du droit de la filiation? J.C.P. 1976 No. 2757.

[73] *Rheinstein, M.S.D.L.* 281.

[74] *Ripert & Boulanger* 495–496; In West Germany the matter is not quite so clear-cut, proof of *"faktische Ehe"* being admissible to cure a formal defect in the legal marriage, H.-F. Thomas, Formlose Ehen 95–97 (1973).

[75] *Clark HB* §2.4. In the view suggested here, the gradual decline in the number of American juridictions which recognize the doctrine of common law marriage loses significance because other devices have simultaneously arisen which bring about functionally analogous legal effects, mostly having to do with the provision of economic benefits – alimony, inheritance rights, wrongful death or workmen's compensation benefits – to members of a *de facto* family.

[76] Boston Evening Globe, May 26 1976 at 2, cols. 1–8.

[77] The drawings of W. Hamilton in *The New Yorker* magazine over the past two or three years are in themselves a concise social history of upper-middle class "living together".

[78] Sussman, *supra* n. 8; and Report of the Commission on Population and the American Future 104 (1972); Macklin, Heterosexual Cohabitation among Unmarried College Students, 21 Fam. Coord. 463 (1972).

[79] E.g. C. Foote, R. Levy & F. Sander, Cases and Materials on Family Law, Chapter 5.C. 1 "The Rights of Illegitimate Children and Informal 'Spouses' " (2d ed. 1976).

[80] The refinements of how to be polite to unmarried couples are now treated in E. Post, The New Emily Post's Etiquette 73, 382–383, 395 (1975).

[81] M. King, Cohabitation Handbook (1975); W. Blaine & J. Bishop, Practical Guide for the Unmarried Couple (1976).

[82] King, *supra* n. 81 at 2.

[83] S. v. J., 367 N.Y.S. 2d 405 (Sup. Ct. 1975). Accord: Christensen v. Christensen, 335 N.E.2d 581 (Ill. App. 1975); Wildermuth v. Wildermuth, 542 P.2d 463 (Wash. App. 1975).

[84] E.g., Brim v. Brim, 532 P.2d 1403 (Okla. App. 1975).

[85] Torrance v. Torrance, 1 Fam. L. Rptr. 2456 (Minn. Dist. Ct. Fam. Div. April 3, 1975).

[86] Holding that cohabitation terminates alimony are: Fahrer v. Fahrer, 304 N.E.2d 411 (Ohio App. 1973); Taake v. Taake, 233 N.W.2d 449 (Wis. 1975) (divorced wife had *"de facto* marriage relationship"); Lang v. Superior Court, 126 Cal. Rptr. 122 (Cal. App. 1975) (pursuant to recently adopted California statute); Latzky v. Latzky, 2 Fam. L. Rptr. 2169 (N.Y. Sup. Ct. Jan. 1, 1975) (pursuant to New York Statute). Holding that alimony must continue in spite of cohabitation are: Garlinger v. Garlinger, 347 A.2d 799 (N.J. Super. 1975): Atwater v. Atwater, 309 N.E.2d 631 (Ill. App. 1974); Sturgis v. Sturgis, 1 Fam. L. Rptr. 2042 (Ark. Sup. Ct. Oct. 14, 1974).

[87] Village of Belle Terre v. Boraas, 416 U.S. 1 (1974); see also Palo Alto Tenants' Union v. Morgan, 321 F. Supp. 908 (N.D. Cal. 1970), *aff'd* 487 F.2d 883 (9th Cir. 1973), *cert. denied,* 417 U.S. 910 (1974).

[88] United States Department of Agriculture v. Moreno, 413 U.S. 528 (1973) (invalidating food stamp eligibility limitation to households consisting of related members).

[89] O'Grady v. Town of North Castle, no. 41751 (S.D.N.Y. Jan. 16, 1975).

[90] In re Marriage of Cary, 109 Cal. Rptr. 862 (Cal. App. 1973).

[91] Vallera v. Vallera, 134 P.2d 761 (Cal. 1943).

[92] In re Marriage of Cary, 109 Cal. Rptr. 862 (Cal. App. 1973).

[93] *Id.* at 867.

[94] *Supra* n. 67.

[95] Marvin v. Marvin, 557 P.2d 106 (Cal. 1976).

[96] *Id.* at 122.

[97] In re Estate of Thornton, 541 P.2d 1243 (Wash. 1972).

[98] Creasman v. Boyle, 196 P.2d 835 (Wash. 1948).

[99] In re Estate of Thornton, 499 P.2d 864, 866–867 (Wash. 1972).

[100] Latham v. Hennessey, 554 P.2d 1057, 1059 (Wash. 1976). Meanwhile, *Thornton* had been followed in a *de facto* "divorce" situation in Omer v. Omer, 523 P.2d 957 (Wash. App. 1974).

[101] E.g. Foote, Levy and Sander, *supra* n. 79 at 701; Note, 9 U.S.F.L. Rev. 186 (1974); Weisberg, Alternative Family Structures and the Law, 24 Fam. Coord. 549, 556 (1975); Weitzman, To Love Honor and Obey? Traditional Legal Marriage and Alternative Family Forms, 24 Fam. Coord. 531, 545 (1975).

[102] Weisberg, *supra* n. 101 at 556–557.

[103] Crépeau, Civil Code Revision in Quebec, 34 La. L. Rev. 921, 934 (1974). This approach raises the problem of whether and how inhabitants can opt out of legal consequences attaching to their union. If a Roman woman did not wish to come under the *manus* of the man she lived with she could prevent this from happening, under the law of the XII Tables, by absenting herself for

three nights in each year. *Jolowicz* 115. A modern version of this "trinoctium" has been proposed in Denmark: *Sundberg, Marriage or no Marriage* 238.

[104] E. Clive & J. Wilson, The Law of Husband and Wife in Scotland 289 (1974).

[105] *Infra* at 266.

[106] *Infra* Chapter 4.

[107] *Infra* Chapter 5.

[108] *Infra* at 101.

[109] Gray, *supra* n. 9.

[110] Purpoole, Legal Oddities, 125 New L. J. 1152 (1975); Poulter, The Death of a Lover – I, 126 New L. J. 417 (1976), says: "[It] seems likely that living together outside marriage is a widespread phenomenon in our society at the present time, both among the unwed and among those who are on the 'rebound' from a divorce or separation."

[111] *Cretney* 4.

[112] Inheritance (Provision for Family and Dependants) Act 1975, adopted pursuant to recommendations of the Law Commission, Second Report of Family Property: Family Provision on Death (Law Commission No. 61) 24 (1974). See *infra* Ch. 6 at 281–282.

[113] Quoted in Poulter, *supra* n. 110 at 418.

[114] Poulter, The Death of a Lover – I and II, 126 New L. J. 417 and 433 (1976).

[115] Even in West Germany, in a dramatic reversal, the hostility of the courts to the *Maitressen-testament* has given way recently to a practical and non-moralistic approach, according to Professor Erik Jayme of the University of Munich law faculty.

[116] Quoted in Poulter, *supra* n. 114 at 434.

[117] *Ibid.*

[118] Hawes v. Evenden [1953] 2 All E.R. 737.

[119] *Supra* n. 90 and n. 93.

[120] Family Income Supplements Act 1970 s. 1(1).

[121] Administration of Estates Act 1925, 15 & 16 Geo.5 c. 23, s. 46(1)(vi) (as amended).

[122] *Cretney* 197.

[123] Eves v. Eves (C.A. 1975), discussed in Bissett-Johnson, Mistress's Right to a Share in the "Matrimonial Home", 125 New L. J. 614 (1975).

[124] *Id.* at 615.

[125] Tanner v. Tanner (C.A. 1975), discussed in Bissett-Johnson, *supra* n. 123 at 615.

[126] *Ibid.*

[127] Barton, Note, 92 L. Q. Rev. 168, 171 (1976).

[128] Morcom, When is a Spouse not a Spouse? 125 New L. J. 593 (1975).

[129] *Ibid.*

[130] Eekelaar 246.

[131] *Sundberg, Marriage or No Marriage* 230; *Rheinstein, M.S.D.L.* 137.

[132] Report of a survey by three international organizations quoted by *Sundberg, Recent Changes* 39.

[133] *Ibid.*

[134] *Sundberg, Nordic Laws* 41.

[135] Quoted in *Sundberg, Marriage or No Marriage* at 233.

[136] Note, *Family Law – Sweden*, 22 Int. & Comp. L. Q. 182 (1973), and Note, *Current Legal Developments, Sweden*, 19 Int. & Comp. L. Q. 164 (1970).

[137] *Sundberg, Louvain Report.*

[138] *Sundberg, Nordic Laws* 40.

[139] *Sundberg, Marriage or No Marriage* 227. The developments described in the remainder of this paragraph are discussed in detail by Sundberg at 227 *et seq.*

[140] *Id.* at 233–234.

[141] Note, *Family Law – Sweden (follow-up)*, 22 Int. & Comp. L. Q. 766 (1973). The reform legislation went into effect on January 1, 1974.

[142] *Sundberg, Recent Changes* 49.
[143] Note, *Current Legal Developments – Sweden,* 19 Int. & Comp. L. Q. 164 (1970).
[144] *Supra* n. 130.
[145] *Supra* n. 132.
[146] *Supra* n. 130.
[147] *Sundberg, Marriage or No Marriage* 224.
[148] See Sage, *Dissolution of the Family under Swedish Law,* 9 Fam. L. Q. 375 (1975).
[149] *Sundberg, Marriage or No Marriage* 237–238.
[150] See in general: England: *Bromley* 228–246 and *Cretney* 309–339; France: Nerson. La situation juridique des enfants nés hors mariage, Rev.trim.dr.civ. 1975, 397 and 631; United States and Comparative: *Krause, Int. Encyc.*; Meulders, Fondements nouveaux du concept de filiation, Ann.dr. 1973, 285.
[151] *Goode* 24.
[152] *Id.* at 30.
[153] "No child should be brought into the world without a man – and one man at that – assuming the role of sociological father...." Malinowski, Parenthood, The Basis of Social Structure, in The Family, Its Structure and Functions 3 (Coser ed. 1964).
[154] *Krause, Illegitimacy* 257–295; *Goode* 24–25.
[155] *Goode* 24.
[156] *Krause, Int. Encyc.* §13.
[157] *Sundberg, Recent Changes* 39.
[158] *Ibid.*
[159] Rheinstein, M.S.D.L. 335.
[160] The landmarks are: Levy v. Louisiana, 391 U.S. 68 (1968) (illegitimate children have right to wrongful death action for death of their mother); Glona v. American Casualty Co., 391 U.S. 73 (1968) (mother has wrongful death action for death of her illegitimate son); Weber v. Aetna Casualty Co., 406 U.S. 164 (1972) (Workmen's Compensation law cannot limit its benefits to dependent legitimate children); Gomez v. Perez, 409 U.S. 535 (1973) (state cannot limit support rights against father to legitimate children). The only area of private law into which the Supreme Court has declined to extend this equalization process is that of intestate succession, Labine v. Vincent, 401 U.S. 532 (1971). In the area of public law however, the distinction between legitimacy and illegitimacy has lost almost all significance: Jiminez v. Weinberger, 417 U.S. 628 (1974); Lewis v. Martin, 397 U.S. 552 (1970); Cahill v. New Jersey Welfare Rights Organization, 411 U.S. 619 (1973); King v. Smith, 392 U.S. 309 (1968). A minor exception remains in the fact that unacknowledged illegitimate children must prove dependency on a deceased father in order to be eligible for Social Security Survivor's benefits, Norton v. Mathews, 96 S.Ct. 2771 (1976) and Mathews v. Lucas, 96 S.Ct. 2755 (1976).
The 1968 Soviet Reform Law and subsequent developments are discussed in Lapenna, The Illegitimate Child in Soviet Law, 25 L. Q. Rev. 156, 169–179 (1976).
[161] Family Law Reform Act 1969 s. 14.
[162] Nichtehelichengesetz 19 Aug. 1969, BGB1. I 1243, effective 1 July 1970.
[163] Grundgesetz (Basic Law) of 1949, Art. 6, par. 5.
[164] Loi No. 72–3 of 3 Jan. 1972 sur la filiation, effective 1 August 1972.
[165] "All children, whether born in or out of wedlock, shall enjoy the same social protection", United Nations Universal Declaration of Human Rights of 10 December 1948 Art. 25, Par. 2.
[166] "Every person, once his filiation has been established, shall have the same legal status as a person born in wedlock." *Krause, Int. Encyc.* §19.
[167] Reported in 125 New L.J. 1196 (1975).
[168] *Krause, Int. Encyc.* §79.
[169] *Supra* p. 90.
[170] French C.C. new art. 340–4.
[171] French C.C. new art. 320. See in general Rémond-Gouilloud, La possession d'état d'enfant, Rev.trim.dr.civ. 1973, 459.

[172] Meulders, *supra* n. 150 at 323.

[173] Rémond-Gouilloud, *supra* n. 171 at 479–481.

[174] Report of the Royal Commission on Marriage and Divorce s. 1180 (1956).

[175] As Cretney points out, this right is not one of equal inheritance. An illegitimate child cannot inherit from an ancestor more remote than a parent or from collaterals. *Cretney* 332.

[176] Grundgesetz (Basic Law) of 1949, Art. 6 Par. 5. As Rheinstein points out, this formulation is not a demand for full equality, especially when read in connection with Art. 6 par. 2 which provides, "Marriage and the family enjoy the special protection of the state." Rheinstein, Book Review, 21 Am. J. Comp. L. 332, 336 (1973).

[177] German C.C. former §1589 II.

[178] E.g. German C.C. new §1615a.

[179] *Krause, Int. Encyc.* §119 and 121.

[180] Labine v. Vincent, 401 U.S. 532 (1971).

[181] *Cretney* 332.

[182] *Supra* n. 154.

[183] See Chapter 6 *infra*.

[184] E.g. Stanley v. Illinois, 405 U.S. 645 (1972) (the State cannot presume that unmarried fathers in general are unsuitable custodians; unwed father entitled to hearing on question of fitness).

[185] Rheinstein, *supra* n. 176 at 333.

4

EFFECTS OF LEGAL MARRIAGE: WHILE THE MARRIAGE LASTS

I. Introduction: Ideals and Reality

Legal treatment of the effects of marriage in any given system of law expresses the basic ideas and aspirations of that legal order concerning the relationship between the spouses. Accordingly, in recent years, as marriage behavior and ideologies have changed, there has been a profound alteration of the legal treatment of interspousal personal and property relationships in all four countries studied here.

This alteration, which amounts to a change in the organizing principles of each country's family law, appears most clearly in the law concerning the effects of the functioning marriage. The reason change is especially apparent in this area is that legal rules on the on-going relationship of spouses everywhere tend more to be pronouncements of general models for behavior than specific rules of conduct with direct sanctions for their violation. In fact, except where they concern property or children, general rules on the husband –wife relationship are often just symbolic descriptions of an ideal of family life. Thus, the present chapter affords a special opportunity to observe how officially expressed ideologies of marriage have changed. The following two chapters – on marriage dissolution and the effects of marriage dissolution – treat legal rules which carry definite legal consequences and sanctions in their wake. But even those rules show the influence of the changes in marriage ideologies and behavior we begin to describe here. Together with Chapter 2, Chapters 4, 5 and 6 show what legal marriage looks like in the late 1970s: its ideals; the way in which specific legal rules have developed to deal with behavior which may fail to meet the ideals; the adaptation of the law to changes in marriage and family behavior; and, finally, overall, the way in which the State has gradually withdrawn from attempting to regulate the manner in which couples form, organize and terminate their married life, contenting itself with trying to deal with the practical economic and child-related problems that legal marriage, like any other form of cohabitation, generates.

The prevailing ideologies of marriage have never been alike for all groups of any large population. In Western society, however, one ideology has been dominant and until modern times has found universal expression in the law. The family law of Western legal systems has traditionally embodied ideas of separate spheres of activity appropriate for women and men. It has carried the image of the woman as principal caretaker of the home and children, the man as principal provider, and of a family authority structure dominated by the husband and father. This should not be understood as meaning that the woman's *exclusive* task has been to care for home and children. In pre-industrial society, the wife was often a co-worker with the husband on the farm, in the craft and in the shop. The exclusively housewife-marriage seems to be a phenomenon of the 20th century.[1] Already this period is beginning to appear to have been a brief interlude in history. Today, as more and more women engage in economic activity outside the home, housewife-marriage is only one of many current marriage patterns.[2] Where housewife-marriage exists, it is now more apt to be a phase of a marriage than a description of the marriage from beginning to end.

Organized around a hierarchical model, with a clear division of roles between the sexes, traditional family law placed primary responsibility for support of the family on the male partner and vested authority in him to determine the place and mode of family life and to deal with all the family property, including that of the wife. Among the wealthy, property matters could to some extent be arranged so that the interests of the wife (and her family of origin) could be protected. The law paid little attention to the needs of the poor, even when large numbers of women began to be employed outside the home in the early 19th century in England, and later in France and Germany. The set of legal rules organized along these traditional lines persisted in England, France, the United States and Germany well into the 20th century, long after behavior of many married people had ceased to correspond to the image enshrined in the laws.

This model was constantly adjusted, beginning in the late 19th century and in the first half of the 20th century, but at last the center could not hold. Laws which might have been appropriate for the family production community, or for the housewife marriage when divorce was rare, no longer worked when many women's economic activity had been transferred to the marketplace and when divorce had become pandemic.

This Chapter describes how the law of the on-going marriage has now been transformed and continues to be transformed, as new ideologies and varying life styles vie for legal recognition. We may begin by mentioning briefly some of the factors which have been instrumental in bringing down the centuries-old system of regulating husband–wife relationships in England, France, the United States and Germany.

First, there is the well-documented change in family structure from a hierarchical pattern headed by the husband and father, to a joint and egalitarian pattern in which husband and wife are equal partners in the decision-making and division of labor within the family.[3] Boundaries between the roles of husband and wife are becoming blurred. Second, there is the shift in emphasis from the character of the family as a unit to the quality of each spouse as an autonomous individual within that unit. These two factors, which have had an important influence on the legal questions discussed in this chapter, are closely related to a third pervasive change in society, namely, the worldwide trend toward female emancipation. A fourth development, of special importance to the law governing the economic relations of spouses, has been the growing economic activity of married women outside the home, and the consequent appearance of many two-earner or two-career marriages. The increased ease of planning the number and timing of children has played its role, too, in enabling women to choose a particular life style or to alternate between marriage styles in a single lifetime. While the average duration of marriages is on the increase through increasing longevity, the growing incidence of divorce has had an important impact on interspousal law.

On the ideological plane, contemporary Western society is a museum of various conceptions of marriage. Classed by some in the antiquities section, but still alive, is the Christian belief in marriage as a sacramental and indissoluble bond through which each partner becomes responsible for the other's material and spiritual welfare. Engels saw this Christian ideal as supplanted by bourgeois marriage in which economic considerations make every marriage one of convenience and a form of legal prostitution. Today it is common to speak of bourgeois marriage as being organized around consumption rather than production. Co-existing with the idea of marriage as an indissoluble undertaking is the view of it as an association which exists primarily for the personal fulfillment of the individual spouses and which should last only so long as it serves this purpose. Finally, there seems to be a tendency to think of each spouse as primarily responsible for his or her own material needs (especially after divorce as we shall see in Chapter 6). When a spouse cannot be self-sufficient, the State is increasingly viewed as an early rather than late resort.

Needless to say, this is not an exhaustive list of all the elements of behavioral and ideological change bearing on the legal ordering of family matters. Nor can these elements be neatly separated from each other. They

are all inter-related, and form part of that process that social scientists sometimes call modernization. When we look at these factors in more detail as a
background for the recent changes in the effects of legal marriage in this and
the following chapters, we will be in a position to take the full measure of
the nature and extent of change in the relationship of the State to the family.
Let us begin by analyzing how changing marriage and sex-role behavior and
ideology have found their way into American, English, French and West
German legal patterns for the functioning marriage and how changing
general norms have in turn provoked further changes in specific legal rules.

II. Law Affecting Interspousal Personal Relations: The Symbolism of the Husband–Wife Relationship

A. Authority Structure of the Family[4]

One measure of how heavily the social institution of marriage became
juridified in Western legal systems is provided by the elaborate manner in
which the 18th and 19th century European codes purport to regulate by law a
matter which is highly resistant to any type of regulation – the personal
relationship of husband and wife and, in particular, the family decision-
making process.[5] One must say "purport" because in general no consequences attached to the violation of the norms established in the Codes for the
conduct of married life unless and until the spouses found themselves in court
in a marriage breakdown situation. Then the norms might be relevant on the
question whether a spouse had committed "fault". Today, however, when
few divorces or separations are denied, and fault is being eliminated as a factor
in granting or denying a divorce (or maintenance or separate support), it may
be doubted whether there is any content to these norms at all beyond the
symbolic.[6]

Therefore this body of law which is not really law gives us the closest look
we can get at the symbols through which any given legal order confers
approval on certain types of conduct. The recent changes are accordingly
viewed here as significant primarily as indicators of changes in the ideology
being communicated through the law of the husband–wife relationship. But
where the symbolic norms also have legal "bite" this is pointed out too.

The French and German Civil Codes dealt elaborately with the allocation
of powers of decision between husband and wife in family matters. From
1804 until 1938, Art. 213 of the French Civil Code read: "The husband owes
protection to his wife, the wife obedience to her husband."[7] In 1938 this

language was repealed, but from 1938 to 1970, revised Art. 213 stated that the husband was the "head of the family". Indeed, as late as 1965 an attempt to change this language was successfully defeated. The original draft by the Commission for the Reform of the Civil Code of the new matrimonial property law of 13 July 1965, which took effect in 1966, had deposed the husband as the head of the family. The opposition to this change was so great, however, that the Commission retained the symbolic leadership of the husband out of fear that otherwise the whole reform project would fail.

Then, in 1967, another draft of Art. 213 was formulated with the approval of the Conseil d'État. This draft would have provided that in the case of an impasse between husband and wife the husband would make a decision in conformity with the interest of the household and the children. In 1970 this proposal was rejected. The 1970 legislature for a time considered retaining the proposal so far as decision-making with respect to the children was concerned but finally rejected it even there.[8]

Finally, in the Law of 4 June 1970, the historic language "The husband is head of the family" was eliminated from Art. 213 of the Civil Code and the following statement was substituted: "The spouses together assure the moral and material direction of the family." The hierarchical principle which at one time had organized French family law was swept away and Art. 215 was amended to include what may be the new organizing principle: "The spouses are mutually bound to a community of life."

The 1970 law had as its principal object the complete reform of Title Nine of the French Civil Code dealing with the father's power over the person and the property of his children, the *puissance paternelle*. Title Nine was renamed *De l'autorité parentale*. The new principle was established that the mother and the father exercise the parental authority in common. For not only was the 1970 law a landmark in the development of legal equality of the sexes in France, it was also the culmination of a steady trend to modify the degree and kind of control to which children are subjected.

The changes wrought by the 1970 law were so widely acclaimed by diverse groups in French society that the Minister of Justice claimed that the new law was a reflection of an evolution of mores and family practices in France.[9] But it can hardly be doubted that the unsettling events of May 1968 had had an effect in causing the legislature, so resistant to change only five years earlier, to recognize this evolution.

It does seem clear that by 1970 political circumstances had changed so much since similar reforms were proposed in 1945 and again in 1965 that the old arguments which were used successfully to resist change in the past did not sound the same any more: "Every human society must have a head";

"The elimination of the head of the family will hasten the dissolution of the family"; "The husband shoud be the head because he is better able to support the family"; "More and more couples will seek judicial intervention and this will lead to marriage breakdown"; "The new marriage will be a *ménage à trois* of husband, wife and judge".

These old arguments did not sound as good as they had twenty-five years before, but Juilliot de la Morandière's response to them at that time had begun to sound better:

> The power of the head of the family can be justified if the family must defend itself by arms; it can even be understood if, because of the social and economic structure, the man is stronger in a social sense, or acts alone in daily affairs. But, this is no longer the case; it is no longer the man alone who earns the living for the family; the wife generally has an education equivalent to that of the husband and she has equal political rights. The notion of a head of the family is contrary to good sense and contrary to reality.

> Real family unity under these circumstances does not depend on the authority given to one of the spouses (such an authoritarian conception can only give rise to conflict); it depends on the unity of the two spouses. If they get along well, (and this will be more difficult if you require the submission of one) the family will last; if they do not get along, the exercise of an authority which is not accepted will only serve to poison the situation.[10]

In 1970 this statement was cited by the Minister of Justice who presented the *exposé des motifs* of the new law as "clairvoyant".[11] The reporter of the law project told the National Assembly that shared authority corresponds to the conception which "young people today" have of marriage and child raising as joint enterprises in which responsibilities are shared equally.[12] The Minister of Justice also claimed that

> The Civil Code can fulfill an educational function by encouraging the spouses to exchange their points of view on all the important questions which arise in connection with the running of the household and the education of the children, as well as to come to agreement, before marriage, concerning a common ethic.[13]

In the same vein the Reporter to the Senate said

> [I]t is good to write down and to say to young husbands when they present themselves before a public official at the dawn of their married life, that the wife has achieved equality with the husband, and that it is up to him to seek out with her the ways of exercising this right.[14]

German law too has undergone a legal and symbolic transformation. The German Civil Code of 1896 (effective 1900) emphasized the unity of the spouses and the predominance of the husband. But it reflected some of the changes that had taken place since the French Civil Code had retained the husband in his customary law position as *"seigneur et maître"* of the family in 1804, and after the Prussian General Code of 1794 had meticulously provided that "The chief purpose of marriage is the procreation and upbringing of children." In the German Civil Code, the husband's powers and rights were predominant but not absolute. And, rather than imposing a duty of obedience on the wife, the German Code described an ideal of *Lebensgemeinschaft*: "The spouses are obliged to live together in a matrimonial community of life."[15] But the division of labor and of decision-making power within the family was still clear. Article 1354 gave the husband the right to "decide all matters of matrimonial life", including the place of residence. But the wife was not obliged to follow the decision of the husband if the decision was an "abuse" of his right. Other provisions of the Code gave the husband a limited right to give notice of termination to his wife's employer and to manage his wife's property.[16] This traditional manner of ordering German family law was upset when the West German Constitution of 1949 proclaimed the principle of equality of the sexes.[17] But the Constitution of 1949 also proclaimed that "Marriage and the family enjoy the special protection of the State."[18] Whether these two ideals could be fully implemented without coming into conflict depended on reinterpreting "marriage" and "the family".

A certain hesitation characterized West German efforts to implement the equality principle. The Constitution of 1949 provided for a delay of four years before the equality provision would become self-executing. This delay was supposed to give the legislature plenty of time to make the necessary adaptations. However the four years passed with no legislative action and the courts were faced with the task, starting on 31 March 1953, of implementing the equality rule on their own. Four more years passed during which the courts struck down provision after provision of the Civil Code. Finally in 1957 the Equality Law, the *Gleichberechtigungsgesetz*, was passed to implement the constitution and to amend the old law.[19]

At the present time, the old legal provisions giving preeminence to the husband have been repealed by the Equality Law, or the Marriage and Family Law Reform of 1976,[20] or declared unconstitutional by the courts. The effect has been that the emphasis on the community aspect of marriage in the original Art. 1353 which still states that husband and wife are obliged to live with each other in marital community of life stands out even more clearly and with new meaning. But if marriage is to be viewed as a community of life, and, at the same time, a union between two free and equal individuals, there will be difficult situations where the law is asked to deal with a conflict

between the community of the two spouses and the autonomy of the individual spouse.[21] The *Lebensgemeinschaft* of the 1970s is not that of 1896.

The 1957 Equality Law itself was ambivalent. It gave the father the final
right to make decisions in the event of disagreement between the spouses on
the exercise of parental authority. This was promptly struck down as a
violation of the constitutional equality principle.[22] On the other hand, the
equality principle was not applied to strike down certain other provisions of
the Civil Code which gave a dominant position to the husband by enshrining
housewife-marriage as the cultural ideal. For example, Art. 1356.I. began
with the statement "The wife's responsibility is to run the household." Then
it provided that the wife was authorized to work outside the home so long
as this was compatible with her marital and family duties. So, up to 1976,
the wife did not have an equal right to independent work outside the
home.

Two law review articles have brilliantly documented the extent to which
West German family law, even after the 1957 Equality Law, still carried the
image and assumptions of "bourgeois" marriage even though explicitly
discriminatory rules had been eliminated.[23] They reveal that constitutional
pronouncements do not transform society and law overnight. But the fact
that this was the state of German law until 1976 renders all the more significant the changes brought about by the Family Law Reforms of that year.

The official family policy statement of the Social Democratic Party of 1972
was prefaced with this paragraph:

The Family between Tradition, Reality and the Future. Society is a process of continuous change. Even the family is changing, in its structure, as well as in its lifestyles.
Family policy should not, therefore, remain bound to the dominant symbols [*Leitbilder*] or ideas of yesterday. It must be open to broader developments and to social
progress.[24]

The statement then went on to distinguish three phases in the current evolution of the family: the traditional family with its clear sex-role differentiation;
the current tendency toward partnership; the likelihood that new forms of the
family will develop in the future. In the Social Democratic government's new
marriage and divorce law promulgated on 14 June 1976, the law is no longer
organized around the image of housewife and maintenance-marriage but
rather around the idea of marriage as a partnership of workers pursuing their
chosen occupations whatever these may be. Article 1356 reads:

s. 1356 (1) The spouses conduct the running of the household by mutual agreement. If
the running of the household is left to one of the spouses, that spouse manages the
household on his own responsibility.

(2) Both spouses have the right to be employed. In the choice and exercise of an occupation they must pay due regard to the interests of the other spouse and the family.

Hence, West German Law has come to reflect not only the principle of equality but an entirely changed concept of marriage – a community of life in which the partners work out their own roles in consultation with or having regard to the interests of the other. This now is the "marriage" which according to the Constitution enjoys the "special protection of the State".

The changes that have occurred in the French Civil Code and in West German family law are highly visible signs of the process of change that is taking place in their normative systems. In the uncodified Anglo-American law, however, the approach to the functioning marriage has traditionally been one of non-intervention. In American law, this principle of non-interference with the on-going marriage has been well-established in a body of law in which the courts refuse to intervene in marital disputes; or even to require a husband to support his wife so long as the couple is still living together.[25] No model of conduct has been explicitly enshrined in the law as it was in the French and German Codes.[26] Yet one can say that while Anglo-American family law lacked general, sweeping statements about marriage and the roles of spouses, its details came to be organized along the same lines as the French and German law. Until mid-twentieth century the various legal rules of Anglo-American family law were also constructed for the model of maintenance-marriage in which the husband was assigned the dominant role. The discussion of specific American and English legal rules in this chapter will show how that model gradually has been modified. On the ideological level, recent developments in the United States have strongly reinforced the traditional approach of non-intervention.

Just as *Loving v. Virginia*[27] ushered in a new approach to marriage formation, if not immediate legal change, the other major statement of the United States Supreme Court on marriage in recent years, *Griswold v. Connecticut*,[28] inaugurated a new approach to the marriage-in-progress.

Like *Loving*, *Griswold* has become remarkable not for its narrow holding (that an archaic state law forbidding the use of birth control devices even by married couples is unconstitutional), but for the potentially far-reaching implications of its articulation of a constitutional right to marital privacy. *Griswold* raises to the constitutional level the principle of non-interference with a functioning marriage.

The idea of a right of marital privacy and the policy of law to interfere as little as possible with family life are both responses to pluralism and diversity in American society. The law in its own way has been digesting the fact that the "melting pot" model is seriously inadequate as a way of thinking about American heterogeneity. Students of ethnicity have now demonstrated that what was described as "melting" was simply a name given to the phenomenon of Anglo-Saxon conformity, and that the diverse groups which come together in the United States do not completely lose their distinctive identities and become merged in some great American amalgam which bears only faint residues and traces of all the groups dissolved in it.[29] Ethnic diversity in the United States merely compounds the problem which exists in all four countries of adapting the law to the practices of persons with different educational and religious backgrounds, of differing social status, and at different economic levels. In American legal thought, the idea has emerged that the only possible democratic response to this situation is neutrality rather than the imposition of the ideology of any one dominant group. A point of great importance from the perspective of this work is that neutrality, in practical terms, is most easily translated into action by withdrawal.

The trend toward withdrawal of regulation of the on-going marriage is not likely to be slowed by the advent of the equality principle. While theoretically it can be applied to extend legal rights and duties connected with marriage to whichever sex previously lacked them, the equality principle may, in combination with other factors, result in diminished legal consequences for both. It has, however, transformed the symbolism of the husband–wife relationship.

In the United States, one must refer to the "equality principle", rather than to any particular law, because the pressures in this direction are diverse. The Equal Rights Amendment to the Constitution of the United States, which was approved by both houses of the Congress on 22 March 1972, cannot take effect until it has been ratified by 38 states by the 1979 deadline. In late 1976, there was some question about whether it would succeed in getting the necessary four remaining state ratifications, as well as about the effectiveness of the attempted withdrawal of ratification by four states which had already given their approval. But the fate of the amendment is not of critical significance to the analysis here for three reasons. One is that the Equal Protection clause of the 14th amendment to the U.S. Constitution has already been used and will continue to be used to eliminate most sex-based discrimination in federal and state laws. Secondly, a great many states already have equal rights amendments to their state constitutions. Finally, at both the state and federal level there are innumerable cases and statutes eliminating distinctions based on sex, particularly in the important areas of employment and salaries. So far as the husband–wife relationship is concerned, the transformation of marriage into a partnership of two individuals of equal rank and dignity is nearly complete in the law of practically all states.

Judicial handling of recent cases brought by husbands asserting a right to participate in the decision whether or not to have an abortion is illustrative of the continuation of the traditional reluctance of American courts to intervene in marital decision-making. The Massachusetts Supreme Judicial Court, declining in 1974 to recognize such a right in the husband, said: "Except in cases involving divorce or separation, our law has not in general undertaken to resolve the many delicate questions inherent in the marriage relationship.... Some things must be left to private agreement."[30] While the legislatures of a few states have not been so reticent and have enacted statutes requiring the husband's consent under some circumstances,[31] the U.S. Supreme Court in 1976 struck this requirement down as unconstitutional.[32]

In England, although the overall situation is now similar to that in the United States, it was not always the case that the law remained aloof from the personal relationship of the spouses. The idea of matrimonial community of life in the English common law is embodied in the concept of *consortium*, the right of the spouses to the society and services of each other. At one time only the husband was viewed as having this right. Until the middle of the 19th century it was thought that the husband's right to consortium might under certain circumstances be enforced by physically confining his wife.[33] It was not until 1891 that it was held that the husband was not allowed to use force to restrain his wife's personal liberty.[34] Even in that case two judges left open the question whether a husband could still physically restrain his wife to protect his honor if, e.g., she was in the act of going to meet her paramour.[35] This question was not finally answered in the negative until 1972.[36]

Meanwhile, however, statutory changes had equated the rights of the spouses to the point where the position today with respect to consortium is, in the words of Professor Bromley, that "...both spouses are the joint, co-equal heads of the family".[37] Under the Domicile and Matrimonial Proceedings Act of 1973, a married woman may acquire or retain an independent domicile. The present situation in England seems to be that consortium, the duty to cohabit, exists as a symbol of the community aspect of marriage but has no legal effects between the spouses unless and until one of the spouses seeks divorce, judicial separation or separate maintenance.[38] Recently, the important Equal Pay and Sex Discrimination legislation of 1975, while limited in its application, has pointed the way for the further evolution of English law so far as equality of the sexes is concerned.[39]

If we turn now from general norms to the recent evolution of specific legal rules affecting the husband–wife relationship, we can see clearly that in all four countries such rules are being recast on the model of equality in the husband–wife relationship. It also appears that the French and West German systems have begun to move toward the Anglo-American posture of non-interference with family authority structure, even in areas where their courts were once active. This development can be seen clearly in the areas involving the choice of residence, the care and education of children, and the management of family property.

Where choice of residence is concerned, since the husband was typically the spouse primarily responsible for the support of the family, the final word was traditionally his. The French Code provided in former Art. 215: "The choice of the family residence belongs to the husband: the wife is obliged to live with him and he is bound to receive her." But in 1970 Art. 215 became: "The spouses are mutually bound to a community of life. The residence of the family is at the place which they choose by common accord." As the line continued, however, the ambivalence which had characterized the early stages of law reform in this area reasserted itself. The left hand took back what the right hand had given by adding the words: "In the absence of accord, in the place chosen by the husband." Then, so as not to entirely deprive the reform of substance, the legislature of 1970 added: "However, if the residence chosen by the husband presents serious inconvenience for the family, the wife may obtain authorization from the court for a separate residence." Then, finally, in the divorce reform law of 11 July 1975, the legislature struck a new balance by making both spouses equally responsible for the support of the family and by eliminating from Art. 215 the husband's right to designate the place of residence in the absence of accord.[40] The 1975 law repealed the first line of Art. 108 of the Civil Code which read: "A married woman has *no* (*n'a point*) other domicile but that of her husband." In its place now stands: "Husband and wife may have separate domiciles without, by this fact, violating the rules pertaining to the community of life."

A similar development has taken place in American law. By case law or statute in many American states a husband was given the right to designate the place of the family's residence in the sense that a wife's refusal to follow her husband to a new home chosen by him was considered desertion, a ground for divorce. While sometimes this right seemed to belong to the husband just because he was the husband, the cases for many years related it to the husband's duty to support the family. American case law, like French law, developed some limitations on the husband's power to select the family residence, e.g. the wife's duty to follow her husband to a residence would not extend to situations where the new residence was manifestly unsuitable from the point of view of health, safety or physical comfort of the family.[41] With or without an equal rights amendment to the U.S. Constitution, it is likely that the husband's right to select the family residence in those states where it was once recognized will not long endure. Recently the Massachusetts Supreme Judicial Court, in a case involving domicile for state income tax purposes, abolished as obsolete the rule that a married woman's domicile had to be the same as her husband's.[42]

Signs of erosion of the rule have been appearing in cases where the courts felt the need to justify the application of the rule on some ground other than the fact that the husband is entitled as husband to decide, and also in cases where the courts have found the rule inapplicable under various circumstances. For example, in a 1952 Maryland case, a husband was refused a divorce on grounds of desertion, the court saying that where the wife contributed more financially to the household than did the husband the reason for the rule permitting the husband to choose the family residence was absent.[43]

Decisions like these, the diminishing importance of fault (and therefore desertion) as a ground for divorce, and the increasing equalization of the duty of support between the wife and the husband will eventually result in the desuetude of the husband's power to designate the family residence.

In England, equality seems to have been achieved in this area by the application on a case-by-case basis of the rule that neither spouse has an absolute right to designate the residence of the couple, but that where the spouses disagree a divorce based on desertion will be granted only if one spouse can be said to have acted unreasonably under all circumstances.[44] In situations where neither spouse clearly has right on his or her side, desertion will not be available to justify a divorce.[45] The older view that the husband as husband is entitled to make the decision seems not to have been expressed since 1940.

In West Germany, where the husband's right to choose the family's place of residence had been qualified already in the Civil Code of 1896, former article 1354 did not survive the Equality Law of 1957.

The law concerning decisions involving a married couple's children has been profoundly influenced not only by the trend toward sex equality but also by increasing concern for the welfare of children.[46] While one can discern an established trend toward an equal sharing of parental rights and obligations, there is at the same time a trend toward diminution of the rights of both. This occurs because as parental equality becomes the rule in decision-making about children, mechanisms have had to be developed to deal with the problem of impasse. If equality is to be maintained at all costs this may mean that at some point the State as a third party in the form of a court or agency has to step in as the final arbiter of such disputes. The trend seems, however, to be toward increased State involvement where the welfare of children is concerned in general, but a pulling-back of the law from involvement in interspousal disputes about the care of the child's person, education or property.[47]

Thus one can say in summary that, at late 20th century, there is marked change on both the substantive and symbolic levels of interspousal law. In law and in fact in the United States, England, France and West Germany husband and wife are nearly equal in their decision-making powers. These trends are of course not confined to the four countries with whose law we are primarily concerned. The traditional law of the on-going marriage has also be repealed and replaced with laws consistent with the ideal of equality between husband and wife in countries where such changes represent a much more abrupt break with the past as, for example, Austria, by the Law of 1 July 1975; Italy, by the Law of 5 May 1975; and Spain, by the Law of 5 May 1975. The trend furthermore seems to be toward the abolition of the remaining distinctions. There is a general tendency for the law to retreat from the area of interspousal relationships altogether, and the new ideology of marriage expressed in the laws emphasizes equality and cooperation rather than hierarchy within the family. The law has moved away from its former express or implicit stereotyping of sex roles within marriage and toward a new model in which there is no fixed pattern of role distribution.

It seems clear that the retrenchment of the law from interspousal disputes is in response to and an official recognition of varied behavior patterns in society and a new ideology of tolerance concerning these behavior patterns.

Historically, until the German Equality Law of 1957, nearly every legislative attempt to regulate the family decision-making process gave the husband the dominant role in that process and required acquiescence from the wife. In societies of the past these arrangements were generally accepted for economic and social reasons and were often reinforced by religious teachings. So long as economic necessity forced the members of a family to cooperate closely with each other for subsistence or material progress it is not surprising that dominance in family politics was legally accorded to that member who, on the basis of common assumption, was the strongest or the principal protector and provider of the family.

This state of affairs, long accepted out of necessity or for its contribution to the economic advancement of the family, was probably perpetuated for social reasons even after the economic reasons had become less pressing. Despite a degree of societal affluence which freed family members from concern about survival of the unit and permitted them to pursue their personal interests independent of the family, social pressures for conformity seem to have long inhibited direct challenge to traditional decision-making roles. Rarely has an aspect of human behavior, sometimes alleged to be instinctive or natural, gained so much reinforcement from society. Now the old patterns have given way under pressure from seemingly irresistible transforming trends.

In Western countries, technology and affluence for the time being have made it possible for more and more spouses to be concerned with such matters as personal development and fulfillment. To the extent that they are different concerns from the economic welfare of the family unit, these preoccupations in the past have been undreamed-of luxuries for all but a few. Also, to the extent that diversity of ideology is increasingly recognized, the attempt to impose a single ideal of marriage becomes more and more futile. Added factors are a growing concern for individual and family privacy and the belief that internal affairs of a family should be free from state interference. In view of and in addition to all these factors, the law, in pulling back from the internal affairs of spouses, may simply be recognizing the running commentary made by folklore upon the law to the effect that the area is one which is difficult to influence through legislation or edict.[48] Withdrawal of regulation may represent acceptance of the fact that where marriage stability is seen as a social goal, giving legal dominance to one partner in case of disputes will not necessarily advance that goal. As a practical matter, if husband and wife are unable to agree on a particular decision the future of the marriage is no more in danger if their status quo is maintained than if the law gave one spouse in these circumstances the power to impose his or her decision on the other. As John Stuart Mill put it over a hundred years ago, "Things never come to an issue of downright power on one side, and obedience on the other, except where the connexion altogether has been a mistake, and it would be a blessing to both parties to be relieved from it."[49]

It seems, and perhaps it has always been so, that if a husband and wife disagree strongly about, say, whether to move to a new place, one of two things will happen if they cannot work it out themselves. Either the status quo will be maintained or one spouse will attempt to take action on his own. If one of these alternatives is intolerable to either of the spouses, the situation may well result in the breakdown of the marriage. If the marriage nevertheless survives, the matter is left to private ordering. The aid of the law is not available or is not invoked by the parties. It is to be expected, except where divorce is not easily available or not considered acceptable by the couple, that couples who reach the point of seeking legal intervention to settle their disputes will also frequently have reached the point of marriage breakdown. In modern times, as divorce becomes increasingly available and couples become less reluctant to resort to divorce, there is less need of courts as arbiters of marital disputes than there may have been in the past. The Anglo-American attitude of noninterference with a functioning marriage seems to be the most compatible, not only with pluralism in society, but also with the principle of equality of husband and wife and the modern view of marriage as a free union of two individuals. Current notions of pluralism, privacy, individual liberty and equality all come together here and for the moment remain in equipoise.

To the extent that modern laws, while getting out of the marriage regulation business, have attempted to announce new ideals or models for conduct, they have encountered a new set of problems. These arise from the tension between the modern vision of marriage as involving cooperation and community of interest on the one hand and marriage as a vehicle for the fullest self-expression of the individual on the other.

These two ideas are always in tension. In a functioning marriage they will be for the most part in equilibrium. But in some marriages the autonomy of the spouses may manifest itself in such a way as to destroy the marital community. Recent cases involving a spouse's exercise of a religion dramatically illustrate this dilemma in all four systems.[50] As this book continues, we will observe repeated contradictions and unresolved problems within the new normative systems.

B. Names

The effect of marriage upon the names of the spouses, like questions about interspousal decision-making, has a symbolic aspect. It is not a question that concerns the spouses alone. It concerns their respective families of origin (especially in societies of patrilineal organization)[51] and it concerns the State to the extent that the State takes an interest in maintaining official identity records. So long as it was the nearly universal custom for a woman to assume her husband's name and rank upon marriage, there was no need to analyze these interests separately from one another. The social custom of taking of the husband's name upon marriage expressed the wife's integration into her husband's family, and the common family name expressed the unity of the new household. The custom was incorporated into the Prussian General Code of 1794[52] and also into Art. 1355 of the German Civil Code of 1896. In England, France, and the United States, however, it never acquired the force of law. So long as the custom was widely followed in the United States, there was a widespread impression there that a woman was legally obliged to assume her husband's name upon marriage. But in the twentieth century, as the aspect of marriage as an association of two separate independent individuals came to be emphasized as much as, if not more than, its community aspect, and as divorce and remarriage became common, the married woman's right to continue using her maiden name has been reaffirmed in American law. The English common law rule, received in the United States, has been that any person, man or woman, may use any name he or she wishes so long as the use in non-fraudulent.[53] No one has a legal name for all time. One's legal name is the name by which one is customarily known. But nothing prevents one from freely changing his name from time to time. Official procedures for changes of name exist for the convenience of those who wish to obtain an official record of their name change, but are not required to make a name change legally effective.[54]

In England, the status of the ancient common law rule has remained clear. The practice of women to assume their husband's names has been consistently seen as nothing more than a custom: "[T]here is, so far as I know, nothing to compel a married woman to use her husband's surname, so that the wife of Mr. Robinson may, speaking generally, go by the name of Mrs.[55] Smith if she chooses to do so."[56]

While this has always been the legal situation in all the United States except Hawaii, the *custom* of women to take their husband's names upon marriage has been so widely followed that, even at the present time, many people and even many lawyers who have not had occasion to consult the law believe that a woman's name changes upon marriage as a matter of law. The interesting point to notice concerning the question of married women's names in the United States is the way that change in the social institution has acted upon the legal institution. Increasingly in American society, a large enough number of women to be visible have chosen not to change their names. Because of the nearly universal belief that the law required them to use their husband's names, these women encountered difficulties when they tried to register to vote or to get driver's licenses. The resulting law suits have caused the courts to reaffirm the ancient common law rule.[57] In some states, the attorneys general have issued opinions for the guidance of municipal clerks, voting registrars and motor vehicle registrars who were confused by the sudden influx of demands by married women to obtain official documents in names other than those of their husband. For example, guidelines issued in 1975 by the Massachusetts Attorney General and Secretary of State on "the law as it applies to commonly encountered situations of name choice" recite: "[I]t has always been the law of this Commonwealth that any individual, male or female, has the right to choose and from time to time change his or her name.... A person may change his or her name simply by using another name." The opinion adds, "There is no law which requires parents to name their children with a particular surname. Thus, the child of John Doe and Mary Jones may be named Baby Doe, Baby Jones, Baby Doe-Jones or even Baby Smith. The choice is left entirely to the parents.[58]

Thus the effect of the changing mores in the United States has been to breathe new life into a long-dormant legal rule. While the great majority of American married women still use their husband's name, the recent lawsuits have in turn begun to chip away at a traditional *social* distinction between the legally married and the unmarried state. They have in addition established that the State will not yet assert an interest in what a married person calls himself. This system, which may seem strange and unworkable to continental Europeans, is possible in part because there is no official system of identity papers in England and the United States.[59] It is not certain how long this will be true in the United States where the social security number is increasingly becoming the basis of a national system of identity.

In England, a married woman is said to have a right, by custom, to assume her husband's name, and, if he is a peer, his title and rank.[60] There is, however, no trace of the idea that she is obliged to do so. Rather, the question has arisen whether a husband may under certain circumstances *restrain* his wife from using his name. In both England and the United States, since a wife is free to use any name she chooses, a husband cannot restrain her from using his name after divorce, so long as the use is non-fraudulent.[61]

When one turns to French law on the effect of marriage on names, there is both a similarity and a contrast with the American situation: a similarity, because in both countries the husband's name has been thought to be of such special importance that the wife's freedom of choice concerning the name she will use has met with obstacles; a contrast, because in America the wife's right to use her birth name has been sought to be limited, whereas in France the wife's right to use the name which belongs to her husband and his family has been challenged under certain circumstances!

In France, marriage does not have the legal effect of changing a woman's name.[62] By custom, however, most women begin to use the name of their husband upon marriage, and, in some regions and among some families, the husband adds the wife's name to his.[63] The wife continues to be referred to in legal papers and official documents by her birth name, with the addition of "wife or widow of so-and-so".[64]

Marriage does, however, give a woman the right to the *use* of the name of her husband. This is a significant right, because in French law, unlike in the United States or England, purely voluntary name change is forbidden. The name on one's birth certificate can only be changed by official act for good reason and provided no one who already has the proposed new name objects.[65] Thus a married woman has two names at her disposition, her birth name and the option to use her husband's name if she wishes. But it is only the *use* of the husband's name which she acquires by marriage. The name does not belong to her, and her right to use it is not absolute. The limited character of the right is clear from the fact that shortly after divorce was re-introduced in France in 1884, an 1893 law amended the Civil Code to provide that upon divorce "each spouse is to resume the usage of his own name".[66] A change made in this provision by the 1976 French Divorce Reform Law was very controversial because it permitted a wife to obtain judicial permission to continue using her husband's name under special limited circumstances.[67]

Art. 264. Following the divorce each spouse is to resume the usage of his own name.

Nevertheless, in the case provided for in articles 237 and 238 [disruption of the life in common] the woman has the right to retain the use of the husband's name if the divorce has been sought by him.

In other cases, the wife may retain the use of the husband's name, either with his permission, or with the permission of the judge, if she demonstrates that it has special importance for her or for the children.

Just as American discussions of these issues have brought expressions of discontent from some who think a married woman *ought* to use her husband's name, the new French law stirred up those who were incensed at the thought that she might *dare* to do so after a divorce.[68] There was discussion of the humiliation to the husband's family of having their name carried around by an ex-spouse, especially if her post-divorce activities were of a kind to embarrass former in-laws. What unites these seemingly different French and American discussions – apart from the common desire to impose a customary or legal rule on women which would not apply to men – is their common increasing emphasis on the separateness of the two individuals who are nevertheless associated in a special way in marriage.

In West Germany, the turn of the century juridification of the customary name practice has run into constitutional difficulties and a search has been made for a way to reconcile equality with the goal of expressing family unity through a common family name. Flexibility to deal with this problem is not so great in West Germany as it is in England and the United States where the questions are not complicated by the existence of a national system of identification.

West Germany is the only one of the four countries (excluding the American state of Hawaii) in which married women were legally obliged to assume their husband's name upon marriage. The rule of Art. 1355 of the Civil Code that the family name is the husband's name was considered, after 1953, to be of doubtful constitutionality. But between that time and the passage of the 1976 Reform Law, the wife's interest in her own family name was taken account of only by permitting her, through a public declaration at the time of marriage, to append her maiden name to that of her husband and to bear a double name. A husband on the other hand was allowed to add the wife's name to his only through a formal name change proceeding.[69] These double names have become increasingly common in West Germany.[70]

The distinguished West German family law authority, Beitzke, points out that because of the public-law interest in the question of names, full equality has been difficult to implement. The only way to offer completely equal rights to both spouses in the matter seems to be to give each spouse the option of retaining his or her birth name, as is the case in England, France and the United States.[71] However, as yet, the West German legislature has been reluctant to give up the idea of the common name as an expression of family unity. One may wonder whether this concern is justified. In the countries where spouses have this option, the overwhelming majority of couples bear a common name. In the United States, where the choice is not limited to the birth name, among those couples who do not follow the traditional custom the desire for a common name is often expressed either through choice of a double name, the husband's adoption of the wife's name, or through selection of a completely new name. In other words, marrying couples may see family name unity as a goal as much as do the Bundestag and Bundesrat. On the other hand, in view of the increasingly frequency of divorce and remarriage, one may question whether it is desirable under modern conditions to encourage anyone's change of name upon marriage.

The 1973 draft of the West German divorce reform law would have amended Art. 1355 to provide that the spouses are to bear a common name chosen as follows:[72]

The spouses are to declare their marriage name at the time of marriage. They are permitted to choose either the birth name of the wife or that of the husband or a double name composed of both, but which can contain no more than two names. The spouse whose name is not the marriage name or part of the marriage name is permitted, by making an official public declaration of his or her intent to do so, to append to the marriage name his or her birth name or any other name legally used before the marriage, such as that of a former spouse.

The draft law also reorganized the law of marriage formation so that a declaration of the marriage name would have become a compulsory marriage preliminary. If the spouses did not make a declaration, the marriage name was, under the 1973 draft, to have been a double name composed of the names of both spouses with the man's name standing first. This scheme was approved by the Bundestag but rejected by the Bundesrat where the majority considered that the spouses should not be obliged to choose a marriage name at the time of marriage.[73] Instead, they should be given the opportunity to choose the wife's name. If no demand to this effect were made, the family name would be the husband's name, not a double name.

The 1976 reform law, as finally adopted, maintained the common name idea and made certain concessions to the Bundesrat. The Registrar must ask the spouses before the marriage is celebrated whether they wish to make a declaration concerning which marriage name they will bear.[74] If they do not make a declaration, the husband's name becomes the common name of the couple. New Art. 1355 limits the choice of the marriage name to either the name of the wife or the husband, with the option given to the one whose name is not chosen to add his or her name to the marriage name. The new section reads:

s. 1355. (1) The spouses bear a common family name (the marriage name).

(2) The spouses can designate as the marriage name, by declaration before the Registrar, the birth name of the husband or the birth name of the wife. If they make no designation, the marriage name is the birth name of the husband. The birth name is the name recorded on the birth certificate of the intended spouses at the time of the celebration of the marriage.

(3) A spouse, whose birth name is not the marriage name, can, by declaration before the Registrar, place his birth name or the name he bears at the time of the celebration of the marriage in front of the marriage name; the declaration must be publicly attested.

Upon divorce, by new Art. 1355(4) a spouse may resume his or her birth name or the name he or she bore upon entering the marriage by making a public declaration before the Registrar of intent to do so.

It is clear that more is stake than appears on the surface. If choice is limited to the name of the husband and the name of the wife only, a stressful situation is created for some couples when tradition has been so clearly in favor of the wife's taking the man's name. The option of the double name for both spouses seems to be the only way to recognize the equality principle while maintaining the ideal of a common name (although it seems that some neutral principle should govern the order of names). The present version has chosen instead to give up the ideal of the common name, despite the flat statement of line (1). It is significant, however, from the point of view of this Chapter, that the reform law has insisted that marrying couples be forced to devote their attention to the family name before marriage. The Bundesrat's proposal, putting the initiative on the spouses to raise the question, and then only if they wished to choose the wife's name rather than the husband's, would have drawn lines tending to aggravate the battle of the sexes and would have been an encouragement to perpetuate the old sex-based differentiation in the matter of names. The requirement of the formal inquiry by the Registrar communicates to the spouses that the matter is of some importance to them as individuals and to the way they see their married life. At the same time, West German law, alone of those we have examined, still tries to transmit the ideal of community symbolized by a common name.

One need hardly elaborate on the symbolic value of names. It is this freight they bear that makes the legal problems of names controversial. When we speak of the names of husband and wife, we speak of their families of origin and of the way in which the husband and wife relate to each other. It is clear that official approval of the symbolism of subordination of the wife to the husband, or absorption of her independent existence into his, is being removed from the law of names. In England, France and the United States change of name on marriage is a question for individual choice. In West Germany, where the law still seeks to channel individual choice to a common name as an expression of family unity as well as for administrative convenience, the equality principle is compromised.

III. Law Affecting Interspousal Economic Relations

A. Introduction

If the law described in the preceding subsection is for the most part law which doesn't bite, the same is not the case with the legal rules governing the spouses' economic relations in the marriage-in-progress. Nevertheless, it has to be said at the outset that the bulk of the law governing the financial aspects of marriage has not been developed for the on-going marriage, but for the situations where the marriage has been terminated by death, judicial dissolution, or separation, or where the spouses are in a state of marital crisis short of separation or dissolution.[75] Thus, the law to be dealt with in this subsection still in large measure reflects society's ideals and hopes for the marriage in being, tempered by the certain knowledge that many marriages will not sail smoothly from beginning to end. But for a complete picture of the effect of marriage on property rights and relationships of the spouses, the subject matter of the present chapter has to be considered together with the law of decedents' estates (or, as is is called in continental systems, succession) and the law regulating the economic consequences of divorce and separation. The present subchapter will continue to explore how social change has affected the law of the existing marriage – this time in its economic aspects. Accordingly, the law of support and the law relating to ownership and management of property as affected by marriage will be the principal topics of concern here.

Let us begin by considering what might be called the traditional manner of legal regulation of these areas.[76] On the eve of the Industrial Revolution, it could be said that the legal systems for regulating the property relationships of husband and wife in England, France, the United States and in the various regions of Germany differed in legal techniques but were similar in their basic characteristics. The husband had the power to manage all the family property, including the property of the wife. He was expected to provide for the material needs of the members of the household; the wife was expected to care for the household and the children. Since some of the family property might have been brought into the marriage by the wife, all the traditional systems were characterized, by the early 19th century, by the development of legal techniques to protect the wife and the wife's blood relatives from the consequences of mismanagement by the husband, and to assure that title to land remained in the family from whence it came.[77] These traditional systems were transformed in the late 19th and early 20th centuries as the law adjusted to the effects of increasing industrialization. As rural families moved to cities, the wages of privates in the industrial army rarely were sufficient to meet the needs of whole families. The wives and children often had to seek employment outside the home or to take in work to be done at home. The model of bourgeois marriage enshrined in the 19th century laws developed for the propertied classes was inappropriate for the wage-earning classes whose voices were increasingly coming to be heard in political life. Gradually the double-earner marriage began to find recognition in the law, first in some of the American states, then in England, then in the German Civil Code of 1896, and finally in the French Law of 13 July 1907, with the rest of American states falling into line along the way. The technique chosen in each system was to give married women the right to dispose freely of at least their own earnings and whatever assets might have been given to them *inter vivos* or by will under stipulations that the assets were to remain subject to the wife's separate control. These innovations were really no more than an extension to the entire population of devices which had been worked out by solicitors for the wealthy and incorporated into marriage settlements in England, *contrats de mariage* in France and *Eheverträge* in Germany, and of exceptions which had appeared early for the special case of the married woman trader.[78] It is probable that the appearance of the first Married Women's Property Acts, starting as early as 1839 in the United States, is related to the fact that marriage settlements were never used in the new country to the extent that they were in England. Thus the need for reform appeared earlier in the United States among sectors of the population who were in a position to do something about it.

The turn of the century reforms, however, turned out to be inadequate with respect to one large group of marriages. When a married woman had no independent means and did not work outside the home, they affected her situation not at all. She was completely dependent on her husband who remained in control of all the family property. In the twentieth century, as the situation of industrial workers improved to the point where one wage-earner could support an entire family, working class families began to emulate the bourgeoisie (which in turn was emulating what it took to be the life styles of the upper classes). Factory work by women, like that of children, had always been associated with the degradation of poverty and families were glad to leave this behind. Hence, a sizeable number of women found themselves, for the first time in history, in circumstances where their exclusive role was the care of a household and children.[79] In the past, women had carried these tasks along with their duties in the agricultural production unit, in the craft, trade or shop. If they were well-to-do (which usually meant their economic welfare was secured by their family of origin), they had made careers of protocol, good works or patronage of the arts or other worthy causes, according to their inclination. Being mistress of a great house was itself a career. The appearance on a wide scale of the exclusively housewife-marriage in the 20th century can be explained in part by the French historian Braudel's theory of luxury:

Luxury does not only represent rarity and vanity, but also social success, fascination, the dream that one day becomes reality for the poor and in so doing immediately loses its old glamour. Not long ago a medical historian wrote: 'When a food that has been rare and long desired finally arrives within reach of the masses, consumption rises sharply, as if a long-repressed appetite had exploded.'...The rich are thus doomed to prepare the future life of the poor. It is, after all, their justification: they try out the pleasures that the masses will sooner or later grasp.[80]

Under modern conditions, where the work place is usually distant from the family dwelling, the devotion of the mother entirely to child-raising and care of the household meant that she ordinarily had to forego outside work. At first this was seen as a luxury. It is only recently, when divorce has become common, that it has become clear what a price women who are not independently wealthy may have to pay for having left the primitive production community and the market-place for the home. It was one thing to be economically dependent in a world where divorce in both the *de facto* and legal sense was exceptional, where the norms of convention, custom, ethics and religion supported the ideal of indissolubility of marriage. It was quite another to be economically dependent in a world where divorce came more and more to be considered a right, necessary for each individual's pursuit of happiness or self-fulfillment.

The legal systems sought to adjust to this new situation by continuing the arrangement of economic dependence after divorce through the device of alimony. But it soon became clear that the financial position of most men, together with problems of new financial responsibilities taken on through remarriage, did not in fact allow much security for the woman who had devoted herself solely to home and family. When the idea of economic responsibility continuing after divorce itself lost support in the mores (either because ideas about duty had changed or simply because there was not enough money to go around) the position of the housewife became risky indeed. This state of affairs is what has led the controversial German writer Stöcker to say that so long as the law continues to channel women into housewife-marriage and into becoming economically dependent, it is in effect systematically turning them into cripples, and then hypocritically rushing to their aid with the nearly useless remedy of alimony.[81] Yet it seems clear that no society wants to discourage parents from devoting themselves as fully as they wish to the care and nurture of future citizens. It is also clear that women, especially, are continuing and will continue to choose this role for at least a portion of their lives. In fact it seems that the major reason why mothers do work outside the home is not to achieve economic independence or personal fulfillment. Rather, as at the beginning of industrialization, it is out of economic necessity or at least desire for improvement of the material circumstances of the family.[82] Thus, all four countries are seeking out ways to make this choice a less dangerous one. At the same time they are seeking to implement the equality principle, and to maintain the ideal of marriage as a community of life. It is no wonder that the current evolution described here and in Chapter 6 is the story of a groping and hesitant search which has not yet achieved its goals.

B. *The Evolution from Support-of-the-Wife to Mutual-Contribution-to-Household-Expenses*

Under the traditional systems of the early 19th century where all family income, including wages earned by the wife, was at the disposal of the husband, he was responsible for the support of his wife and children and for all the needs of the family.[83] These traditional schemes were usually accompanied by the wife's legal power to obtain "necessaries" upon the credit of her husband, e.g. the married woman's agency of necessity in the common law and the German "power of the keys" (*Schlüsselgewalt*).

The various alterations made in the support provisions of the French Civil Code since 1804 are illustrative of the effect that changes in the social and economic roles of women have had on the husband–wife relationship and eventually on the law. The original version of Art. 214 read:

The wife is obliged to live with the husband and to follow him to whatever residence he deems appropriate: the husband is obliged to receive her and to furnish her with the necessities of life according to his ability and station.

In 1938 this article was amended to add that the wife was obliged to furnish, from any funds subject to her separate administration, a contribution, in proportion to her and her husband's resources, to the expenses of the household and the upbringing of the children. A 1942 law changed the article again to read:

If the marriage contract does not regulate the contribution of the spouses to the expenses of the marriage, they are to contribute in proportion to their respective abilities.

The principal obligation to assume these expenses falls on the husband. He is obliged to furnish the wife with the necessities of life according to his ability and station.

The wife discharges her obligation for the expenses of the marriage by her dowry or separate property brought into the community and by deductions made from the personal funds subject to her separate administration....

In 1965, there was belatedly added to this scheme the idea that the wife could also discharge her obligation to contribute to the expenses of the household "through her activity in the home or her collaboration in the profession of the husband". At the same time, also belatedly, the wife was given the right to engage in an occupation separate from that of her husband without his consent or judicial authorization.

Through this series of changes one can trace the development in France from the 1804 family unit headed by the husband, to recognition in 1938, 1942 and 1965 of the wife's economic activity outside the home, to recognition in 1965 of the economic value of the wife's activity within the home. All these developments were within a scheme in which the husband bore primary responsibility for the needs of the family. But in 1975, the mold was broken. The divorce reform law which became effective in 1976 eliminated the husband's primary responsibility for the support of the family and left the first line of Art. 214 standing alone to state the basic principle that husband and wife are to contribute according to their respective abilities.

In West Germany, the Equal Rights Law of 18 June 1957, established as the basic principle that both spouses are obliged to support the household during their life together, and freed the wife to work outside the home without obtaining her husband's permission. But it went on to elaborate the duties of the spouses in a way which was so bound up with the model of housewife-marriage that it was necessary to revise the scheme in the 1976 Reform Law. The former section read:

§1360. The spouses are mutually obliged to adequately maintain the family by their work and property. As a general rule, the wife performs her obligation to contribute to the maintenance of the family through her labor, by conducting the household. She is obliged to engage in a gainful activity only insofar as the working capacity of the husband and the income of the family do not suffice for the maintenance of the family, and insofar as an inroad into their capital is not commensurate with the circumstances of the spouses.

§1360a. The proper (*angemessene*) maintenance of the family includes all that is required in the circumstances of the spouses, to cover the costs of the household and to satisfy the personal needs of the spouses and the support of those common children of theirs who are entitled to be supported.

Maintenance is to be supplied in that fashion which is demanded by the marital community of life. The husband is obliged to render for the wife's disposition a proper amount in advance for a reasonable period of time....

§1360b. If one spouse has furnished for the maintenance of the family more than he is obliged to furnish, it is to be presumed that he did not intend to obtain restitution from the other spouse.

The Reform Law amended §1360 so as to eliminate sex-based classifications:

§1360. The spouses are mutually obliged to appropriately maintain the family through their work and with their property. If the running of the household is left to one spouse, that spouse as a rule fulfills his duty to contribute to the support of the family through work by managing the household.

The Reform Law also amended §1360a, par. 2, line 2:

The spouses are mutually obliged to make available, a suitable time in advance, the necessary means for the common support of the family.

In the United States, a similar evolution is taking place in the statutory and case law. In England, the traditional common law rules that the husband is obliged to support the wife, that the wife is obliged to render services in the home and that these duties are reciprocal, still form the basis of the law.[84] These reciprocal duties of husband and wife are inextricable from the English concept of *consortium*, which connotes the sharing of a common home and domestic life, and is thus roughly analogous to the French and German ideas of marital community of life.[85] In some of the American states this version of the common law was declared by statute. But later statutes have imposed a corresponding duty on the wife to support the husband, and the Family Expense Acts now widely make both husband and wife equally liable for basic expenses.[86] Under the influence of the equality principle, whether or not it is elevated to state or federal constitutional status, it is to be expected that the states will increasingly equalize the rights and duties of husband and wife in this area to the extent they have not already done so. It is likely that the current evolution of the common law will result in a doctrine similar to the mutual obligation to contribute money or labor to the maintenance of the household now found in the French Code, rather than in a mutual support obligation as such. The fact that legal enforcement of support obligations generally awaits marriage breakdown in all four systems, however, means that the legal provisions under discussion are still, in part at least, that special kind of law we saw in section II of this Chapter – law which in good measure simply expresses an ideal of proper conduct. The current ideal seems to be that in the absence of special circumstances of need, husband and wife do not "support" each other; rather, they cooperate in the running of their joint enterprise. During the marriage the spouses are essentially left to work out their own arrangement. The most extreme version of this attitude of non-interference is in the United States. There the courts will not order support so long as the couple is living together, and a husband and wife in a functioning marriage may not even make a legally enforceable contract concerning support.[87]

C. Matrimonial Property: Efforts to Combine Autonomy, Equality and Sharing

1. Introduction

In Western legal systems it has traditionally been possible for the property relationships of spouses to be determined within certain limits by private agreement concluded either between the marriage partners themselves or with the participation of their parents or other members of their families. In fact, the current evolution of family law in the four countries with which we are concerned is characterized in part by the great measure of freedom that spouses are given to regulate their property affairs as they regard best to fit their ideals about married life and their practical needs. But for those situations in which there is no contractual regulation, the law keeps in store a scheme of its own. In both the French and the West German systems the scheme regulated by the law itself is called the "legal regime" (*régime légal, gesetzlicher Güterstand*). However, as Professor Müller-Freienfels and others have pointed out, the property relationship of the partners to a normal, amicable marriage is apt to be a *de facto* community, each contributing according to his ability and each receiving according to his needs, regardless of the system of marital property law that happens to be in force.[89] During such a marriage, the law of matrimonial property is of little interest to the spouses, although it may be important to their creditors and other third parties. It is when family life is disrupted by divorce; the death, insolvency, or incapacity of a spouse; or some other pathological circumstance, that the matrimonial property law in all systems comes to the fore. Most disputes concerning marital property law actually arise as a consequence of marriage dissolution, the subject of Chapter 6.

Among the owners of great wealth, persons about to marry, together with their families, regularly make their own arrangements through marriage contracts. For them, as for persons who accumulate little or no property, the law of marital property is of marginal interest. The legal regime is of most concern to those couples who live on income and savings of their own rather than on inherited wealth, and who own little or nothing when they enter their first marriage but who accumulate property later on. The law, however, must also be adapted to the needs of those who enter remarriages and those whose economic wellbeing is affected by the termination of their marriages.

Forty years ago, in 1937, it was possible for the distinguished French civil law scholar Georges Ripert to write that eleven national reporters to a symposium on matrimonial property law sponsored by the *Semaine Internationale de Droit* in Paris, had arrived at the conclusion that the legal matrimonial property regimes of their respective countries were "...responding admirably to the desires and needs of the population and that any modification of the legal regime would be difficult or unnecessary".[90] The eleven countries represented included England, where marital property has since been gradually but fundamentally transformed, and France, where a completely new system of marital property law was instituted in 1965. Germany and the United States were not represented at the 1937 Paris conference, but most American states have either completely reformed their systems or have begun the process of reform since that time, and West Germany has been through two major reforms.[91]

As we have already seen, by 1937 all four countries had already accorded to married women the freedom to deal with earnings resulting from their own labor. Why did further reforms become necessary?

Most legal activity in the area of matrimonial property since 1937 has concerned: (1) the attempt to implement more fully the principle of equality of husband and wife; (2) the need to respond to the ever-increasing incidence of marriage termination by divorce; and (3) in some systems the attempt to permit a spouse who works inside the home to participate in the earnings of the spouse who works outside the home. The legal problems to which these efforts have given rise are chiefly those of distribution of powers of management between the spouses during marriage, and of financial settlements upon divorce.

Problems relating to management powers have appeared in the French and American community property systems as problems of how to bring the wife into the scheme of management of the community fund. In England, West Germany and the 42 separate property states of the United States, they take on the aspect of determining to what extent, if at all, the spouses are to be subject to limitations on their freedom to dispose of their respective funds.

Efforts to resolve these problems have been complicated by the fact that many reforms of the post-World War II period were organized around the image of housewife-marriage and on the assumption of marriage stability. But even as such reforms were taking place, the phenomenon of housewife-marriage was giving way to a plurality of marriage models in society and divorce was spreading.

When Rheinstein and Glendon examined existing marital property systems in industrialized countries from the point of view of the extent to which equality had been implemented; the extent to which each spouse shared in the other's property; and the extent to which the existence of marriage models other than housewife-marriage were recognized, we concluded that in systems where reforms have begun, that is, nearly everywhere, the traditional classification of marital property schemes according to the existence or non-existence of a community fund, and by the extent of that fund, was obsolete.[92] Our comparative analysis of marital property law and of the technical devices through which changes had been effected in the so-called separate, community and deferred community systems, indicated that the systems seemed to converge insofar as separate systems have adopted devices to assure sharing of property between the spouses, and community systems have adopted devices to provide for equal rights to management. At the same time, we found a growing divergence among systems according to the degree of emphasis they give to the solidarity of the spouses or to the autonomy of each spouse.

In some reforms, sharing ownership and control of property between spouses has been seen either as required by the principle of equality, or as desirable in and of itself, perhaps as reflecting the needs and desires of the population, or perhaps reflecting the extent to which the law reformers or legislatures have in mind the model of housewife-marriage or an ideal of community. Other reforms have emphasized the independence of the spouses either because it is thought to be required by the principle of equality, or desirable in itself. We did not see one or the other trend clearly prevailing. Rather they are interacting in each system.

Our study led us to conclude that under modern conditions the whole idea of "matrimonial regime" should be abandoned if the different functional problems of the property aspects of the on-going marriage, of divorce and of death are to be clearly analyzed. What follows here is a presentation of laws affecting the ownership and control of property by the partners in a functioning marriage according to the degree of emphasis placed on sharing, equality and autonomy in each national system. Property relations upon divorce and death will be treated in Chapter 6.

2. The French and American Communities: Toward more Equality

a. France

In France, where the Civil Code of 1804 made community property the legal regime and gave the wife a half share in the community fund, the goal of sharing was built into marital property law. The "community of movables and acquests" of the Code Napoleon included in the fund to be shared all assets of the spouses except: (a) immovables[93] owned separately at the time of marriage or acquired thereafter by gift or succession; (b) movables gratuitously acquired with a stipulation that they were to remain separate; and (c) movables of a peculiarly personal nature. But shared ownership did not mean shared control. Except for the wife's separate earnings after 1907, the husband had control of the community fund. Thus the problem was presented of bringing about equality of the wife and the husband in the management of the community.

The Nordic countries had confronted this problem in the early twentieth century. There the traditional marital property system was a form of community property. Management had been in the hands of the husband. Joint management seemed at the time to be unworkable, but to give up community property would have gone against ingrained tradition. Hence, the idea of "deferred community" was developed. In outline form, such a system had already existed in Costa Rica, for certain groups as a legal system in Hungary, and as an optional system in Austria. In Sweden and in the other Nordic countries the system was carefully elaborated and made the basic legal pattern. So long as the marriage lasts or, more correctly, so long as the regime operates, either spouse autonomously manages the assets he or she brings in, but when the marriage (or the regime) comes to an end, the funds which remain are shared equally as if there had been a community scheme all along. This system has widely been regarded as a model where demands for equality have required change of an existing scheme of shared ownership.

When France embarked on its major matrimonial property law reform in 1965, it was not ready to go so far from its community tradition, and it sacrificed the goal of equality instead. Since the 1965 reform also purported to reduce the scope of the community fund, there are those who think that the goal of sharing lost out as well.

The tension between the aims of equality and sharing was apparent in the debates on the choice of the new French legal regime. Public opinion polls taken in 1963 at the behest of the government as an aid in the reform of the Code indicated that the popular view of marriage was a relatively egalitarian one *and* that the majority of those interviewed approved of some sort of community regime.[94] Both within the Commission on Reform of the Civil Code and in the French National Assembly, there were those who favored a system of deferred community and there were those who favored a more traditional community system. The arguments of the latter were largely based on an idea that the community regime corresponded better to the prevailing conception of marriage. The opponents of the community regime tended to be proponents of absolute equality between husband and wife, while the partisans of community property tended to think the husband ought to be recognized as having the dominant voice in matters of the administration of the family funds.[95]

Deferred community was thought by many to strike the ideal balance between concern for equality of the married woman and the French conception of marriage as a union of the financial, as well as other, interests of two people. But the choice was made to adopt a community system and to replace the community of movables and acquests with a community reduced to acquests, which excludes from the community all assets which are not acquired during marriage by gainful activity. The content of the community is defined by new Art. 1401 as "...the acquests made by the two spouses together or separately during the marriage, originating from their personal industry as well as from economies made from the fruits and revenues of their separate property". Thus, the scope of the separate funds of the spouses has been seemingly enlarged, and the scope of community funds seemingly diminished. Not only has the community been reduced from one of all movables and acquests to one of acquests, but even the acquests made during marriage remain at least initially subject to the separate management of the spouse by whom they are made. But since, in all cases in which there is doubt whether a particular asset is personal or community, the presumption is in favor of the latter, the difference between the new community of acquests and the old system of movables and acquests is less dramatic than it would first appear. As proof of separate ownership will ordinarily be available in the case of immovables but not in the case of movables, all of a couple's movables will be treated as community property in many cases no matter when or how they were acquired. Thus in the case of an average couple who started married life with no property of any considerable value, nearly all of their assets except real estate will be common property under the new regime – just as they were under the old one.

With respect to the problem of the management powers of the spouses, the 1965 law retained the husband as manager of the community, but his powers were circumscribed and the wife's participation greatly increased. The husband is the sole manager of that part of the community which is not under the management of the wife as her reserved fund. The wife's reserved property is defined by Art. 224 as "...the assets that the wife acquires through profits and income from her exercise of a profession separate from that of her husband". The husband needs the wife's consent to transactions of major importance involving the community fund; and the husband's consent is now required for the same group of transactions concerning the wife's reserved fund. In practice, if the couple is not engaged in a joint business, the assets subject to the husband's control are probably no more than those which have been acquired through his own gainful activities, or property which can be traced to such assets. If there are no other assets but the acquests of the husband and those of the wife, the situation is to all practical effects that of deferred community with equal rights of management by each spouse over his or her respective fund.

If the wife is not engaged in a separate gainful activity, but assists her husband in his occupation or business, her earnings are not reserved property but are ordinary community property administered by the husband. However some of the protection which the wife had under the former system against misfortune (as distinct from mismanagement) during the existence of the regime has been eliminated. Other guarantees which had previously been accorded to the wife alone have been extended to the husband.

The matrimonial home and its contents receive special treatment in French law regardless of title. Neither spouse may dispose of the "rights which assure the family's lodging and furniture" without the consent of the other. If the husband, even as apparent sole titleholder, attempts to convey such property to third parties the wife is protected by Art. 215 of the Civil Code, which gives the non-consenting spouse the right to bring an *action en nullité* within one year.

To help assure that there will be a community fund to be divided when the time comes, various devices are provided by French law to prevent its dissipation. One of these devices is the provision of Art. 220–1 that if either husband or wife defaults seriously in his or her duties, so as to jeopardize the family's interest, the president of the local *tribunal de grande instance* may order "all the urgent measures that those interests require", and in particular forbid him or her "to make any acts of disposal of his own property or that of the community" without the consent of the other. This article was applied in a recent case to authorize the wife of a corporation president to have shares of stock, belonging to the community and registered in the husband's name, transferred to her control and registered in her name on the books of the corporation, where the husband was shown to be "captivated by a young mistress" and to be endangering the interests of the family.[96]

If need be, a spouse may resort to two additional measures. First, one spouse may obtain a court order authorizing him or her to exercise the powers of the other in certain cases. This authorization may be obtained under Art. 1426 if a spouse becomes legally incompetent, or where a spouse's management of the reserved property (in the case of the wife) or the community is manifestly inept or fraudulent. The spouse so authorized can carry on the day-to-day exercise of the other spouse's powers and, with the special authorization of the court, even the acts for which joint consent would otherwise have been required. In this way a husband is protected against the wife's mismanagement of her reserved property and the wife is protected against the husband's mismanagement of the rest of the community.

Second, a spouse may sue to put an end to the community. If, in the words of Art. 1443, "...due to the disorder of one spouse's affairs or his mismanagement or misconduct, it is clear that to maintain the community imperils the interests of the other partner, he or she can sue for the separation of property".

The foregoing protections are characteristic of devices traditionally used in community systems to preserve the community fund. Involving as they do, restraints on individual action, (even, in the case of Art. 220–1, of one's freedom to deal with his or her own separate property) they tend to be eliminated from those systems (such as the American community property states) which are moving furthest toward incorporating ideas of equality in the sense of autonomy. In the separate property systems such restraints are exceptional and limited to a few special situations, such as the protection of the family home and the protection of a surviving spouse against disinheritance.

b. American Community Property Systems

In the eight American states where a form of community of acquests has been the system of marital property either from the beginning of settlement or from a very early date (Arizona, California, Idaho, Louisiana, Nevada, New Mexico, Texas and Washington) a series of reforms appeared at the turn of the century restricting the broad powers of the husband and providing protection to the wife against abuses of his managerial power. As in France, these laws required the wife's consent for certain important transactions and gave her managerial powers over her own earnings. Now the American community systems, like the French, are again in motion, and seven of them have moved well beyond France in implementing equality between the spouses. Texas in 1967, and Washington in 1972, deposed the husband as head of the community and provided for schemes of co-management. Arizona, California, Idaho and Nevada have since adopted systems similar to that of Washington, while New Mexico has worked out a scheme of its own. The system introduced in Arizona, California, Nevada and Washington permits either spouse acting alone to deal with community property, joinder of both spouses being required only for certain important transactions such as gifts of community property, disposition of community real property, purchase of community real property, sale or encumbrance of community household goods, and purchase or disposition of a common business enterprise.[97] In Idaho only sales of community real estate are beyond the power of mutual representation.[98]

Texas has taken a different approach to equality. Under the Texas Family Code, each spouse has during marriage the sole management, control and disposition of those assets of the community property that he or she would have owned if single.[99] But if community property subject to the sole control of one spouse is "mixed or combined" with community property subject to the sole control of the other, then such mixed property becomes subject to the "joint management" of both spouses, unless the spouses provide otherwise in writing. "Joint management" means that *both* spouses must join in any transaction affecting such property, not that either can act for the other, as in the Washington model. Community property, other than that which each spouse would have owned separately if single, is also subject to the "joint management, control and disposition" of the spouses unless they provide otherwise. Presumably, this would subject all joint acquisitions of the spouses (such as those earned in a family business) to joint control. Cooperation of both spouses is also necessary for disposition of the homestead whether it is an asset of the community fund or the separate fund of one of the spouses.

New Mexico has started down the road, well trodden by France, of trying to implement its constitutional equality principle while still providing "continuity" with its "four hundred year tradition of husband headship of the community".[100] Louisiana is in the midst of a major code reform project which will result in some form of co-management.[101]

Thus, in less than 10 years, the law in all American community property states has been affected profoundly by the equality principle. But the chief interest of all this is in the *way* the principle has been implemented. Except to a very limited degree in New Mexico, the new laws do not try to impose the old hierarchical *or* a new conjugal pattern on everyone. All the new laws emphasize the separateness and autonomy of the spouses. They say nothing about how family life should be organized, neither that the husband is the head of the family nor that marriage is a community of life. At the same time, they tend to chip away at the legal differences between the legally married state and other forms of cohabitation in which the partners may mingle or jointly acquire property.

In contrast to the French system, none of the American community systems has anything resembling the complicated network of restraints designed to protect the community. Indeed, the scope given to mutual representation, especially in Idaho, gives each spouse the power to diminish the community fund to the other's detriment. Only the matrimonial home is singled out for special legal protection.

3. Anglo-American Individualism: Toward More Sharing

The preceding section demonstrates how equality in management has been introduced into marital property systems in which shared ownership of certain assets is a standard feature. In the Anglo-American systems established by the various Married Women's Property Acts around the turn of the century, where separate ownership is the distinctive feature, each spouse's equal right to manage and dispose of his or her own property was built in, and the problem has been whether and how to secure to each partner a share in the acquests of the other.

The American and English Married Women's Property legislation responded to the demand for a married woman's autonomy in the use of her own earnings by transforming the traditional common law system into one of complete separation of assets. The laws gave married women the same rights to deal with their own property and earnings as had been enjoyed previously by men and single women.

The married women's property laws did make spouses equals in property matters, in a strict, formal sense. But these laws did not affect or improve the position of married women who were not employed outside the home and had no property of their own. Their activity in the home was not recognized as contributing to their husband's acquests. Furthermore, the common practice in two-earner families of using the husband's earnings to acquire capital assets (mortgage payments, investments) and the wife's earnings for purchases which are consumed (vacations, groceries, clothing, entertainment), means that the separation system can work hardship even in those families where the wife has a considerable measure of economic independence.

Individual couples can and often do introduce sharing of ownership into these systems by agreement. Like any individuals who are not married to each other, spouses may make agreements by which they establish co-ownership of some specific asset or assets. Like any other persons, spouses may jointly engage in business as a partnership, of which they may be the only partners or partners together with other persons (except possibly in some American states where old common law restrictions on husband–wife contracts have not yet been officially discarded).

In civil law terminology the system introduced in England and 42 American states by the Married Women's Acts is known as the matrimonial regime of separation of assets (*régime de séparation de biens, Gütertrennung*). The common law, however, has no special term for its rules governing the property relationships of husband and wife. An English or American lawyer, contemplating the system, would simply observe that in a marriage a husband owns and manages his property and the wife owns and controls hers, but that the fact that they are married to each other has certain effects in the event of death, divorce or insolvency, and on their tax situation.

At first glance, the separation system appears to be both simple and just. On closer inspection, it is not always simple in practical application, nor does it necessarily function in full accordance with presently prevailing ideas of fairness. Difficulties in practice arise because in the great majority of marriages the assets of the spouses tend to be intermingled rather than to be kept separate and earmarked. The system has been felt to be unjust in those frequent cases where the parties enter marriage without owning any property, where the husband is the sole or the principal breadwinner, and where, as a consequence, practically everything belongs to the husband when the marriage or marital harmony has come to an end, or when one of the parties becomes insolvent. These problems have given rise to much litigation and discussion in England and the United States.

a. England

In a separate property system there is no doubt that the acquests made from a spouse's earnings and to which title is taken in that spouse's own name are his or hers alone. But considerable uncertainty surrounds the ownership rights of the spouses with respect to assets such as savings or real property to which both have contributed – normally in unequal degrees – and which are held in various ways. These assets may include the marital dwelling and certain of its contents to which there may or may not be documents of title. It is a great weakness of English matrimonial property law that, if marital discord arises and a spouse wishes to know his or her rights, the only answer a solicitor can give is that it depends in the first instance upon what the husband and wife *intended* at the time the property was acquired.[102] Obviously, the trouble with this answer is that in a normal functioning marriage the parties do not ordinarily form an intention as to the allocation of title to their acquests. They do not think that the television set, the washing machine or the furniture was acquired for one spouse or the other and in what proportion. Thus, the cases are inevitably resolved by the court's imputation of a "reasonable" intent in view of the circumstances at the time the acquisition was made.[103] This resolution naturally leaves wide discretion to the judge.

Under present English case and statutory law, a *prima facie* case of co-ownership in equity is made out in the following situations regardless of whether title is taken in the husband's name, the wife's name or in the names of both spouses together: where property is acquired through the direct cash contributions of both spouses; where property is acquired from a joint fund to which both spouses have contributed directly in cash; and where one spouse has contributed in money or money's worth to the improvement of real or personal property.[104] Proof of contribution by the spouse who is not the title holder may be exceedingly difficult in all of these situations, just as proof of intent at the time of acquisition is difficult, if not impossible, in most cases. Especially troublesome in all separate property jurisdictions is the problem of determining whether and how a contribution of substantial physical labor, as distinct from direct cash contribution, should be recognized in property division.[105]

When and if it can be established that both spouses are beneficially interested in an asset, the problem then arises of ascertaining the exact share of each spouse. If it can be established that the parties contributed in distinct and unequal shares, it will be presumed that they are tenants in common in equity, in shares proportionate to the amounts they advanced.[106] But the problem becomes more complex when, as is often the case, the parties' financial affairs cannot be so neatly sorted out.

In cases where there is clear evidence of substantial contribution by both spouses to the acquisition of assets for their common use, the English courts have developed a doctrine of "joint enterprise", which *usually* results in equal division of the acquisition or its proceeds.[107] But the state of the law in 1976 seems to be that there is no *presumption* in favor of equal division of property acquired through joint contribution. The case law is so uncertain that it seems likely that Parliament will eventually act to clarify the situation. For the time being no answer can be given in any individual case until a final decision has been obtained in potentially lengthy and expensive judicial proceedings.

Property acquired through the earnings of one spouse and held in the names of both will be presumed to have been intended, by the spouse who acquires the property, as a gift of a one-half interest to the other.[108] But the presumption is rebuttable and the question is again ultimately one of intent.

The foregoing summary indicates the uncertainty about ownership rights which an English spouse may have during the marriage. He or she can apply to a court for emergency injunctive relief against the other spouse's disposing of any of the property as to which title is in doubt. But he or she will be faced with the difficulty of proof of intent in order to establish his or her rights, except in the case of the marital home where an occupational right is preserved.

In Scotland the strictness of the system of separation of assets has been so little mitigated by presumptions of the type just described that the authors of a 1974 treatise were able to say that, "In general, so far as property is concerned, the position of a man living with his wife is the same as that of a man living with a mistress."[109]

In New Zealand and in the Australian State of Victoria reforms have been adopted in order to mitigate some of the harsh effects of the English system of separation of property during marriage. Under the 1962 Victoria law, and the 1963 New Zealand law, if any dispute arises between husband and wife concerning the title or possession of property, either spouse may apply for a judicial determination of the property rights of the spouses.[110] No other matrimonial proceeding need be pending. The judge, in such case, may make any order he thinks fit and is not bound by the way in which legal title is held, except that he cannot disregard a common intention expressed by the spouses with respect to the property. Other limits on the judge's discretion are, in Victoria, that the matrimonial home, in the absence of evidence to the contrary, is presumed to be jointly owned and, in New Zealand, that the judge must have regard to the contributions of the parties to the property in dispute. In New Zealand the court is expressly forbidden to consider marital misconduct in making a property division. It is said that thus far the New Zealand courts have used their discretion to effect an approximately equal division of property in nearly all of the cases which have come before them since the Act was passed.[111] For this reason the New Zealand system has been characterized as a "deferred community".[112] But it is a deferred community only at the discretion of the judge. The New Zealand judges are said to have accepted the broad grant of discretion given to them as "a charter which entitles them to range over the whole of the parties' matrimonial history".[113] This system, while it may work well in New Zealand, would probably be regarded as unacceptable in many other countries, where the degree of discretion and uncertainty might be regarded as too high a price for the system's potentially greater fairness in individual cases. A similar system is proposed in the latest version of the marital property sections of the American Uniform Marriage and Divorce Act except that the UMDA provisions would apply only after proceedings for marriage dissolution or judicial separation have been instituted.[114]

Singled out for special treatment in the English system is the matrimonial home. If the legal title to the matrimonial home is in one spouse, the Matrimonial Homes Act of 1967 protects the other against eviction by giving him a "right of occupation".[115] The statute applies both to cases where the home is owned absolutely by one spouse, and to cases where the other spouse may have a right to share in the ownership of the home by virtue of economic contributions even though the outward legal title does not reflect this fact. The right to occupation is not absolute. In deciding whether to enforce it the court is to take into consideration the needs of the spouses, their conduct and all the circumstances of the individual case.

If the home is leased by only one spouse, the non-lessee spouse is protected by the Rent Acts which were passed in the housing shortage following World War II and which have developed a complicated system of regulation of the landlord–tenant relationship. Provisions of these Acts assure the non-lessee spouse that he or she will not lose the right to possession. Ordinarily when a tenant abandons leased premises the landlord is entitled to repossess them. But if the tenant-spouse leaves the non-lessee spouse on the premises, the Rent Acts treat the non-lessee's possession as the lessee's. The non-lessee then becomes the statutory tenant and becomes entitled to all the protection the Rent Acts give to tenants in possession.

In Scotland, the absence of any special treatment of the matrimonial home is seen to be one of the worst defects of the Scottish separate property system.[116] Since it is often the husband alone who acquires property, the wife is often without rights in the home and its contents. It is the separate property system in all its purity.

A related question which has given rise to much litigation in England is whether and under what circumstances one spouse may exclude the other from the matrimonial home, regardless of the state of title. The English courts have been reluctant to enjoin one spouse from occupying the matrimonial home, even where full title is in the other spouse. But if the circumstances are grave enough, the fact that one spouse has complete title will not prevent the court form enjoining that spouse from occupying the home whild divorce proceedings are pending.[117] By the Domestic Violence and Matrimonial Proceedings Act 1976 courts may enter orders excluding either spouse from all or part of the matrimonial home even though no other matrimonial proceedings are pending.

It is thus clear that at least as to one type of property, the matrimonial home, the English separate property system has been significantly modified. The fact of marriage limits the rights of the owner of the marital dwelling to something less than Blackstonian "absolute and despotic dominion" with the right to exclude all others. The exact nature and extent of these limits are unclear, however, and the need for reform has been recognized. In 1973, a working party of the Law Commission was working on draft legislation to introduce a principle of co-ownership of the matrimonial home (in the absence of agreement to the contrary) and to regulate the spouses' rights of occupation.[118] The working party is also preparing recommendations for protecting a spouse's use and enjoyment of household goods.

At one time it seemed that England might implement the idea of sharing by adopting some form of community property. In 1956, seven of the 19 members of the Royal Commission on Marriage and Divorce (Morton Commission) advocated that step.[119] This was seen at the time as such a striking departure from traditional English law as to be practically unthinkable. The majority of the Commission rejected it as too unfamiliar and novel to be a practical system for England. Nonetheless, the idea persisted. In 1969, a member of Parliament introduced a bill for the establishment of a unified matrimonial property system with community features. The bill was withdrawn upon the Government's undertaking to request the Law Commission to study the subject and prepare systematic family property legislation.[120] The Law Commission's first working paper, published in 1971, indicated that it was leaning strongly in favor of some form of community property.[121] But by 1973, when the Law Commission issued its First Report on Family

Property, it was clear that the moment had passed. The Law Commission confined itself to recommending the introduction of a principle of co-ownership limited to the matrimonial home. [122] Meanwhile, the Matrimonial Proceedings and Property Act of 1970, consolidated in the Matrimonial Causes Act of 1973, had implemented sharing in another way by giving the courts broad discretion to redistribute spouses' property upon divorce. The reason why the Law Commission backed off from more extensive sharing lies in part in the fact that by 1973 changes in the divorce rate, and in the functions and expectations of families and their members had made it increasingly difficult to identify needs and desires common to most groups of the population. At least one English writer has recently spoken up against the introduction of forms of shared ownership in a time of flux and has defended the old system of the Married Women's Act of 1882 as perhaps the most appropriate for modern conditions after all. [123]

b. United States
In those jurisdictions of the United States which do not have community property, there are presented some interesting comparisons and contrasts with the situation under English law. In the United States the system of separation of ownership and control exists in 42 states, the District of Columbia and the Territory of the Virgin Islands. As we shall see in Chapter 6 there are considerable differences among American jurisdictions in the ways in which property relations of the spouses are treated when marriage comes to an end by death or divorce. Especially where the law is under pressure for change, as in the field of marital property, the American federal system can and often does function as a laboratory in which the various states experiment with different approaches to common social problems. In cases where determination of ownership must be made in connection with death, divorce, marital discord or attachment of assets for debt, the problems and the approaches are basically similar to those in England. However, published judicial decisions in the United States are less concerned than English cases with title to such assets of small value as household goods, and more with rights to such assets as joint bank accounts, or securities or real estate held in joint tenancy. Except among the affluent groups of the population where estate and gift tax considerations counterindicate the use of joint ownership with right of survivorship, the custom of holding savings and real estate in joint tenancy with right of survivorship has become so widespread in the United States that it amounts to a form of quasi-community property, a system of community property voluntarily entered into as to each asset rather than as to a fund so designated by the law. The main reason for the popularity

of this device among groups where the assets of the predeceasing spouse are not substantial enough to be subject to federal estate tax and where state inheritance and estate taxes are not a major concern is that it avoids the expense and delay of probate and administration through its automatic survivorship feature. But, in addition, its aspect as an expression of the fact that many couples think about marriage as a joint enterprise cannot be discounted. With the net worth of the average American family estimated at $38,200 in a 1976 study, and with the pre-1976 federal estate tax exemption set at $60,000, it is clear that the number of couples in this category has been considerable. The category is expanded by the Tax Reform Act of 1976 which replaces the exemption with an estate tax credit which can operate to relieve estates of up to approximately $175,000 from estate tax.

Among affluent couples in the United States, tax avoidance considerations are apt to be of overriding significance in estate planning and therefore in the way such couples choose to hold their property. Except for the marital home and small bank accounts, joint tenancies will not normally be chosen by such couples. As to such couples, it can be said that their matrimonial property regime is written in the tax laws.

The power of a married person in the United States to dispose freely of his or her assets, or at least of real property, is or can be restricted by the existence of the other spouse's interests of dower, curtesy or homestead;[124] by the other spouse's right to a forced share in succession;[125] and by case law doctrines developed to protect these statutory rights. The ancient institution of dower, and its counterpart, curtesy, have now been abolished in the great majority of American jurisdictions, as they have been in England. But a modern counterpart of dower and curtesy is provided by the legislation on homestead. In the present context, homestead means that, no matter which spouse is the owner, neither spouse can dispose of the land on which the couple has its home without the consent of the other. The details vary from state to state.

The legal situation with respect to assets which have been commingled or toward whose acquisition or improvement both spouses have contributed is similar to the situation in England. Determination of the ownership rights of each spouse may remain unsettled until the court has spoken; and for each asset the decision will be based in the first instance on the supposed intent of the parties at the time of its acquisition. Until that determination is made, a spouse's property rights are not secure against a transfer by the other to third parties of assets of which the other is the apparent owner. In the determination of ownership, the source of funds is not controlling. An Illinois case illustrates this. It was held that the fact the parties used furniture and other household items in the normal way justified the conclusion that the property was intended to be held by them as tenants in common in equal parts, regardless of its source.[126] The court stated that while the source of funds is an important element in determining title to property, it is not determinative. The court noted, however, that its decision might have been different if there had been evidence that the parties had intended some other form of ownership. The case indicates that upon death or divorce household property used by both spouses will ordinarily be divided equally, unless the presumption of ownership in common is rebutted by evidence over and above source of funds or by evidence that one spouse made a gift of his or her half-interest to the other. With respect to other types of property however, the situation is apt to be, as in all separate property systems, that the husband will have acquired the property, and there is no evidence either of contribution by the wife or intent by the husband that she should share its ownership.

Property paid for by one spouse is frequently held in both names by couples in the United States. In form, bank accounts, securities, or real estate held in joint tenancy give the survivor complete ownership and may in fact represent a gift from the funding spouse of a joint interest in the asset. But the title to joint assets may nevertheless be uncertain. The mere form of joint tenancy has been held in a number of cases not to be conclusive on the question of ownership. The funding spouse or his or her personal representative has been permitted to show the court that the intention was to create some relationship other than an absolute gift (such as an agency relationship) thereby securing for the funding spouse the exclusive right to the property.[127] The funding spouse also has prevailed in such cases by proving that he had put the property in joint names only as a will substitute, with no intent to create a present gift.[128]

When an asset is acquired in one spouse's name, but with funds of the other, it may be treated as a gift from one spouse to the other; or it may be treated as a resulting trust, with the spouse who holds legal title being a trustee for the funding spouse.[129] Ultimately, the answer depends upon the intention of the parties and any presumptions can be rebutted by evidence "of a convincing character".[130]

The laws of the American states, like English law, provide special treatment for the matrimonial home. In some states, one spouse is expressly forbidden by statute to exclude the other from the family home unless he or she provides another suitable home. Thus, as against one spouse, the other has a right of occupancy, as in England, regardless of who has title. Furthermore, if one spouse attempts to transfer his or her interest in the home or leasehold to a third party who wishes to remove the other spouse, a certain amount of protection is afforded in most states by homestead laws which protect a deserted spouse, not through a right of occupancy as such but through a "homestead estate" in a certain dollar amount of its value.

In the United States the matrimonial home also receives protection under the homestead laws against creditors. All or part of the "homestead estate" is exempt from execution if it is owned by a debtor who is the principal provider of a "household", which can be a married couple, or a parent and minor children. The scope and details of protection vary from state to state.

As we shall see in Chapter 6, a steadily increased share in the estate of a deceased husband has been given to his surviving wife in all American common law jurisdictions, and the extent to which the share of the surviving spouse can be reduced or excluded by last will and testament is strictly limited. Also in Chapter 6 we will see that in the case of divorce a steadily increasing number of states grant the courts discretion to divide all property of the spouses, however and whenever acquired, "equitably" between the parties. The draftsmen of the Uniform Marriage and Divorce Act of 1970 suggest that the division of spouses' property should be treated, "as nearly as possible, like the distribution of assets incident to the dissolution of a partnership".[131]

c. Summary

Current English and American law reform efforts have concentrated on the problem of mitigating the sometimes harsh effects of the system of strict separation of title through legal devices designed to give each spouse a share of the family property regardless of its source or how it is held. For the most part, participation by one spouse in the property of the other has been introduced indirectly through the techniques of the law of succession and divorce. These techniques will be treated in Chapter 6 on the effects of marriage dissolution.

In both England and the United States, reform movements for some time have searched for techniques to incorporate more directly the idea of sharing in the sense of recognizing the contribution of one spouse to the acquests of the other. Thus it is now possible to say that although a property owner does not ordinarily gain or lose ownership rights upon marriage, he or she does become subject to a system of legal rules which apply mainly to married people and which either affect property directly or permit a court, in its discretion, to interfere substantially with property rights in certain cases. This kind of reform represents one idea, but not the only idea, of what is required by the principle of equality. Sometimes these reforms are described as a recognition of the activity of one spouse in the home, and as compensation not only for this activity but for opportunities lost. Sometimes they are thought of as an expression of the pooling of the fortunes of husband and wife on an equal basis, share and share alike. Whatever the rationale, devices designed to introduce increased sharing of property have penetrated separate property systems and, in so doing, have transformed these systems into something closely resembling what several community systems have become when they introduced separate management as a means of implementing equality, namely deferred community. Inasmuch as these transforming devices were devised primarily for the kind of marriage in which the wife is occupied mainly with household activities while the husband performs the role of breadwinner, the question must be posed whether such devices continue to be suitable where this is no longer the prevailing marriage pattern.

d. The Zugewinngemeinschaft: Equilibrium at Last?

The preceding sections show a movement of the separate property systems toward increased sharing and of the community property systems toward increased equality. This double movement has in fact brought both systems close to the accommodation of these two goals worked out in the Scandinavian countries and West Germany.

In the Scandinavian countries, where the starting point was a form of community property, each spouse is in control of his property so long as the marriage or the regime exists, just as if the regime were that of separation of assets. But once the marriage or the regime terminates by death or divorce or otherwise ceases to function, the funds of the two spouses are pooled, and the common mass is evenly divided. Hence the name "deferred" community. Since this result has to be anticipated by the spouses during their marriage, neither has unlimited freedom in the control of his property. Each partner requires the consent of the other to certain transactions of special importance; and either may become liable to pay damages to the other if he or she gravely disregards the other's expectation of future sharing. This scheme of marital property is supplemented by generous inheritance rights of the surviving spouse and by the possibility of an alimony award upon divorce, limited to cases of need but independent of guilt.

In West Germany the starting point was different. In the late 19th century, when the Married Women's Property Acts were being passed in England and the United States, the matrimonial property provisions of the German Civil Code were being prepared. The property system selected for the legal regime in the Code of 1896 was the *Güterstand der Verwaltung und Nutzniessung*, which, like the turn of the century French and Anglo-American reforms, to some extent took account of a married woman's right to her own earnings and property. This regime, which remained the legal regime (through both the Weimar Republic and the Third Reich) until 1953, was a system of separation of ownership under which the husband had the right to administer, possess, and keep the income from, most of his wife's real and personal property. He could not, however, transfer ownership of her property. With respect to one important category of her property, the *Vorbehaltsgut*, the wife had not only title but also the exclusive right to administer, enjoy, and dispose. The *Vorbehaltsgut* included the wife's profits and earnings acquired in the exercise of a separate occupation. It also included objects exclusively destined for her personal use, any property designated by the marriage contract as *Vorbehaltsgut*, and any assets acquired by the wife through succession or donation with the express condition that they should become part of her reserved property.

West Germany began to reform the Civil Code provisions on family law in general, including matrimonial property, after the end of the Second World War, at about the same time the commission to reform the French Code began its work. But no new regime of matrimonial property was adopted by the legislature before the 31 March 1953 constitutional deadline for implementation of the equality command.[132] The West German courts then had to decide whether the existing legal provisions were in conformity with the constitutional equality rule. With respect to matrimonial property, the courts held almost unanimously that the only regime fitting the equality rule that could be imposed by the courts was the regime of separation.[133] As a result, West Germany for a while became a separate property jurisdiction.

Even though the goal of equality thus had been fully achieved, the West Germans were not satisfied with the system. A need was felt there, as elsewhere in the 1950s, to give the married woman more of a share of the family property than she had received either under the new system of separation or under the old system of the Civil Code. After extensive comparative studies, a new matrimonial property system was fashioned and was put into effect by the 1957 Equality Law on 1 June 1958.[134]

The Nordic system of deferred matrimonial property was the principal model for the West German system. But it was altered in important respects. The fund ultimately to be shared by the two spouses was reduced to something similar to, but not identical with, the parties' marital acquests. In order to simplify the liquidation, the subject matter to be shared is the *Zugewinn*, i.e. the increase of the monetary value of the parties' estates that has occurred during the marriage or, more correctly, during the existence of the marital property regime which may be terminated by agreement or by court decision even while the marriage continues. The increase, if any, of one spouse's estate is compared with the increase, if any, of the estate of the other party. If the increase of one partner is higher than the other's, he or his heir, as the case may be, has to pay to the other side one-half of the difference (the so-called *Ausgleichsforderung*, or equalization claim). In computing the difference between the final value and the initial value of each of the two estates, one has to consider not only the value of newly acquired assets but also the *increase* in value of existing assets that may be due merely to conditions of the market.

Thus, the basic difference between the West German and the Nordic systems is that the former provides merely a share in the marital increase rather than a share of the total combined assets of both parties. The sharing of the *Zugewinn,* or increase, is reduced to an arithmetical operation resulting in mere money claims.[135]

During the parliamentary debates, the influence of the West German notaries brought about another deviation from the Nordic model. In the Scandinavian countries, sharing occurs in the same manner in the case of death and in the case of divorce or other termination *inter vivos.* In the course of the deliberations of the West German Bundestag, the above-described scheme of the equalization claim was rejected for the most frequent case of marriage termination, i.e., of the death intestate of one spouse. In this case, sharing was believed adequately to be provided by giving the surviving spouse a fixed share in lieu of any claim of equalization.[136]

So far as freedom of disposition during marriage is concerned, the position of the spouses is freer than under the Nordic laws. In principle, neither spouse has any interest in specific assets of the other. There are only two limitations on one's freedom of individual disposition. Neither spouse can engage in a transaction involving his estate in its entirety *(Vermögen im Ganzen),* or involving household goods *(Hausrat),* without the other's consent.[137] In order to be treated as involving a spouse's estate in its entirety, a transaction does not need to include each and every asset. As interpreted by the courts, the term may apply to the matrimonial home, but only if it constitutes the main economic value owned by the spouse.[138] Transactions involving the family home as such are not among those which require spousal consent. Household goods[139] are all those articles which are used in the household such as furniture, tableware, television sets etc.

Is this an ideal accommodation of individual liberty, equal rights and the notion of the community of life of spouses? Law reformers in many other countries have thought so. Yet even as their systems serve as a model to others, there are signs in West Germany and Sweden of discontent with the deferred community. In Sweden, law reforms are in progress which seem likely to result in curtailment or abolition of the deferred community and its replacement with another system more suited to current needs and desires. The existing system has been described as "inconsistent with the goal of independence of the spouses", and the Swedish government's proposal for reform envisions the restriction of co-ownership to the matrimonial home and its contents.[140] Thus the new legal regime would be in effect that of separation of assets, which a large number of couples already choose by contract. A similar development seems to have begun in West Germany, where contracts providing for separation of assets are said to be widely combined with tax-saving contracts of employment of wives by their husbands. Significantly, the West German Marriage and Family Law Reform of 1976 provides that in case of divorce a wife shall be entitled to such social security benefits as she would have acquired if, during the marriage, she had been the employee of the husband.[141]

In both West Germany and Sweden, the feeling is expressed in some quarters that legal devices developed for the situation where one spouse works outside and the other works inside the home are increasingly inappropriate.[142] In Sweden, the exclusively housewife-marriage is said now to be becoming uncommon.[143] In West Germany, the two-earner marriage (*Doppelverdienerehe*) is said to have replaced *Hausfrauenehe* as the dominant pattern.[144] The official family policy statement of the Social Democratic Party and the new Divorce Law are designed to reflect and respond to the changing social situation.

The official family policy statement of the Social Democratic Party says that "the law should not be bound to the dominant symbols (*Leitbilder*) and ideals of the past but must be open to broader development and progress".[145] The statement announces that there is presently a trend away from the traditional family structure with its clear sex-role differentiation and toward a partnership model.

The fact that exclusively housewife-marriage is no longer the dominant pattern does not in and of itself explain the new West German–Swedish interest in separation of property any more than it constitutes a reason for reexamination of law reform efforts designed to introduce more sharing elsewhere. So far, the intermittent economic independence of married women has not made them the economic equals of men nor has it eliminated the arguments in favor of sharing marital acquests.[146] The explanation and the reason, if there be any, must lie not only in changing economic behavior of spouses, but in a combination of factors including changing ideologies of marriage.

There is an eternal tension in matrimonial law, in social attitudes, and in every marriage, between the community of life that marriage involves and the separate, autonomous existence of the individuals who are associated in that community of life. "Same bed, different dreams", as Dean Carbonnier has put it. Emphasis on one or the other aspect varies from time to time in the law, in societies, and in the lives of couples. John Stuart Mill's idea that marriage ought to be likened to a partnership,[147] and its expression in the marital property provisions of the Uniform Marriage and Divorce Act, emphasizes the community aspect of marriage.

But there is another idea that has regained great currency in contemporary society and which is in conflict with the ideology of community. This is the notion that marriage exists primarily for the personal fulfillment of the individual spouses and that it should last only so long as it performs this function to the satisfaction of each. This idea is not new. It has roots in the so-called Enlightenment, and found legal expression in the Code of Frederick the Great of Prussia and the short-lived revolutionary French law of 1792[148].

Since 1915, the ideology of personal fulfillment has been expressed in the required opening words of Swedish marriage ceremonies: "The end of marriage is the welfare of the individuals who desire to enter matrimony." [149] At the present time, unilateral divorce upon the application of one party after the expiration of a short waiting period is permitted in Sweden and the American state of Washington.[150] Upon the fulfillment of various conditions, or after more or less lengthy waiting periods, one party is permitted to obtain a divorce upon proving the breakdown of the marriage in steadily growing numbers of countries and states. So long as the waiting periods are lengthy, the significance of these breakdown laws is primarily ideological, showing the acceptance of a principle which is transforming marriage and divorce law. Divorce by mutual consent and unilateral divorce are already, as we shall see in the following chapter, available one way or another, no matter what the apparent state of the law is.

Another change which is fast being incorporated into English, French, Swedish, West German, and American law, concerns the economic responsibility of the spouses for each other after divorce. No longer is it considered self-evident that marriage involves an economic responsibility to a spouse which may continue even after the legal tie has been dissolved.

From one point of view it might seem that the stage is thus set for the introduction of more mechanisms to enable each spouse to share in the other's acquests. Despite increased employment of married women outside the home, economists and demographers predict that the upward trend for women's employment will be moderate in years to come.[151] Furthermore the increased labor force participation of married women includes so much part time and intermittent work that it cannot be seen as a move toward imminent economic independence of most married women. High divorce rates have put the economically dependent married woman at risk. Like the man who becomes a coal miner, the woman who becomes a housewife chooses a dangerous occupation. However it is not clear where these facts lead so far as marital property policy is concerned.

In the first place, the factual economic dependence of great numbers of married women must be distinguished from their *potential* for being economically independent. The changing alimony law already makes this distinction.[152] Therefore, we must ask whether women's potential, as distinguished from their actual, status should be emphasized in framing laws affecting the economic relations of spouses.

Second, how much weight should be given to the fact that laws emphasizing and responding to the factual economic dependence of married women may tend themselves to perpetuate dependence and to discourage the acquisition of skills and seniority needed to make married women economically independent and equal in the labor market? In West Germany, one segment of opinion attacks the *Zugewinnideologie* itself, taking the position that it is pure fantasy, and a harmful one at that, to pretend that the work of a wife in the home is either worth the same as her employment outside the home or that it in some way contributes to the wage-earning husband's acquests or to the joint achievement of the marital life-style. In this view the often-repeated theory of community property as a just recognition of the value of a spouse's work in the home and of the joint achievement of the life style of the marriage is but a "fig leaf" – an "ideological concealment" of the real economic basis of housewife-and-maintenance-marriage:

> For the man this demand signifies nothing other than the substitute price that he must pay, beyond support in the event of divorce, for the enjoyment of companionship. For the wife on the other hand this demand fulfills an appeasing function: her total economic dependence on the husband in the housewife-and-maintenance-marriage becomes concealed when these marriages, whose subsidy character is obvious, are disguised as blooming family enterprises by the virtue of the marital property rights fiction. Such constructions placed upon the situation create an alibi, allowing the wife to accept the existing relationship. But such constructions change none of the economic relations. They are not even capable of completely hiding the structures that

result from the tendency of the housewife-and-maintenance-marriage to assume an economic character.[153]

Finally, there is the question of how, even conceding the compatibility of sharing mechanisms with current economic behavior of spouses, we can assess their compatibility with current marriage behavior and ideologies. Is ideology at cross-purposes, in the short run at least, with economic reality? A leading French writer, Dean Savatier, advises married women that their choice is between *"la finance"* and *"la gloire"*, and counsels them to be practical.[154] Others think, as does the West German Stöcker, that it is not just a question of choosing between financial security here and now and an illusion of glory later. They feel that opting for devices which shore up the economic role of housewife will, in the long run, work to the economic detriment of women. Certainly a factor to be considered here is the question whether the role of housewife should be discouraged before a solution to the problem of child care can be found.

These questions are thorny but cannot be overlooked by law reformers. Many different conceptions of marriage coexist in society at the present time. It is impossible to say which predominates. But when the widespread expectation that marriage will last only so long as it performs its function of providing personal fulfillment is put together with the reality of unilateral divorce, a diminished sense of economic responsibility after divorce, the increasing economic independence of married women, and the expansion of social welfare, the resulting state of affairs does not lead inevitably to the sharing of worldly goods. Compulsory sharing, and the kind of restraints that even deferred community property can put on the freedom of each spouse to deal with his own property, may come to be seen by increasing numbers of spouses as undesirable, in much the same way that the French revolutionaries felt that marriage, if conceived of as an indissoluble undertaking, was incompatible with the principle of individual liberty.[155]

5. The Decline of Matrimonial Property: Ideals and Reality Again

The factors which have led to doubts about the deferred community in Sweden and West Germany may or may not lead to increasing separation of spouses' economic affairs there and in England, France and the United States. But from another point of view, these problems of marital property law which appear to be on the frontier are actually of declining importance, and the question of how they are resolved is not critical. For other changes have taken place which must eventually unsettle the assumptions on which all matrimonial property law is currently based. These have to do with changes in forms of wealth.

Individual liberty, equal rights and the community of life of spouses are all ideals, but the law governing the economic relations of spouses operates in the realm of economic and political reality. At this level changes have taken place which have made much of even the most modern matrimonial property law irrelevant to the daily lives of the majority of citizens. What has happened, quite simply, is that matrimonial property law has been losing its traditional subject matter, as what Professor Charles Reich has called "the new property"[156] becomes more important than land, investments and tangible objects, and as the process of what Dean Carbonnier calls the "proletarization" of family law continues.[157] Add to these factors, that the difficulty of adapting any one marital property pattern to the diverse marriage styles co-existing in modern societies has led in all systems to diminished regulation and to increasing reliance on private contract as a principle of order.

a. The "New Property"

What has recently been called "the new property" in the United States is not really new.[158] The law of property has a constantly shifting subject matter. As early as 1937, Thurman Arnold wrote:

It is obvious today that private property has disappeared. The writer, for example, owns some furniture which he can use without the assistance of any large organization, though not to the extent his parents could, because he is unable to repair it as his father was. For transportation he has an automobile, but he does not know what is going on under the hood and could not run it without a great organization to assist him. His father owned a western ranch and raised his own horses. These horses burned hay, but the hay did not come from a filling station, which in turn required a still larger organization to supply it. Yet today furniture and automobiles are the nearest we come to private property generally owned by any large group of our population.

The other things the writer 'owns' are all claims to rank or privilege in an organizational hierarchy. He is a professor at The Yale School and hopes that Yale will feed and lodge him. He has a piece of paper from an insurance company which he hopes will induce that organization to take care of his wife if he dies.[159]

In the 1940s American property lawyers were already speaking of an employee's protected interest in his job as a new property right.[160] Charles Reich in the 1960s called attention to the emergence of the government as a major source of wealth:

Government is a gigantic syphon. It draws in revenue and power, and pours forth wealth: money, benefits, services, contracts, franchises, and licenses. Government has always had this function. But while in early times it was minor, today's distribution of largess is on a vast, imperial scale.

The valuables dispensed by government take many forms, but they all share one characteristic. They are steadily taking the place of traditional forms of wealth – forms which are held as private property. Social insurance substitutes for savings; a government contract replaces a businessman's customers and goodwill. The wealth of more and more Americans depends upon a relationship to government. Increasingly, Americans live on government largess – allocated by government on its own terms, and held by recipients subject to conditions which express "the public interest". [161]

Reich elaborated on the idea which had been expressed earlier by Arnold:

But today more and more of our wealth takes the form of rights or status rather than of tangible goods. An individual's profession or occupation is a prime example. To many others, a job with a particular employer is the principal form of wealth. A profession or a job is frequently far more valuable than a house or bank account, for a new house can be bought, and a new bank account created, once a profession or job is secure. For the jobless, their status as governmentally assisted or insured persons may be the main source of subsistence.

The kinds of wealth dispensed by government consist almost entirely of those forms which are in the ascendancy today. To the individual, these new forms, such as a profession, job, or right to receive income, are the basis of his various statuses in society, and may therefore be the most meaningful and distinctive wealth he possesses. [162]

French civilists, who tend to be competent scholars in all fields of private law, rather than specializing in one area as their English or American counterparts tend to do, naturally have related such trends in property to the major tendencies of family law. They do not see the increasing importance of individual earning power and the declining importance of acquired wealth as meaning that family law is losing any of its economic emphasis. What has happened is that in family law such emphasis is increasingly on support relationships and on their enforcement through rights and obligations in salaries or other income, or sometimes in savings, if any, made from these, or in such relatively modest assets as the family home or shop.

As Dean Carbonnier says,

A theme which has been sounded a hundred times is that the family has ceased to be that plutocratic entity, that institution for consolidation and devolution of capital, that reservoir of dowries and inheritances, that it ostensibly was in the time of Balzac. The transformation is related to the two world wars which impoverished, if they did not ruin, the propertied classes, and as evidence one points notably to the very substantial diminution in the past 50 years of lawsuits involving marriage contracts, decedents' estates and gifts, in short, in the capitalistic aspect of the family.[163]

But Carbonnier himself thinks this point of view is overstated. It is, he thinks, useful in its postulation of a certain change in psychological attitudes toward such matters as dowries and inheritance, but erroneous in its suggestion that in the 19th century there were only capitalist families or that in the 20th century there are no more. In keeping with the notion of the "new property", Carbonnier points out that in the area of employment and of entry into other economically important social institutions a sort of non-patrimonial "succession" takes place:

Social rank continues to be conserved in and by families. In this sense, the institution of the family has not essentially changed: It remains the possible source of considerable economic advantages. What has changed is the nature of these advantages.[164]

Historically, marital property law was developed by and for the well-to-do. As affluence spread in the 20th century more persons have come within the potential scope of this law. Most of the reforms discussed in the preceding sections represent an attempt in mid-twentieth century to make marital property law more generally applicable. But economic conditions in the latter half of the 20th century seem to be making it less widely applicable again. Examples from the United States should serve to illustrate the point. In 1975, the Labor Department reported that a typical urban family of four needed $15,500 a year to maintain a moderate standard of living, and $22,500 a year to live on a level allowing some luxuries, such as a new car every four years and more household goods and services.[165] (Neither of these budgets allows for savings or investments apart from the acquisition of household goods and perhaps the eventual building up of equity in a home.) But the U.S. Census Bureau's analysis of income distribution as of December 31, 1974, showed that only 21.8% of American families have an annual family income over $20,000.[166] The two government agencies' definitions of "family" do not exactly coincide, but these figures do give a rough idea of the relatively small size of the group of the population which has even the possibility of accumulating "marital property" in the traditional sense. The application of marital property law even to this group, supposing they do not consume all they earn, is limited by the fact that as their income level reaches the point where the couple has to be concerned about estate taxes, the manner in which they order their property relationship tends to be dictated by the tax laws and not left to the application of rules of marital property law. Thus, as was traditionally the case, the well-to-do make their own marital property law in their contracts, trusts and wills – in what Max Weber called the cautelary jurisprudence.

The French public opinion studies done in connection with the 1965 marital property reform indicate obliquely that a similar state of affairs may exist in France.[167] An extensive study in 1963 concluded, on the basis of a large sample, that the general public in France "remains largely ignorant of the legal rules of their matrimonial regime". At the same time little dissatisfaction with existing marital property law was found. 82% of the respondents said that they would not choose a different regime if they had it to do over again. But when the sample of persons engaged in business, professional persons and their spouses is broken out from the whole, one finds that those who have married under a contract are more satisfied (91%) than those who have not (63%).

The fact that the great majority of couples spend what they earn on food, shelter, clothing and a few modest luxuries, leaves a restricted field of application to marital property law as traditionally conceived and validates the result to which modern systems seem to be coming, namely, that a marital property system will typically operate only on the marital home and household goods. Existing American and English law everywhere contains some type of restraint on a spouse's power to deal with the matrimonial home. It is interesting that this is the only type of restraint on individual action the Swedish reform proposal contemplates retaining.[168] Sweden would expand the restraint to embrace household goods as well as the home, a change similar to that recently proposed for England. These developments with respect to the nature of wealth also explain why Professor Sundberg is able to say that in the Swedish welfare state there is generally a "disappearance of interest" in marital property and that such interest is indeed regarded by many as evidence of a "squirrel mentality".[169]

Put in a general way, what seems to have happened in the 20th century is this: more and more groups of persons who would once have been entirely propertyless began to be owners of property. Marital property law began to pay attention to their needs. This is part of the expanding process of application of family law generally which Dean Carbonnier has called "proletarization". The direction the law had begun to take in responding to the needs of the steadily increasing number of owners of modest amounts of traditional forms of property was toward equality and sharing between the marriage partners. Changes in the forms of wealth and in the frequency of divorce and remarriage have now called the evolving solutions to the problem of equality and sharing into question. But even though marital property (in the traditional sense of that term) is declining, the need continues as strongly as ever for legal regulation of the property relations of spouses in those characteristic situations where trouble arises: between the spouses and creditors or purchasers;

between parties to a divorce or separation proceeding; and between a surviving spouse and heirs of a deceased spouse. In these situations, the solutions developed for the future will have to take account not only of new forms of wealth but of those unmarried cohabitants whose problems can be the same as those of legally married persons.

b. Contract as an Ordering Mechanism

In Anglo-American discussions of the role which law ought to have in interspousal personal and economic relations during the on-going marriage, there is a burgeoning literature which sees private contractual regulation of these matters as an ideal approach which preserves the neutrality of the State, promotes sex equality, and respects individual liberty.[170] However, leaving these matters to private contract is not so simple as it has been made to sound. The proponents of such "marriage contracts" (not to be confused with *contrats de mariage* or *Eheverträge* which regulate matrimonial property regimes in French and West German law) have correctly pointed out that the reasons traditionally given in the family law setting for the unenforceability of such contracts have an anachronistic ring. But it is to contract law that they must ultimately resort. Contract theory seems still to furnish good reasons why the State will not and should not become involved in enforcing certain kinds of agreements, particularly those about division of labor and decision-making within the family.

As Morris R. Cohen has pointed out, there is a common "intuitionist" idea that promises ought to be kept and that a properly organized society ought to enforce all promises:

This may also be said to be the common man's theory.... But while this intuitionist theory contains an element of truth, it is clearly inadequate. No legal system does or can attempt to enforce all promises. Not even the canon law held all promises to be sacred.[171]

In contract theory, it is taken for granted that the armed might of the State will not be put behind every promise or every bargain fulfilling all the formal requirements of "contract":

[I]t may be wondered why the law has not made contracts out of all promises. The reason why it has not is probably a reason of public policy. Some promises are not of enough importance to make it worthwhile to make contracts out of them. The legal enforcement of all promises is expensive. No more expense should be incurred for the enforcement of promises than the needs of our social order make imperative. There is a social interest in personal liberty; and personal liberty, even the personal liberty to lie, ought not to be delimited unless the social interests of other people are thereby injured enough so as to warrant the delimitation of personal liberty.[172]

It seems clear that "contracts" which purport to regulate who will wash the dishes and take out the garbage are no more enforceable than the famous "invitation to dinner".[173] Furthermore, the general retreat of the State from involvement in the arrangement of interspousal relations which is observable in the law of England, France, the United States and West Germany is not likely to be halted in favor of enforcing hitherto unenforceable contracts.

Where the economic relations of the spouses are concerned, however, contract may have more of a role to play in England and the United States than it has had in the past. It is not unreasonable to expect that there, as in France and West Germany, couples will eventually be allowed to contract in advance of marriage concerning at least some of the economic consequences of divorce.[174] But even in the economic area, it is unlikely that contracts between spouses will come to be treated just like other contracts. Their enforceability will continue to be subject to uncertainty arising from the need to screen such contracts for unconscionability (and set them aside if need be), and to make support contracts modifiable or terminable upon changed circumstances. The principle of non-interference with a functioning marriage as well as the overall withdrawal of the State from regulating husband–wife relations during marriage make it unlikely that contracts to require cash flow from one partner to the other during marriage would be any more enforceable than support rights presently are.

In France and West Germany, the role of contract in interspousal economic relations has been expanded by the lifting of restrictions on freedom of contract which had been designed to protect the wife or her family from overreaching by the husband. Today, both the French and West German systems have increased the spouse's freedom to choose alternative regimes and to change the regime or details of it during marriage.[175] Unlike the traditional legal regimes, the current legal regimes are designed for people who live on income and savings of their own rather than inherited wealth, who own little or nothing when they enter upon their first marriage and who accumulate property through their earnings during the marriage. Thus, marriage contracts in France and West Germany today perform a rather different social function from the one they performed in traditional systems. Up to the end of the 19th century, the marriage contract was apt to be a bargain struck between the families of the two spouses. The law was strongly influenced by the idea that the spouses should not be able to undo the scheme of regulation that their parents had carefully worked out. Thus in France until 1965 the marriage contract became immutable upon the conclusion of the marriage. In the twentieth century, however, marriage contracts tend to be used by individual spouses for their own purposes, not the least of which may be to obtain optimum savings under the tax laws. Apart from regulating the economic relationship of the spouses themselves, marriage contracts are often concerned with the special circumstances of spouses who have children from previous marriages, a situation which has become more frequent as divorces have increased. Marriage contracts are also sometimes used as will substitutes, as in the *institution contractuelle* of French law.[176] It is thus not surprising that the legal regulation of freedom to make marriage contracts has changed along with the uses being made of them.

Impetus for increased contractual freedom in arranging an individual couple's regime in the French legal system came from the fact that it was difficult to devise a new legal regime which was equally suitable for any and all couples within the population. A couple's needs and desires in this respect may depend on whether theirs is a first or later marriage, whether both or only one of the spouses work, and whether either or both owned substantial property before entering the marriage. In addition, such factors as family and regional tradition and religious custom may be important.

It should not be forgotten, however, that, in the light of the discussion of changing forms of property in the preceding section, contracts regulating economic relations of spouses will be of most interest and help to those couples who accumulate substantial property. It is unlikely that contracts will be used by large numbers of spouses. For most people, attention will continue to focus on the matrimonial home and on rights of one spouse in the salary, pension, insurance, and social security rights of the other. Here, freedom of contract tends to be limited by concern for the public treasury, as we will see in Chapter 6. Keeping in mind that in an amicable functioning marriage, the economic relationship of the couple will be a *de facto* community, each giving and receiving according to his abilities and needs, it is apparent that generally speaking most problems of marital property, new or old, will appear and be resolved in the context of the dissolution of the marriage by divorce or death.

IV. Conclusions: Freedom, Individualism and Community, or Autonomy, Estrangement and Anomie?

A. Dejuridification of Internal Spousal Relationships

When we compare the forgoing survey of the changing effects of the ongoing legal marriage with the effects of informal marriage in Chapter 3, we begin to discern some of the ways in which the relationship of the State to the family is changing. It is less likely that the State will go into business on a large scale regulating the shadow institution, than that it will leave the effects of the on-going legal marriage, if not its formation, to regulation by the social norms of convention, custom, ethics or religion.

As legal marriage is gradually being deprived of legal effects, the developments described in Chapter 3 now appear not so much as signs of the increasing legal existence of informal cohabitation as they are of the gradual assimilation of the married to the unmarried state. Many different factors are coming together at once to diminish the legal effects of marriage. Here the ideological banner of freedom to marry is joined by those of the right to privacy and equality. In addition, as various interest groups in society become more and more vocal, the law has had to respond by adapting more and more to diverse life styles and attitudes in pursuit of what Rheinstein has called the "ideology of tolerance".[177] The idea of individual liberty has been important, especially in Europe. The idea of marriage as "an association of two individuals" rather than as a unit, as expressed by the United States Supreme Court,[178] has played its part. Finally, the virtual accomplishment of free and easy exit from legal marriage has already transformed and will continue to affect the legal institution of marriage. The tendency of each one of these factors has been to cause the legal system to withdraw from marriage regulation. Together, they seem irresistible.

In the United States, just as *Loving v. Virginia* brought into question much traditional State control of marriage formation,[179] the Supreme Court's other major recent pronouncement on marriage in recent years, *Griswold v. Connecticut*, has established at the constitutional level the idea that the State should interfere as little as possible with the on-going marriage.[180] Even more significant than any specific constitutional trend is the fact that the Supreme Court has begun to blur the distinction between the legal and social institutions of marriage in various ways whose significance is not yet clear nor widely recognized. This is one way of looking at the zoning cases described in Chapter 3.[181] So far as public law is concerned, the distinction has been practically erased. This blurring has also occurred in an interesting way with respect to the *Griswold* case. The basis for striking down the Connecticut birth control laws in *Griswold* was a supposed "right of marital privacy". Over and over again the majority and concurring opinions in *Griswold* emphasized the fact that it was interference with the *marriage* relationship which was being held unconstitutional. But, in 1972, in *Eisenstadt v. Baird* the Supreme Court held the birth control laws of Massachusetts unconstitutional as applied to *unmarried* persons on the basis of the Equal Protection Clause saying:

If under *Griswold* the distribution of contraceptives to married persons cannot be prohibited, a ban on distribution to unmarried persons would be equally impermissible. It is true that in *Griswold* the right of privacy in question inhered in the marital relationship. Yet the marital couple is not an independent entity with a mind and heart of its own, but an association of two individuals each with a separate intellectual and emotional make-up. If the right of privacy means anything, it is the right of the *individual*, married or single, to be free from unwarranted governmental intrusion into matters so fundamentally affecting a person as the decision whether to bear or beget a child.[182] (Court's emphasis).

Because *Eisenstadt* did not offer any explanation of why the right of marital privacy which was the rationale of *Griswold* should be extended to unmarried persons, nor did it advance any new explanation of *Griswold*, constitutional law scholars have dismissed it as only one more instance of poor reasoning by the Court. But the decision is not astonishing. The result was politic and practical. What is interesting to speculate about is whether some day, in similar crab-like fashion, the Supreme Court will move to further erasure of the differences between the legal status of being married and that of being unmarried.

Another influence which converges with *Eisenstadt* to draw the law away from marriage regulation comes from the growing number of state Human Rights laws which prohibit discrimination not only on the basis of sex, race, and national origin, but also on the basis of marital status.[183] Similarly, it will be interesting to watch the English courts elaborate on that part of the British Sex Discrimination Act of 1975 which prohibits discrimination on the ground of marital status.[184]

In France, the phenomena which we have described as part of a pattern of dejuridification have been seen as part of an effort to "save" the institution of legal marriage:

The progression of the free union in the legal area cannot fail to act as a counterforce on the very structure of marriage. In order that the institution of marriage will not be completely abandoned, it has been necessary to modify it so far as its obligatory ties are concerned. In this way, individual liberty has been aided in its progress against the traditional "categories" of marriage by an external action, a sort of flanking and enclosing maneuver on the institution of marriage.[185]

Professor Bénabent sees in the divorce case law an increasing recognition of the individual liberty of the spouses: it is not marital "fault" for a spouse to hold and act upon a wide variety of opinions, and divorces have been granted against spouses who have interfered with the other's freedom of expression or association.[186] Bénabent believes that there is a new idea of marriage being expressed in French law: the idea of marriage as a means to the fullest possible development of the individual.[187] If this is so, it is still balanced by a conservative countertrend which figured importantly in the 1976 Divorce Reform.[188]

Current French law still limits a spouse's freedom of behavior when it substantially interferes with the obligations of marriage. On a case-by-case basis many freedoms of the spouses have been qualified when the freedom is expressed in a way harmful to the other spouse. Thus a spouse's freedom of expression may give grounds for divorce if it takes the form of execessive criticism of the other spouse, a cold and distant attitude, or an excessive though innocent friendship with a third party. The freedom to choose one's leisure activities does not extend to the point that the household is completely neglected.[189] Even the conscientious exercise of religious duties, a highly individual matter, can come into conflict with the duties and obligations inherent in marriage to such an extent that one spouse's religious activities will be considered an injury to the other spouse and thus grounds for divorce. When the expression of one spouse's individuality seriously disrupts the community of life the court will step in to grant a divorce.

West German law up to the 1976 reform has been similar. The spouses are obliged by Art. 1353 to live together in marital community. To the extent that this obligation is anything more than an expression of an ideal, it seems to impose some limit on the freedom of each spouse to act. Thus while each spouse has the power to decide personal matters for himself or herself, neither may thereby impair the matrimonial community of life. In making personal decisions concerning religious affiliation, dress, reading, smoking, etc. each spouse must have regard for the other.[190] Conversion to a new religious faith does not release one from one's duties toward one's family.[191] But what "marital community of life" shall mean is left largely to the determination of the parties. It does not even necessarily imply a duty of the parties to live together. With the drastic curtailment of the role of fault under the 1976 Divorce Reform Law, the idea of *Lebensgemeinschaft* is almost completely deprived of content, except as an expression of the aspirations of the society for marriages. But heavy with meanings yet to be revealed, like the recent marriage pronouncements of the United States Supreme Court, is Article 2 of the 1949 Constitution: "Everyone has the right to the free unfolding of his personality...".

B. Spouses and the Outside World: Unit or Association of Two Autonomous Individuals?

We have thus far confined our discussion of the legal effects of the on-going marriage to a consideration of the relationship between spouses. An examination of the changing law governing the relationships of the spouses with *others*, be they private individuals or agencies of the State, furnishes further evidence of spreading tendencies to minimize the legal effects of marriage and to assimilate the status of legal marriage either to the status of being unmarried or to the situation of a partner in an informal union.

One type of third party who takes more than a passing interest in the degree to which marriage constitutes a community of life is a creditor who wants recourse against two individuals rather than just the one he originally dealt with. In the Anglo-American systems of separation of assets, the starting point is, and has been since the Married Women's Property Acts, that each spouse is liable for his and only his transactions. However, because of the mingling of affairs typical of persons who live together, problems are immediately posed concerning the rights each person may have in property apparently belonging to the other and in assets whose title is not clearly apparent, and the extent to which those rights can be asserted by third parties. Yet the answers to these problems depend on the application of the same general principles of the law of property that would apply to two strangers.[192] Creditors are assisted by the policy in favor of protecting good faith reliance on appearances. Thus, creditors of either spouse are able to reach everything held in their debtor's name, and also their debtor's interest in jointly held property. But if they attempt to reach any equitable interests their debtor may have by virtue of contributions to the acquisition of property held in the other spouse's name they encounter the same difficulties of proof that that spouse himself would have.

An exception to treating the spouses like any other cohabitants exists in many American states, where Family Expense Statutes provide that "The expenses of the family and of the education of the children shall be chargeable upon the property of both husband and wife, or of either of them in favor of creditors therefor."[193] But under some of these statutes, the spouse who has not engaged in the transaction – by himself or through his agent – cannot be held liable so long as payment can be obtained from the other, or his liability may be limited to those assets which he owned at the time of the transaction.

In England, the Matrimonial Proceedings and Property Act of 1970 abolished the married woman's agency of necessity by which at common law she had had the power to pledge her husband's credit for such items as housing, food, clothing, medical attention and education for the children. Today, if a spouse is to be liable at all on transactions of the other, it is on the general agency principle of apparent authority, which applies not just to married people, but to any one who has given a third party reason to believe someone has his authority to pledge his credit.[194] The presumption of implied authority applies not only to a wife but to anyone who has apparent power to make purchases for the household. Neither in England nor the United States is a spouse any longer liable as such for a tort committed by the other.

The situation under the West German version of deferred community is broadly similar. Obligations incurred by one spouse can be enforced against his property only. But, in favor of a creditor of either spouse, movable assets which are in the possession of either or both are rebuttably presumed to be owned by the debtor spouse. Negotiable bearer instruments are covered by this presumption. If the spouses do not live together, the presumption does not apply to assets in the possession of the spouse who is not the debtor. Assets which exclusively serve the use of one spouse are presumed to be owned by him.[195]

Under the French legal community property regime, in contrast to both the Anglo-American systems of separate property and the West German system, a creditor may have recourse in some situations not only to the assets of the separate fund of his debtor, but also to the community fund or at least to a certain part of it. The law also provides that for certain obligations incurred by one spouse, the other automatically becomes a co-obligor. As in some American states, the unity of the married couple is recognized by treating as joint obligations those which are incurred by one of the spouses for a "family expense".[196] But in France, a creditor also may resort to the personal fund of the obligor and the totality of the community fund for:[197] obligations of support due by either the husband or the wife; premarital obligations of the husband or the wife or obligations which encumber an inheritance or a donation acquired by either during marriage, provided movables thus acquired have been so intermingled with the community that they can no longer be distinguished; and obligations which are incurred by the wife during the existence of the regime and which arise out of tort, quasi-contract or some other non-contractual cause or out of a contract which has been consented to by the husband or by the court. Creditors of the husband can resort to the community fund, but not that part of it which is composed of the wife's reserved property.[198] Third parties receive substantial protection against possible surprises arising from the complexity of the property relationships which may exist between the spouses themselves. The presumption that any given asset is community property operates to protect them in many cases. In those cases where the presumption of community may be to their detriment, or may be rebutted, they receive further protection from dispositions of the code establishing presumptions of power of either spouse to act alone and bind the common fund. All in all, it seems that French law still treats a married couple more as a unit and more differently from other units than do any of the other legal systems.

While creditors are probably the third parties most interested in enforcing legal rights against spouses, the spouses themselves are often interested in suing a variety of individuals for harm done to one of the spouses or even to the marital relationship itself. The community aspect of marriage seems to shine forth clearly when a spouse sues a third party who has injured or killed his partner, just as it does when the rights of a surviving spouse in the estate of the predeceasing spouse are involved.[199] In the case of those actions which are known in the United States as the "heartbalm" torts, there is a definite trend to deny the injured spouse any civil remedy against a third party for diverting the affection or depriving him of the company of the other.

In the United States a number of states long ago abolished actions for interference with the marriage relationship because such actions were thought to be susceptible to abuse by spiteful persons or even to encourage blackmail. But a new idea concerning these actions has appeared in the wake of *Griswold-Eisenstadt*. In 1976, the tort of criminal conversation (adultery) was held unconstitutional by a lower Pennsylvania court which relied on the two U.S. Supreme Court decisions. The Pennsylvania Court said that the tort was a "violation or infringement of the right to privacy of individuals to engage in natural consensual sexual relations".[200] The court said the tort was an anachronism in view of the "...moral, ethical and sexual, if you will, standards and mores under which we live in this last quarter of the twentieth century". In view of the Pennsylvania legislature's recent abolition of criminal penalties for adultery, the court believed that "...it is no longer in the state's interest to impose upon a married person's right to natural, voluntary sexual relations with other persons".

In England, the heart-balm actions of enticement, harbouring and damages for adultery, were abolished in 1970.[201] According to Professor Bromley, "...it was doubtful whether it was any longer socially desirable to give either spouse a remedy if the loss of the other's consortium was due to the latter's voluntary act, even though the defendant had induced or encouraged it".[202] In France, under general principles of tort law, causes of action for heart balm exist against a third person but seem not to be much utilized.[203] In West Germany, causes of action against a third party for disturbing the marriage relationship (*Ehestörungsklage*) began to be cautiously allowed only after World War II, and are now extremely controversial.[204]

Another area in which there are signs of a shift to emphasizing the separate quality of each spouse rather than the aspect of the married couple as a unit is that of taxation. Here, as in other areas, Sweden has taken the most far-reaching steps. In 1960, in reaction to the great number of "tax divorces" which married couples had undergone in order to gain more favorable tax treatment, Sweden established a system of separate taxation for married couples in which the taxation of each spouse follows the rules applicable to single persons.[205] Nevertheless, with respect to some types of income, there is still unfavorable joint taxation of married couples.[206] In this connection, it is interesting that Swedish law equates some informal marriage-like households with formal legal marriages for tax law purposes, as well as in its legislation on social insurance.[207] In England, France and the United States, the married couple in general receives more favorable treatment than the single tax-payer through income splitting, split rates or through using different tax scales for married and single persons. But changing economic behavior of spouses has put these systems in tension. In the United States, for example, married couples in which only one partner works outside the home receive more favorable tax treatment than single taxpayers. But married couples with approximately equal incomes or even with a 60–40 or 70–30 income differential pay a "marriage penalty".[208] This has resulted in demands for a marriage-neutral tax system, as described in the following excerpt from an article by Professor Boris Bittker:

> It is increasingly argued that the income tax on two persons who get married should be neither more nor less than they paid on the same income before marriage. This call for a marriage-neutral tax system stems sometimes from the conviction that the state should neither encourage nor discourage marriage by a tax incentive or penalty, and sometimes from a belief that ceremonial marriages in today's society are not sufficiently different from informal alliances to warrant a difference in tax liability. A legislative bill to achieve a marriage-neutral federal income tax has gained a large and diverse Congressional following in both the House of Representatives and the Senate.[209]

But, as Professor Bittker points out, given a progressive rate schedule, demands for marriage-neutrality in the tax system confront the problem that a neutral system cannot be reconciled with a regime of equal taxes for married couples with equal income. So far, the decision has been made to let the partners in certain types of marriages pay more tax than they would pay if single. But as these two-worker marriages become more common, the United States may be pushed in the direction of the Swedish solution. The

New York Times has already carried accounts of many couples who have obtained "tax-divorces". In 1974, The American Bar Association adopted a resolution calling for the study of the tax laws with a view toward determining whether they improperly discriminate on the basis of marital status, and for the passage of employment and housing laws to eliminate discrimination on the basis of marital status. [210]

The tendency to treat the spouses as separate individuals in their relations with the outside world continues in other ways. The New Jersey Supreme Court in 1976 held that spouses of members of the judiciary in that state could no longer be forbidden to run for public office, citing the "emergence and the social and legal recognition of spousal autonomy and retention of separate identities and interests." [211] In 1975, the American Bar Association was asked to rule on the ethical question of whether husband and wife lawyers are prohibited from representing differing interests or from being associated with firms representing differing interests. In a formal opinion, the ABA, noting that the "...problem undoubtedly will arise with increasing frequency", ruled that,

It is not necessarily improper for husband and wife lawyers...to represent differing interests. No disciplinary rule expressly requires a lawyer to decline employment if a husband, wife, son, daughter, brother, father, or other close relative represents the opposing party in negotiation or litigation. [212]

C. The Empty Community

Taken together, the various recent changes in the law concerning the effects of the on-going marriage present a pattern similar to that which emerged from the study of marriage formation in Chapter 2. Like the freedom to marry, the heightened symbolism of marriage as a community of life or of marital privacy has appeared in all four legal systems just as the legal effects of marriage are being eliminated altogether or assimilated to those of informal unions. To say the least, the social reality to which the ideology of spousal unity or family privacy may once have corresponded has become more diffuse and evanescent. The concrete legal changes in each system have moved decisively in the direction of emphasis on the separate and equal individuality of the spouses even during the on-going marriage.

A recent French case provides a revealing glimpse into the actual content of the command of the Civil Code that the spouses are mutually bound to a community of life. A husband, having failed in his efforts to obtain a divorce, rented an apartment in another city and declared that this apartment, not the luxurious house in which he and his wife had been living, would henceforward be the marital dwelling. He then endeavored to remove his wife from the house, and install her in the apartment. The Paris Court of Appeals held the dispute could be resolved by the "simple" application of the requirement of Art. 215 that the spouses are bound to a community of life.[213] It gave the wife the right to remain in the house, adding hopefully, "It is not impossible that a peaceful coexistence can be established in the interest of the children", and that in any case "...it is up to the spouses to deduce the consequences of their reciprocal attitudes".

What then does "community of life" in article 215 mean? What content can the court give to this expression of the aspirations of society for married couples?

[I]t is certain that this community of life will not take on the same form, nor the same intimacy in each household; it is not up to the law, but to each family to work out the modalities of the community of life between spouses who may have serious difficulties and whose personal and material potential may be quite diverse.[214]

Community of life in French law, then, has no more meaning than *Lebensgemeinschaft* in West German law and consortium in English law. The United States Supreme Court has contented itself, wisely perhaps, with dropping the mantle of "privacy" over the complexity, diversity and fluctuations of marriage behavior.

In this Chapter we have seen many instances where, as society and law both change, old problems are solved and new ones are generated. To the extent that modern laws, while withdrawing from the marriage regulation business, have attempted to announce new ideals, they have encountered a new set of problems arising from the internal contradiction between the modern visions of marriage as involving cooperation and community on the one hand, and marriage as a vehicle for the fullest self expression of the individual on the other. The tensions among equality, individuality and community may eventually turn out to be dynamic and creative. On the other hand, the banner of community may be flying over societies where family behavior is characterized by the less imposing reverse sides of the coinage of freedom, equality and individuality – disorganization, estrangement and anomie. The standard of privacy may have been raised over societies where the State constantly undermines conditions that are needed to make privacy meaningful.

The law, in struggling with these problems, merely reflects the ambivalence that actually exists in society and in individuals. It is likely that most persons who enter marriage still entertain ideals of community and cooperation, and that these ideals guide a functioning marriage, more or less. It is also likely that an individual's ideas will change if he finds himself in a deteriorating marriage situation. The lack of firm and fixed ideas about what marriage is and should be is but an aspect of the alienation of modern man. And in this respect the law seems truly to reflect the fact that in modern society more and more is expected of human relationships, while at the same time social conditions have rendered these relationships increasingly fragile.

NOTES

[1] F. Nye & F. Berardo, The Family 249 (1973); Rossi, Equality between the Sexes: An Immodest Proposal, 93 Daedalus 607, 615 (1964). See *infra* at 135–137.

[2] On varying marriage patterns in contemporary society generally see *König* 38–44.

[3] *König* 24–26, discusses the American, English, French and German studies among others. See also, Kerckhoff, The Structure of the Conjugal Relationship in Industrial Societies, and Kandel & Lesser, The Internal Structure of Families in the United States and Denmark, in Cross-National Family Research at 53 and 70 respectively (Sussman & Cogswell eds. 1972).

[4] Portions of the material in this section IIA have appeared in *Glendon, Family Power and Authority*, and in *Rheinstein & Glendon, Int. Encyc.*

[5] The difficulty of regulating these matters must have appeared along with the first efforts to do so. The Book of Esther tells us that when Assuerus, the King of Persia, gave a great feast in order to show off the riches and power of his kingdom he commanded that Queen Vasthi be brought out in all her finery so that he could show her beauty to the guests. But the Queen refused to come. The King was advised by his wise men that if the Queen went unpunished all the women in the kingdom would ignore the commandments of their husbands. Accordingly Vasthi was banished forever and it became part of the unalterable law of the Medes and the Persians that wives must obey their husbands. There is no evidence that these or any other such measures have ever succeeded in making wives obey their husbands.

[6] Cf. E. Ehrlich, Fundamental Principles of the Sociology of Law 491 (1962; orig. publ. 1936): "The first thing that attracts the attention of the observer is the contrast between the actual order of the family and that which the codes decree. I doubt whether there is a country in Europe in which the relation between husband and wife, parents and children, between the family and the outside world, as it actually takes form in life, corresponds to the norms of the positive law; in which the members of the family, in which there is a semblance of proper family life, would as much as think of attempting to enforce the rights against one another that the letter of the law grants them."

[7] The duty of obedience was not in the original draft of the Civil Code. It was inserted at Napoleon's personal insistence. The record of debates on the code reveals him saying "Women ought to obey us. Nature has made women our slaves! The husband ought to be able to say to his wife: 'Madam, you will not go to the theatre; Madam, you will not see such or such a person; Madam, you belong to me body and soul.' " Recounting this story, the great French civil law scholar, Dean Savatier, has commented: "When one hears this impassioned tone, one realizes that this was not simply a legal question. It is a domestic question. Bonaparte was thinking about Josephine! 'You are preventing me from seeing whomever I please!' It has to be said that during the Egyptian campaign, there were a certain number of men whom Josephine found pleasing; and this fact rankled in the memories of Bonaparte! But it is the spiteful act of a man who did not succeed in making his wife obey him, which was responsible for the insertion of this historic phrase in our Civil Code: The wife owes obedience to her husband. One should not attach more importance to it than that. I do not think in spite of the autocratic nature which produced this intervention in the Civil Code, that it was within Bonaparte's power, or even within the power of Napoleon, to make his wife always obey him!"
Savatier, La femme et son ménage dans le mariage français, in Le Droit dans la Vie Familiale 173, 177 (Boucher & Morel eds. 1970).

[8] Colombet, Commentaire de la loi du 4 juin 1970, D.S. 1971. Chr. 1, 11.

[9] *Id*. at 3.

[10] *Id*. at 5.

[11] *Ibid.*
[12] Id. at 3.
[13] *Id.* at 5.
[14] *Id.* at 11.
[15] German C.C. §1353.
[16] German C.C. §§1358 and 1363 *et seq.*
[17] *Grundgesetz* (Basic Law) of 1949, art. 3.
[18] *Grundgesetz* (Basic Law) of 1949, art. 6 §I.
[19] GleichberG, of 18 June 1957, BGB1. I 609.
[20] Erstes Gesetz zur Reform des Ehe- und Familienrechts of 14 June 1976 (1. EheRG) I BGB1 1976. 1421–1464.
[21] See *Markovits* 125–135, and *Beitzke* 512.
[22] BVerfG, 29 July 1959, FamRZ 1959, 416.
[23] *Markovits* 125–35, and *Stöcker* 553.
[24] Familienpolitik der Sozialdemokratischen Partei Deutschlands, Entwurf 10 (1972).
[25] E.g., Maguire v. Maguire, 59 N.W.2d 336 (Neb. 1953).
[26] It is true that the words "The husband is the head of the family" crept into an occasional state statute, e.g. Ohio Rev. Code §3103.02 (1972): "The husband is the head of the family. He may choose any reasonable place or mode of living and the wife must conform thereto." But American state laws do not have the national monument character of European codes and symbolic statements in such laws do not have the same significance as the ideals embodied in codes.
[27] 388 U.S. 1 (1967).
[28] 381 U.S. 479 (1965).
[29] A. Greeley, Ethnicity in the United States: a preliminary reconnaissance 3 (1974).
[30] Doe v. Doe, 314 N.E.2d 128, 132 (Mass. 1974).
[31] Citations collected *Id.* at 131 n. 3–5.
[32] Planned Parenthood of Central Missouri v. Danforth, 96 S. Ct. 2831 (1976).
[33] Re Cochrane (1840), 8 Dowl. 630.
[34] R. v. Jackson [1891] 1 Q.B. 671 (C.A.).
[35] *Id.* at 679–80.
[36] R. v. Reid, [1972] 2 All E.R. 1350, 1352 (C.A.); [1973] Q.B. 299, 302.
[37] *Bromley* 94.
[38] Loss of consortium is still widely the basis of an action by one spouse against a third party who injures the other spouse, however.
[39] Equal Pay Act 1970, c. 41. Sex Discrimination Act 1975, c. 65.
[40] Law No. 75–617 of 11 July 1975; J.O. 12 July P. 7171(1); D.S. 1975. Leg. 248.
[41] 29 A.L.R.2d 474 (1953).
[42] Green v. Commr., 305 N.E.2d 92 (Mass. 1973). For other cases indicating that the common law rule that the husband chooses the domicile of the couple is being eroded, see *Restatement* (Second) of Conflict of Laws §21 (1971).
[43] Blair v. Blair, 85 A.2d 442 (Md. 1952).
[44] *Bromley* 95–96.
[45] *Ibid.*
[46] On the latter development, see generally *Stoljar* §§155–157.
[47] See generally *Rheinstein and Glendon, Int. Encyc.*
[48] A well-known American study of the interspousal decision-making process concluded: "[T]he power to make decisions stems primarily from the resources which the individual can provide to meet the needs of his marriage partner and to upgrade his decision-making skill. Because it is based on such tangible and relevant criteria, the balance of power may be said to be adapted to the interpersonal relationship of the two partners involved." R. Blood & D. Wolfe, Husbands and Wives: The Dynamics of Married Living 44 (1960). John Stuart Mill put it

somewhat more concisely: "The real practical decision of affairs, to whichever may be given the legal authority, will greatly depend, as it even now does, upon comparative qualifications." The Subjection of Women, in Essays on Sex Equality 170 (Rossi ed. 1970).

[49] *Ibid.*

[50] Discussed in *Glendon, Family Power and Authority* at 28–31; and Müller-Freienfels, Zur Scheidung wegen Glaubenswechsels, JZ 1964, 305–310, 344–349.

[51] Montesquieu helps us to understand the relative seriousness with which legal questions concerning names are treated in France: "Names, whereby men acquire an idea of a thing which one would imagine ought not to perish, are extremely proper to inspire every family with a desire of extending its duration. There are people among whom names distinguish families: there are others where they only distinguish persons; the latter have not the same advantage as the former." The Spirit of the Laws, Book XXIII. Ch. 4.

[52] Prussian General C., Part II art. 192.

[53] Daum, The Right of Married Women to Assert their own Surnames, 8 J.L. Reform 63 (1974).

[54] Rheinstein, The Transformation of Marriage and the Law, 68 Nw. U.L. Rev. 463, 465 (1973).

[55] On the use of titles which disclose a woman's marital status, while the titles used for men do not, see Karst, "A Discrimination so Trivial": A Note on the Law and Symbolism of Women's Dependency, 35 Ohio St. L.J. 546 (1974).

[56] Vaisey, J., in Re Fry [1945] Ch. 348, 354.

[57] Many of the cases are collected in Daum, *supra* n. 53.

[58] Reported in The Boston Evening Globe, Dec. 10, 1975, at 47, 65.

[59] See Ch. 2 *supra* at n. 181.

[60] *Bromley* 95.

[61] *Ibid.*; Richette v. Ajello, 2 F.L.R. 2716 (Pa.C.P. 1976).

[62] *Marty & Raynaud* 675; cf. *Carbonnier, 1 Droit Civil* 243.

[63] *Marty & Raynaud* 675.

[64] *Ibid.*

[65] Carbonnier, 1 Droit Civil 245–247.

[66] French C.C. former art. 299.

[67] French C.C. new art. 264.

[68] See *Lindon* Nos. 311–316.

[69] *Beitzke* 50.

[70] New York Times, May 20, 1971, at 2.

[71] *Beitzke* 50.

[72] Böhmer, Die Neuregelung des Eheschliessungsrechts, Das Standesamt, Jan. 1975, at 5, 9.

[73] *Ibid.*

[74] EheG, new s. 13a(1).

[75] The present section of this chapter deals with economic relations between the spouses, but the internal financial relations of the spouses are also often of interest to third parties such as creditors and purchasers. These problems are discussed *infra* at 175–179.

[76] What follows is but a brief, schematic description. For more details, see *Rheinstein and Glendon, Int. Encyc.*

[77] An exception should perhaps be noted for those few German regions where, under the system of universal community property, a share of land would shift from one family to another, unless private contracts provided otherwise.

[78] Universally, it seems, the fund embarked upon her business by the married woman merchant was under her own management. But the opportunity to act as a trader depended upon the husband's revocable permission. Widely, but not universally, the withholding or revoking of such permission was subject to judicial control.

[79] *Supra* n. 1.

[80] F. Braudel, Capitalism and Material Life: 1400–1800, 122 (Kochan transl. 1973; orig. publ. 1967).

[81] *Stöcker* 556–557

[82] Blake, The Changing Status of Women in Developed Countries, Scientific American, Sept. 1974, at 144.

[83] *Rheinstein & Glendon, Int. Encyc.*

[84] *Cretney* 181. But cf. Glover, A Wife's Duty to Support her Husband, 126 New L.J. 356 (1976).

[85] *Bromley* 94.

[86] *Clark HB* 186.

[87] *Clark HB* 185–186.

[88] Portions of the material in this Section C are adapted from *Rheinstein and Glendon, Int. Encyc.*

[89] Müller-Freienfels, Equality of Husband and Wife in Family Law, 8 Int. & Comp. L.Q. 249, 261 (1959).

[90] Travaux de la semaine internationale de droit 1 (1937).

[91] Glendon, Matrimonial Property: A Comparative Study of Legal and Social Change, 49 Tul. L. Rev. 21, 22 (1974).

[92] *Rheinstein & Glendon, Int. Encyc.*

[93] In French law, "immovables" and "movables" correspond roughly but not exactly to what would be called real and personal property in common law systems.

[94] Sondages, La Réforme des régimes matrimoniaux, Rev. fr. opin. pub. 1967, 13.

[95] *4 Mazeaud* 113.

[96] Ribatto v. Ribatto, Trib. Digne 1 July 1972, D.S. 1973, 259.

[97] Ariz. Rev. Stat. Ann. §25–214, 25–215 (Supp. 1973); Cal. Civil Code §5125, 5127 (Supp. 1974); Nev. Rev. Stat. §123.230 (1973); Wash. Rev. Code §26.16.030 (Supp. 1973).

[98] Idaho Code 32–912 (1963), *as amended,* (Supp. 1975).

[99] Tex. Family Code Ann. §5.22 (1971).

[100] N.M. Stat. Ann. §57–4A–7, 57–4A–7.1, 57–4A–8 (Supp. 1973).

[101] Pascal, Updating Louisiana's Community of Gains, 49 Tul. L. Rev. 605 (1975).

[102] Pettitt v. Pettitt, [1970] A.C. 777; Gissing v. Gissing, [1971] A.C. 886.

[103] Where the parties have not formed a common intention, the court will "…impute to them a constructive common intention which is that which in the court's opinion would have been formed by reasonable spouses". Pettitt v. Pettitt, [1970] A.C. 777, 823.

[104] Latimer v. Latimer (C.A. 1970), noted in 114 Sol. J. 973 (1971); Peck v. Sheridan (C.A. 1971), noted in 115 Sol. J. 709; Cracknell v. Cracknell, [1971] P. 356 (C.A.); Matrimonial Proceedings and Property Act 1970, c. 45, §37; Davis v. Vale, [1971] 1 W.L.R. 1022 (C.A.).·

[105] This problem is, of course, not presented in community property jurisdictions.

[106] In re Roger's Question, [1948] 1 All. E.R. 328 (C.A.).

[107] Rimmer v. Rimmer, [1953] 1 Q.B. 63 (C.A.); Gissing v. Gissing, [1971] A.C. 886.

[108] See Re Figgis, [1969] 1 Ch. 123 (1968).

[109] E. Clive & J. Wilson, The Law of Husband and Wife in Scotland 289 (1974).

[110] Victoria: Marriage (Property) Act 1962, no. 6924, 20 Nov. 1962, 1962 Vict. Acts of Parl. 351; New Zealand, Matrimonial Property Act, no. 72, 23 Oct. 1963, 1 N.Z. Stat. 666 (1963).

[111] Davis, Recent Developments in Matrimonial Property Law in Australia, New Zealand and England, RabelsZ 35 (1971) 685–686.

[112] *Id.* at 688.

[113] *Id.* at 685.

[114] UMDA §307.

[115] The following discussion of the English treatment of the matrimonial home is based on A. Kiralfy, Comparative Law of Matrimonial Property 188–191 (1972).

[116] Clive & Wilson, *supra* n. 109 at 321–322.

[117] Denyer, Excluding the Husband from the Matrimonial Home, 123 New L.J. 664 (1973); cf. Ellis, The Right of Occupation of the Matrimonial Home and its Enforcement by the Courts, 4 Anglo-Am. L. Rev. 59–68 (1975).

[118] The Law Commission, First Report on Family Property Law (Law Comm. no. 52) (1973).

[119] Royal Commission on Marriage and Divorce (Morton Commission), par. 644, 650–653 (1956).

[120] Kiralfy, *supra* n. 115 at 180–181.

[121] The Law Commission, Working Paper No. 42, Family Property Law (1971); Matrimonial Property – Towards the Principle of "Community", 121 New L.J. 983–985 (1971).

[122] The Law Commission, First Report No. 52 (1973).

[123] See Deech, The Matrimonial Cash Problem, 123 New L.J. 1107–1108, 1117–1118 (1973).

[124] These property rights of one spouse in the other's real property arise as a matter of law upon marriage (or in the case of common law curtesy upon the birth of a live child from the marriage) but become possessory only when and if the property-owning spouse predeceases the other. See in general *Rheinstein & Glendon, Decedents' Estates* 89–90.

[125] See *infra* Ch. 6 at 279.

[126] In re Estate of Smith, 232 N.E.2d 310 (Ill. App. 1967). To the same effect is Rubenstein v. Mueller, 225 N.E.2d 540 (N.Y. Ct. App. 1967).

[127] Doucette v. Doucette, 279 N.E.2d 901 (Mass. 1972); Blanchette v. Blanchette, 287 N.E.2d 459 (Mass. 1972).

[128] Blanchette v. Blanchette, 287 N.E.2d 459 (Mass. 1972).

[129] Bowman v. Peterson, 102 N.E.2d 787 (Ill. 1951); Lutticke v. Lutticke, 92 N.E.2d 754 (Ill. 1950); Nickoloff v. Nickoloff, 51 N.E.2d 565 (Ill. 1943); Spina v. Spina, 22 N.E.2d 687 (Ill. 1937).

[130] Baker v. Baker, 107 N.E.2d 711 (Ill. 1952).

[131] UMDA, Prefatory Note p. 5.

[132] *Grundgesetz* (Basic Law) of 1949, §31.

[133] *Rheinstein, Family and Succession* 34.

[134] GleichberG, BGBl. I. 609.

[135] German C.C. §1378.

[136] German C.C. §1371.

[137] German C.C. §1365, 1369.

[138] I H. Dölle, Familienrecht 750 (1964–1965).

[139] German C.C. §1369.

[140] Note, *Current Legal Developments – Sweden*, 19 Int. & Comp. L.Q. 164 (1970).

[141] Cf. Gitter, Die soziale Sicherung der "Nur-Hausfrau", FamRZ 1974, 233; Höfer, Die soziale Sicherung der nichtsberufstätigen Hausfrau in Frankreich, Belgien und Italien (Stuttgart 1972).

[142] *Sundberg, Louvain Report*; the German reform law has been said to proceed "on the theory that both spouses were gainfully employed prior to the divorce and that they enjoy economic independence". Giesen, Divorce Reform in Germany, 7 Fam. L.Q. 351, 372 (1973).

[143] In a speech before the Women's National Democratic Club of Washington, D.C., in 1970, Swedish Prime Minister Olof Palme said "The public opinion is nowadays so well informed that if a politician today should declare that the woman ought to have a different role than the man and that it is natural that she devotes more time to the children he would be regarded to be of the Stone Age", reported in K. Davidson, R. Ginsburg & H. Kay, Sex-Based Discrimination 938, 942 (1974). According to the Prime Minister, 43% of married women in Sweden were estimated to be working outside the home in 1970. *Id.* at 943. In West Germany in 1970, 35.5% of married women were so working, Bericht der Bundesregierung über die Massnahmen zur Verbesserung der Situation der Frau, 46–47 Drucksache VI/3689 (1972). In Sweden, as in West Germany and the United States, statements that housewife-marriage is no longer the dominant pattern have to be understood as referring to the fact that most women work outside the home at some time during their married lives, not to the numbers of married women working at the time of any given survey.

[144] Ramm, Gleichberechtigung und Hausfrauenehe, JZ 1968, 41, 44; see also Ramm, Der Funktionswandel der Ehe und das Recht, JZ 1975, 505.

[145] Familienpolitik der Sozialdemokratischen Partei Deutschlands, Entwurf 10 (1972).

[146] See *Rheinstein & Glendon, Int. Encyc.*, for Tables and analysis of data on married women's labor force participation and economic dependency.

[147] Mill, The Subjection of Women, in Essays on Sex Equality 168 (Rossi ed. 1970).

[148] *Rheinstein, M.S.D.L.* 25–27, 202. Dörner's study has revealed that it is likely that Frederick's ideas about population policy were probably more at work in the family law provisions than the notion of individual liberty as such, *Dörner* 59–60. See *infra* Chapter 5 at 215.

[149] *Rheinstein, M.S.D.L.* at 127 n.1.

[150] *Infra* Chapter 5 at 231.

[151] See generally Blake, *supra* n. 82.

[152] *Infra* Chapter 6 at 247–264.

[153] *Stöcker* 555.

[154] Savatier, *supra* n. 7 at 187.

[155] See Chapter 5 *infra* at 202.

[156] Reich, The New Property, 73 Yale L.J. 733 (1964). See *infra* 165–169.

[157] *Carbonnier, Flexible Droit* 131.

[158] I. R. Powell, Real Property 22–34 (Rohan ed. 1973).

[159] T. Arnold, The Folklore of Capitalism Chs. V, VII (1937).

[160] Moore, The Emergence of New Property Conceptions in America, 1 J. Leg. & Pol. Soc. 34, 53 (1943).

[161] Reich, *supra* n. 156 at 733.

[162] *Id.* at 738–739.

[163] *Carbonnier, Flexible Droit* 131–132.

[164] *Id.* at 132.

[165] Boston Sunday Globe, April 11, 1976, at 1, 28.

[166] U.S. Census Bureau, Current Population Reports, Series P–60, No. 99, July 1975.

[167] Reported in F. Terré and A. Sayag, Conscience et Connaissance du Droit, Annex A at 4–10 (1975).

[168] *Supra* n. 140.

[169] *Sundberg, Marriage or No Marriage* 224.

[170] E.g. Weitzman, Legal Regulation of Marriage: Tradition and Change, A Proposal for Individual Contracts and Contracts in Lieu of Marriage, 62 Calif. L. Rev. 1169, 1170 (1974); Note, *Marriage Contracts for Support and Services: Constitutionality Begins at Home*, 49 N.Y.U.L. Rev. 1161 (1974). Such proposals are extensively discussed and evaluated in B. Babcock, A. Freedman, E. Norton and S. Ross, Sex Discrimination and the Law 647–657 (1975) and have attracted the attention of most other recent books on family law and sex discrimination law.

[171] Cohen, The Basis of Contract, 46 Harv. L. Rev. 553, 571 (1933).

[172] Willis, The Rationale of the Law of Contracts, 11 Ind. L.J. 227, 230 (1936).

[173] H. Hart & A. Sacks, The Legal Process 477 (Tentative ed. 1958).

[174] An indication of the likely future trend is Dawley v. Dawley, 551 P.2d 323. (Cal. 1976), where traditional public policy objections to advance pre-marital planning for the possibility of divorce were brushed aside, and "realistic planning that takes account of the possibility of dissolution" upheld.

[175] See *Rheinstein & Glendon, Int. Encyc.*

[176] French C.C. arts. 1081–1090. See also Ch. 6 *infra* at 287.

[177] *Rheinstein, Int. Encyc.* §10.

[178] *Infra* n. 182.

[179] Chapter 2 *supra* at 65–66.

[180] *Drinan* 53.

[181] Chapter 3 *supra* at 93.

[182] Eisenstadt v. Baird, 405 U.S. 438, 453 (1972).

[183] *E.g.* N.Y. Exec. Law §291 (McKinney Supp. 1975).

[184] Sex Discrimination Act 1975 s. 3; see Birtles and Hewitt, Equal Pay and Sex Discrimination – I, 126 New L.J. 205, 207 (1976).

[185] *Bénabent* 446.
[186] *Id.* 480–486.
[187] *Bénabent* 489–490.
[188] Ch. 5 *infra* at 202 *et seq.*
[189] *Bénabent* 485.
[190] *Beitzke* §12 III.
[191] *Müller-Freienfels, supra* n. 50.
[192] *Bromley* 359. The most thorough examination of the regulation (or perhaps one should say non-regulation) of the property relationship of husband and wife with respect to creditors in the United States is Landers, The Bankrupt's Spouse: The Forgotten Character in the Bankruptcy Drama, 1974 Utah L. Rev. 709–759.
[193] E.g. Ill. Ann. Stat. ch. 68 §15 (Smith-Hurd 1959).
[194] *Bromley* 121–124.
[195] German C.C. §1362.
[196] French C.C. art. 1409.
[197] French C.C. arts. 1409, 1411, 1414.
[198] French C.C. art. 1413.
[199] On the latter situation see Chapter 6 *infra* at 279 *et seq.*
[200] Kyle v. Albert, 2 Fam. L. Rptr. 2361 (Pa. Ct. C.P., March 16, 1976).
[201] Law Reform (Miscellaneous Provisions) Act 1970 s. 4, 5(a) and (c).
[202] *Bromley* 103–104.
[203] *Carbonnier, 2 Droit Civil* 22, 68.
[294] *Beitzke* 58.
[205] *Sundberg, Marriage or No Marriage* 231.
[206] Higher rates are applied notably to what is called "non-work" income of married persons. LVIIa Cahiers de Droit Fiscal International, Le régime fiscal des unités familiales (revenus, fortune, successions) I(/)11 (1972). *Sundberg, Louvain Report.*
[207] *Id.* 1/5. Informal unions in which the partners have a common child or were once married to each other receive such treatment.
[208] Bittker, Federal Income Taxation and the Family, 27 Stan. L. Rev. 1389, 1430 (1975).
[209] *Id.* at 1395.
[210] 60 A.B.A.J. 454 (1974).
[211] Application of Gaulkin, 351 A.2d 740 (N.J. 1976).
[212] Professional Ethics Opinions, Formal Opinion No. 340 (September 23, 1975), 61 A.B.A.J. 1542 (1975).
[213] Cour d'appel de Paris, 2 Feb. 1973, D.S. 1973. Jur. 524.
[214] *Ibid.*

EFFECTS OF LEGAL MARRIAGE: FREE TERMINABILITY

I. Marriage Dissolution: A Legal and a Social Phenomenon

One of the reasons for introducing the tinkers Michael and Sarah in the first chapter of this book was to fix, for the purposes of analysis, the distinction between marriage as a legal institution and as a social or religious institution. Long before marriage became encrusted with all the legal features by which it was characterized on the eve of the series of changes described in this book, Thomas Aquinas had found it useful to distinguish between marriage as a "civil contract" and marriage as a phenomenon of nature; and further, between those two views of marriage and the view of marriage as a sacrament. Just as marriage itself is both a legal and a social phenomenon, so is the subject matter of this chapter – marriage termination. Just as Michael and Sarah, despite their failure to come to terms with the priest, may have been "married" in the social sense, so a man or woman who ceases to live in a formal or informal marriage has "dissolved" that marriage. There has never been a society where divorce, or some functional equivalent, did not exist.[1] In Ireland, where legal marriage is indissoluble and where the Constitution expressly provides, "No law shall be enacted providing for the grant of a dissolution of marriage",[2] the only forms of marriage dissolution available are the very limited ones afforded under ecclesiastical law,[3] and that which is effected informally by the simple departure of one of the spouses. An unhappy modern-day Michael or Sarah might well choose the latter route on much the same reasoning which led the tinkers to give up on the priest.

When the common life between the spouses is at an end, the marriage in a social sense is also at an end. But what this chapter is concerned with is the *legal* termination of marriage. As with legal marriage, legal marriage termination overlaps but does not exactly coincide with the social phenomenon it purports to regulate. Legal marriage termination itself has two aspects which claim our attention: it releases the spouses from the legal marriage bond thus enabling them to legally remarry, and it terminates or alters the effects of legal marriage. The present chapter will be concerned primarily with the first aspect. So far as the second aspect is concerned, we have just seen in Chapter 4 how marriage is already being deprived of many of its legal effects through the evolution of the law of the on-going marriage, thus leaving less for the divorce law to operate on when it comes in to finish the job. On the other hand, in the following chapter, Chapter 6, we will see that it is not necessarily the case that a dissolution of the marriage bond will terminate all the economic effects of marriage, and that in fact divorce itself may produce legal effects which resemble the continuation of the economic ties between married persons.

But in the present chapter, our attention will be concentrated on the dissolution of the legal bond. Even here, however, it is necessary to distinguish between the terminating event (the divorce proceeding) and the resulting state of being divorced and therefore capable of entering another legal marriage. With respect to the event itself, we are once again dealing with a phenomenon which has important social, as well as legal, aspects. For even where legal divorce is unknown, the termination of the married state is often marked by a rite of some sort. In fact the modern divorce proceeding resembles a ritual change of social status much more than it does an ordinary lawsuit.

König has postulated that the complexity of divorce rituals bears a direct relationship to the elaborateness of the marriage rite.[4] Where the marriage rite is attended with great pomp and ceremony, the chances are the reverse rite, divorce, will be also. The analysis of legal developments in Chapter 2 and in the present chapter seems to bear out König and those whose work he relies on. In Chapter 2 on the formation of marriage we saw a steady movement toward reducing legal regulation, especially the compulsory ceremonial aspects, of the formation of marriage. The present chapter will show that exactly the same process is occurring in divorce law. What social factors are characteristically associated with elaborate marriage and divorce rituals? König tells us that where there is a high degree of family involvement in and control of marriage formation, it is usual to find the practice of producing arguments and reasons for its termination, presumably in order to neutralize objections from involved groups of relatives.[5] Similarly, he notes that emphasis on property exchange before a marriage and property relations during marriage is characteristically associated with elaborate procedures for undoing such arrangements.[6] As we have just seen in Chapters 2 and 4, legal changes, themselves reflecting underlying social and economic changes, have greatly diminished family involvement in, and the property aspects of, modern marriages. The economic dimension has not of course disappeared. Rather, as we will see in Chapter 6, it is being put on a new basis and in the process being freed from dependence on the existence of formal legal family relationships.

Viewing marriage dissolution as a social phenomenon as well as a legal institution enabled Rheinstein to demonstrate convincingly that if marriage stability is a problem in modern society, attention has to be focused on marriage breakdown and its causes; that "divorce" is not a cause but a symptom of marriage breakdown.[7] The search for "causes" of marriage breakdown can really do no more than identify factors characteristically found associated with the incidence of marriage breakdown. When such factors are identified, however, they turn out to include many matters over which law has little or no control, or as to which most persons would not want to see legal control: life styles in which the work place is separate from the home and family members spend large parts of their day apart; the greater educational and employment opportunities enjoyed by women; family pressure; younger age at marriage; longer life expectancy and consequent longer duration of marriages; long-lasting unemployment; separations such as those caused by military service; and other aspects of what is often called "modernization".[8]

Thinking of marriage dissolution as a social phenomenon casts doubt, however, on whether a high incidence of marriage breakdown is a peculiarly modern phenomenon.[9] Parsons and Bales, for example, have estimated that more "divorce" took place (through separation and desertion) in 19th century America than at the relatively quiescent period during which they were writing in the 1950s, even though the official rates for the 19th century were low.[10]

These puzzles concerning the causes, extent and modernity of marriage breakdown will have to be left to others. The modest aim of this chapter will be to demonstrate how the legal institution of divorce has changed radically within less than 10 years in five countries. During this period, law reformers seem increasingly to have been influenced by an awareness of the growing discrepancy between the sets of social and legal marriages, so much so that in recent legal writing in all five countries the emphasis is strongly on the positive aspects of legal divorce – its role in terminating conflict and in permitting the regularization of new family situations.[11]

II. *Patterns of Change in the Legal Phenomenon*
A. *England: Divorce Reform Act, 1969*

1. Prelude

Judicial divorce was not available in England until the passage of the Matrimonial Causes Act of 1857, which went into effect in 1858.[12] Previously,
divorce was obtainable only by a special act of Parliament, a system which
restricted divorce to a wealthy few.[13] By the end of the 18th century, the
practice of Parliament was to admit only petitions on the ground of adultery.
For social and economic reasons, access to divorce in practice seems to have
been further restricted by sex. There are only four reported cases of parliamentary divorces on a wife's petition.[14] Apart from transferring jurisdiction from Parliament to the courts, the 1857 law made little change in this
state of affairs.

Following the prior parliamentary practice, the new law made divorce
available only on grounds of adultery, which was judged according to
different standards for men and women. While a man could divorce his wife
for a single act of adultery, a woman could divorce her husband only if his
adultery was aggravated by special circumstances such as desertion or
extreme physical cruelty. It was not until 1923 that a woman was finally
enabled to divorce her husband for a single act of adultery without aggravat-
ing circumstances; and not until 1937 that a law made divorce available on the
following grounds besides adultery: desertion for three years, cruelty, and
supervening, incurable insanity.[15] This latter ground was, of course, an initial
recognition of the idea that a spouse might be divorced without being
chargeable with any "fault". In addition, the 1937 law expanded the grounds
for nullity.

More significant changes took place in the aftermath of World War II. The
divorce courts were made much more widely accessible when the Legal Aid
and Advice Act went into effect in 1950.[16] Then began that process, so well
described in the studies conducted by Rheinstein, through which the strict
divorce laws on the books of various countries were converted by the courts
into a system of easy divorce by mutual consent.[17] According to the Law
Commission, 93% of the petitions under the pre-1969 law were undefended.[18] In many of the remaining cases, cross-petitions were filed by both
spouses – each wanting the divorce, but for economic reasons wanting the
other spouse to appear as the guilty party of record.[19] In England, as elsewhere, the high post-war incidence of divorce cases, the great majority of

which were undefended, raised the question of whether any changes should be made in the law.

The question was examined in the Report of the Morton Commission of 1956, and in the Reports of the Archbishop of Canterbury's Group and of The Law Commission, both of which were published in 1966.[20]

The searching, meticulous and extensive studies done by all three groups of the social and legal aspects of divorce law reform had great influence not only on the course eventually taken by English law, but also on the thinking of law reformers in other countries. For our purposes it is interesting to see the contrast between how the case for eliminating fault from the divorce laws looked to the Morton Commission in 1956 and how it looked just 10 years later to the Law Commission and to the Archbishop's Group. Only one member of 19 on the Morton Commission thought that fault should be eliminated from the divorce laws. Of the remaining 18 members who thought fault grounds should be retained as the basis of the law, nine thought that breakdown of the marriage should not be introduced even as an additional ground for divorce. Even the nine members who were *for* breakdown as an added ground, thought that it should be available in principle only where husband and wife had lived apart for seven years *and* the petition was not objected to by the defendant spouse. It was due to the introduction in Parliament in 1963 of a bill providing for divorce on this type of added ground that the matter once more came in for intensive study.[21] The Report of the Archbishop of Canterbury's Group, *Putting Asunder: A Divorce Law for Contemporary Society*, drew a clear distinction between religious law and the secular law of the State and set itself the task of developing a Christian position with respect to a social problem affecting both believers and non-believers.[22] The report expressed dissatisfaction with the existing system of collusive divorce. To the surprise of many at the time, it favored reorganization of the law with breakdown of the marriage as the exclusive ground for divorce. But to guard against abuse, the fact of breakdown was to be established by an elaborate judicial inquest.[23] The Report of the Law Commission, which appeared late in 1966, considered the Report of the Archbishop's Group along with other proposals. It agreed with the Archbishop's Group that the matrimonial offense principle did not provide an adequate basis for a good modern divorce law. But it found the idea of breakdown with inquest to be too elaborate, expensive and time-consuming to be practicable. As the Law Commission saw it, the "Field of Choice" for reform narrowed down to three alternatives:[24] (1) A system of breakdown, but without the elaborate inquest foreseen by the Archbishop's Group, might be established as the sole ground for divorce, with proof of a period of separation sufficing as evidence of breakdown unless evidence to the contrary were produced. The Commission judged that this system would not be feasible as the *sole* ground for divorce if the period of separation were much more than six months. It recognized that Parliament would probably not adopt a law which afforded a divorce so quickly in all cases, and thus set forth two other alternatives. (2) Mutual consent divorce might be added to the other grounds for divorce. It could not be the sole ground because although the majority of divorces are in fact consent divorces there are still cases where one spouse remains opposed. A spouse who had been guilty of conduct which would have justified divorce under the prior law should not be allowed to block a divorce by withholding his consent. (3) Finally, the Law Commission suggested that breakdown might be added to other grounds in the form of divorce after a period of separation. Where the other spouse consented or did not object, the period would be two years. After a period of five or seven years, divorce would be granted even if the other spouse did object.

All three of the Law Commission's proposals contradicted certain basic ideas of the Archbishop's Group: the first because it did not provide for adequate judicial inquiry; the second because it permitted the parties themselves to dissolve their marriage; the second and third because they retained fault grounds alongside no-fault grounds, thereby perpetuating the defects of the old fault-based law.

2. The 1969 Reform

In November 1966, the members of the Law Commission entered into discussions with the Archbishop's Group concerning the points of difference between their two reports. As a result of these discussions, the Law Commission put forward proposals that became, with slight modifications, the Divorce Reform Act, 1969, which went into effect on 1 January 1971. (This delay was to enable Parliament to reform the law of maintenance in a statute which went into effect at the same time as the divorce law.)[25]

The Divorce Reform Act, now consolidated in the Matrimonial Causes Act, 1973, was, as Professor Bromley has characterized it, an "unhappy compromise".[26] Section 1(1) of the Act declares that the sole ground of divorce will be the irretrievable breakdown of the marriage. But Section 1(2) of the Act makes it clear that all the reform law really does is preserve the traditional offense grounds and add the separation grounds to them. Section 1(2) provides:[27]

(2) The court...shall not hold the marriage to have broken down irretrievably unless

the petitioner satisfies the court of one or more of the following facts, that is to say

(a) that the respondent has committed adultery and the petitioner finds it intolerable to live with the respondent;

(b) that the respondent has behaved in such a way that the petitioner cannot reasonably be expected to live with the respondent;

(c) that the respondent has deserted the petitioner for a continuous period of at least two years immediately preceding the presentation of the petition;

(d) that the parties to the marriage have lived apart for a continuous period of at least two years immediately preceding the presentation of the petition and the respondent consents to a decree being granted;

(e) that the parties to the marriage have lived apart for a continuous period of at least five years immediately preceding the presentation of the petition.

Even when one of these five situations has been proved, the divorce is not to be granted unless the court is satisfied on all the evidence that the marriage has in fact broken down irretrievably. The court has the duty "to inquire, so far as it reasonably can, into the facts alleged" by the petitioner or respondent.[28] As we shall see, in most undefended cases, "so far as it reasonably can" has come to mean little more than that a Registrar will scrutinize the affidavit evidence of the allegations in a petition before certifying that all is in order.[29] Further restriction on the availability of divorce is provided by the continuation in the 1969 law of a provision, introduced in 1937, that no divorce petition can be presented in the first three years of marriage unless "...the case is one of exceptional hardship suffered by the petitioner or of exceptional depravity on the part of the respondent".[30] Furthermore, the divorce decree, once granted, does not become absolute until a period of three months has passed. Provisions designed to promote reconciliation figure prominently in the Act, as they did in the discussions that preceded it.

Thus the modest innovations of the Act are simply that mutual consent divorce (which, disguised as fault divorce, accounted for the overwhelming majority of divorces in the past) is brought out in the open and permitted after a two year separation; and that unilateral divorce is permitted after a five year separation. This latter ground was greeted by some as a "Casanova's charter."[31] (Impetuous, these English Casanovas!) As a practical matter, its primary use is probably to regularize stable unions. Since the two-year separation ground requires the active consent of the respondent (as distinguished from mere lack of opposition to the petition), this ground cannot be

used to divorce an insane spouse.[32] Thus presumably resort will also be had to
the five-year separation ground in that special case.

Special provisions were included for the protection of the respondent when
the two new grounds for divorce are used. In the case of unilateral divorce
after five years' separation, the court must dismiss the petition if it believes
the respondent's allegation that the dissolution of the marriage will result in
"grave financial or other hardship" to him or her and that it would "in all the
circumstances be wrong" to dissolve the marriage.[33] Also, where the only
grounds on which divorce is sought are the grounds of two or five years'
separation, the court may refuse to make the decree absolute until it is
satisfied that the financial provision, if any, to be made by the petitioner for
the respondent is reasonable and fair, or the best that can be made under the
circumstances.[34] Finally, a court may not in any case pronounce an absolute
decree unless it has made an order with reference to arrangements for any
children of the marriage.[35]

Judicial separation, under the Divorce Reform Act of 1969, is now available
on the same basis as is divorce, except that the breakdown of the marriage is
not an issue.[36] The decree for separation is granted upon proof of any of the
five sets of facts that in a divorce case would prove breakdown. After five
years' separation, the decree can of course be converted into a divorce. It is
said that the separation provisions are of interest primarily where a decree
of divorce cannot be obtained because three years have not elapsed
from the time of the celebration of the marriage, or where neither party
wishes to remarry but one party wishes to take advantage of the court's
ancillary powers.

Meanwhile, the Finer Committee estimated in 1974 that at least 11,000
marriages a year are being effectively terminated through "non-cohabitation
orders" by Magistrates' Courts under the Matrimonial Proceedings (Magistrates' Courts) Act of 1960. These orders, which have the same effect as a
decree of judicial separation, can be made only upon showing that the
defendant is guilty of a matrimonial offense. "The result", as the Committee
pointed out, "has been to produce two sets of laws dealing with matrimonial
breakdown, operating concurrently, but in different courts, and standing,
both in the spirit and the letter, in the most remarkable contrast to each
other".[37] In its highly-regarded Report on One-Parent Families, the Committee has recommended the establishment of a unified Family Court system
to deal with matrimonial disputes and with children.

3. The Aftermath of Reform

The years that have passed since the 1969 Act went into effect furnish an opportunity to form some judgments about how it has worked and how it can be expected to work in practice. It is now clear that the "unhappy compromise" is not serving the hopes and expectations of either the Archbishop's Group or the Law Commission.

The Archbishop's Group and the Law Commission were agreed that when a marriage has failed to the point where there is no reasonable likelihood of the parties again living together as husband and wife, the legal tie should be dissolved in a way which involves "maximum fairness, and the minimum bitterness, distress and humiliation".[38] But marital fault not only remains important in proving the first three types of "breakdown" under the Act; it has also continued to be important in maintenance and child custody questions.[39] Despite the addition of objective grounds to fault grounds, in 1972 the most popular single ground for divorce remained adultery (32,960 of 106,560 decrees) and many decrees were still based on the general misconduct ground (21,710).[40]

Furthermore, there is reason to believe that the percentage of divorces granted on objective grounds may go down. The figures for 1972 (20,669 divorces on 2 years' separation and consent; 22,030 on five years' separation) may simply reflect the regularization of long-standing *de facto* separations. The fault grounds may be expected to retain or even gain popularity because they offer two advantages over the objective grounds: speed, and leverage in bargaining over maintenance or child custody questions.

Accordingly fault grounds will still be chosen by many couples when both desire a quick divorce, or where one party's desire for a quick divorce has resulted in a trade-off of financial advantages to the other.[41] Fault grounds are also employed when the spouses have not been able to agree on financial or child custody matters. They then often file cross-petitions alleging the other's fault as part of their jockeying for position with respect to the ultimate judicial settlement of these matters.[42] Conduct remains an important factor in the judicial disposition of these questions, which are called "ancillary," but which are actually, as Bromley points out, *the* vital issues.[43]

While fault remains important, the concept of fault has undergone subtle changes in the case law. Attention has shifted from the blameworthiness of the acts of one spouse to the effect the conduct has on the other spouse; and from misconduct in the traditional categories to a more generalized idea of responsibility for the breakdown of the marriage.[44] Professor Finlay, remarking on this tendency of the courts to take up where the legislature left off in eliminating marital misconduct, nevertheless concludes that Parliament ought to act:[45]

[I]t may well be that legislation will complete the process more quickly and deliver the *coup de grace* to what has clearly proved to be outmoded and out of touch with modern thinking. It would on the whole be preferable, it is submitted, for the community to take a clear stand than to prolong the inevitable: a lingering death for the principle of matrimonial fault.

Along with the desire to eliminate from marriage dissolution the bitterness which fault divorce engendered or at least exacerbated, both the Archbishop's Group and the Law Commission had thought that the divorce law should perform a positive social function by facilitating and encouraging reconciliation between estranged couples.[46] The Reform Act thus introduced provisions designed to aid in bringing such couples together.[47] Five years later, it is agreed that the effort was futile. Cretney says, "[I]t is doubtful if they have had any significant effect."[48] Jackson puts it more bluntly, "The fact is that the reconciliation provisions are a dead letter."[49] To Freeman, they are a "sham".[50]

Another feature of the Act which reflected strong views of the Law Commission and the Church of England group was the provision that unilateral divorce should be denied where it would result in "grave financial or other hardship" to the respondent.[51] However, there have in fact been few cases where a decree has been refused under this provision. As Cretney says, "The section seems to be used primarily to protect middle-aged and elderly wives against the loss of pension rights, and then only very sparingly."[52]

As for the provision of the Act that the court must "...inquire, so far as it reasonably can, into the facts alleged by the petitioner and into any facts alleged by the respondent", it now seems clear that in practice in all except in the small minority of contested cases, the form of judicial inquest is but an empty ritual and the result is but a rubber-stamping of the parties' agreement.

A 1973 Bristol University study of undefended divorce petitions in three county courts found that the great majority of cases (85%) took less than 10 minutes each.[53] In two of the three courts studied, 61% of the cases took less than five minutes, and in the courtroom of one judge, the average case time was four minutes. Furthermore, regardless of how the hearing was conducted, "the result was invariably the same. A decree was granted."[54]

This finding is not surprising. The judges have little choice but to accept evidence in an undefended case at face value.[55] The perfunctory nature of the hearing not only means that the Act's aspiration toward judicial inquest has resulted in mere form in most cases; more importantly, it has also served to undermine the aim to eliminate, so far as possible, bitterness and humiliation from divorce proceedings. For, in the four to ten minutes allotted to each case, the proceeding consists typically of nothing but a long recital in open court by one party of the other party's misconduct or of embarrassing details of the couple's private life.[56] The 1973 survey, which included interviews with petitioners, found this one of the most distressing aspects of divorce under the new act. In this respect divorce under the new act has remained much the same as under the old law.[57]

It is thus not surprising that the requirement of this pro forma hearing was quietly done away with for most undefended petitions through amendments in 1973 and 1975 to the rules of procedure for matrimonial cases, and a new "special procedure" established under which the judge pronounces the decree after a Registrar certifies that he is satisfied with the allegations of the affidavits in support of the petition.[58] The parties need not appear in court, either to testify or to hear the decree. In 1976, the Lord Chancellor recommended that this "special procedure" be extended to all uncontested cases, even those involving children, and that legal aid be withdrawn from such cases. Thus, although the language of the 1969 Act remains unchanged, judicial inquest divorce is being converted unobtrusively into registration of the parties' agreement.

The failure of the Act to deal adequately with the very problems which led up to law reform in 1969 has now produced new calls for reform. But current discussions of reform have a new tone. The issues now seem to be between outright unilateral divorce with no inquest and a short waiting period and other versions of the breakdown principle with the element of misconduct eliminated; and between retaining the judicial process or developing other fora for settling marital disputes.

Eekelaar proposes a system of divorce available to either spouse on proof of one year's "estrangement".[59] Estrangement would be presumed if there is no evidence presented to the contrary and if the parties have not shared a common life for twelve months. Estrangement would be conclusively presumed (i.e. the court would have no choice but to grant the decree) if not less than 12 nor more than 13 months have passed from the institution of divorce proceedings or filing of a "notice of intention" to divorce.

In fact it would probably make little practical difference whether further reforms moved to open unilateral divorce or to a pure breakdown ground, since, as Lord Simon of Glaisdale has pointed out, there is really no answer to the firm insistence by one spouse that a marriage has broken down:

If even one of the parties adamantly refuses to consider living with the other again, the court is in no position to gainsay him or her. The court cannot say, 'I have seen your wife in the witness-box. She wants your marriage to continue. She seems a most charming and blameless person. I cannot believe that the marriage has really broken down.' The husband has only to reply, 'I'm very sorry; it's not what *you* think about her that matters, it's what *I* think. I am not prepared to live with her any more.' He may add for good measure, 'What is more, there is another person with whom I prefer to live.' The court may think that the husband is behaving wrongly and unreasonably; but how is it to hold that the marriage has not irretrievably broken down?[60]

The eventual adoption of these proposals, should it occur, will do no more than conform the law to reality since, as Cretney has observed and the experience of other countries with similar laws has confirmed, "there will be few cases in which a divorce will not ultimately be granted, if even one party wants it".[61] If the matter does come up for reconsideration in England, the comparative law context will be considerably different from what it was in 1969. At that time there were no working models of pure no-fault or unilateral divorce statutes to look to. The Law Commission in 1966 had been influenced strongly by the fact that systems of mixed no-fault grounds were operating in Australia, New Zealand, and the United States.[62] In 1975 however, Australia adopted a new Family Law which abolished matrimonial fault and substituted a system of irretrievable breakdown to be established by the simple fact of 12 months' separation.[63] "Separation" is expressly made to include situations where termination of cohabitation is due to the conduct of only one of the spouses and where the spouses continue to share the same dwelling. In the United States, marriage breakdown was established as the sole ground of divorce in 1970 in both the California divorce law and in the Uniform Marriage and Divorce Act, and, in late 1976, such laws had been adopted by a total of 11 American states.

So far as divorce procedure is concerned, English discussions increasingly distinguish between the granting of the divorce itself and the handling of the economic and child-related matters. Although discussion is not framed in these terms, the dissolution of a particular marriage is being seen more and more as a matter in which there is little State concern. The "vital issues" are, as Professor Bromley says, financial provision and child welfare. The 1973 Bristol study shed some interesting light on the view which divorce "consumers" take of the present system from this point of view. The research group found that many petitioners were "puzzled" about the nature of the proceeding in which they had to recite their wrongs.[64] Most saw little point in going to court at all. But at the same time the majority were surprised at how little attention was paid to their children's welfare.[65] For many, the primary reason for getting a divorce was said not to be to get a "license to remarry" but, precisely, to sort out financial details and make arrangements concerning their children.[66] The investigators, wondering whether there might be some felt need for a ceremony or ritual to mark the change of a social status, asked the petitioners whether they thought a divorce should involve some sort of ceremony. Only 27 of 102 replied that they thought it should. One of the majority who disagreed, summed up the present system as "a lot of hoo-haa for nothing".[67]

The study concluded:[68]

In the light of our research findings we seriously question whether such hearings command the confidence and respect of the petitioners themselves. We also question whether, in issues where there is seldom any legal dispute, the traditional adversary procedure is the most appropriate, efficient and economic way of granting decrees and adjudicating on the matters that result from broken marriage.

But at the same time the study clearly identified a desire on the part of divorce consumers for more procedures to investigate the welfare of their children, and for more supervision of financial arrangements. Thus, from the point of view of those directly affected the system is topsy-turvy: the vital issues as to which weaker parties may need protection and help being arranged privately out of court.

Jackson, Q.C., commented recently:

Whether divorce should remain a matter of judicial process remains to be seen: it certainly cannot be taken for granted that it will, particularly as the fight seems to be between the protagonists of consensual divorce and the protagonists of the right of unilateral divorce (divorce by rejection), none of whom are satisfied by the compromise of the Act of 1969 and none of whom require an adjudication.[69]

In any event, proposals, such as that of the Finer Committee, for a comprehensive family court system, have not found a warm official reception in the present day climate of governmental austerity in Britain. Rather, the demise of judicial inquest in divorce seems to be taking place in England, without reports, debates or discussion, not in furtherance of any particular family policy, but simply in response to over-crowded courts and the need for economy.[70]

B. France: Divorce Reform Law, 1975

1. Prelude

Up to 1 January 1976, when France's new divorce law went into effect, the prior law had been virtually unchanged for 92 years. In comparison with England, however, the history of divorce in France had been eventful and colorful.

While England made only timid inroads on the ecclesiastical principle of the indissolubility of marriage, the French revolutionary divorce law of 20 September 1792 made an all-out assault. It established several forms of divorce, among them divorce obtainable upon mutual consent and upon unilateral application on grounds of incompatibility of temperament.[71] The 1792 divorce law in general and this ground in particular, though hedged in by time-consuming formalities, were thought to express the idea that any indissoluble tie is an infringement of individual liberty and that, therefore, the principle of individual liberty presupposes a natural right to divorce.[72] By 1804, when the Code Napoleon was adopted, this was far from being the dominant ideology in France; indeed, were it not for the personal interest which Napoleon himself took in the drafting of the divorce provisions of the Code, it is doubtful whether even divorce by mutual consent would have survived.[73] As it happened, divorce by mutual consent did not long endure. The uneasy balance in the realm of ideas, politics and law between what has often been characterized as "les deux Frances"[74] – the France of conservative, Catholic, family-oriented tradition on the one hand, and the France of the spirit of the liberal-individualistic ideas of the Enlightenment and the "men of '92", on the other – had shifted, and in 1816 divorce was completely abolished. Its demise was accompanied by this comment of a member of the Law Commission of 1815: "For twenty years in France men have made laws like themselves – feeble and fleeting. Let us now finally establish those eternal laws which make men rather than being made by them".[75]

Eternity turned out to last for 68 years – until 1884 when divorce was re-introduced by the Loi Naquet (so named after its author), under which divorce was available only on grounds of adultery, condemnation to an infamous punishment[76] and grave violation of marital duties.[77] This scheme of divorce-sanction lasted without substantial change until 1975 by which time there was wide consensus in French society on the need for, although not the direction of, reform.

When the government of Giscard d'Estaing prepared to make good its promise to reform the divorce laws, it discovered that in the France of the 1970s there were still *"deux Frances"*. The spirit of '92 was flourishing in some of the learned writing,[78] and the divorce reform proposals of the socialist and communist parties were seeking to eliminate fault divorce completely and replace it with divorce for objective grounds[79] such as irretrievable break-down of the marriage or permanent disruption of the life in common. A proposal for divorce upon the unilateral allegation of marriage breakdown was also presented by the *Association Nationale des Avocats de France* who argued that such a change was desirable on practical grounds.[80]

In addition to substantial opposition to this solution from the expected strongholds of conservative family policy, the public opinion surveys which were made at the behest of the government for the express purpose of aiding in the preparation of reforms showed considerable ambivalence within the population on the subject.[81] The survey results suggested further that this ambivalence is not just a reflection of age, regional, class, educational or income differences in the French population but also an ambivalence of individual Frenchmen and Frenchwomen.[82] As Rheinstein had already pointed out in his 1971 study of marriage stability and divorce in several countries, the two Frances, since they are in the realm of ideas, can and do co-exist within the souls of many individual French people.[83]

Thus it is not surprising that the principal architect of the new law, Dean Jean Carbonnier, has said, in explaining the hypotheses along which the preceding government had asked him to proceed, that divorce for objective grounds was rejected as the guiding principle of the reform, although two limited forms of it were added to fault grounds.[84] In spite of the draftsmen's full awareness of the kinds of arguments which had won the day for objective grounds in Sweden, in the Uniform Marriage and Divorce Act and similar acts in force in several American states, and in the West German reform proposal then pending before the Bundestag, the discussion of objective grounds in France still, in Dean Carbonnier's words, "...comes down to divorce by repudiation, a tragedy for the wife, the object of horror for our Western societies".[85] Divorce on fault grounds, the object of so much criticism from practitioners as well as academic experts, was retained in the reform law because, as Dean Carbonnier explained further,

There are some marital conflicts which the popular mentality continues to characterize in terms of culpability and to resolve in terms of sanctions – all the more vigorously when, in the popular view, the faults which have caused the divorce are those which flaunt the very duties which constitute marriage. To underestimate the force of these elementary reflexes would gratuitously compromise the reception of the reform in the nation.[86]

Thus, he said, the reform envisaged a "pluralistic system of grounds for divorce".[87]

2. The 1975 Reform Law

Once again, then, as in 1804, the legal response to the social reality was to offer a compromise, and, as a primary solution, divorce by mutual consent. But of course the social reality of 1975 was not that of 1804, and the legal solution offered to the problems of divorce in late 20th century France is a far different law from the short-lived solution built into the Code of 1804. The new system offers so many altenative forms of divorce that it has already been characterized as the "divorce *à la carte* law". It is clear, however, that the legislature intended one of these forms, divorce by mutual agreement, to be the "preferred form", and that the other forms (fault divorce, *"resignation-divorce"*; divorce after legal separation; and two limited types of divorce on objective grounds) would be resorted to only in exceptional cases.[88] In this respect, too, there is a historical resonance between the new divorce law and the Code Napoleon of 1804. For under the divorce provisions of that Code, which were in force only from 1804 until 1816, when the restoration of the Bourbon monarchy brought about the complete abolition of divorce in France for the next 68 years, divorce by mutual consent was also established as the form of divorce which the draftsmen hoped would be the most frequently utilized.[89]

The bases for divorce will be examined here in the order in which they are set out in the Act, under the headings of "Divorce by Mutual Consent", "Divorce for Prolonged Disruption of the life in Common", and "Divorce for Fault". Thus, contrary to the great tradition of French cuisine, the *pièce de résistance* comes first.

a. Divorce by Mutual Consent

Two versions of divorce by mutual consent are offered. They have been characterized by the commentators as *"divorce-convention"* and *"divorce-resignation"*. These are, respectively, divorce upon the joint petition of the spouses, and divorce sought by one spouse and accepted by the other. The latter ground seems to be, as one writer has put it, for spouses who want to leave marriage "by the same door, but not hand in hand".[90]

(1) Divorce-Convention

This form of mutual consent divorce in which the spouses jointly petition for termination of their marriage, is the one which was most favored by the authors of the reform law, and which secured the widest base of support in the legislature.[91] The three new Articles of the Civil Code which govern "Divorce by Agreement" are as follows:

Art. 230. When the spouses petition together for a divorce, they need not make known the cause; they must only submit for the approval of the judge the draft of an agreement which will regulate the consequences.

The petition may be presented either by the respective lawyers of the parties, or by one lawyer chosen by common accord.

Divorce by mutual consent may not be sought during the first six months of marriage.

Art. 231. The judge is to examine the petition with each of the parties, then to call them together. Then he is to call in the lawyer or lawyers.

If the spouses persist in their intention to divorce, the judge is to advise them that their petition should be renewed after a three-month period of reflection.

In the absence of a renewal within the six months following the expiration of this period of reflection, the joint petition will lapse.

Art. 232. The judge is to pronounce the divorce if he is convinced that the intention of each spouse is real and that each of them has given his consent freely. In the same judgment he approves (*homologue*) the agreement governing the consequences of the divorce.

He can refuse his approval and the granting of the divorce if he judges that the agreement does not sufficiently secure the interests of the children or of one of the spouses.

This system of joint petition is supposed to avoid the judicial comedy, as familiar to Americans, English people and Germans, as it is to the French, which has traditionally been played out by spouses in fault-divorce jurisdictions who are in agreement on the divorce and its economic and child custody consequences.[92] The system is also devised so as to spare the spouses the necessity, still theoretically imposed in England, of revealing details of their personal lives in order to secure the legal ratification of their agreement.

That this will not be a speedy form of divorce is apparent, not only from the delays provided for in the text, but from the commentary of those who are familiar with the everyday affairs of the divorce courts.[93] The text itself provides for four successive court appearances: first that of one spouse, then of the other, then the two together, and finally, both of them together with their lawyers or lawyer. Then, there is the three-month waiting period after which, if the suit is to be pursued, the parties must renew their petition.

Furthermore, the judge has the option under new Art. 251, to attempt conciliation between the spouses.

Even after all these appearances and the three-month delay, judicial approval of the agreed-upon divorce is not automatic. The law reserves, in form at least, an important role for the judge. There are two bases on which he can withhold his approval under Art. 232 – those relating to the quality of the intention and consent of the spouses and those relating to the adequacy of their agreement in protecting the interests of any children or of one of the spouses. These provisions give the judge so much discretion that it has been justly observed that, through successive denials of approval, the judge can in effect force the parties to adopt an agreement of which he himself is indirectly the author. [94]

(2) Divorce-Resignation

Under the heading of "Divorce by Mutual Consent" the new law describes first, "divorce by agreement", then, as a second form of divorce by mutual consent, "divorce sought by one spouse and accepted by the other". The four articles governing this consent-judgment type of divorce are as follows:

Art. 233. One spouse may petition for divorce by setting forth the fact of a set of acts, proceeding from both spouses, which make the continuation of their life in common intolerable.

Art. 234. If the other spouse acknowledges the facts before the judge, the judge is to grant the divorce without ruling on the allocation of fault. A divorce granted in this manner produces the legal effects of a divorce granted for shared fault.

Art. 235. If the other spouse does not acknowledge the facts, the judge is not to grant the divorce.

Art. 236. The statements made by the spouses may not be used as evidence in any other legal action.

The system here described, for the situation where one spouse alleges certain facts and the consequent impossibility of continuing the life in common, and the other spouse acquiesces, leaves the economic and other consequences of divorce up to the judge.

It is not expected that the dish here offered will be found appetizing by many. It was apparently prepared with the idea in mind that certain spouses, while not opposing a divorce, for religious or ethical reasons would not wish to participate actively. It is said that practitioners feel that cases will not be frequent where a defendant in a divorce action will be so indifferent to the effects of divorce as to abandon those questions to judicial discretion. [95]

From the legislative history, it appears that the section on mutual consent divorce by joint petition providing for four successive appearances before the judge applies here as well.[96] As with divorce by agreement, new Art. 251 gives the judge the option to attempt conciliation.

b. Divorce for Prolonged Disruption of the Life in Common

As with divorce by mutual consent, the French reform law, in introducing the new form of divorce which can be sought unilaterally without allegation of fault, by a spouse who may himself have committed fault, offers to the consumer two varieties of the product. One is addressed to the situation where the prolonged disruption of the life in common has been accompanied by a *de facto* separation of six years, the other where it has been accompanied for at least six years by the apparently incurable mental illness of the other spouse. The sections pertaining to these two forms are as follows:

Art. 237. One spouse may petition for divorce, by reason of the prolonged disruption of the life in common, when the spouses have been factually separated for six years.

Art. 238. The same is the case where the mental faculties of the other spouse have been so seriously impaired for a period of six years that the community of life no longer exists between the spouses and cannot, according to the most reasonable conjectures, be reestablished in the future.

The judge may on his own motion dismiss this petition, without resorting to the provisions of Article 240, if the divorce would entail the risk of too serious consequences for the illness of the other spouse.

Art. 239. The spouse who petitions for divorce for disruption of the life in common is to assume all of the costs of the suit. In the petition he is to specify the means through which he will fulfill his obligations to his spouse and children.

Art. 240. If the other spouse establishes that the divorce would entail, either for him, taking account of his age and of the duration of the marriage, or for the children, material or moral consequences of exceptional hardship, the judge is to dismiss the petition. He can even dismiss it on his own motion in the situation provided for in Article 238.

Art. 241. The disruption of the life in common can be invoked as a ground of divorce only by the spouse who presents the initial petition, called the principal petition.

The other spouse can then present a petition, called the cross-petition, (*demande en revendication*) by alleging the fault of the spouse who took the initiative. This cross-petition can only be for divorce and not for legal separation. If the judge accepts the cross-petition, he dismisses the principal petition, and grants the divorce on the ground of fault of the spouse who took the initiative.

When it is recalled that the similar provision of the English Divorce Reform Act of 1969 was often referred to as "Casanova's Charter", it is perhaps not surprising that this provision of the French divorce reform bill was controversial and attracted the label, which its government sponsors vigorously rejected, of "divorce by repudiation".

In the case of France, as in England, divorce on objective grounds gave rise to lively debate centering about the hypothetical situation of the blameless wife and mother who is put aside by her husband after many years of marriage, in favor of a younger woman.[97] In both countries, the debate on the question of principle – whether a spouse who may himself have brought about the disruption of the life in common nevertheless should be allowed to divorce a spouse who has committed no fault – was lost by the defenders of the bond, as it were. But the legislation which resulted has so hemmed in the exercise of this reluctantly-granted opportunity, that it seems likely that the underlying factual situations on which this part of the law was meant to operate will continue to be dealt with under other guises, as they were in the past. Just as divorce by mutual consent existed in France prior to the reform in the form of the judicial comedy, so unilateral divorce resulted, in effect, when the consent of the unwilling spouse was purchased or coerced by the spouse seeking divorce. Then the judicial comedy was played out as in the ordinary old version of divorce by mutual consent, disguised as divorce for serious violation of marital duties.[98]

The government had to tread a difficult path, denying on the one hand that this ground permitted unilateral repudiation, but asserting that broad social concerns supported the necessity of permitting one spouse to divorce a blameless partner on the other: "Is it advisable to promote illegitimate unions, by preventing the legal reconstitution of a new home? In the present state of the mores and living conditions, the law no longer is responding to these concerns."[99]

The mental impairment ground, new to French law, was likewise controversial, the original version passing the Senate but not the National Assembly.[100] After a modification giving to the judge the power to dismiss the petition on his own motion, it was passed, although in one of the two Frances it seemed to undermine the notion that spouses take each other for better or worse, in sickness and in health.

These sections of the new law bear the mark of the pen of French President Giscard d'Estaing, who was perhaps inspired by the example of Napoleon when he undertook to redraft them, and then permitted a photograph of a page of the draft law with his own corrections to be published in *Paris-Match*.[101] The changes he made were in fact crucial. As originally drafted, this section of the bill sponsored by the government provided in three successive sections: (1) that one spouse could seek divorce for prolonged disruption of the life in common, (2) that a spouse might seek such a divorce in the case where the spouses had lived apart for six years, and (3) that a spouse might seek such a divorce when the mental faculties of the other spouse had been gravely impaired for six years.[102] In that scheme, the first article seemed to announce a principle of which the following two articles were but applications, exemplifying but not limiting the scope of the principle. As the sections were reformulated by the French president, however, it is clear that there is now no divorce on objective grounds apart from the two cases established in the law.

Quite apart from the strictly limited scope of availability of this concession to the demand for a form of *"divorce-libération"*, there are other features which make it unlikely that these grounds will be frequently utilized. In the first place, as Art. 239 indicates, and as we shall see when we examine the economic effects of this type of divorce, it entails economic disadvantages for the plaintiff which may well be greater than those involved in the old system of purchasing the consent of the reluctant spouse.

Secondly, under new Art. 251, the judge is obliged to make conciliation efforts, where divorce is sought on these grounds. As elaborated in new Art. 252 and 252-1 the conciliation procedures alone could consume more than six months.

Third, a proceeding begun under these sections is not automatically to result in divorce, even where the conditions of Art. 237 or 238 are satisfied. Under both sections, the judge has discretion to deny a divorce. It remains to be seen however whether the exceptional hardship clause means that a divorce will be refused in any but rare cases. The English experience with such a clause is probably relevant.

But, it does seem that until the practice is settled, one bringing a suit under these new sections will be dependent on the luck of the judicial draw, especially since it is not at all clear that the Court of Cassation will consider varying interpretations of the hardship clause to present reviewable questions of law.

c. Divorce for Fault

The divorce reform law, in retaining fault-based divorce, did not simply continue the former law under which divorce could be granted for specified categories of fault: adultery, conviction and sentence for serious crime, or for serious violation of marital duties. Instead, fault divorce is completely reformulated and is now available on one generally stated ground, or for conviction and sentence for a serious crime. As under the prior law, the fault of the plaintiff does not bar him from pursuing a divorce. But under the new law divorces under such circumstances are called divorces for "shared fault" rather than "reciprocal fault".

The new style of fault divorce is regulated by the following four articles:

Art. 242. Divorce can be sought by one spouse for acts imputable to the other spouse when these acts constitute a serious or repeated violation of the duties and obligations of marriage and render intolerable the maintenance of the life in common.

Art. 243. It can be sought by one spouse when the other has been sentenced in a criminal case to one of the punishments set forth in Article 7 of the penal code.

Art. 244. The reconciliation of the spouses taking place after the occurrence of the facts alleged bars them from being invoked as cause for divorce.

The judge in such case is to declare that the petition is inadmissible. A new petition can however be presented on the basis of facts occurring or discovered after the reconciliation, the earlier facts then being admissible in support of this new petition.

The temporary maintenance or resumption of the common life are not to be considered a reconciliation if they result only from necessity or from an attempt at conciliation or from the requirements of the upbringing of the children.

Art. 245. The faults of the spouse who took the initiative in the divorce do not prevent the examination of his petition; they can however, deprive the acts with which he reproaches the other spouse of that character of seriousness which would have made them a cause for divorce.

These faults can also be invoked by the other spouse in support of a cross-petition for divorce. If both petitions are admitted, the divorce is granted for shared fault.

Even in the absence of a cross-petition, the divorce can be granted for shared fault of both spouses if the trial reveals fault attributable to both of them.

Because French divorce law since 1884 has been developed under the fault provisions of the *Loi Naquet*, it becomes important to inquire into the relationship of the new fault provisions to the old law and into the extent to which the settled case law (*jurisprudence constante*) under the old provisions can be expected to be relevant in the interpretation and application of the new.

One general observation which can be made with some confidence is that the case law developed under the former law interpreting the language of former Art. 232, "*excès, sévices ou injures*, constituting a serious or repeated violation of the marital duties" will continue to be relevant in interpreting the new general ground based on "acts constituting a serious or repeated violation of the duties and obligations of marriage". However, given the fact that the old ground has been used in the same way as the American all-purpose cruelty and mental cruelty grounds have been – to turn fault divorce into no-fault divorce – this observation cannot reveal much about how the new language will be interpreted by any particular judge in any given case. As before, the general language can be expected to be susceptible to widely varying interpretations, meaning one thing in Paris to a busy judge who may himself have been divorced, and quite another in the provinces.

The legislature has attempted in three ways to take some of the sting out of this version of divorce which apparently was politically impossible to eliminate. First, as with divorce for prolonged disruption of the life in common, conciliation efforts are made mandatory in fault divorce by new Art. 251. Secondly, in keeping with the central place given in the new law to divorce by mutual consent, the legislature has provided that, at any time before judgment is rendered, the spouses in a fault divorce case, or any other type of divorce case, can transform their suit into a divorce based on agreement and proceed under the system laid down in Articles 231 and 232.[103] It seems clear that this is meant not only to be a permission but an encouragement.

Third, if the spouses do proceed to judgment on fault grounds and if the divorce is granted, Art. 248-1 of the new law's provisions on divorce procedure gives the parties the opportunity to request the judge to confine himself in the decree to the simple statement that a cause for divorce existed, without setting forth the various accusations and wrongs of the parties.

d. Legal Separation

Legal separation was enormously important in French law, as might be imagined, in the period from 1816 to 1884 when divorce, in the sense of release from the matrimonial bond with permission to remarry, did not exist.[104] The same law which repealed the divorce provisions of the Civil Code in 1816, then proceeded to enact them *in haec verba* as the grounds for legal separation, except for the ground of mutual consent.[105] Thus, a considerable body of case law was built up which long continued to inform the cases on divorce when that institution as such was re-introduced in 1884.

The institution of legal separation has continued to be important, functioning as a substitute for divorce for that part of the population which, for religious reasons, is reluctant to use the institution of divorce. Estimates in the legislative history of the percentage of matrimonial actions expected to be brought under this section of the new law, rather than under the divorce sections, ranged from 5 to 13%.[106]

The approach to legal separation under the new law resembles the mode of regulation under the prior law. As before, legal separation is available on the same basis as divorce. Thus with the addition of the new divorce grounds, the availability of legal separation has been broadened. The right of either party to convert the legal separation into a divorce after three years is continued from the prior law in substantially the same language. It is noteworthy, however, that the fact that legal separation by mutual consent can only be converted to divorce if both spouses agree may discourage some people from seeking legal separation on the "favored" ground.

3. Summary

In discussing the problems involved in drafting the reform law, Dean Carbonnier has said,

All divorce by mutual consent must steer between two dangers: either it is very accomodating in accepting the reality of the consents, and the risk is great that the better-armed of the spouses surprises, extorts or buys the consent of the other; or it multiplies the precautions, the formalities and the delays, and the spouses (who are by hypothesis in agreement to divorce) prefer to bring a simulated lawsuit, rather than to confront this procedure fraught with complications.[107]

It seems that the reform law has sought to avoid both these dangers by providing *no* form of divorce which is not fraught with complications.

It is ironic, inasmuch as one of the main reasons for divorce reform was the slowness of divorce procedures under the former law, that the *Premier Avocat Général* has given it as his opinion that the multiplication of stages of litigation, the increase in the tasks of judges combined with the shortage of judicial personnel, and the complexity of the systems of economic guarantees, will greatly slow down all aspects of divorce.[108] Lawyers, he said, need never have feared that divorce reform would take away some of their business: in fact it will increase.[109]

Certain other effects, probably unintended, are foreseeable. Fault divorce will probably be sought for financial reasons in those situations in which divorce for disruption of the life in common was supposed to operate. Fault divorce will be sought by others because the supervised mutual consent divorce is too complicated and time consuming.[110] Mutual consent divorce will probably be favored by many who might have sought fault divorces, not because of its "civilized" nature, but because of the possibility it offers to modify the financial effects upon future change of conditions.

Mutual consent divorce out in the open will not only be much more cumbersome and costly than the prior version disguised as fault divorce in which the spouses had only to go on stage once, but, as the *Association*

Nationale des Avocats de France has pointed out, "It does not solve the real problem which remains that of...spouses who are in disagreement on the very principle of divorce and who find themselves in a situation of confrontation poisoned by the system of fault divorce."[111] For these divorce clients, it seems that recourse will be had to the old system of forced or purchased consent more often than to the formidable new set of rules governing what some have called "repudiation–divorce". As before, many simply will not bother to terminate their marriages legally before entering a new liason.

The *Premier Avocat Générál* has said that the only solution will be to increase the number of judges.[112] There is, of course, another solution. The judges may treat the new law with the same seriousness as they treated the old, and as English judges have treated the "inquest" provisions of the 1969 Divorce Reform Law. Before the Divorce Law reform, the average time for hearing a divorce case in Paris was four to seven minutes, and the number of divorces denied or conciliations effected was said to be "infinitesimal".[113]

Probably it is the admission of the principles of availability of divorce by mutual consent and on unilateral application that will in the end turn out to be important.

In the case of mutual consent, one cannot help but be reminded by the present provisions of the fact that the mutual consent provisions of the Code of 1804 were mostly a dead letter even before they were repealed in 1816 because they were too cumbersome.[114] The same has been true of the mutual consent provisions which remained in force in Belgium even after the end of Napoleonic rule.[115] The true significance of the innovation may be concealed in this remark by the *Premier Avocat Général*:

One has the impression that implicit in this text [divorce by agreement] is the idea that since it suffices for the purpose of getting married to establish an agreement in front of a public official, it should also suffice to go before a public official and establish a disagreement in order to get divorced.[116]

Similarly, in the case of divorce upon unilateral application and objective grounds it may be true that the legislature has made this form of divorce practically unavailable for the time being. But at least from now on in conflict of laws matters, it can no longer be said that unilateral divorce is contrary to French public policy.

One need not expect further developments in the near future. France has chosen to adopt the same type of compromise legislation as have England and a great many American states, retaining fault divorce, but adding objective and consent grounds, or both, to try to do away with the pretense that there is fault when there is agreement, and to offer the possibility of regularizing new unions entered into by spouses who may themselves have caused the break-down of their marriages.

Whether and when the further step of absorbing all these grounds into one general marriage breakdown ground will be taken as has been done in West Germany and Sweden, in the socialist countries of Eastern Europe, in 11 American states, and under the American Uniform Marriage and Divorce Act, is hard to say. Even harder to predict is whether the next step, that of doing away with the pretense that the court is adjudicating when it is in reality acting as a registrar, will be taken, as it has in Sweden and the State of Washington. Certainly the course of French reform has showed the continued existence of *les deux Frances*. And, as Dean Carbonnier and Professors Rheinstein and Kahn-Freund have all shown us from a comparative perspective, in family law, if anywhere, distinct cultural differences make themselves felt.[117] Yet, the recent evolution of French family law furnishes a number of examples of how an exception cautiously opened up has gone on to swallow the rule.[118] One need only reflect on the complete political impossibility of deposing the husband as "head of the family" in connection with the matrimonial property reform of 1965,[119] and the casual ease with which this historic provision was dropped in the parental authority reform of 1970.[120] Perhaps after all it will be the law of 1792 with its objective grounds, its administrative rather than judicial tribunals, its lack of inquest, and above all, its libertarian ideology, which, rather than the Code Napoleon, will provide the inspiration for future French reforms.

C. West Germany: Marriage and Family Law Reform, 1976

1. Prelude

Unlike the English and French reforms which replaced very old, traditional, fault-based divorce laws, West Germany's 1976 reform was against the background of a 38-year-old law which was not too different either from the 1969 English Reform Act or the 1975 French Reform law.[121] Like these liberalization efforts, the prior German law provided for divorce on fault grounds and on the added ground of "marriage breakdown" (*Zerrüttung*) following a period of separation. Divorce on the no-fault ground of insanity had been available from the time of the German Civil Code. As under the new English and French laws, divorce for marriage breakdown could be denied if special circumstances made it unjust in a given case.

Thus it is particularly interesting to examine the background of the West German reform, to see what led up to the relatively liberal 1938–1946 law, why further and fundamental change was thought necessary, and what eventually emerged from the political process after six years of parliamentary struggle and compromise.

Prior to the legal unification of the German empire which occurred when the Civil Code went into effect on 1 January 1900, there had been three major groups of legal patterns for divorce in Germany.[122]

One of these patterns was that of the Code Napoleon, which had been maintained in effect in the Rhineland and was also in force in the Grand Duchy of Baden. Another was that of the so-called common law of Germany which referred questions of marriage and divorce to ecclesiastical law, that is, to canon law for Catholics and to Protestant ecclesiastical law for Protestants. Hence, in regions such as Southern Bavaria, where common law applied, marriage was indissoluble for Catholics, and divorce was available to Protestants only on narrow fault grounds (not by mutual agreement as was the case under the Code Napoleon). The third and best known predecessor of the German Civil Code was the Prussian General Code which was in effect in about half the territory of the State of Prussia and in a few small territories outside Prussia. This code, inspired by King Frederick II of Prussia, did not come into effect until 1794, eight years after his death.[123] Under the Prussian Code, marriages could be dissolved not only for fault, as under Protestant law, but also without fault, i.e. by mutual consent, and even upon unilateral application. As the Prussian Code is known to have been influenced decisively by the secular thought of Frederick the Great, its divorce provisons have usually been thought to embody the libertarian ideas of the so-called Enlightenment. However, recent research by Dörner has convincingly demonstrated that the no-fault divorce provisions were not so much the product either of ideas of extreme individualism or of marriage as a civil contract as they were consequences of Frederick's pro-natalist thinking.[124] Dörner traces the Prussian Code's principle of free divorce to a cabinet directive of 1783 in which Frederick wrote that divorce

...must not be made too difficult, lest the population be hindered. For when two spouses are so angry and irritated with each other, that no further connection between them is to be hoped for...then also will they produce no children with each other, and that is detrimental to the population. On the other hand, if such a pair is divorced, and the wife then marries another fellow (*Kerl*), then surely children are likely to come along.[125]

The divorce provisions of the Prussian General Code lend themselves to the interpretation that their purpose was the social one of encouraging population growth. Mutual consent divorce was made available only where the marriage was "entirely childless" (*ganz kinderlose*).[126] Unilateral divorce was

216 *Chapter 5*

available only when the petitioner could prove "...the existence of such a violent and deeply-rooted aversion, that no hope remains for reconciliation and for achievement of the purposes of the state of marriage".[127] It will be recalled from Chapter 4 that under the Prussian Code there was no doubt about the chief purpose of marriage: it was the procreation and upbringing of children.

The three prior patterns of German law, each so different from the other, had to be replaced by a single pattern in the German Civil Code of 1896. The pattern chosen by the draftsmen of the Civil Code resembled that chosen by the French when divorce was re-introduced into the French Civil Code in 1884. Except for the case of insanity, divorce was to be granted only for the misconduct of one spouse.[128] Thus, divorce was made possible for Catholics in former regions of the common law, but was rendered more difficult for residents of those regions previously under the Code Napoleon or the Prussian Code. However, studies of divorce in Germany for the period beginning 19 years before the new Code went into effect and ending 16 years afterwards showed no appreciable effect either on the incidence of divorce or on the behavior of judges.[129]

Unlike France and England, Germany did not retain the fault principle as the basis of its divorce law until well into the second half of the twentieth century. In 1938, under the National Socialist regime, a new marriage law for Greater Germany introduced the breakdown principle into German law in the form of divorce after a period of separation. The 1938 law, with slight modifications made by the Allied Control Council Law No. 16 of 1946, remained the divorce law of West Germany until the 1976 reform law went into effect.[130]

It had been the original idea of the draftsmen of the National Socialist divorce law to eliminate the concept of fault entirely and to have only one ground of divorce – the breakdown of the marriage to such a degree that the marriage had become "valueless to the *Volksgemeinschaft*", i.e. the community of all racially pure Germans.[131] But the idea of making such a radical break with the past all at once was eventually rejected. Instead it was decided to modify the old fault grounds and add new grounds.[132] Some of the new grounds, such as "unreasonable refusal to beget offspring," were thought to be so intimately related to National Socialist ideology that they were eliminated in 1946 when the Allied Control Council re-enacted the Marriage Law of 1938.[133]

The 1938 law, as retained in 1946, provided for divorce upon proof of two types of matrimonial misconduct: adultery, and other "violations of matrimonial duties" so serious that they have led to disruption of the marriage and that restoration of the life in common cannot be expected.[134] In addition divorce was made available in two types of cases where neither partner could be charged with fault. In one of these types, divorce is granted on the ground of the physical or mental condition of the defendant.[135] In the other type of case, a version of breakdown divorce is provided on proof of three year's separation without reference to misconduct of the defendant:[136]

s. 48. (1) If the marriage partners have not kept a common household for three years and if, owing to a deep-rooted incurable breakdown (*Zerrüttung*) of marital relations, restoration of the life in common cannot be expected, either of the marriage partners can petition for a divorce.

(2) If the spouse petitioning for divorce is wholly or predominantly responsible for bringing about the breakdown, the divorce cannot be granted against the other spouse's opposition, except if the opposing spouse lacks attachment to the marriage, and such readiness to continue it, as may fairly be expected of him or her, (amended in 1961).[137]

(3) The petition for divorce must not be granted if a true understanding of the interests of one or several minor children of the marriage requires the maintenance of the marriage (Added by the Allied Control Council Law of 1946).

In 1946 the breakdown principle, even in the limited form in which it appeared in the 1938 German law, was novel enough so that the English, French and Soviet members of the quadripartite Committee on the Reform of German Law, established by the four allied powers to purge German law of National Socialist ideology, were initially of the view that the breakdown ground, like the racial and eugenic aspects of the Marriage Law, should be eliminated.[138] The American member of the Committee eventually persuaded his colleagues that the provision was not tainted – in part by pointing out that the American state of Louisiana which had long had no-fault divorce after three years' separation could hardly be said to be under the sway of National Socialist ideas.[139]

Despite the fact that section 48 of the Allied Control Council Law of 1946 (and its predecessor Section 55 of the Marriage Law of 1938) is the best-known and most-discussed feature of German divorce law, it has not played a very important role in practice for reasons which eventually produced agitation for further reform in Germany and which should have given pause to the English in 1969 and to the French in 1975.

In the first place, in West Germany, as in England, France and the United States, it is estimated that over 90% of all divorces are uncontested. Most of these are collusive divorces.[140] But such "mutual consent" divorces are most often disguised as divorces for marital misconduct, not as divorce for breakdown. One reason for this has been that consideration of guilt had been brought into contested cases by the courts through paragraph 48(2). Another reason is that under paragraphs 48(2) and (3) the court under certain circumstances has power to deny a divorce. In fact, the Bundesgerichtshof for a long time showed great favor to objecting spouses in interpreting paragraph 48(2),[141] but by the time of the 1976 Reform had turned completely in the other direction. This reversal was facilitated by the vagueness of 48(2), a fact which in itself gave rise to considerable dissatisfaction and criticism.

But the main reason for the desuetude of s. 48 seems to be that s. 48 is the long road (three years) to a divorce, whereas fault divorce has been the speedy route.[142] Hence, the breakdown ground has played a diminishing role. In 1950, it accounted for 12.2% of all divorces; in 1968 the percentage was only 4.4.[143] The general misconduct clause of s. 43 permitting one spouse to obtain a divorce if the other's behavior has seriously disrupted the marriage was, as misconduct grounds have been in England and in many American states, by far the most popular ground for divorce, accounting for 93% of the divorces in West Germany by 1968.[144]

The plans of the West German government for a divorce law reform which would strengthen the breakdown principle and eliminate the fault principle were explained in a 1970 speech by the Minister of Justice, Gerhard Jahn:

> The parties involved, as well as the courts, must be relieved of the necessity to search for responsibility in a sphere that cannot be clarified and to find in this search the justification for a divorce. They must confine themselves to the objective and more easily demonstrated establishment of whether a marriage has in fact broken down.[145]

A discussion draft of a reform bill, based on the report of a commission appointed in 1968 to examine the questions of divorce and support law reform, was circulated in 1970 and a draft law was introduced by the government in the Bundestag in 1971.[146]

From the time the government's draft bill reforming divorce and many other aspects of family law was introduced until the eventual adoption of a compromise version in 1976, it was the subject of persistent controversy. It was debated no less than two dozen times in the legal committee of the Bundestag and no less than 45 times in the subcommittee on divorce law reform.[147]

The controversy aroused by the proposed law, however, was less attributable to its changes in the grounds for divorce than to its proposed innovations with respect to post-divorce economics.[148] Yet many opponents sincerely believed the traditional ideology of marriage was at stake. And they were correct – so far as the ideology expressed in the laws was concerned.

The 1973 government draft appeared certain of adoption in December 1975, having passed the Bundestag on December 11 and needing only the approval of the Bundesrat. Then, an intervening change of a representative in Lower Saxony suddenly gave the Christian Democrats a one-vote majority in the Bundesrat which served to defeat the bill – by one vote – in January 1976.[149] This gave the Christian Democrats the leverage they needed to secure a few important last-minute modifications in conference committee before the bill was finally adopted in April 1976 and promulgated on 14 June 1976.

2. The Marriage and Family Law Reform of 1976

The West German Marriage and Family Law Reform Law begins with the words, "Marriage is concluded for a lifetime" (*Die Ehe wird auf Lebenszeit geschlossen*).[150] With this brave beginning (inserted at the last moment to please the Christian Democrats), the Reform law replaces all specific grounds for divorce with a single no-fault ground. The new ground is called *Scheitern* (literally, "foundering", as of a ship upon the rocks; figuratively, failure), rather than *Zerrüttung* (breakdown) of the marriage. The articles of the divorce law, for the first time since 1938, are put back into the body of the German Civil Code. The basis for divorce is set forth in just five sections. They read:

1564. A marriage can be terminated only through judicial decision upon the petition of one or both spouses. The marriage is dissolved by the legal force of the judgment [when the judgment becomes *res judicata*]. The conditions under which divorce can be sought are set forth in the following provisions.

1565. (1) A marriage can be terminated, if it has failed (*wenn sie gescheitert ist.*). A marriage has failed, if the community of life of the spouses no longer exists and it can not be expected that the spouses will restore it.

(2) If the spouses have lived apart for less than one year, the marriage can only be dissolved if the continuation of the marriage would pose an insupportable hardship for the petitioner for reasons which repose in the person of the other spouse.

1566. (1) It is irrebuttably presumed that the marriage has failed, if the spouses have lived apart for one year and both spouses petition for divorce or the respondent consents to the divorce.

(2) It is irrebuttably presumed that the marriage has failed, if the spouses have lived apart for three years.

1567. (1) The spouses are living apart, if no household community exists between them and one spouse perceptibly refuses its restoration by rejecting the marital community of life. The household community no longer exists in such case even if the spouses live apart within the marital dwelling.

(2) Cohabitation for a short time, that should serve the reconciliation of the spouses, does not interrupt or stop the time periods specified in s. 1566.

s. 1568. The marriage may not be dissolved, although it has broken down, if and so long as the maintenance of the marriage is especially necessary for exceptional reasons in the interest of minor children produced by the marriage, or if and so long as the dissolution, for the respondent who opposes it, would pose such exceptional hardship by reason of extraordinary circumstances, that the maintenance of the marriage, even taking into consideration the interests of the petitioner, appears exceptionally required.

(2) Paragraph (1) is not applicable if the spouses have lived apart for more than five years.

It will be noted that, unlike the English and French reforms, the 1976 West German reform retains no fault grounds. Further, it does not make any period of actual separation mandatory before a divorce can be granted. The marriage can even be found to have "failed" though the parties are still living under the same roof.

Under the general clause of art. 1565(1) a spouse can obtain a divorce if he convinces the court that the marriage has failed. This general rule is qualified by 1565(2) which was added in the haggling that went on between the government Coalition and the Opposition between January and April 1976, as a concession to the Christian Democratic and Christian Social Unions who then held the upper hand in the Bundesrat. Where the couple has not been separated for one year, the marriage can be dissolved only if its maintenance, for the divorce-seeking partner, "would be an insupportable hardship" for reasons attributable to the other spouse. This compromise has correctly been described as a reintroduction of the guilt principle,[151] but it is at least limited in application to a one-year period.

If the divorce is by mutual consent (either on joint petition or with consent of one party) and the parties have lived apart for one year the presumption of failure is conclusive and the court must grant the divorce under 1566(1). If only one spouse seeks the divorce and if the spouses have lived apart for three years, the petitioner is aided in making out his case of marriage failure by the irrebuttable presumption established in paragraph 1566(2). The irrebuttable presumption in this case, however, will not automatically lead to divorce.

The hardship clause in s.1568 permits the court, in exceptional circumstances at least, to deny a divorce even where a marriage has failed unless the couple has lived apart for five years. It will be recalled that such clauses were included in the French and English divorce reforms, primarily, if not exclusively, to protect middle-aged wives from financial hardship. The 1973 draft of the West German law had expressly excluded these circumstances from consideration, reflecting the insistence in the Minister's Report that "Marriage must not be degraded into an institution that is merely to guarantee economic security."[152] In the 1976 compromise law this exclusion of economic factors came out, but the five-year outside limit was imposed.

Unlike the English draftsmen, the West Germans rejected the idea of making divorce unavailable in principle during the first years of marriage. In contrast to the view taken by the English, the Germans thought that when it was clear at the outset that a marriage was a failure, the best course for everyone would not be to preserve it.[153] Unlike both the English and the French, and perhaps with the benefit of knowledge of the failures of conciliation and reconciliation efforts in England and the United States, the West Germans repealed their compulsory system of attempted reconciliation, and rejected proposals for counselling or conciliation provisions as useless and impracticable.[154]

3. Summary

The West German Reform, like the English and the French, was a compromise. But it differed in significant ways from the two earlier reforms. The principle of elimination of marital misconduct from consideration was much more fully accepted, as was the principle of availability of unilateral divorce. Judicial inquest into the fact of breakdown was completely eliminated under s. 1566(2) in mutual consent divorces after one-year's separation, which will probably turn out to be the great majority of cases. The role of the judge was diminished even in other types of divorce although the procedural rules require the appearance of the spouses, in principle, in every divorce case. Of equal importance is the fact that, in the law itself and in all the discussion that led up to it, the focus is much more on the satisfactory resolution of the economic consequences of divorce than on the fact of divorce itself. And even with respect to these matters, the law eventually adopted was a compromise measure, as will be described in Chapter 6. But in future West German discussions of divorce law it is probable that emphasis will center more and more on the financial relationships of the ex-spouses.

The breakdown principle and, in the words of *Die Zeit*, "the withdrawal of the modern State with its civil marriage law from the sphere of marital privacy",[155] have been accepted. In the end, as *Die Zeit* put it in its front page article on the reform:

The silence, in the Coalition and Opposition last week, their compromise on divorce law reform having been concluded, expressed above all, embarrassment. It demonstrated in retrospect that the parliamentary arguments about the future of marriage in Germany had been in good measure only an exhibition match.[156]

Yet, the article went on, so far as the change in official marriage ideology is concerned,

No one should expect much concerning the influence of the new divorce law on the condition of marriage and the family. The withdrawal of State regulation will presumably develop neither marriage-preserving nor marriage-destroying force. It is no more than a declaration of neutrality.[157]

In its aspect as evidence of the shift of the State toward a neutral position with respect to the institution of legal marriage, and in its emphasis on the functional problems associated with the breakup of a household, the West German law leads naturally to a consideration of Swedish law, where these trends have reached their furthest point − so far as contemporary West European law is concerned.

D. Sweden: The Family Law Reform, 1973

1. Prelude

If the German Divorce Reform of 1976 was of a prior law which appeared liberal in comparison with pre-1969 English law, pre-1975 French law, and the laws of many American states prior to the reforms of the 1970s, the Swedish Divorce Reform of 1973 was of a prior law which had long been thought to be remarkable for the ease with which it made divorce available without allegation of fault and even upon unilateral application.

The pre-1973 Swedish law was enacted in 1915[158] in reaction to a situation which had grown up under the exclusively fault-based divorce law of the Swedish Code of 1734. The Code, following the ecclesiastical law of the Lutheran State Church, permitted divorce only for adultery or desertion.[159] But the king was empowered to depart from the strict application of the Code provisions. Professor Folke Schmidt says that by the end of the 18th century the Swedish kings, acting in accordance with the philosophy of the Enlightenment, were liberally granting divorces in cases where the spouses were actually separated.[160] But obtaining a royal dispensation was a time-consuming process. Thus, in Sweden, as elsewhere where divorce was not easily available, the means were found to dissolve marriages quickly. For spouses who were in agreement on divorce *and* well-to-do, the answer was the "Copenhagen divorce", described as follows in an 1879 Swedish Parliamentary Law Committee Report:[161]

The matter is arranged thus, that one of the spouses, e.g. the husband, travels to the nearest foreign city, usually Copenhagen. Then the wife sues him in court for divorce on the ground that he maliciously and willfully deserted her, and went abroad with the intention not to be and cohabit with her any more. Having been served the writ, the defendant admits the circumstances of the case by attorney, whereupon the court grants its decree of divorce without more ado.... With the rapid communications of today, all this can be managed within the period of a few weeks.

For those who could not afford the trip to Copenhagen or who could not obtain the agreement of the other spouse, the answer was the "Stockholm marriage", an informal union believed to have been popular among the urban working class population.[162]

A Law Revision Commission charged with looking into the matter of divorce reform in 1913 came to the conclusion, as had a Swiss Commission in 1907, that the true basis for divorce should be the breakdown of the marriage:

> Ordinarily, it is not desirable, either from the point of view of the community or with regard to the spouses, that in such situations [of breakdown] a marriage can be held together by force. The State can enforce the external bond alone; but a community of life which carries into effect the moral content of a marriage cannot be enforced by external pressure.[163]

The Minister of Justice, referring to the Copenhagen divorce and the delay involved in the royal writ, said, "Here we have an abuse to be countered, but also a need which should be recognized."[164] Thus, in 1915 a law was passed to eliminate the practice of fictitious trips to Copenhagen but to make available a simpler and more expeditious form of divorce than that offered by petitioning to the king. The law had wide support, and met little opposition from the Lutheran clergy.[165] It abolished the royal divorce jurisdiction and made divorce available on no-fault grounds as well as several fault grounds, in addition to the old grounds of adultery and desertion.

The new no-fault grounds permitted divorce on application by either spouse in the following situations:[166] (1) where the two spouses acting together obtain a judicial decree of separation on the ground that they are unable to continue living together because of profound and lasting breakdown, and the spouses live apart for one year thereafter; (2) where one spouse obtains such a decree of separation, and the spouses live apart for one year thereafter (one spouse acting alone had to prove the breakdown was caused by differences in temperament and outlook, but this burden was said not to be heavy); (3) where the spouses had in fact lived separately for three years even though there had been no decree of separation.

Where both spouses acted together, the court could not look behind the allegation of breakdown and had no discretion to deny a divorce after the period of separation. In cases where one spouse acted alone, however, there was a clause permitting the court to deny a divorce if special circumstances made it proper to continue the marriage even though it had broken down. [167] Denial of a divorce under this clause however was "almost unheard of". [168] In the entire history of the act there seem to have been only two published cases where a decree is known to have been refused. [169] As Rheinstein says,

> Observation of life and literature seems to have convinced the judges that it is inane to search for guilt in matters of marital discord and that it is futile to attempt by governmental coercion to restore harmony among spouses who, by actually living apart from each other, have demonstrated that their marriage has become a failure. [170]

Under the 1915 law, legal separation for one year was by far the most popular ground for divorce, but the number of divorces sought on fault grounds was sufficiently high to indicate that these grounds remained important either because fault divorce continued to be a speedier route than separation, or because a decree based on one spouse's fault still gave the other some advantage in economic or child-related matters. [171]

This system of divorce in which the principal ground was the factual breakdown of the marriage, proved by a period of separation and the mutual consent of the parties, and in which unilateral divorce was obtainable with little difficulty, was described in Max Rheinstein's 1971 study of divorce in several countries as the full legal expression of the predominance of liberal individualism. [172] He so characterized the Swedish law of 1915 and similar laws adopted in Norway in 1918 and in Denmark, Finland and Iceland in the 1920s. [173] We now turn to the question why Sweden made a radical change in this system in 1973.

2. The Divorce Law Reform of 1973

Legislative cooperation with a high decree of coordination in the handling of problems of private law has long been characteristic of the Nordic countries. Thus it was a remarkable event when Carl Lidbom of Sweden announced at the 1969 meeting of the Nordic Council a new "pioneer" theory, rather resembling the American idea of the 50 states as "laboratories" where various legal approaches to common social problems can be tested. As Professor Sundberg has described the Swedish departure,

> Mr. Lidbom announced that he did not regret but rather rejoiced 'when the one or the other Nordic country tries to find new ways to solve social and economic problems by

legislation. It is often found that new creations that are inserted into one country's legal system eventually are also adopted by the neighboring countries."[174]

Thus the ground was prepared for a divorce reform in Sweden that would not be, as was the 1915 marriage law, the product of coordinated effort with the other Nordic countries. Later in 1969, the Swedish Minister of Justice, Herman Kling, appointed a committee to prepare new marriage legislation, and laid down certain directives to guide their work. He charged the Committee that, "[L]egislation should not under any circumstance force a person to continue to live under a marriage from which he wishes to free himself",[175] and that, "A new [family] law should...as far as possible be neutral as regards different forms of cohabitation and different moral ideas."[176]

In accordance with these directives, the Committee on Reform of Family Law produced a draft based on the principles that, "...not only entry into marriage but also its continued existence, should be based on the free will of the spouses" and that "the wish of one of the spouses to dissolve the marriage should always be respected".[177] But as we have seen above the practice in Sweden already conformed to these principles. Thus, Professor Folke Schmidt in 1971 seems to have over-estimated the change the new law would bring about when he said:

> The law of marriage...will be the law of the young generation to whom it appears a matter of course that women will continue to be wage-earning when married. The new law will be revolutionary in character since it will reflect the ideas of young people; it will not, like the present law, be based upon the experiences and evaluations of earlier generations.[178]

The changes made in the law, proposed by the Committee and adopted in 1973, do not constitute radical departures from the prior practice. The divorce provisions of the Swedish Marriage Code now read as follows:[179]

1§. If spouses agree to the dissolution of their marriage, they are entitled to a decree of divorce. If a spouse has children under the age of sixteen who are in his care, the divorce shall be preceded by a period of consideration.

2§. If only one of the spouses desires to have the marriage dissolved, he is entitled to divorce after the lapse of the period of consideration.

3§. The period of consideration begins when the spouses jointly petition for divorce or when one spouse's petition for divorce is brought to the notice of the other spouse. If the period of consideration has been running for no less than six months, divorce will be decreed upon petition therefor by one of the spouses. If such a petition has not been presented within a year from the beginning of the period of consideration, the question of divorce has terminated....

4§. If spouses have lived separate at least two years, each spouse has the right to obtain divorce without a previous period of consideration.

5§. If a marriage was entered into contrary to Chapter 2, §3 para. 1, a spouse is entitled to a divorce without any previous period of consideration. The same will apply if the marriage was entered into contrary to Chapter 2, §4, and the previous marriage has not been dissolved.[180]

If there is bigamy, the spouse in the first marriage is entitled to have it [the first marriage] dissolved by a decree of divorce without any previous period of consideration.

In the cases referred to in the first paragraph the petition for divorce may also be initiated by a prosecutor.

The principal changes from the prior law can be summarized as follows: (1) all fault grounds have been eliminated; (2) unilateral divorce is now made a matter of unqualified legal right; (3) no reasons for the divorce need be given, no "breakdown" of the marriage need be alleged, and therefore the court need not even appear to make findings concerning these matters; (4) the conciliation provisions of the prior law are eliminated; (5) divorce is available without any waiting period unless one spouse is opposed or one spouse has custody of children under 16, in which cases a six month period of consideration must be observed. After six months, if the plaintiff persists the court must grant the divorce. There is no discretion to deny a divorce under "special circumstances".

Thus, Sweden, pursuing its pioneer country theory, has simultaneously eliminated all trace of "fault" and even the appearance of judicial inquest from its divorce laws. At the same time, it has shifted attention to those matters which are elsewhere still often called ancillary and has made them of paramount significance. As Professor Folke Schmidt has said, "In a divorce case the custody of the children and the questions of alimony and support are the truly important matters", and

[T]o the Swedish courts, to the attorneys, and to the social welfare officers it has become increasingly evident that in divorce matters one should look rather to the future than to the past, or rather to the interests of the children and to economic long-term relations than to the question whether there was a proper ground for divorce.[181]

The new Swedish approach to economic and child-related matters will be discussed in the following chapter.

There are signs that the other Nordic countries, to varying degrees, may follow the Swedish lead.[182] In Denmark, Iceland and Norway, uncontested divorces have long been under the jurisdiction of adminstrative, rather than judicial, tribunals, so that in this sense a step in the process of "dejuridification" of divorce was taken there long ago.[183]

It is too soon to have any reports from the "laboratory" where the new law went into effect on 1 January 1974. But since in so many ways the reform merely conforms the law to the practice, and since the "Stockholm marriage" flourishes today more than ever, it may be that we should not expect to hear much more about it. The law, for the time being, seems to have been harmonized with the underlying social reality.

E. The United States: the Uniform Marriage and Divorce Act and Other Reforms of the 1970s

Like the Nordic Countries, the various American states have long engaged in coordinated law reform efforts, notably through the work of the National Conference of Commissioners on Uniform State Laws which was founded in 1892 with the aim, among others, of preparing uniform divorce legislation. But unlike in Scandinavia, such legal cooperation has co-existed with enthusiastic support for the idea that the experiments of one state, striking out on its own, may prove instructive and beneficial for the other states.

Thus, if French divorce law after 1976 is "à la carte", it is the United States, and not the Scandinavian countries, which offer a smorgasbord. Every stage in the recent evolution of the divorce laws described in this Chapter can be found there.

It is true that cooperation finally produced a Uniform Marriage and Divorce Act in 1970 with "irretrievable" marriage breakdown as the sole ground for divorce.[184] But as of 1976, this Act or similar laws had been adopted in only 11 states.[185] A tiny minority, three states out of 50, clung to exclusively fault-based divorce laws, but at least two of these states were on the verge of reform.[186] One state – Washington – had surpassed even Sweden in making divorce available on demand, and another – Colorado – had come close. In the great majority of states, as in England and France after their 1969 and 1975 reforms, and in Sweden and West Germany before their reforms of 1973 and 1976, fault grounds still co-existed with no-fault grounds and the characteristic rituals associated with that state of affairs were being played out by courts and litigants.

In the United States, as in the other countries whose laws we have examined, uncontested divorces have been consistently estimated to account for over 90% of all divorces pronounced.[187] Before the reforms of the 1970s, fault divorce on the books was converted into no-fault divorce in action by collusion and by expanded definitions of the general cruelty grounds for divorce.[188] In addition, the American federal system offered the possibility of migratory divorce through which a person living in a place where divorce was difficult could (if he or she were sufficiently well-to-do) resort to the courts of another jurisdiction where divorce was more readily available.[189]

In his 1971 book, Rheinstein has described in detail this "judicial compromise" and how it has increasingly been replaced by "legislative compromises".[190] As of this writing, most of the states have a combination of no-fault grounds (such as breakdown of the marriage, incompatibility or separation), and fault grounds. Some of these statutes are quite old, but many reflect recent compromises of the English or French type. In addition, many of these states have greatly broadened the availability of divorce on fault grounds by eliminating the traditional defenses of recrimination, condonation or collusion, and by permitting divorce to be awarded to both parties where each alleges the other has been at fault.

These American developments are not significantly different from the developments we have just described under similar European statutes, except that in the United States the possibility of migratory divorce makes it difficult for any one state to maintain for long a divorce law much stricter than those of other states. As we saw in Chapter 2, for the same reason it is also difficult for any one state to enforce a strict marriage formation policy, even if it desired to do so. Thus, the process of legal change is hastened in the United States by the ease of evading any one state's attempt to enforce a legal policy which is much different from that of neighboring states. Such provisions as the English prohibition of divorce within the first three years of marriage would be impossible to enforce, as would such "hardship clauses" as are found in the English, French and West German reforms.

It is not proposed in the present chapter to discuss in detail the process through which the divorce laws of the American states are presently being transformed. There is an abundant literature on this subject.[191] Rather I will show how this process, taken as a whole, is nothing more than a part of the gradual but steady "dejuridification" of marriage that has been described up to this point.

Let us turn therefore to the Uniform Act of 1970 and to the growing number of state statutes under which marriage breakdown is the sole ground for divorce. If one excludes the English type of law where "breakdown" is provable by fault grounds, there were 11 such states in 1976.[192]

California was the first state to enact a "pure" no-fault statute. Under the California Family Law Act of 1970, "irreconcilable differences, which have caused the irremediable breakdown of the marriage" and "incurable insanity" are the only grounds for the "dissolution" (as it is called) of marriage.[193] The insanity ground is rarely used. The original draft of the California bill required the court to take the allegations of irreconcilable differences in the petition at face value.[194] But it is not surprising that the California legislature was unwilling to move so abruptly to an open system of divorce on demand. The form of judicial inquest was preserved. Six years later, it is clear that under the California and other no-fault laws the "inquest" is nothing more than a ritual; and that divorce is, in fact if not in form, available upon unilateral demand.[195]

Actually, divorce has become so ritualized and automatic, even in fault or mixed jurisdictions as well as in no-fault jurisdictions, that judges speak quite openly about it. The April 1976 issue of *Trial magazine* carried an article, "Divorce without Trauma", by a trial judge seeking to instruct lawyers how to properly conduct a divorce case.[196] He explains that in a typical case the parties first work out mutually agreeable divorce terms. "A court hearing is then held where unopposed testimony of the plaintiff is taken to affirm the grounds for divorce alleged in the complaint." Despite the fact that, "[f]or run-of-the-mill stipulated cases, the presentation of testimony need take no more than five minutes", the judge has observed that the hearing is often "needlessly protracted" by poorly-prepared attorneys. The judge therefore sets out a suggested script for lawyers to follow, so that they may earn the gratitude of their clients and the court for "economy of time".

The ritual in California quickly became so concise that it naturally occurred to some judges and lawyers that an uncontested divorce case, like any other uncontested lawsuit, could be handled entirely on paper, through affidavits, without the necessity of any court appearance by either spouse.[197] However, this procedure was held inadequate by the California Supreme Court in 1972. Ruling that a person seeking a divorce must appear in court unless there are exceptional circumstances (such as hospitalization or imprisonment), the Court condemned plaintiffs, lawyers and judges to continue the weary acting out of formalities until the legislature shall ordain them to cease.[198]

The divorce provisions of the Uniform Act,[199] too, preserve the form of inquest. Sections 302 and 305 of the Act provide that the court must find that the marriage is irretrievably broken and that its "finding" must be "supported by evidence" either that the parties have lived apart for 180 days prior to the commencement of the action *or* that there is "serious marital discord adversely affecting the attitude of one or both of the parties toward the marriage". The draftsmen's comment to section 305 states that the "...determination of breakdown should be a judicial function rather than a conclusive presumption arising from the parties' testimony or from the petition".

Thus, theoretically, a court under the new no-fault grounds retains even greater discretion to deny a divorce than under the old fault grounds where it had to grant a divorce if the plaintiff's allegations were proved. As Rheinstein has pointed out, a judge, as a matter of strict logic, could take the position that no marriage is "irretrievably" broken, at least while the parties are still alive.[200]

Like the California law, the Uniform Act as originally proposed would have allowed the court less discretion. The court would have been required to dissolve a marriage when both parties agreed or when the petition was unopposed, and one party would have had the right to dissolve a childless marriage.[201] Professor Herma Hill Kay, who played an active role in preparing both statutes, has stated that the original proposals in both cases

...rest ultimately upon notions of family privacy: namely, that married persons ought to have the right to terminate their relationship just as they had the right to begin it, subject only to the law's power to insist that the custody and support of their children be provided for adequately and that their financial affairs be settled equitably.[202]

An early draft of the Uniform Act was in fact adopted in Colorado where a court now *must* grant a divorce if the testimony that the marriage has broken down is uncontroverted.[203]

There is agreement among the observers that divorce in California and the other pure no-fault states is in fact available on unilateral demand.[204] One commentator sums up the situation as follows: "The difference between divorce by demand and no-fault divorce as it is practiced is one of degree and appearance rather than kind, and in most instances, even these differences have been slight."[205]

Lately, objections to even the form of inquest are being raised. It has been said that the marriage breakdown laws, praised for doing away with hypocrisy, are themselves open to the charge of hypocrisy since the ritual recitation of reasons for breakdown can bring "fault" considerations back into the process.[206] The kinds of recitals petitioners often make in uncontested hearings are also thought to justify the criticism that the inquest is an unwarranted intrusion on individual privacy.[207] It has even been argued in the United States, as in France, that a corollary of the right to marry is the right to terminate a marriage.[208] Some have questioned the constitutionality of various restrictions on divorce.[209] As in the areas of marriage formation and the legal effects of marriage, there is a recent Supreme Court decision on divorce, the full import of which is at this point still unclear. In the 1971 case of *Boddie v. Connecticut,* the Supreme Court held that welfare recipients cannot be denied access to courts for the purpose of obtaining a divorce because of their inability to pay court fees and costs.[210] Although the case does not purport to go any further than simply assuring equal access to the courts for the poor, it has been understood by some as, together with *Loving v. Virginia*,[211] potentially establishing that freedom to marry includes the right to remarry or to simply terminate the marriage relationship.[212] This reading seems too broad in view of a 1975 Supreme Court case upholding Iowa's one-year residence requirement for divorce.[213] But *Boddie*, together with *Loving, Eisenstadt*,[214] and *Griswold*,[215] may have implications yet to be revealed.

Meanwhile, divorce on demand is already practiced in a number of states where separation for a certain length of time is a ground for divorce. Where this period is lengthy, however, shorter routes are often chosen.[216] As Rheinstein has pointed out, separation will not work as the sole ground for divorce unless the period involved is short.[217]

The movement for change in the United States has not spent itself in bringing about a system of divorce which is in fact available upon unilateral demand. Changes are still taking place with the effect of further disentangling the State from involvement in the marriage dissolution process as such.

So far the only state which has explicitly made unilateral divorce available on demand and which has drastically limited the role of the judge is Washington. Whereas the other no-fault laws provide that a court shall grant a divorce *if it finds* that the marriage is irretrievably broken, the State of Washington's Marriage Dissolution Act of 1973 provides that the court *must* dissolve the marriage as follows:[218] If both parties allege the marriage is irretrievably broken, or if no denial is entered by one party to such an allegation by the other, the court must decree dissolution 90 days after the action is begun. If one party denies the marriage is broken, the court may either (1) dissolve the marriage, (2) transfer the case to the family court, (3) refer the parties to a counselling service, asking the service to report back within 60 days, or (4) continue the matter for not more than 60 days. As a Washington state judge has commented, the Washington Act differs from the others in that it does not require presentation of evidence of irretrievable breakdown and the exercise of judicial discretion. Rather it has elected to proceed on the basis of a conclusive presumption arising from the allegations of the petition.[219] As Judge Holman straightforwardly acknowledges, the Washington Act "...places the burden of resolving or terminating marital conflicts squarely upon the parties rather than upon the state".[220]

Yet it is clear that the primary significance of the Washington law is in making explicit what was already the practice under fault grounds, mixed grounds, and no-fault-with-inquest statutes. Washington has merely conformed its law to its social reality, as did Sweden in 1974.

Apart from the advent of unilateral divorce on demand, there are other signs of the retreat of the State from the matter of marriage termination in the United States. Conciliation provisions, often built into the American divorce reform statutes as part of the legislative compromises, are typically little used and many, having served their purpose to aid in securing adoption of reforms, have already been repealed. The growing realization that divorce is a matter of agreement-plus-ritual has led to the proliferation of manuals and "kits" designed to enable private individuals to obtain divorces without the assistance of lawyers.

But, at the same time, withdrawal of legal regulation of the termination of the marriage has spotlighted the economic and child-related problems which often arise when a cohabitation, formal or informal, is terminated. Divorce law reform is thus increasingly turning away from "divorce" as such and to the *consequences* of marriage termination.

The old system, in which fault grounds or the existence of defenses which might bar a divorce were used to obtain advantages in the pre-divorce negotiating process, has increasingly been replaced by systems in which one spouse may terminate the marriage regardless of the wish of the other.[221] Many American writers, chief among them Professor Henry Foster and Doctor Doris Freed, have insisted that a system of divorce on demand must be accompanied by fair and equitable provisions for maintenance and property division and by provisions to secure the welfare of children.[222] Foster and Freed have well documented the deficiencies of American state laws, old and new, with respect to these matters. They have pointed out that while divorce reform, which costs little and may even result in savings in terms of state machinery required to implement it, has passed relatively easily, movements for specialized family courts to aid in conciliation and to bring expert attention to resolution of interspousal disputes concerning money and children have failed to win legislative support because of the expense they would entail.[223] Ironically, when the fault element has been eliminated from the grounds for divorce and from consideration in post-divorce economic matters, it has surfaced in a particularly vicious form in the area of child custody. Since "fitness" of a parent can always be made an issue in custody matters, many spouses are not above using the threat of contesting the other spouse's fitness as custodian in order to avoid paying maintenance or child support.[224] As Foster and Freed have warned, "[n]o fault divorce...has enhanced the risk that the welfare of children may be downgraded or overlooked".[225]

Thus, the United States, like Sweden, is coming to the realization that

The focal points for judicial inquiry should be economic justice as between the parties and the protection of the welfare of children.... [I]nstead of merely holding a mock inquest for allegedly dead marriages, courts should...help the family to pick up the pieces and plan for the future.[226]

The Chief Justice of the Supreme Court of the United States has lent his support to these ideas by calling frequently in his public speeches for the transfer of family matters from the court system to specialized administrative agencies.[227] But so far these matters remain to a great extent unresolved problems. The state of Washington seems to have pioneered even here, however, with a family court system which provides the possibility of facilitating conciliation where that is appropriate and for giving the required degree of attention to economic and child-related matters, which are treated separately from the question of divorce itself.[228]

The device of making the entry of the divorce decree conditional upon satisfactory regulation of financial and custody questions is not practical within the federal system of the United States where a court may have jurisdiction to grant a divorce but not over property or children of the marriage.

The Uniform Act contents itself with providing that a divorce decree is not to be granted until the court has,

...to the extent it has jurisdiction to do so,...considered, approved, or provided for child custody, the support of any child entitled to support, the maintenance of either spouse, and the disposition of property; or has provided for a separate later hearing to complete these matters.[229]

III. Summary: Free Terminability as an Attribute of Marriage

The general aim of Chapters 2, 4 and 5 has been to describe the transformation of the legal institution of marriage. The events related in the present chapter have gone far toward transforming that institution from a relationship which was legally terminable only for serious cause to a relationship dissoluble at will. In terms of the relationship of the State to the family, the movement of the divorce law described here can only be seen as evidence of the diminishing willingness of the State to be involved in the matter of marriage termination. It is but one aspect of the State's gradual divestment of its marriage regulation business.

Some may object that I have overstated the case: that, except in Sweden and Washington, there is no unilateral divorce, or even, in many places, no divorce by mutual consent. At most, it might be argued, there is increasingly, in pure no-fault jurisdictions, divorce available upon a judicial finding that a marriage has irretrievably broken down. The facts that a reason (marriage breakdown) must be given and that a finding by a court that the marriage has in fact broken down must be made, are evidence, it might be said, of the State's continuing interest in, involvement with and supervision of marriage dissolution. Further, it can be pointed out that the progress of pure no-fault divorce has been by no means uniform. England and France and the majority of American states have been content for the moment with mixed grounds. Even West Germany has retained a trace of the fault concept. Only in Sweden and in 11 American states is divorce available on purely objective grounds.

To these arguments there are the following answers: In the first place, fault divorce, wherever we have seen it to exist, has been converted to divorce by mutual consent through collusion and perjury, and, in the United States, by migration. In all the countries here examined, the percentage of uncontested divorces has consistently been estimated as over 90%. The courts have co-operated with the litigants, by transforming general fault grounds such as cruelty into no-fault grounds by interpretation. Everywhere but in three American states no-fault grounds, first inserted in the divorce law by judicial interpretation, have now been added to or substituted for fault grounds through legislation.

Secondly, we have observed that not only has every system here examined embraced divorce by mutual consent in practice, but they also make uni-lateral divorce available, no matter what the law is. What Henri Mazeaud has said about French law is also true about the other systems where the law still appears to give a judge discretion to deny a divorce under certain circum-stances: a persistent individual who wants a divorce can get one by purchas-ing or coercing the consent of the other spouse.[230] The exceptional cases where an unwilling spouse is able to keep a determined partner from getting a divorce are not merely exceptional. They are everywhere said to be rare.

Furthermore, not only have we seen that divorce at will exists everywhere in fact, but the law is steadily being brought into harmony with reality. The process described in this chapter appears to have acquired such momentum that it is difficult to imagine its reversal. The requirement of a judicial finding of irretrievable breakdown in practice means no more than that the court must enter a finding on the record, as has been the case in England and in the American no-fault states. As a practical matter, no answer can be made to the allegation of breakdown if one spouse firmly insists the marriage is at an end, and in fact it is practically unheard of that divorces are denied under such statutes. The draftsmen of what might be called the first wave of no-fault statutes felt the necessity to provide for at least the appearance of judicial inquest, in order to secure acceptance of and support for the no-fault prin-ciple. The Archbishop of Canterbury's group, it will be recalled, supported divorce on the sole ground of breakdown only on condition that it be accompanied by a thorough investigation of the circumstances of each case. But now that the principle of breakdown divorce has been accepted, the palliatives of inquest or conciliation necessary to secure passage of no-fault legislation can be seen to be dropping away through repeal or disuse.

The 1973 legislation in Sweden and Washington, coming along after the ground had already been prepared and experience had been accumulated under no-fault statutes, dropped the pretense of inquest. Under both laws the court *must* grant a divorce upon the petition of one party. The Swedish law moves closer to total disengagement of the State from the divorce process in that it does not require a reason (breakdown) to be stated, and repeals its former conciliation measures. The state of Washington still preserves the formula of breakdown and makes conciliation services available. But in another sense, the Washington law is more liberal than the Swedish, because in a case where the petition is opposed, it seems to permit a maximum delay of only five months whereas in Sweden there is a six-month waiting period in such cases. (Another difference is that while the Swedish law has attracted a great deal of international attention, the Washington law has gone unnoticed, classified as simply another no-fault divorce law.)

While the movement in England, France, West Germany and the United States is by no means snowballing toward total reform on the Swedish-Washington model, formal legal change is less important than that marriage is in fact increasingly terminable at will and that the legal divorce proceedings are increasingly being seen as the mere formalities they are. The laws themselves are gradually coming to reflect these facts, Sweden and Washington at present being the only places where the facts are fully reflected.

Finally, with legal divorce as with the legal marriage, one must not forget the shadow institutions. Cases dealing with custody or visitation rights with respect to children born outside marriage increasingly imitate divorce cases in their approach. Terminating a legal marriage by simply walking out was known until recently as "the poor man's divorce". Increasingly, it is becoming the property of many persons who are not poor but do not feel the need of a legal death certificate for their marriages nor for a legal permit to marry. The spread of this kind of social conduct reacts back on the law, on the one hand as an impetus for divorce reform lest legal divorce become simply irrelevant; on the other hand, as an impetus to seek ways of fixing economic responsibility upon providers who abandon their families.

It is probably not an accident that outright divorce on demand has been admitted first in places such as Washington and Sweden where informal cohabitation has made important claims upon the legal system. One has the impression from Professor Sundberg's writing that in Sweden unilateral divorce, like the elimination of the vow for life from the marriage ceremony, is in a curious way almost a conservative measure, intended to "save" legal marriage by winning back persons who live in informal unions.

As free exit becomes established as an attribute of marriage, either in fact or in law, this inevitably interacts with the increasing freedom of entry seen in Chapter 2, and the increasing withdrawal of regulation of the on-going marriage in Chapter 4. The trends react upon and reinforce each other.[231] Together, they amount to a dejuridification of marriage. A relationship which can be freely entered or left is, Professor Sundberg suggests, "not a legal relationship", whatever else it may be.[232] He sees the Swedish development as having reached this point. Congressman Drinan, writing in 1968, before the wave of major divorce law changes, approached the same view: "If American divorce law in the near future formally endorses the idea that spouses may rescind their contract of marriage by mutual choice and without any allegation or proof of fault, American law may well have explicitly or implicitly rejected the concept of marriage as a status or as an institution."[233]

In fact, it is believed that the trends described in Chapters 2, 4 and 5 do represent the dejuridification of marriage. The present chapter has described the transformation of divorce from an institution characterized by a seemingly high degree of State interest and involvement, to yet another empty structure in the ghost town left behind as the modern State retreats from the regulation of marriage, its formation, effects and finally its termination. As the process unfolds, one cannot help but wonder how it was that these matters became subject to governmental regulation in the first place. That story, fascinating in itself, is the subject of Chapter 7 of this book.

But for the moment we must return to the distinction taken at the outset of this Chapter between divorce as the event which terminates marriage, and the economic and child-related consequences of marriage termination. For, the withdrawal of the State from regulation of marriage termination as such has brought about an increasingly clear separation between the divorce proceeding itself and economic and child custody questions which may be generated by marriage dissolution. As to these issues one can make three general observations: (1) It now seems to be almost universally agreed that, from the point of view of practical legal and social policy, these matters, and not the grounds for divorce, are the "vital issues". (2) While the State has withdrawn from involvement with the formation and dissolution of marriage, it has by no means withdrawn from involvement with e relations of spouses so far as economic and child-related matters are concerned. (3) But in dealing with such matters, the law seems increasingly to be taking a functional approach, to be solving practical problems which arise from cohabitation and its termination regardless of whether a legal marriage has taken place, or simply to be responding to individual needs. The extent that the law is becoming marriage-neutral in these matters, one can say that even the remaining "effects" of marriage and of divorce, are really just consequences of cohabitation and regulated as such. Conversely, where the law has not become neutral, we can see the extent to which legal marriage still retains distinctive features. The following chapter explores the current legal treatment of these issues in the context of dissolution of marriage by divorce or death.

NOTES

[1] *König* par 103.

[2] Constitution of Ireland, Article 41(3) 2°.

[3] Except for dissolution by the so-called Pauline Privilege under Canon 1120 "in favor of the faith", these forms are, of course, treated as declarations that no valid marriage ever existed between the parties. See generally, *Bouscaren & Ellis* 611–633.

[4] *König* par. 96.

[5] *König* par. 97.

[6] *König* par. 97, 98.

[7] *Rheinstein, M.S.D.L.* 247–307. See also *König* par. 98, 101.

[8] *König* par. 104, 105.

[9] *Konig* par. 99, 103.

[10] T. Parsons and R. Bales, Family Ch. 1 (1955).

[11] *König* par. 109 puts it this way: "If we depart from the distinction between breakdown of the marriage and legal divorce then the latter appears from the outset in a neutral light. The breakdown is the crisis, with the legal divorce being simply an adaptation to the new situation."

[12] *Bromley* 204.

[13] *Id.* at 203.

[14] *Id.* at 204 n. 10.

[15] *Id.* at 204.

[16] *Rheinstein, M.S.D.L.* 320.

[17] *Id.* esp. at 247–260.

[18] *Field of Choice* par. 20.

[19] *Bromley* 217.

[20] Report of the Royal Commission on Marriage and Divorce (Morton Commission) Cmnd. 9678 (1956); *Putting Asunder; Field of Choice.*

[21] Rheinstein, M.S.D.L. 323.

[22] The Archbishop's Group had clearly in mind the distinctions between marriage as a social, legal and religious institution: "Today, it is manifestly impossible that the Church should accept the matrimonial law of the land as satisfactory for its own purposes." *Putting Asunder* 7. "When...a modern court 'dissolves' a marriage, it is not making a pronouncement about the *vinculum matrimonii* in the traditional Christian sense of that term; for it does not take cognizance of any such thing. What it dissolves is the legal complex of rights and duties that make up the legal status of marriage." *Id.* at 11.

[23] *Putting Asunder* 67–70.

[24] *Field of Choice* par. 120.

[25] The Divorce Reform Act of 1969 and the Matrimonial Proceedings and Property Act of 1971 were consolidated in the Matrimonial Causes Act of 1973.

[26] *Bromley* 213.

[27] Matrimonial Causes Act 1973 § 1(2).

[28] *Id.* at § 6 (2).

[29] See *infra* at 199.

[30] Matrimonial Causes Act 1973 § 3. This section has been criticized for its obvious retention of the fault principle, e.g. *Cretney* 110.

[31] *Bromley* 213.

[32] In the original draft of the Act, active consent was not required, *Cretney* 121.

[33] Matrimonial Causes Act 1973 s. 5.
[34] *Id.* at s. 10(2)–(4).
[35] See *Bromley* 288–289.
[36] See *Cretney* 140–141.
[37] I *Finer Report* 89.
[38] *Field of Choice* par. 15. Cf. *Putting Asunder* 23–24.
[39] *Bromley* 217.
[40] *Cretney* 137.
[41] *Cretney* 135; *Eekelaar* 247–248.
[42] *Cretney* 137; *Eekelaar* 248; Finlay, Reluctant, but Inevitable: The Retreat of Matrimonial Fault, 38 Mod. L. Rev. 153, 171 (1975).
[43] *Bromley* 217.
[44] Finlay, *supra* n. 42.
[45] *Id.* at 173.
[46] *Field of Choice* pars. 29–32; *Putting Asunder* 63–64.
[47] Matrimonial Causes Act 1973 s. 6.
[48] *Cretney* 134.
[49] Jackson, Book Review, 89 L. Q. Rev. 423, 424 (1973).
[50] The Search for a Rational Divorce Law, 1971 Curr. Leg. Prob. 210.
[51] *Field of Choice* par. 119; *Putting Asunder* p. 53.
[52] *Cretney* 131.
[53] *Elston, Fuller & Murch* 626, 636.
[54] *Id.* at 635.
[55] *Id.* at 633; *Cretney* 112.
[56] *Elston, Fuller & Murch* 612–633.
[57] *Id.* at 633.
[58] Bradley, Realism in Divorce Law, 126 New L. J. 1204 (1976).
[59] *Eekelaar* 252.
[60] Quoted in *Cretney* 111.
[61] *Cretney* 135.
[62] Finlay, *supra* n. 42 at 157–158.
[63] Australia, Family Law Act 1975, No. 53 of 1975 s. 48, 49.
[64] *Elston, Fuller & Murch* 637.
[65] *Ibid.*
[66] Ibid.
[67] *Id.* at 639.
[68] *Id.* at 609–610.
[69] Jackson, *supra* n. 49 at 422.
[70] Bradley, *supra* n. 58.
[71] *Rheinstein, M.S.D.L.* 201.
[72] *Bénabent* 486.
[73] *Rheinstein, M.S.D.L.* 211. It has often been said that Bonaparte insisted on the inclusion of divorce by mutual consent among the grounds for divorce in the Civil Code because he already intended to terminate his marriage to Josephine in order to be able to enter a marriage that would produce an heir. But while he may have had his personal situation on his mind during this period, he seems to have wanted the Code to offer a method of divorce to the French people which would not involve dishonor and embarrassment. As for himself, in fact he never used the divorce provisions of the Civil Code. The dissolution of his marriage was pronounced by the *Senatus-Consult*; it was a political act outside the domain of civil law. Roughol-Valdeyron, Le divorce par consentement mutuel et le Code Napoléon, Rev. trim, dr. civ. 1975, 432, 484–487.
[74] *Rheinstein, M.S.D.L.* 195.
[75] Roughol-Valdeyron *supra* n. 73 at 487.
[76] *"La condamnation de l'un des époux à une peine afflictive et infamante"* under former Art. 231 was

understood to mean sentence to death or lengthy imprisonment. In the former case, if the granting of a pardon prevented the marriage from being terminated by death, the death sentence remained a ground for divorce. See D. 1954. Jur. 566 (Cass. civ. 2e).

[77] *"Excès, sévices ou injures* [excesses, cruelty or abuse], constituting a serious or repeated violation of marital duties", under former Art. 232 came to be understood and treated in the same way as American courts have treated physical and mental cruelty. Using this ground, French courts have transformed the fault divorce of the law of 1884 into no-fault divorce. *Rheinstein, M.S.D.L.* 214, 217, 219.

[78] *Bénabent* 486; and Bénabent, note J.C.P. 1975. II. 17934.

[79] *Lindon* Nos. 22, 38.

[80] Chaumié, À propos du projet de loi sur le divorce, Gaz. Pal. 1974. 786–801.

[81] *Carbonnier, Mémoire* 116.

[82] *Ibid.*: "There are different feelings about divorce, which can give rise to different forms of the institution. Public opinion, for its part, is divided with respect to the idea of reform. One can discern one bloc – young (is it their age or their generation?) – which is disposed to go very far; another bloc is opposed to any innovation; and between the two the "centrists" who, while manifesting an attachment to the principle of indissolubility of marriage or at least to the exceptional character of divorce, take indulgent positions with respect to concrete situations described to them. It seems, in any event, that the general widespread sense of justice, which supported the reforms on behalf of children, (and therefore the reform of the law of filiation), is not so easily identified when it is the parents who are at issue."

[83] *Rheinstein, M.S.D.L.* 195. Many interesting examples of this fact were observable in connection with the *affaire* Gabrielle Russier described by Mavis Gallant in "Annals of Justice-Immortal Gatitio", The New Yorker, June 26, 1971.

[84] *Carbonnier, Mèmoire* 117. Dean Carbonnier had been asked by M. Taittinger, the Minister of Justice in the Pompidou government, to prepare a draft, which in essence became the proposal put forward by the government of Giscard d'Estaing. This proposal, with certain modifications, in turn became the present law.

[85] *Carbonnier, Mèmoire* 117. In preparing the draft law, the systems of nine countries (not including the United States) were studied and extensive sociological investigations were undertaken. *Id.* at 116.

[86] *Id.* at 118.

[87] *Ibid.*

[88] Loi No. 75–617 of 11 July 1975 *portant réforme du divorce,* (J.O. 12 July p. 7171(1)); D.S. 1975 Leg. 248; amending the French Civil Code; and Decree of 5 Dec. 1975, D.S. 1975. 426 on divorce procedure. References herein are to the new Civil Code articles.

[89] Roughol-Valdeyron, *supra* n. 73 at 487. Concerning divorce by mutual consent, Savoye-Rollin, the reporter for the divorce provisions of the Code, stated before the Tribunate: "All the law of divorce is there. Recourse to specific grounds is never frequent in our mores. They [our mores] may not be good, but they are polite.... We earnestly sought for a device which would conceal all evils and cure them without publicity." Quoted *id.* at 487.

[90] *Lindon* No. 34.

[91] *Id.* at No. 138. The National Assembly and the Senate voted on the law section by section, rather than as one single piece of legislation.

[92] See Chesné, Le divorce par consentement mutuel, D. 1963. Chr. 95; *Lindon* at No. 8. Dean Carbonnier has said: "It is notorious that we already have in France, de facto, divorce by mutual consent, in the innumerable cases of 'divorce by accord' where the spouses collaborate to simulate wrongs and injuries. The comedy discredits the law and (as sociological inquiry has revealed) leaves the spouses with bitter memories. To introduce a procedure of joint petition would be thus a healthy step." (*Mèmoire* at 117.)

[93] *Lindon* Nos. 23, 24, 421.

[94] *Id.* at No. 145.

[95] *Id.* at No. 131.

[96] *Id.* at No. 133.
[97] *Lindon* Nos. 90, 95, 110.
[98] H. Mazeaud, Le divorce par consentement forcé, D. 1963, Chr. 141.
[99] *Lindon* No. 102.
[100] *Id.* at Nos. 76–86.
[101] *Id.* at Nos. 25–27.
[102] *Ibid.*
[103] New Art. 246.
[104] *Rheinstein, M.S.D.L.* 216.
[105] *Ibid.*
[106] *Lindon* No. 357.
[107] *Carbonnier, Mèmoire* at 119.
[108] *Lindon* Nos. 23, 404, 411, 412.
[109] *Id.* at No. 421.
[110] This was already the case after 5 months of operation of the 1976 law according to two practitioners who spoke at the 18 June 1976 meeting on the Divorce Reform, sponsored by the Famille et Droit Association at the National Assembly in Paris.
[111] Chaumié, *supra* n. 80 at 787.
[112] *Lindon* 411.
[113] Commaille, Divorce: la loi suit, Autrement No. 3 at 122, 127 (1975).
[114] *Rheinstein, M.S.D.L.* 213.
[115] *Ibid.*
[116] *Lindon* No. 18.
[117] *Carbonnier, Flexible Droit* 127; Kahn-Freund, On Uses and Misuses of Comparative Law, 37 Mod. L. Rev. 1, 13 (1974); *Rheinstein, M.S.D.L.* 8.
[118] See Chapter 4 *supra* at 117.
[119] *Carbonnier, 2 Droit Civil* 79.
[120] See Chapter 4 *supra* at 117.
[121] Marriage Law for Greater Germany (Grossdeutsches Ehegesetz) of 6 July 1938 RGB1. I 807; reenacted with minor changes as Allied Control Council Law No. 16 of 20 February 1946, referred to herein as "EheG". The 1938 law is discussed in detail in Schoch, Divorce Law and Practice under National Socialism in Germany, 28 Iowa L. Rev. 225 (1943). The background of the Allied Control Council law is discussed in *Rheinstein, Family and Succession* 27, 46–47.
[122] *Rheinstein, Family and Succession* 44; *Rheinstein, M.S.D.L.* 293–294.
[123] *Rheinstein, M.S.D.L.* 25.
[124] *Dörner* 59.
[125] Quoted in *Dörner* at 59.
[126] Prussian General C. §716.
[127] Prussian General C. §718a.
[128] German C.C. former §§1564–1587. The grounds for divorce included adultery, bigamy, insanity, unnatural practices, attempt on a spouse's life, wilful desertion and a general fault ground.
[129] *Rheinstein, M.S.D.L.* 295–301.
[130] 1.EheRG of 14 June 1976.
[131] Schoch, *supra* n. 121 at 234–236.
[132] *Id.* at 237.
[133] I. E. Cohn, Manual of German Law 229 (2d ed. 1968).
[134] EheG §§42, 43.
[135] EheG §§44, 45, 46.
[136] EheG §48.
[137] Law of 11 August 1961 BGBl. I 1221. This amendment merely adopted the existing judicial practice which had made it difficult for a plaintiff to overcome the defendant's opposition in contested cases, *Rheinstein, M.S.D.L.* 287. Ironically, since the amendment the 4th Civil Senate

of the Bundesgerichtshof has failed to follow its earlier practice and has interpreted §48(2) so as to deny few divorces.

[138] *Rheinstein, Family and Succession* 46.

[139] *Ibid.*

[140] Rheinstein, M.S.D.L. 287–288; Giesen, Divorce Reform in Germany, 7 Fam. L. Q. 351, 360 (1973).

[141] *Rheinstein, M.S.D.L.* 346.

[142] Giesen, *supra* n. 140 at 360.

[143] *Rheinstein, M.S.D.L. 393.*

[144] *Ibid.*

[145] Quoted in Bohndorf, Recent Developments in German Divorce Law, 19 Int. & Comp. L. Q. 705, 710 (1970).

[146] *Rheinstein, M.S.D.L.* 392.

[147] The German Tribune, December 21, 1975, at 4.

[148] *Rheinstein, M.S.D.L.* 394–395.

[149] Boston Globe, January 31, 1976, at 2.

[150] German C.C. §1353. Citations of the reform law are to the new articles of the German Civil Code.

[151] Die Zeit, April 23, 1976, at 1 (Overseas Edition).

[152] *Rheinstein, M.S.D.L.* 394.

[153] *Rheinstein, M.S.D.L.* 395.

[154] *Ibid.*

[155] Die Zeit *supra* n. 151.

[156] *Ibid.*

[157] *Ibid.*

[158] Re-enacted with slight modifications as the Marriage Code of Sweden (*Giftermalsbalken*) of 11 June 1920, now amended by Law of 5 June 1973, No. 645.

[159] *Schmidt (1963)* at 110–111.

[160] *Schmidt (1971)* at 198.

[161] *Schmidt (1963)* at 111–112.

[162] *Rheinstein, M.S.D.L.* 139.

[163] Quoted in *Schmidt (1963)* at 117.

[164] *Ibid.*

[165] *Id.* at 112.

[166] *Rheinstein, M.S.D.L.* 141–142.

[167] *Ibid.*

[168] *Ibid.*

[169] *Sundberg, Louvain Report.*

[170] *Rheinstein, M.S.D.L.* 144

[171] *Schmidt (1963)* at 121; Rheinstein, *M.S.D.L.* 142–143.

[172] *Rheinstein, M.S.D.L.* 126.

[173] *Id.* at 155.

[174] Quoted in *Sundberg, Louvain Report.*

[175] Quoted in *Sundberg, Recent Changes* 44.

[176] Quoted in Note, *Current Legal Developments – Sweden*, 19 Int. & Comp. L. Q. 164 (1970).

[177] Quoted in Note, *Sweden – Family Law*, 22 Int. & Comp. L. Q. 182, 183 (1973).

[178] *Schmidt (1971)* at 218.

[179] Marriage Code of 11 June 1920, as amended by Law of 5 June 1973, §§1–5.

[180] This section refers to prohibited marriages formerly treated under the law of nullity.

[181] *Schmidt (1963)* at 114; Rheinstein, *M.S.D.L.* 155.

[182] *Sundberg, Louvain Report.*

[183] *Rheinstein, M.S.D.L.* 131.

[184] National Conference of Commissioners on Uniform State Laws, Uniform Marriage and Divorce Act (1970) with 1971 and 1973 amendments.

[185] Arizona, California, Colorado, Florida, Iowa, Kentucky, Michigan, Montana, Nebraska, Oregon, Washington. I am relying on the lists prepared by Freed, Grounds for Divorce in the American Jurisdictions, 8 Fam. L. Q. 401 (1974) and Freed & Foster, Taking out the Fault but not the Sting, Trial Magazine, April, 1976 at 10, 11, but I have eliminated those jurisdictions where breakdown must or can be proved by proving specific fault grounds. In some of the states listed here, insanity is retained as a separate no-fault ground.

[186] Illinois, Pennsylvania and South Dakota. Change in Illinois and Pennsylvania was said by Freed and Foster to be imminent in Taking out the Fault but not the Sting, Trial Magazine, April, 1976 at 10, 11.

[187] *Id.* at 10; *Rheinstein, M.S.D.L.* 63.

[188] *Rheinstein, M.S.D.L.* 316.

[189] *Id.* at 63–91; *Wheeler* 155.

[190] *Rheinstein, M.S.D.L.* 316.

[191] *Foster & Freed*; Levy, Uniform Marriage and Divorce Legislation (1969); *Rheinstein, M.S.D.L.*; *Wheeler*; and many other books and articles treat the subject.

[192] See n. 185 *supra*.

[193] Cal. Civil Code §§ 4506, 4507, 4508.

[194] Kay, Making Marriage and Divorce Safe for Women (review of *Rheinstein, M.S.D.L.*), 60 Calif. L. Rev. 1683, 1685–1686 (1972).

[195] *Foster & Freed* 446; *Wheeler* 22–23.

[196] Maxwell, Divorce without Trauma, Trial Magazine, April 1976, at 13.

[197] The fate of these efforts is discussed in *Wheeler* at 22–23.

[198] *Id.* at 26.

[199] The Uniform Act or a version of it has been adopted in Arizona, Colorado, Kentucky, and Montana and is under active consideration in a number of states.

[200] *Rheinstein, M.S.D.L.* at 368.

[201] Kay, *supra* n. 194 at 1685–1686.

[202] *Id.* at 1686.

[203] Colo. Rev. Stat. §46–1–10(1) (Supp. 1971).

[204] *Wheeler* 27–30; *Foster & Freed* 446–447.

[205] *Wheeler* 48.

[206] *Id.* at 37.

[207] *Ibid.*

[208] Comment, *Untying the Knot: The Course and Patterns of Divorce Reform*, 57 Corn. L. Rev. 649, 652 (1972).

[209] *Foster* 74–78.

[210] *Boddie* v. *Connecticut*, 401 U.S. 371 (1971).

[211] See Chapter 2 *supra* at 65.

[212] Comment, *supra* n. 208 at 652. See also, Gold, The Poor and Divorce, 3 Fam. L. Q. 281 (1969), commenting on the early stages of the *Boddie* litigation.

[213] *Sosna* v. *Iowa*, 419 U.S. 393 (1975).

[214] See Chapter 4 *supra* at 173.

[215] See Chapter 4 *supra* at 173.

[216] Foster, Divorce Reform and the Uniform Act, 7 Fam. L. Q. 179, 198 (1973); Comment, *supra* n. 208 at 657.

[217] *Rheinstein, M.S.D.L.* 313.

[218] Washington Marriage Dissolution Act 1973, §26.09.030.

[219] Holman, A Law in the Spirit of Conciliation and Understanding: Washington's Marriage Dissolution Act, 9 Gonz. L. Rev. 39, 44 (1973).

[220] *Id.* at 56.

[221] *Foster & Freed, Divorce Reform* 446.

[222] *Id.* at 448.

[223] *Id.* at 456.

[224] *Id.* at 488, 490.

[225] *Id.* at 490–491.

[226] *Id.* at 491.

[227] E.g., New York Times, December 30, 1973 at 24; New York Times, April 8, 1976, at 27.

[228] Holman, *supra* n. 219.

[229] UMDA §302(a)(4).

[230] H. Mazeaud, *supra* n. 98.

[231] Drinan put it this way at 54: "Inevitably, this new concept of marriage as a mere contract rescindable at the will of the parties will have an enormous influence upon whatever American law may decide to do in order to regulate the formation of such a contract. For if the marriage contract is seen as an agreement between a man and a woman, which can be dissolved by mutual wish or even unilaterally by one spouse without fault on the part of the other spouse, then the law need not reassert and seek to implement all those safeguards now present in the law, most of which clearly presuppose that the marriage contract is made for life,…and that only in extreme cases will the state permit the dissolution of any marriage bond which has been created in compliance with all the dictates of the law."

[232] *Sundberg, Marriage or No Marriage* 234.

[233] *Drinan* 53–54.

EFFECTS OF LEGAL MARRIAGE: CONSEQUENCES OF DISSOLUTION

I. Introduction

If the process of dejuridification whose unfolding has been narrated in the preceding chapters might be described as moving toward the withering away of marriage as a legal institution, it is time to make clear that this delegalization of marriage in no way implies the withering away of the State so far as its relationship to the family is concerned. What becomes plain when we turn our attention to the economic and child-related consequences of marriage dissolution in the present chapter is that State interest in these areas, as expressed through laws, not only continues but is higher than ever. But it is being manifested in new ways. These new forms of State involvement with the family are consistent both with the dejuridification of marriage and with the tendency to blur or erase distinctions between legal and *de facto* marriage as well as between the married and the unmarried states.

The present Chapter is concerned with the effects produced by the fact that two persons have been legally married when that marriage is dissolved by death, divorce, or, as is less frequently the case, by legal separation or annulment. The pressure from the sweep of current legal and social developments is such that the inquiry of this chapter sooner or later leads to the question of the extent to which any given legal effects attach to dissolution of *legal* marriages alone, and the extent to which the legal effects traditionally attached to the dissolution of legal marriages are falling away or else becoming attributes of the dissolution of *de facto* marriages as well. The inquiry of the Chapter does not end there, however, for it is also necessary to consider the extent to which the needs of dependent or needy individuals are being directly responded to through programs in which an individual's eligibility is independent of any legal *or* de facto family relationships.

As these questions are pressed, it will be apparent that it becomes less and less useful to use the term "family law" (tied as it is to the touchstone of legal marriage and the legitimate family) to describe the current interaction between State and family. Rather one must think in terms of "laws affecting the family" in order to reach and include for consideration not only family law but all the ways in which the modern State, both intentionally and accidentally, interacts with the various forms of families now present in the different societies with which we are here concerned. In this latter connection, recent studies suggest that there has been significant recent change in the prevalence of various family forms.[1] In the United States, for example, in 1975 the family model of husband-breadwinner and wife-homemaker was valid for only 34 out of 100 husband-wife families, compared with 56 out of 100 in 1950.[2] A 1975 Labor Department survey showed that in 47.1% of husband-wife families, both spouses were employed, the wives' earnings averaging 26.3% of family income. In 1975, single-parent families were 15.7% of all families, and the single-parent family headed by a woman (the fastest-growing household type in the United States) had grown almost ten times as fast as two-parent families between 1965 and 1975 to become 13% of all families.[3] The female head of family may be divorced, separated, widowed or unmarried. But the connection with the present Chapter is apparent if, as the study by Ross and Sawhill indicates, the breakup of husband–wife families is the major cause of this growth.[4] One-third of these female-headed families subsist at or below the officially defined poverty level; the great majority of them are on welfare; and female-headed families comprise 46% of all poverty level families.[5]

The 1974 Finer Report on One-Parent Families has made similar findings and assertions for England. This meticulous survey established that in England the largest group of female-headed households consists of married women living apart from their husbands, followed by divorced and widowed women in groups of approximately equal numbers.[6] In 1971, out of a total of 520,000 fatherless families in England, 238,000 were receiving public assistance and, for 200,000 of these, public assistance was their main source of income.[7] In West Germany, one quarter of the persons claiming public assistance are in one-parent families, according to a 1972 government report.[8]

In the United States, where the divorce rate for 1974 was the highest reported anywhere in the world, the association of poverty with female-headed households means that, in a family with dependent children, the decision to leave the marriage by a spouse who is the caretaker of the children and is economically dependent will often mean entering a life of severe deprivation, at least until a new marriage is entered.[9] Similarly, the decision to leave by an economically independent non–custodial spouse will often mean that the family left behind is precipitated into poverty, especially if he or she enters a new marriage. Obviously, in such cases, the dependent custodial spouse's freedom to quit an intolerable marital situation, let alone to pursue happiness, is substantially restricted by economic factors, while the economically independent non-custodial spouse's freedom is limited only by whatever moral considerations he or she personally deems appropriate to the situation.

Reaction to the growing awareness of the problems of one-parent families, many of which are spun off by serial polygamy in Western societies, is by no means uniform, even within a single country. But as we saw at the end of the preceding Chapter, what does seem to be happening everywhere is that legal retrenchment in the areas of marriage and divorce has laid bare several problems of family policy which are serious, controversial and unresolved. Many of these problems, having to do with spousal and child support and child custody, and the different ways in which they are beginning to be approached, will be discussed in subsection II of the present chapter which treats the consequences of marriage dissolution by divorce. By contrast, section III, which treats the legal effects of marriage dissolution by death, will seem peaceful and harmonious, the policy conflicts by and large being resolved in roughly similar fashion by the various systems, and the community ideal at last and for once taking precedence over all others. Indeed one might say that inheritance law is the last outpost of legal marriage and the legitimate family. But, it is an outpost under siege.[10]
The concluding section of this Chapter will be devoted to an exploration of the new bases which have begun to supplement or replace legal marriage and the legitimate family as the focal points of the interaction between the modern State and the various modern family forms.

II. *Legal Marriage Dissolution by Divorce*[11]

A. Interspousal Economic Relations after Divorce

In reality a number of problems are intertwined here. Although the problems of divorce as such, spousal support, child support and property division will be analyzed here separately, in fact they rarely occur in isolation. A few examples will make this clear. As we have already seen in Chapter 5, to the extent that one spouse has the power to delay or even occasionally prevent a divorce until the desired financial or child custody arrangements are agreed to, one cannot say that the divorce itself is separate and distinct from the consequences of divorce. A second complicating factor is that while the problem of whether and how continuing support arrangements after divorce should be made is analytically distinct from the problem of how the existing property of the spouses should be allocated, the two problems are rarely kept separate, either in law or in practice. Similarly, while the question of spousal support is analytically and morally distinct from the problem of child support, in fact, because support of a child often involves custodial care and because the custodian is usually one of the ex-spouses, the distinction is often lost. Frequently the distinction between spousal support and child support is not lost but deliberately buried, either where a spouse trades financial benefit for the children in exchange for some benefit to herself or himself, (either financial or in the form of quick escape from the marriage); or where, as in the United States, alimony is labelled as child support and *vice versa*, in order to gain tax advantages for whichever spouse was able to prevail in bargaining. In spite of these practical difficulties, we will hew for the moment to the distinctions between spousal support, marital property division and child support, because it is here, at the level of the principles announced, if not implemented, in the law, that changes are taking place – changes so profound that they will eventually transform current practices.

1. Spousal Support: Patterns of Change

As part of the historical process of "juridification" of marriage which will be described in the following chapter, marriage became indissoluble, first in ecclesiastical doctrine, then in law (canon and secular). Where Roman Catholic influence has remained strong, marriage has remained indissoluble, in the legal sense, into the latter half of the 20th century. This is so, for example, in the land of the tinkers, Michael and Sarah, whose presence in these pages serves to remind us of the chasm that can exist between behavior and law, whether of the canon or secular variety. In England until 1857, and in many American states at the beginning of the 19th century the only way to obtain a divorce was by private legislative act.[12] In the Protestant countries and those of the Orthodox Church, divorce was possible but only under limited circumstances and was in fact rarely sought.[13]

In the 20th century, however, as we have seen in the preceding chapter, divorce has had to be considered as an ordinary way of terminating marriage and legislators have had to rethink its economic consequences. So long as divorce was rare, it was natural that legal adaptation to it proceeded along the lines of existing institutions. Thus the typical technique was the claim for continuing support by a legally innocent ex-wife against a legally guilty ex-husband.[14] But as divorce became a mass phenomenon dissatisfaction appeared, first with the system's attention to technical "fault" rather than need and then with the frequent insufficiency and precariousness of the support claim itself. Naturally, the principle of sex equality has been seen to require equalization of the support rules between men and women where that has not already taken place. The four legal systems which concern us are in various stages of wrestling with the problems. In general one can say that all these systems have in common their basic reliance on private agreement as the principal mechanism for adjusting economic and child-related disputes at divorce. In this sense the area has already in fact largely been drawn into the private order, even though, theoretically, the desirability of providing protection of weaker parties might argue for increased State intervention here in the form of more supervision of divorce settlements. But where the parties do not agree, each system holds a set of rules in store to guide the judge in determining whether spousal support shall be allowed and, if so, what its modalities shall be. It is to these rules, revealing the basic underlying policies of each system, to which we now turn.

2. France: Divorce Reform Law of 1975

An innovation of the 1975 French Divorce Reform Law, with its variety of grounds for divorce, was to establish different systems of economic consequences devised specially for the different forms of divorce.

Under the former law, where divorce itself was exclusively fault-based, spousal maintenance was available only to the spouse who obtained the divorce. Inasmuch as divorce, in addition to terminating the marriage, also brings to an end the matrimonial property regime that exists between the parties, any assets of the spouses acquired during the marriage will at that time be divided equally between them, unless the spouses have made some other arrangement by marital contract or divorce settlement. But because in most cases a spouse's share of the marital property will not be large enough to assure the future support of that spouse, the matrimonial property law is supplemented by provisions of the divorce law which determine whether and how economic transfers besides the division of marital property should be accorded to either spouse.

With the exception of divorce for disruption of the life in common, the guiding principle of the 1975 law, so far as effects of divorce are concerned, is said to have been to try to minimize "after-divorce" contact and conflict between the ex-spouses.[15] To this end, the Code provides now in new Art. 270 that "divorce puts an end to the duty of support". The economic effects, if any, are to be regulated by a new technique, the "compensatory payment".[16] But the basic technique for adjusting post-divorce financial matters, in the French as in the other systems examined here, is the parties' own agreement. The rules governing this method are set forth as the economic consequences of that kind of divorce which is the preferred form under the 1975 law, *divorce convention*, i.e. divorce by mutual consent expressed in a written agreement. Just as the divorce itself is by an agreement approved by the judge, so are the economic effects of such a divorce. However, it will be recalled from Chapter 5 that the judge can refuse his approval and thus delay the divorce if he does not find that the agreement adequately protects the interests of either spouse or the children. The sections on the economic effects of divorce by agreement repeat this idea in more precise terms:

Art. 278. In the case of joint petition, the spouses are to fix the amount and the details of the compensatory payment[17] in the agreement which they submit for the approval of the judge. The judge is invariably to refuse approval of the agreement if it allocates the rights and obligations of the spouses inequitably.

Art. 279. The agreement once approved (*homologuée*) has the same executory force as a judicial decision. It can be modified only by a new agreement between the spouses which must likewise be submitted for approval. The spouses nevertheless have the option to provide in their agreement that either of them may, in the case of unforeseen change in their resources and needs, petition the judge to modify the compensatory payment.

This then is the legislature's preferred system of economic effects following from its preferred system of divorce. When the spouses are not able to come to agreement, or when one spouse has opposed the divorce and has not been guilty of "fault" in the technical sense of the divorce laws, three other systems are potentially brought into play: compensatory payment fixed by the judge, support and damages.

a. The System of Compensatory Payment

In those cases where the parties have not reached an agreement and the decision on the effects of divorce is left to the judge, the judge is required to follow the guidelines which are established for the system of "compensatory payment" (*prestation compensatoire*) except in those cases where divorce was granted for the prolonged disruption of the life in common. Thus the types of divorce in which this new system is called into play are: the form of mutual consent divorce known as "resignation-divorce"; divorce for shared fault; and fault divorce granted for the fault of one spouse only. In the case of fault divorce granted for the fault of one spouse only, the compensatory payment is available to the plaintiff but not, in principle, to the defendant, although an exception is made even here where the denial of such a payment would be manifestly inequitable.[18]

The rule which determines whether a compensatory payment is to be made at all is as follows:

Art. 270. Except where it is pronounced by reason of the disruption of the life in common, divorce puts an end to the duty of support established in Article 212 of the Civil Code; but one spouse may be required to make to the other a payment designed to compensate, so far as possible, for the disparity which the disruption of the marriage creates in the conditions of their respective lives.

It will be observed that the compensatory payment does not automatically follow from the fact of divorce. Also, unlike alimony under the prior law, it is not in the nature of a sanction against the person against whom the divorce was pronounced. Nor has it been formulated as a support or maintenance provision, but rather is supposed to depend on the establishment of the fact of disparity between the situations of the two ex-spouses.

If the payment is to be made, its amount is to be determined in the following manner:

Art. 271. The compensatory payment is to be fixed according to the needs of the spouse to whom it is made and the resources of the other, taking account of their situations at the time of the divorce and of developments in the forseeable future.

Art. 272. In the determination of needs and resources, the judge is to take into consideration notably:
– the age and the state of health of the spouses;
– the time already devoted or which they will have to devote to the upbringing of the children;
– their professional qualifications;
– their existing and forseeable economic rights;
– the eventual loss of such rights in connection with terminable pensions;
– their wealth, in income as well as capital, after the liquidation of the   matrimonial regime.

Taking account of the fact that these sections require the judge to look into the economic future and that article 273, following them, provides that in principle the compensatory payment is unmodifiable,[19] these sections have been criticized in France as requiring judges "to foresee the impossible and yet forbidding them to make any mistakes".[20] The legislative intent to avoid post-divorce litigation has, in this view, "promoted the creation of drastic and irremediable situations".[21] However, from a comparative perspective one can see underlying the obvious purpose to avoid post-divorce litigation, the beginning of acknowledgment of another idea which is gaining adherence in Sweden, West Germany and the United States. This is that basically, after divorce, the spouses (but not the children) are to be on their own, and that if the economic situation of an ex-spouse requires attention, this attention should be forthcoming from the society as a whole through public assistance, and not from the ex-spouse. [22] The "compensatory payment" may be the germ of the "severance pay" idea which has become influential in other systems.

In keeping with the idea that post–divorce contact and conflict should be minimized, the reform law has provided that the compensatory payment should in principle be constituted as a lump sum payment and should in principle be non-modifiable. The rules which are to guide the judge are as follows:

Art. 274. When the assets of the spouse who owes the compensatory payment permit it, the payment is to take the form of a lump sum.

Art. 275. The judge decides on the method according to which assets are allocated or charged for the lump sum:
1. Payment of a sum of money;
2. Transfer of property in kind; movables or immovables, but where usufruct only is concerned the judgment operates as a forced assignment to the creditor-spouse;
3. Deposit of revenue-producing securities into the hands of a third party charged with the duty of paying income to the creditor-spouse for the period fixed;

The divorce decree can be subordinated to the effective payment of the lump sum or to the constitution of the guarantees provided for in Article 277.

Art. 275–1. If the debtor-spouse of the compensatory payment does not presently dispose of liquid assets, he may be authorized, subject to the guarantees provided for in Article 277, to make up the lump sum in three annual payments.

Art. 276. In the absence of a lump sum, or if the lump sum is insufficient, the compensatory payment can take the form of a pension.

Art. 276–1. The pension is to be granted for a time equal to or less than the life of the creditor-spouse.

It is to be indexed; the index is to be determined as in the case of support payments.

The amount of the pension prior to being indexed can be made uniform for its entire duration or may vary in successive stages according to the probable evolution of needs and resources.

Art. 276–2. At the death of the debtor-spouse, the responsibility for the pension passes to his heirs.

Art. 277. Independently of any statutory or court-ordered security interest, the judge may require the debtor-spouse to give a pledge or other security to guarantee the pension.

Laudable as this scheme may be in its effort to eliminate litigation and the difficulties so often encountered when periodic payments are sought to be collected, it is unrealistic, because the lump sum payment method in practice will usually be possible only in the cases of relatively few well-to-do individuals.[23] That case which the law establishes as the exception – compensatory payments made periodically – will in fact be the rule in the majority of cases where the payment is allowed. Likewise, it may turn out that the exception to the general rule of non-modifiability provided in Art. 273 in practice will envelop the rule.[24]

b. Divorce for Prolonged Disruption of the Life in Common

It has already been observed that divorce ends the duty of support, except in the case of divorce on the limited objective grounds established in the 1975 law[25] and that in these special cases the system of the compensatory payment does not operate.

In fact it does not seem to be an exaggeration to say that the system of economic effects prescribed under the reform law for the two types of divorce permitted on objective grounds represents the full continuation of the matrimonial duty of support, even though the other incidents of marriage have been severed by divorce. We have already seen that in this kind of divorce the plaintiff must assume all the costs.[26] The sections regulating its economic effects add to the impression that the legislature had in mind that any one who wished to have this kind of legal death certificate for his marriage and permission to remarry would have to be prepared to pay and to keep paying for the privilege. None of the efforts made to reduce post-marital contact between spouses are present here. In fact the situation is the inverse of that of the compensatory payment:

Art. 281. When the divorce is granted for disruption of the life in common, the spouse who took the initiative in the divorce remains completely bound to the duty of support.

In the case of Art. 238, [impairment of a spouse's mental faculties] the duty of support includes everything which is necessary for the medical treatment of the ill spouse.

Art. 282. The accomplishment of the duty of support is to take the form of periodic alimony. This may always be modified in accordance with the resources and needs of each spouse.

Art. 283. Periodic alimony terminates as a matter of law if the spouse who is the creditor contracts a new marriage.

It is terminable if the creditor is living in open and notorious concubinage.

It will be noted that this system in effect binds the ex-spouses economically for better or worse, in sickness and in health. Even when death does them part, alimony lives on if it is the debtor-spouse who has died, and it terminates only upon the death of the creditor spouse, according to Art. 284, which makes alimony a responsibility of the heirs of the deceased debtor. Exactly contrary to the scheme of the compensatory payment, Art. 285 provides that in an exceptional case the duty of support can be fulfilled by a lump sum payment rather than by periodic payments.

Certain other provisions of the new law reinforce the impression that this form of divorce is like a continuation of a limited form of marriage. For example, an amendment to the Social Security law provides that when an insured does not remarry after divorce granted on his initiative for prolonged disruption of the life in common, the divorced spouse will be deemed a surviving spouse for social security purposes. [27] If the insured does remarry, then social security benefits upon his death are made payable to both spouses in proportion to the duration of each marriage. [28] To the same effect is a new amendment to the civil service and military pensions law which extends a widow's right to *any* divorced wife, except one whose fault was the sole basis of the divorce. [29]

How all of these provisions will work out has a great deal to do with the efficacy of the new collection procedures. As Dean Carbonnier has pointed out,

The idea of maintaining something of the conjugal tie between the divorced spouses is certainly a very morally elevated idea; but sociological inquiry...has put its finger on the principal reason for its practical failure: it is that the majority of the population of divorcés is a population that aspires to flee from its past. [30]

c. Action for Damages

Under the prior fault-based law, there was available to the spouse who obtained the divorce, not only alimony, but the possibility of an action for damages for reparation of "the material or moral prejudice caused him by the dissolution of the marriage". [31] The new law, in Article 266, continues this possibility, but limits it to the two special cases of the plaintiff in a divorce granted for the exclusive fault of the defendant, and the defendant in a divorce granted for prolonged disruption of the common life. Under the prior law, "material and moral prejudice" has been interpreted to be separate and distinct from the loss of support which may be occasioned by divorce. Compensation, sometimes very substantial, has been awarded under former Art. 301 for such alleged harms resulting from the divorce as: the loss of esteem suffered by a divorced person; loneliness; and loss of social position by one who has become accustomed to a high standard of living. [32]

Finally, independent of marital fault, there is the possibility of bringing a regular tort action, under Art. 1382 of the Civil Code, for damage caused by one spouse to the other. Under the prior law, the Court of Cassation had sanctioned an action under Art. 301 for "material and moral prejudice" in a case where the husband had squandered community property on a mistress, and where, in addition, the wife had been damaged in the equal division of the community because the community consisted largely of property she had contributed.[33] While this case was criticized as an improper application of the "material and moral prejudice" provision in that the harm complained of did not result from the dissolution of the marriage, the result was approved in the *doctrine* as properly flowing from Article 1382.[34]

The shadow institution imitates the legal institution in the area of damages on the occasion of the termination of the relationship. *De facto* spouses have been successful in a number of cases in recovering tort damages, usually based on the idea that the male partner incurred responsibility through the original wrongful seduction of the female partner.[35] The transparency of this reasoning is obvious when the "wrongfully seduced" woman brings the action after many years of stable cohabitation have come to an end. A Paris Court of Appeal case[36] which awarded damages on the basis of "wrongful unilateral rupture of the free union" differs from the other cases only in that the court does not trouble to conceal its assimilation of the *de facto* to the legal situation.

d. Legal Separation

The economic effects of legal separation are, by new Art. 304, governed by the same rules which govern the consequences of divorce, with certain enumerated exceptions. In the first place, legal separation, as before, automatically results in separation of the assets of the parties if they previously had been living under a matrimonial property regime other than that of separate property. Since most French married couples live under the regime of community of acquests, the provision affects most couples who seek legal separation. Secondly, as before, legal separation leaves the duty of support between the spouses in force and, under new Art. 303 the duty can be enforced by a judgment awarding maintenance to a needy spouse without regard to fault save in exceptional instances.

3. England: Matrimonial Proceedings and Property Act, 1970

The English set of rules on the economic effects of divorce, unlike the French, is uniform for all types of divorce. Under the Matrimonial Proceedings and Property Act of 1970, consolidated with the Divorce Reform Act of 1969 into the Matrimonial Causes Act of 1973, the court has the power, upon the grant of a decree of divorce, nullity or judicial separation, to order one spouse to make financial provision for the other by way of periodical payments; a lump sum; a transfer or settlement of property; or by various combinations of these devices. The purpose of the statutory scheme is to assure continuing family provision, and the court is so to exercise its powers

...as to place the parties, so far as it is practicable and, having regard to their conduct, just to do so, in the financial position in which they would have been if the marriage had not broken down and each had properly discharged his or her financial obligations and responsibilities towards the other.[37]

It is now recognized that the aspiration of Parliament to place the parties in the same position as if there had been no breakdown is wholly unrealistic, except for the affluent few.[38]

In attempting to fulfill its impossible task, the court is directed by the statute to have regard to all the circumstances of the case and to take into consideration the following enumerated factors relating to the needs and resources of the spouses: the present and probable future financial situation of the spouses; their financial needs and obligations; their standard of living during the marriage; their ages; their mental and physical health; the duration of the marriage; and the loss of marriage-related benefits (such as a pension) in the future. The contributions of the spouses to the marriage are to be taken into account at this time, and the law expressly states that these contributions include housework as well as financial payments.[39]

It is said that judges expect a divorced wife to work, and will presume that she has the appropriate earning capacity, unless she is old, or ill, or responsible for the care of young children.[40]

The English were under no illusions that a payment in a lump sum would be feasible as means of assuring financial provision in the ordinary case. Maintenance through unsecured payments is by far the most common method of financial provision, and the rule of thumb in assessing mainte-nance seems to be to try to bring the wife's income up to one third of the joint incomes of herself and her husband.[41] But when the 1970 Act was passed, hopes were expressed by the Law Commission and in Parliament that the lump sum technique (which usually would involve redistribution of the spouse's property) would be used more widely, and that the courts would make ample use of their new power to make orders for the splitting up of family assets.[42] Often the courts combine the lump sum technique with periodic maintenance, giving the wife the matrimonial home and/or a share of the family assets.[43] Because of the broad discretion and flexible powers of the courts, spouses can expect that upon the termination of the marriage a court will effect some kind of redistribution of their property. If the husband has been the sole wage-earner during the marriage, the rule of thumb seems to be that the wife will be allocated one-third of the joint assets.[44]

But unlike the French system where spousal support supplements fixed rights to a share of the property acquired during the marriage, the English system makes both property division and support discretionary with the judge. Even though there are statutory guidelines for the exercise of the judge's discretion, an English spouse, unlike his or her French counterpart, can have no sense of security during the marriage about his or her financial position in the event of marriage breakdown.[45] The status of their property and the availability of support will be in doubt until the court renders its decree. The continuing presence of "conduct" as a factor in assessing maintenance renders the outcome all the more uncertain. This attention to conduct represents an important difference between the English system and most systems where property rights of the spouses are fixed by law. Typically, in the latter systems, certain property is designated a fund subject to equal division irrespective of the conduct of the parties, although conduct may become relevant in deciding questions of maintenance and damages. In those American community property systems, such as Washington, which have moved from equal to discretionary division of the common fund, the court is still forbidden to consider the parties' marital misconduct in making the division.

A split of authority has developed between two different divisions of the English Court of Appeal on the question whether conduct is always relevant or relevant only in extreme cases. In the well-known 1973 case of *Wachtel v. Wachtel*, Lord Denning said that misconduct, in order to justify reduction of financial provision, would have to be "both obvious and gross", and not merely "what was formerly regarded as guilt or blame" under the prior fault-oriented English divorce law.[46] However in other English cases conduct has been considered quite important as a factor in fixing maintenance,[47] and there is Court of Appeal authority that relevant conduct is not confined to obvious and gross misconduct.[48] Further confusion has been introduced by disagreement about what constitutes obvious and gross misconduct.

The presence of the conduct factor in maintenance decisions has an unfortunate effect on the announced policy of the English Divorce Reform to try to reduce the distress, humiliation and bitterness of divorce proceedings. Fault bases for proving "breakdown" are often chosen as the battleground even though financial issues are really at stake.[49]

Although the English law directs the court to consider the effect of the possible loss of derived pension rights upon divorce, it does not tell the judge how he is to make up for such loss. In fact the assumption of the statutory scheme seems to be that some sort of property transfer to the wife is appropriate in lieu of the expectancy. But this solution will only be effective where there is substantial property to be transferred, not in those numerous cases where the "wealth" of the couple was mostly in the form of expectancies based on the husband's earnings. Practitioners have apparently been working out techniques for securing, at the time of divorce, assignment of the pension rights or contracts to pay over such benefits in the future.[50] In England, as elsewhere, enforcement is a serious problem.

If a spouse seeks separate maintenance in a Magistrates' Court, instead of the Divorce Court, the governing law is the Matrimonial Proceedings (Magistrates' Courts) Act 1960 which still provides that no petition except those pertaining to children can be granted unless the petitioner proves the respondent has been guilty of a matrimonial offence. Two 1966 surveys showed that the amounts payable under Magistrates' Court orders were small (two thirds of the wives with two children were awarded less than 3 pounds 5 shillings a week); and that 39% of all orders were in arrears.[51]

4. West Germany: Marriage and Family Law Reform of 1976

In the area of post-divorce spousal support, the 14 June 1976 West German family law reform constituted much more of a break with the past than did the 1975 French or the 1970 English reforms. Until 1976, in West German support law (as in the French and English prior law), the post-divorce support rights of the parties depended in important respects on the judicial determination of "guilt".[52] If the husband was the party at fault, he was obliged to maintain the wife at the standard of the married life insofar as her own resources were insufficient to do so.[53] Markovits has concluded, on the basis of her study of the cases under the provisions of the 1938–1946 law, that lower court decisions have tended to reflect the idea that an ex-wife ought to support herself by her own labor, while the appellate court cases have reflected a notion that a wife should not be deprived of her part of the marriage "bargain" (of services in exchange for continuing support).[54] A wife found to be at fault in the divorce suit was, under the prior law, to maintain her husband only if he were incapable of supporting himself, and even then only at a subsistence level.[55]

The 1976 reform law drastically changes this scheme.[56] Not only is regulation of support independent of guilt but, as a general rule, spousal support is not to be available after divorce except for the transitional period needed by the economically weaker partner to adjust to the new situation and to become economically self-sufficient. The amount received by each spouse when the marital property regime is terminated is thought to aid in this readjustment period.[57] A duty of support continuing beyond the transitional period is to exist only in cases enumerated by the law.[58] A right of support is provided where a spouse cannot be self-supporting because of age,[59] incapacity,[60] or because he or she is caring for a child of the marriage.[61] In addition a spouse has a support claim if he or she is unable to find suitable employment.[62] A new provision, reflecting concerns that have also appeared in recent American cases,[63] permits one spouse to claim support from the other in order to be able to finish an interrupted course of studies or to secure more advanced training in a professional field.[64]. If a spouse is in possession of sufficient income and or property of his or her own, then no support is allowed even in the above cases.[65] No claim for support is given where the marriage was of short duration and the claimant spouse is not caring for common children or where the claimant had long neglected his or her duty to contribute to the maintenance of the common household and is not caring for the common children.[66] The law also amends the laws on social security and other pensions so that housekeeping, like any other gainful activity, is treated as work for which benefits may be obtained.[67] The wife's claim to social benefits is in her own right, not derived from her husband. Pension rights and similar benefits accumulated during the marriage are to be shared between husband and wife. The equal sharing of such benefits applies to national insurance pension rights, civil service pensions, and supplementary plans run by the employer or a professional organization or accruing from private insurance arrangements. This plan was devised to take care of the problems arising from the fact that the principal "wealth" of many couples is in such "new property" related to previous earnings. Housewives often have had no "new property" except that derived from their relationship to their husband. These derivative rights were generally destroyed with divorce. Where such rights cannot be fairly apportioned, the new West German law provides that the beneficiary must pay the other an indemnity. The highly detailed, minute regulation by the new West German law of this "*Versorgungsausgleich*" at divorce and the question of how it will work in practice, should be of interest to lawmakers in other countries.

Under the Government draft as it stood until last minute compromises were made to secure the passage of the Bill in the *Bundesrat* in April 1976, couples would have been allowed to make different private arrangements with respect to benefits only in exceptional circumstances. But one of the concessions wrested by the CDU/CSU from the Coalition diminished the

housewife's right to one-half the pension rights earned by the husband during
the marriage by permitting the claim to be foreclosed by contract.[68] A
front-page article in *Die Zeit* commented that this compromise, "bullied" out
of the Coalition, should make the members of the Opposition "ashamed of
themselves before their female constituents".[69]

5. A Scandinavian Perspective

Although there was a thoroughgoing reform of Swedish divorce law in 1974,
the preparation of a reform project concerning the economic aspects of family
law was not yet complete in mid-1976. So far as spousal support after divorce
is concerned, the Minister of Justice laid down the guiding principle of the
reform in his 1969 Directives, stating that the starting point should be that
there should be no maintenance between spouses after dissolution of marriage.[70] In Sweden, if this principle becomes the basis of a new reform, it will
not be much of a change from present practice, where alimony already plays
an extremely limited role. In Sweden, as in Denmark, Finland and Norway,
spousal support is already available only on the basis of one spouse's need and
the other's ability to pay.[71] The present Swedish provision regulating what is
called the "contribution to support" reads as follows:

If after divorce one of the spouses needs contribution to his adequate support, the
court may impose upon the other the duty to so contribute. The court is to determine
what amount is appropriate in view of the latter spouse's possibilities and of the
other's circumstances. In its determination the court is to consider that a spouse may
be in special need of a contribution to his support during the period immediately
following the divorce.[72]

In practice, according to Sundberg, alimony is awarded only to women
married to men with either very high or very low incomes.[73] In the latter case,
he says, payments are "never" made.[74] Thus what really seems to be happening with respect to the pending reform project is that (like the 1974 Swedish
divorce law) it simply conforms the law to reality. It recognizes that no
matter what the law says marriage no longer functions as a support institution when the community of family life has come to an end. Yet, if it is true, as
Sundberg says, that only a quarter of Swedish married women can be
regarded as economically independent,[75] some mechanism has to be found to
respond to the fact of economic dependency after divorce. The eventual
Scandinavian resolution of this problem may be found in the 1972 Report of
the Committee appointed by the Finnish Government to suggest changes in
the Finnish Marriage Act:[76]

If a divorced spouse is unable to provide for her own subsistence, the primary responsibility for organizing the subsistence lies with society and not with the other spouse, as is presently the case. This point of departure as a matter of principle, can be argued first and foremost by the fact that the need of the divorced spouse generally is caused either by unemployment or by inability to work, and traditionally caring for citizens who for such reasons have been left without subsistence has been considered to be a task for society.

The Finnish Committee thus recommended that the problem of economic dependency after divorce be approached along the lines of "...expanding the social security and employment security programmes of society, by intensifying vocational training and by developing the social security system so as to guarantee the basic security of all citizens, regardless of their family relations".[77] The role of spousal support in the Finnish committee's view "...should be limited to providing a transitory protection: it should not be possible to decree alimony for a longer period than three years".[78]

In fact, the social insurance and other security arrangements in Sweden are now so extensive and generous that, according to Sundberg, "...fewer and fewer people in Sweden are today dependent on support from relatives".[79]

6. United States

The diversity of the support laws of the various American states ranges from a few states where support is available only to an "innocent" wife against a "guilty" husband, to the growing number of states where support is awarded or not to either spouse on the basis of relative need and resources alone, to two states where permanent alimony is not given at all.[80] Nonetheless, out of all the legal diversity, a fairly uniform picture emerges from accounts of the social reality of post-divorce spousal support. The reality is not significantly different from the situation in Sweden. Alimony figures in only a small percentage of cases.[81] It is infrequently sought, infrequently awarded, and even less frequently collected.[82]

In all states the law of alimony itself has been undergoing change. In one respect there is the trend to limit alimony to a temporary period and to cases of genuine need, and not to give one spouse a "lifetime profit-sharing plan" in the fortunes of the other.[83] In another respect there is the trend to extend alimony to the husband where it had not been so extended before, to make marital misconduct irrelevant, and (when alimony is granted) to strengthen enforcement procedures for its collection.[84] This latter development, motivated by a desire to protect the public purse, especially in those cases where the financially responsible ex-spouse moves to another state, does not seem to have been effective in stemming the widespread practice of defaulting on support orders.[85] There is a definite trend in the cases where alimony is awarded to give "short term" alimony only, limited to the time necessary for children to reach the age where custodial care is no longer necessary or for the wife to become trained or retrained in marketable skills.[86]

Where the resources of the payor spouse are sufficient to permit it one sees in the American cases judicial innovations resembling features of the new West German legislation. In 1975, for example, a New York court ordered a lawyer-husband, whose wife had given up pre-medical studies in order to work as a secretary to put him through law school, to pay $200 a week for alimony and child support so that the wife could complete her medical training even though she was in fact capable of being self-supporting as a secretary and data analyst.[87]

American legislation and cases are also developing responses to the problems arising from the fact that a woman who has not worked outside the home frequently loses the right to her husband's social security, pension and insurance benefits upon divorce and has no such benefits in her own right. Thus an increasing number of courts are holding that assets of a spouse available for equitable division upon divorce include unliquidated workmen's compensation claims,[88] pension benefits from private plans to which either the employee-spouse[89] or his employer[90] has contributed, and military benefits.[91] Divorced wives whose marriages have lasted for at least 20 years are entitled to share in their ex-husband's social security benefits,[92] and proposals to shorten this period have been made with increasing frequency and volubility.[93]

Periodic alimony is increasingly felt to be an inadequate mechanism for dealing with the economic aspects of divorce and separation. As the institution of marriage changes and the idea gains ground that household activity deserves to be compensated like any other kind of work, American courts, and occasionally legislatures too, are casting about for alternatives.

The main legislative trends are well exemplified by the Uniform Marriage and Divorce Act. According to the draftsmen,

The Act authorizes the division of the property belonging to either spouse, or to both spouses, as the primary means of providing for the future financial needs of the spouses, as well as doing justice between them. Where the property is insufficient for the first purpose, the Act provides that an award of maintenance may be made to either spouse under appropriate circumstances to supplement the available property. But because of its property division rules, the Act does not continue the traditional reliance upon maintenance as the primary means of support for divorced spouses.[94]

Like the French compensatory payment scheme and the English goal of keeping the post-divorce standard of living at the pre-divorce level, this aspiration is unrealistic in the majority of cases where economic need exists and is likely to continue beyond a transition period. If support is needed at all, it will usually be needed at a higher level than can be supplied by most persons in a lump sum transfer. For example, a non-farm family of four in the United States with income of less than $5038 is classified by the Bureau of the Census as below the poverty level in 1974.[95] Yet a capital of nearly $100,000 would be required to yield an annual income of this amount at $5\frac{1}{2}\%$ interest.

So whether they are meant to or not the maintenance provisions of the Uniform Act will continue to play an important role. But the implicit starting point of UMDA Article 308 on maintenance is that there is *no* continuing financial responsibility of one spouse for the other after divorce. The section provides

the court may grant a maintenance order for either spouse, *only* if it finds that the spouse seeking maintenance:

(1) lacks sufficient property to provide for his reasonable needs; and

(2) is unable to support himself through appropriate employment or is the custodian of a child whose condition or circumstances make it appropriate that the custodian not be required to seek employment outside the home.

(b) The maintenance order shall be in amounts and for periods of time that the court deems just, without regard to marital misconduct, and after considering all relevant factors including:

(1) the financial resources of the party seeking maintenance, including marital property apportioned to him, his ability to meet his needs independently, and the extent to which a provision for support of a child living with the party includes a sum for that party as custodian;

(2) the time necessary to acquire sufficient education or training to enable the party seeking maintenance to find appropriate employment;

(3) the standard of living established during the marriage;

(4) the duration of the marriage;

(5) the age and the physical and emotional condition of the spouse seeking maintenance; and

(6) the ability of the spouse from whom maintenance is sought to meet his needs while meeting those of the spouse seeking maintenance. [Emphasis added]

The draftsmen's comment to the section reinforces the intention that in principle no maintenance should be awarded and that spouses are expected to be self-supporting after divorce:

Only if the available property is insufficient for the purpose and if the spouse who seeks maintenance is unable to secure employment appropriate to his skills and interests or is occupied with child care may an award of maintenance be ordered.

B. Property Division at Divorce

Analytically distinct from the question of whether and how financial relations of the spouses should be continued after divorce is the question of what to do with any property the spouses may have owned prior to divorce. One approach to the problem would be for each spouse to take back whatever he or she brought in. Another is to divide all the property of the spouses, or perhaps just all the property acquired during the marriage, between the spouses without trying to find out which spouse might have brought which property into the marriage. If the latter approach is adopted, the choice must be made between establishing a rule for division of the property in fixed proportions in principle, or leaving the modalities of division to the discretion of a judge and perhaps setting guidelines for the exercise of this discretion. No matter which solution is chosen (unless all the property of the spouses no matter when and how acquired is to be subject to division upon divorce), some rule must be established for determining who owns what or which property belongs in the fund to be shared and which property is to be excluded from such fund. The simplest rule is the presumption that any given asset is to be subject to sharing unless it can be proved that it belongs to the class of assets which need not be divided. The effect of such a presumption (a form of which is present in all systems examined here) is to reduce some of the apparent distinctions between the Anglo-American systems of so-called separate property and the various continental European systems of so-called community property. Rheinstein and Glendon's study of the laws governing property relations between spouses concludes that these systems are converging as the community systems accord more autonomy to each spouse in dealing with his or her earnings and other assets during the marriage, and as the separate property systems enforce more sharing of the spouses' property upon dissolution of marriage.[96] We concluded that comparison of systems according to traditional categories of "separate" and "community" is no longer useful, but that functional comparisons had to be made according to whether property questions are raised in the context of the on-going marriage; divorce, separation or annulment; testate and intestate succession; or creditors' rights; and according to the degree of solidarity or separateness of the spouses' interests which is recognized by each legal system in each of these situations. When this functional comparison is made, we found that modern marital property systems do differ considerably from one another in the degree to which they emphasize the community-of-life aspect of marriage through enforced sharing of property, or the independence of the spouses through limited sharing. We found, further, that differences among systems in this respect were sharpest in the divorce situation and least where marriage is terminated by death. Finally, we noted a tendency to treat the matrimonial home and household goods as a special category of property subject to sharing regardless of the other features of each system.

Among the four countries with which we are here concerned, the system of no-sharing of property in principle upon divorce exists only in a small minority of American states where, theoretically, either party upon divorce walks away with what he or she owns and the court's role is merely to unscramble the ownership situation if dispute develops about who owns what.[97] The law of New York is frequently referred to as an example of this legal situation. In such jurisdictions, if a wife's contribution to the acquests of the marriage through her work in caring for the home and children is recognized at all, it is only as a factor in fixing support. But where support, as is usually the case, can be awarded in a lump sum instead of or in addition to an award of periodic payments, the distinction between alimony as the means of support and property division upon divorce is easily lost.[98] The practical result *can* be a division of marital property which closely resembles that achieved in states or countries where the property of the spouses is designated as a common fund subject to division upon divorce.

Another factor which weakens the distinction between systems of sharing property upon divorce and systems of returning to each spouse his or her property is the difficulty of determining what belongs to each. A few couples may keep neat inventories and accounts which at any time clearly indicate who owns what. But such earmarking is unusual. Savings are likely to be invested in the joint names of the spouses; both are likely to have contributed to the purchase, upkeep and improvement of the home; and they will rarely have thought about whether the car, the furniture or the household utensils are his or hers or the property of both. Not until the break has occurred between the parties or its possibility is being considered (or until family assets are levied upon by creditors of the husband or the wife), do the parties think about questions of title. Hence, when the judicial determination has to be made, the court frequently has a range of open or disguised discretion; and in the exercise of this discretion the court is likely to consider the role the wife played during the marriage. The various presumptions established for the guidance of the court push in the direction of sharing.[99] Finally, it must be remembered that most property settlements upon divorce are made by private contract where sharing can be introduced along the lines negotiated by the parties. However, as the movement of the divorce law lessens the leverage the economically weaker spouse has in such negotiations, the background law becomes increasingly important.

With the exception of a few American states, however, the systems we are examining here start out from the premise that divorce is an occasion upon which some sort of property sharing is appropriate. The ways in which they implement this idea differ.

In the majority of American states, and in England, the court as part of its power to assure financial provision after divorce has broad discretion to redistribute *all* the property of the spouses in the manner that seems fair to it. This carries the at least theoretical advantage, which the minority American states lack, of being able to adapt the economic consequences of divorce to the individual circumstances. But in fact both systems have in common the feature of unpredictability arising from open or disguised judicial discretion.[100]

The proposed Uniform Marriage and Divorce Act differs from both approaches by neatly separating the problem of maintenance from that of property division. Although initially committed to a system of limiting the court's discretion to division of post-marital *acquests* upon divorce, the proposed Uniform Marriage and Divorce Act in its 1973 revision proceeds upon the principle that *all* property of the spouses, however and whenever acquired, should be regarded as assets of the married couple, available for distribution between them "without regard to marital misconduct" but upon consideration of various factors including "the contribution of a spouse as a homemaker or to the family unit".[101] Recognizing that the concept of making available for division this "great hotchpot of assets" may not appeal to legislatures in all jurisdictions, particularly those with community property systems which limit sharing upon divorce to the marital acquests, the Uniform Law Commissioners have provided an alternative section limiting the fund to be divided to the property acquired during the marriage.[102]

Although the 1973 revision has brought the Uniform Act into line with the system which actually exists (under the guise of maintenance) in the majority of states, it may be questioned whether this concept is the one which best corresponds to current mores in view of the frequency of divorce and changing attitudes toward marriage in general and the financial responsibility of the spouses for each other in particular. It may be that the American community property states will not be alone in questioning the desirability of giving a court the discretionary power to range over and reallocate all of the property of the spouses. In this connection it is especially noteworthy that although the Uniform Act directs the court to "consider" any antenuptial agreement executed by the parties, it does not appear to have been the intent of the commissioners that the court should be *bound* by any such agreement.[103] The 1970 version of the Uniform Act which limited the court's discretion to division of "marital property", defined as acquests, may turn out not only to correspond more fully to the desires of the community property states, but to current and developing conditions in the others.[104] The 1970 version of the Act would have had the effect of expanding the court's discretion in minority states while cutting down its discretion in other states.

The methods by which sharing of property at divorce is implemented in France and West Germany differ from the systems of England and the majority of the American states. The French and West German systems, like most American community property states, start out from the premise that only the property acquired during the marriage ought to be subject to sharing. They differ from the Anglo-American systems discussed above in that they provide that sharing should be in fixed 50–50 proportions, rather than discretionary with the court. As to the first difference, however, the presumption that assets are marital acquests and the practice of most couples not to keep records operate to increase the amount of property which is in fact subject to division. The rule of 50–50 division has the advantage of assuring more predictability than the English and the majority American systems which presuppose great confidence in the judiciary. The 50–50 rule probably reduces litigation. But a flat halving is not fair under all circumstances. With increasing divorce, there is a widespread trend to limit the equal division principle, especially where the marriage has been of short duration. Most American community property states have moved from the original Spanish equal division rule to submitting distribution of acquests in every case to the discretion of the court, to be exercised along statutory guidelines and without reference to marital misconduct. The best solution seems to be that chosen by the Russian Republic of the Soviet Union and West Germany: to provide for an equal division in principle, but to leave open a narrowly defined possibility of judicial correction in exceptional cases.[105] Under the West German Equal Rights Law of 18 June 1957, the 50–50 rule can be corrected if it would result in "gross unfairness" (*grobe Unbilligkeit*) under the circumstances of the case. Gross unfairness is interpreted to mean unfairness or misconduct of an economic sort, but not to permit reference to other types of marital misconduct.

As to the technique of liquidation of the spouses' property relations, the French and West German systems present two contrasting methods. The first is to partition all the property which the system designates as available for distribution, as is done with acquests in France. The second method is found in the West German law of 1957. What is to be divided there is not a conglomeration of individual assets but the increase in monetary values of the estates of the parties that has occurred during the marriage. The sum to be divided and the distribution of the increase is achieved by arithmetical operation. The smaller increase is subtracted from the larger and one-half of the difference constitutes the "equalization claim" which is payable by the party whose estate has had the greater increase to the party who has had the lower.

On the surface it would appear that the legal systems of England, France, West Germany and all but a small minority of American states are firmly committed to the view that the spouses' property ought to be shared upon divorce. In each system the techniques for implementing such sharing resemble those first worked out by the Nordic countries in the 1920s: leave the spouses free to deal with their property as they wish during the marriage, but marshall all or some of their assets and divide them at divorce. But beneath the surface there are countercurrents to the trend toward sharing. In Sweden, the pending proposal for reform of the economic aspects of family law would restrict the property subject to sharing to the matrimonial home and the household goods.[106] Discontent has been expressed in Sweden with the system of more extensive sharing because it is seen as inconsistent with the independence of the spouses.[107] Already in Swedish law equal sharing of marital property upon divorce is excluded by statute if one spouse brought in most of the property and the marriage was short.[108] Existing Swedish law also confides in the judge discretion to award the marital home or lease to the spouse who is found to "need it most".[109] Usually this will be the spouse with custody of children. Thus, as Sundberg points out, the custody decision frequently controls the most important property decision.[110]

In West Germany, sharing is said to be excluded by marriage contract in a great number of cases. But perhaps the most significant way in which sharing of property at divorce is everywhere avoided is through each spouse's power to diminish the *amount* of property left to be shared at the end of the marriage through transactions entered into during the marriage. Traditional community property systems were characterized by an elaborate network of restraints on each spouse's power of disposition in order to assure that something would be left to divide. But these restraints, where they existed, have been dropping off as the systems are becoming modernized.[111] In all the systems examined here, one spouse needs the consent of the other for certain transactions of particular importance and, except in West Germany, each spouse's rights in the matrimonial home receive special protection against transfer by the other spouse. Only in France is there an extensive list of transactions for which one spouse needs the consent of the other. In West Germany, only transfers of substantially all of one spouse's assets (*Vermögen im Ganzen*) and of the household goods, and in England and most American states, only the marital home, are so protected. Thus, to the extent that a spouse can unilaterally dispose of all or most of his or her property prior to divorce, he has the power to undermine the promise of sharing held out by the system. Only in France, among the countries discussed here, does the concept of marriage as a partnership clearly prevail at the present time over the individual liberty of each spouse to deal freely with his or her earnings and assets.

Where, as under the proposed Swedish system or in the minority of American states, the aim of the law is simply to restore to each spouse his or her own property (except for the marital home), the property situation of legally married persons becomes the same as that of any other cohabitants who break up their common household.[112] Ordinary rules of property law apply to sort out the relationships. In Sweden, the convergence of the legal and social institutions under the proposed reform would be nearly total in this area because under the 1974 reform law the common dwelling or lease of a couple living in "marriage-like cohabitation" is to be awarded, on the same principles that apply to married couples, to the one who needs it most.[113] Of course, as we have seen in Chapter 3, in systems where sharing at divorce is a firm policy, the legal and social institutions can still converge but in a different way. In California and Washington, the community property has been divided between the *de facto* cohabitants, and in France and West Germany such unions are often liquidated as though they were implied partnerships.[114] If a court does not find an implied partnership, the cohabitants are, under French law, each supposed to take back their separate property, but as to assets whose origin cannot be proved, they are deemed to be co-owners in equal shares.[115] Once more the differences evaporate.

The truth is that the legal conflicts and ambivalence in the area of property division upon divorce reflect the difficulty the law is having in adjusting to different marriage patterns and ideals in society. Rather extensive sharing has been seen as an appropriate means to give a woman who has worked inside the home, and who has not accumulated property of her own, a share in the property of her husband, either on the theory that she has in some way contributed to his acquests or on the theory that the spouses have pooled all their resources of labor and capital and were thus engaged in a venture in which the results should be shared.[116] The proliferation of the double-earner marriage and the decreasing economic dependence of wives upon husbands has caused some to question the continuing appropriateness of extensive sharing. Despite the likelihood that an increased labor force participation by married women in England, France, Sweden, West Germany and the United

States will continue and expand at a moderate rate the fact is, as the comparative economic data assembled by Rheinstein and Glendon show, that substantial numbers of married women are still completely dependent economically and even those who are independent or potentially so are not the economic equals of men.[117] Thus it seems unlikely that the problem of the wife's *de facto* economic dependency on her husband is soon to disappear. From this point of view, then, sharing of marital property seems to continue to be appropriate – and not only because of the economic dependency of many wives. Even though the exclusively housewife-marriage may become obsolete, it still makes sense to many couples to view marriage as a pooling of lives, expectations and even fortunes.

But if sharing mechanisms do comport well with present economic needs and current marriage behavior, how can the appearance of a countertrend toward decreasing the sharing of marital property be explained? What are the reasons for the Swedish re-examination of deferred community and interest in separate property? In both West Germany and Sweden, the feeling is being expressed in some quarters that legal devices developed for the situation where one spouse works outside and the other works inside the home are increasingly inappropriate. The criticism has been raised against current law reform efforts which promote sharing of acquests that they will tend to channel women into positions of economic dependence and to perpetuate the inferior economic status of women.[118]

But the fact that exclusively housewife-marriage may no longer be the dominant pattern does not in and of itself explain the West German-Swedish interest in separation of property because great numbers of married women are still economic dependents for at least part of their married lives. The explanation must lie, not only in changing economic behavior of spouses, but in a combination of factors including changing ideologies of marriage.

There is an eternal tension in matrimonial law, in social attitudes, and in every marriage, between the community of life that marriage involves and the separate, autonomous existence of the individuals who are associated in this community of life. Emphasis on the one or the other aspect varies from time to time in the law, in societies and in the lives of couples. John Stuart Mill's suggestion that marriage ought to be likened to a partnership, and its expression in modern community property laws and the marital property provisions of the American Uniform Marriage and Divorce Act, emphasizes the community aspect of marriage.

But there is another idea that, as we have seen, has regained great currency in contemporary society and which is in conflict with the ideology of community. This is the notion that marriage exists primarily for the personal fulfillment of the individual spouses and that it should last only so long as it performs this function to the satisfaction of each. This idea seems to be a factor in the changes which are fast being incorporated into Swedish, West German and American law concerning the economic responsibility of the spouses for each other after divorce. No longer is it seen as self-evident in those countries that marriage involves economic responsibility to a spouse which may continue even after the legal tie has been dissolved.

Underlying these reforms is the issue of who should care for those casualties of divorce who cannot be economically self-sufficient. Should this responsibility fall on the other ex-spouse or on the State as social insurer? The Swedish welfare state has undoubtedly played a major role in the Swedish reform of alimony law. In West Germany, too, there seems to be a shift to thinking of public, rather than private, law solutions to the problem. This shift need not be seen as solely ideological. It may simply be a practical recognition, by our serial-polygamist societies, of the fact long understood in countries where simultaneous polygamy is permitted, that most men cannot support more than one family.

When the widespread expectation that marriage will last only so long as it performs its function of providing personal fulfillment is put together with the reality of unilateral divorce, a diminished sense of economic responsibility after divorce, the increasing economic independence of married women, and the expansion of social welfare, the resulting state of affairs does not lead inevitably to the sharing of worldly goods. Compulsory sharing, and restraints on the freedom of each spouse to deal with his own property, may come to be seen by increasing numbers of spouses as undesirable, in much the same way that the French revolutionaries felt that marriage, if conceived of as an indissoluble undertaking, was incompatible with the principle of individual liberty.[119]

Seen in this light, the system of separation of assets with the possibility it has always offered for purely voluntary co-ownership may come to have the most appeal for the greatest number of people in the Anglo-American jurisdictions.

In France and West Germany, the most important corrective of the statutory fixed proportions of distribution may well be constituted by the parties' freedom to provide for a different disposition in advance of the divorce.[120]

In common law countries contractual advance regulation of the financial consequences of a divorce not yet contemplated or immediately impending is still generally regarded as legally invalid.[121] This is so even though the law allows and even favors contractual settlements where divorce or legal separation is already pending.

But as Rheinstein has argued, the rule of invalidity is ripe for abandonment.[122]

The need for admission of contractual advance regulation clearly exists in jurisdictions in which the proportion of property division is fixed. But the need of recognition exists with at least equal pressure in those jurisdictions in which the property distribution is left to judicial discretion. Marrying parties nowadays know that their marriage may end in divorce and they must be enabled to provide for the reduction of controversy in that eventuality.

The case law is finally beginning to recognize this fact. A 1972 Illinois appellate court has acknowledged, in upholding an antenuptial agreement concerning financial arrangements to be made if the marriage should end in divorce:

The incidence of divorce in this country is increasing, and consequently more persons with families and established wealth are in a position to consider the possibility of a marriage later in life. Public policy is not violated by permitting these persons prior to marriage to anticipate the possibility of divorce and to establish their rights by contract in such an event as long as the contract is entered with full knowledge and without fraud, duress or coercion.[123]

In 1976 the California Supreme Court also approved such an agreement.[124]

Nevertheless, the expansion of contractual regulation will not dispense with the necessity of legal regulation and supervision. The contracting parties need to know what the likely outcome will be if the matter is entrusted to a court.[125] Furthermore, there is a special need for judicial supervision of marriage and separation contracts in order to prevent over-reaching and unfairness. Yet if parties are to be able to rely on financial arrangements made upon marriage or later, judicial control must be limited to extreme cases.[126]

C. Child Custody and Support

The unifying principle that runs through modern custody[127] law is that custody of children must be so awarded as to promote the "interests", "best interests", or "welfare" of the child.[128] However, these notions are so general and have been interpreted in so many different ways that they are not of much help in understanding current trends in custody law. There has been considerable change in recent years in ideas about what the best interests or welfare of children may require. Whatever these vague standards may mean, they are being increasingly interpreted *not* to mean that young children should always be placed with their mother; or that marital "fault" makes a parent an unfit custodian; or that biological or legitimate family relations should always take precedence over others.

As a practical matter, most custody and child support arrangements are made by the parties themselves, just as are most property settlements, and, as we have seen, most divorces. However, the state of the positive law has had an important effect on the negotiating leverage of each party where the law permits one to prevent or delay a divorce until a satisfactory financial settlement is made. One of the principal arguments in favor of no-fault divorce was that it would eliminate leverage based on fault. However, a disadvantage of no-fault divorce may turn out to be that the arena where the battles over money take place will simply be *shifted* from the question of the divorce itself to the question of custody of children, and that children will be used more than ever as pawns in financial or emotional battles between their parents.[129] While the no-fault concept has been incorporated into modern custody laws in the sense that the court is not to take into consideration conduct of a proposed custodian which does not affect his relationship to the child, the fitness of a custodian will always be an issue. One spouse can always make a divorce proceeding extremely unpleasant by calling into question the fitness of the spouse who desires custody.

An aspect of custody which is changing in law if not in fact under the influence of the equality principle in the United States is the elimination from the interpretation of the "best interests of the child" of that rule of thumb that the interests of a child of "tender years" are best served by placing him with the mother.[130] The new French divorce law has abolished the prior French rule under which custody was in principle awarded to the spouse who obtained the divorce.[131] In fact there seems to be little reason to expect that the practice will vary much from the past where custody has generally been given to the mother. Sociological studies and opinion surveys made in connection with the French reform law showed that the great majority of fathers were content with this system.[132] Practitioners in the United States say that, apart from a few well-publicized cases, it is still rather rare for fathers to seek to undertake the primary responsibility for children after divorce.

A new theory which seems to be gaining acceptance in the United States is elaborated in the recent book, *Beyond the Best Interests of the Child*.[133] Among its other controversial proposals this book, the product of collaboration between two psychoanalysts and a law professor, recommends that paramount weight in child custody disputes should be given to continuity in a familiar situation, even where a new and in some ways more advantageous alternative is available for the child. Under the slogan, "the psychological parent is the real parent", the authors have urged that mere biological parentage should be given less weight in custody and visitation disputes than a child's bonds to that parent or persons with whom he has formed a close

day-to-day relationship. Because of the extreme importance to the child of
stability and continuity the authors likewise urge that after divorce the
non-custodial parent should be given no visitation *rights*, and that visitation
should be a *privilege* within the discretion of the custodial parent. Finally, the
authors urge that the "best interests of the child" test itself should be replaced
by a "least detrimental alternative" test, a formulation which is supposed to
alert the court to the fact that a child who is the subject of a custody dispute is
already at risk, and that the real choice is usually not between two good
alternatives but in deciding, in the light of all the circumstances, which
alternative is least harmful. All these ideas have gained surprisingly rapid
acceptance in the American case law, and have received wide attention in the
scholarly writing.[134]

In Sweden it has been explicitly established that child custody questions
arising between unmarried parents are to be determined in the same manner
as between parents who were once married to each other, that is, in accordance with the best interests of the child.[135] Thus a father of a child born out of
wedlock can apply for custody of a child and his petition will be judged by the
"best interests" test.[136] A government reform proposal, not yet adopted,
provides that separated unmarried couples, like divorced couples, may be
granted joint custody of mutual children.[137]

Support of children is everywhere increasingly the responsibility of both
spouses, or ex-spouses, and with the advent of reforms assimilating the status
of illegitimate to legitimate children,[138] the distinction in legal effect between
the legally married and the unmarried states breaks down here as well in favor
of concern for the *de facto* consequences of cohabitation. The tendency to
disregard legal and biological ties which may not correspond to actual family
relationships is apparent also in the emerging law concerning support of
children "treated" as children of the family, such as stepchildren. Under
English financial provision law, a child of one spouse has support rights
against the other if that child was "treated" as a child of the family.[139] A recent
American case has enforced support rights against an ex-husband, where the
child in question was not the biological or adopted child of either ex-spouse,
but had been cared for by them and treated as their son for 12 years.[140]

But the ascertainment of *liability* for spousal or child support is not in itself
an exceptionally difficult legal problem. It is only the beginning of the story,
for it is easier to fix liability than to enforce it. The problem has been well
stated by the English family law specialist, Alec Samuels:

The problem in society today is that H has two women to support, his wife or ex-wife,
and his mistress or second wife, and the children by both women. And he has only one

pay packet, barely sufficient to support one family, let alone two. And he prefers the second family, and the second woman can get her hands on to the pay packet. The obligation, legal or moral, to the mistress or second wife must be taken into account, and H will not be left below subsistence level in the second family, even though this may well mean that W will inevitably be forced upon social security, or forced to remain on social security. As the obligations in the second family increase so the orders in favour of the children of the first family may be reduced.[141]

The new West German law, like its predecessor, and like English law, recognizes, in an oblique fashion, that financial obligations to a later family can take priority over obligations to earlier ones.[142]

In the United States a great deal of data has now been collected which shows that child support judgments, whether arrived at by consent or imposed by a court, typically furnish considerably less than half the support of a child, and that even these small payments are frequently not adhered to.[143] A Wisconsin study for example showed that within one year after the divorce decree, only 38% of fathers were in full compliance with the support order and that 42% had made no payments at all. By the 10th year only 13% of the fathers were fully complying and 79% were in total non–compliance.[144] A nationwide survey by the U.S. Department of Health Education and Welfare has indicated that 46.9% of all families with one or more court orders for child support were not receiving any.[145] Collection procedures, although there have been many statutes passed to facilitate them, have not been much utilized by private individuals because of their expense and because even when successful they may only result in a new decree cutting down the amount owed, followed by a new period of non–compliance.

The American writers Foster and Freed, discussing the "notorious difficulties in collecting support and alimony awards", say,

This unprecedented wholesale defiance of court orders by embittered men may be accounted for, at least in part, by the failure of courts to be realistic and to appreciate that an automatic imposition of the support duty is not in accord with current values and in many cases is highly penal.... [W]here a poor or low income husband is involved, even a minimal order may constitute a great hardship or impossible burden.... Moreover, if he remarries or establishes a new family, further complications inevitably arise, making his primary obligation to the first family unrealistic.[146]

Because of the difficulty of enforcement, any discussion of child support, like that of spousal support, inevitably leads back to the State through the questions of how support obligations should be enforced, how economic independence can be fostered, and how needs of individuals can be met when support obligations cannot be enforced and their own efforts cannot suffice.

D. The City of the Rich and the City of the Poor

Watching the ball go back and forth between the proponents and opponents of alimony and property sharing is a fascinating pastime. For those whose financial situation permits the support of an extra family or two, and who have managed not to consume all that they earned in the course of a marriage, the game is worth the candle. But if one wishes to grasp the economic reality of after-divorce in society as a whole, these vigorous battles over property may distract the eye from the real action. In every city, as Aristotle said, there is the city of the rich and the city of the poor. The law which we have been examining in this Chapter up to now has for the most part been the law of the propertied classes. In the city of the poor, the law pertaining to post-divorce economic dependency is public law. Who lives in the city of the poor? In the United States the majority of poor families with children are headed by women.[147] The major cause of the growth of female-headed families in the U.S. is marriage dissolution.[148] As stated above, the Finer Report indicates that a similar situation prevails in England.

It has long been recognized that private enforcement of support orders has been inadequate to assure the continuing support of women and children after divorce. Thus the United States in 1975 and France in 1976 put into operation national systems of public recovery of maintenance orders.[149] While the American law was controversial (on grounds that it represented too much federal intrusion in private life), the French law was enacted as a compromise measure only after a more radical program of state intervention narrowly missed adoption. In England, the system of the Social Security Act of 1966 operates to furnish the spouse in need of support with public assistance, and to permit the public agency (the Supplementary Benefits Commission) to try to recoup from the "liable relative". The Finer Report has recommended against the implementation of any new system which would involve direct involvement of the needy spouse in the recoupment effort.

Whereas the new American federal law is limited to providing federal assistance for the collection of child support orders, the French law provides that the Treasury will assume the task of recovering child and spousal support orders and the compensatory payments described above. In this, it resembles laws of the various American states providing public assistance in certain cases for the recovery of support orders. Studies taken in connection with divorce law reform in France revealed that 40% of support orders were being regularly paid, and 27% were never complied with.[150] Although these figures are better than the corresponding ones available for the United States,[151] the pressure for further reform nearly led in France to the adoption of the proposals of the socialist and communist parties for a public insurance program through which the payment of support orders would be guaranteed by the state which in turn would try to recover the sums due from the debtors.[152] The supporters of such a program at first included the Cabinet Secretary for Women's Affairs, Mme Françoise Giroud. However, it was in great measure due to Mme Giroud's influence, after she became convinced that such a solution was unacceptable, that the law in its present form was eventually adopted.[153] This occurred however only after a law providing for a public guarantee fund had passed the National Assembly, had been discussed widely, and, upon resubmission to the National Assembly, was defeated.[154] The arguments which finally prevailed against the establishment of a primary rather than a secondary role for the government in the recovery of support orders were, first and foremost, those relating to the cost of establishing the system. But it also seemed there was concern about certain social and moral aspects of the idea. Fear was expressed that the establishment of collective responsibility for maintenance of spouses and children would diminish the sense of individual responsibility and further reduce the amount of voluntary compliance. Likewise, there was concern that the "good payers" would feel that it was unfair for them to have to share the burden of the responsibilities neglected by the "bad payers". Finally Mme Giroud expressed reservations about the distinctions which such a system would establish between judgment-creditors in support cases on the one hand, and other unfortunates in society who would not be eligible for the benefits of the Act on the other:

How can one isolate the situation of the child whose provider is insolvent or absent from that of a child who has only one parent to minister to his needs? How can one prefer the child of a divorced person to a child whose father or mother is dead, or a child of an unmarried mother, or a child whose parent, even if present at home, is incapable of supporting himself and perhaps is even an added burden?... Even if there are no children,...how can one prefer a divorced wife to a widow without resources?[155]

Under the American Social Services Amendments Law of 1975, a vast federal program is set up for enforcing support orders of state courts. The law puts the forces of the Social Security system, the Internal Revenue Service, and other federal agencies at the disposal of divorced, deserted and unwed mothers, whether they are solvent or receiving public aid, in order to assure collection of support orders. Non-support of a welfare mother is made a federal crime, and a welfare mother is required to cooperate in the civil or criminal prosecution of a non-supporting father as a condition of receiving public aid. In one sense, this law is a reaction against the assumption by the state of family functions, fixing economic responsibility for the casualties of broken legal or *de facto* families on the family members themselves, rather than on the taxpayers. But at the same time it reaches deeply enough into the private lives of citizens and family members that it was vigorously opposed by civil liberties groups. The law is also evidence of the trend we have already noticed for the state to be concerned with functional problems of economic dependence without regard to legal or non-legal relationship.

In spite of the real efforts now being made to solve the problems of post-divorce poverty through public aid in finding the "liable relative", as he is called in English law, and collecting amounts due under support orders, the problem stated by Alec Samuels persists. What if the liable relative is found in the bosom of his new family where, once again, one paycheck is barely enough to go around? Public enforcement of support orders will perhaps help some of the persons who have been left in economically precarious circumstances by divorce, but as Congressman (then Dean) Drinan S. J. had already written in 1969: "...mere strict enforcement of support orders...is not and cannot be, in the vast majority of cases, a program that will even begin to take care of the needs of the children of divorce".[156] Sooner or later Drinan's point must be directly faced. According to 1975 U.S. Department of Labor figures, an urban family of four needs $9800 a year to live at "an austere level",[157] but U.S. Census Bureau figures for 1974 show that over 35% of all American families had less than $10,000 income that year.[158] A disproportionate number of these families are female-headed.[159]

Where the flow of unearned income to family members in need cannot be assured by enforcing private transfers, there are two other ways in which the State can seek to respond to the situation. One is to try to enable a dependent ex-spouse, or an ex-spouse who is the custodian of children, to be wholly or partly self-supporting. In the case of the former, State aid may be limited to vocational training or help in finding employment; in the case of the latter publicly-funded child-care facilities may be required. Working mothers and would-be working mothers in the United States have found allies in their efforts to secure more child-care facilities among the persons who make up the education industry, where supply of personnel for the moment exceeds demand for their services.

Ultimately, the fact has to be faced that the question often comes down to which family is to be preferred, the old or the new, when the breadwinner's means are sufficient for one family only. Basic approaches to this question range from that of the Archbishop of Canterbury's Group that the obligations of the original marriage are "inescapable", to Stöcker's view that it is "unjust" for the state to pass on its own responsibility as social insurer to the ex-spouses. But the practical answer is that if the State must support one family, it might as well support the one the breadwinner has left behind, rather than spend money to force him to do it, leaving the family he will voluntarily support in need. When matters are put this crassly, it is easy to see why legislatures have been reluctant to proceed along the lines suggested by Drinan, Stöcker and the Finnish committee and to openly assume primary responsibility for the victims of broken homes.[160] Even if one can imagine good citizen taxpayers who are not opposed to assuming more and more responsibility for such social risks as illness, disability and old age in society, it would take an almost saintly taxpayer to cheerfully assume the cost of other people's serial marital adventures. It is frequently forgotten that for the economically dependent spouse, especially a mother of young children, the choice is often between enduring an intolerable marriage or a life of grinding poverty. Should escape from an unbearable situation be facilitated only for those who are well-to-do or otherwise self-sufficient?

The end result of course is that the public *does* assume the burden, but grudgingly and at a niggardly level (except possibly in Sweden where public assistance is said to make the position of a female-headed household quite strong). In England and the United States, the majority of female-headed one-parent families are on welfare and in poor circumstances. The words of a Massachusetts judge interviewed by the U.S. Citizens Advisory Council on the Status of Women are an appropriate comment on the situation:

> The whole problem is one of complete frustration since no middle class person can actually afford divorce. Our only consolation is that public welfare supplies the balance, but this, of course, means that the taxpayer is assuming the parental burdens.[161]

This does not mean that the taxpayer can go to sleep at night feeling like a good parent. As the American and English studies show, public assistance to female-headed families in those countries assures at present only a life of bare subsistence. Increasingly, therefore, claims have been made that humane and sensible family policy requires a program of broad income maintenance for all poor families with children, without regard to whether the parents are married or divorced, or single, or cohabiting; employed or unemployed; or whether the children are born in or out of legal marriage.[162] In the concluding section of this chapter, we will return to these problems as we continue our exploration of the changing relationship of the State to the family.

III. Legal Marriage Dissolution by Death of a Spouse

In traditional legal systems limited provision was made for the continued support of widows and widowers. It would have been simple to do this by giving the surviving spouse a generous share of the property of the predeceasing spouse, secured against defeat by testamentary disposition or transactions *inter vivos*. But this would have entailed a consequence that appeared unacceptable in social systems where wealth was thought to belong not so much to individuals as to families, i.e., to groups of kindred related by blood. To permit a surviving spouse to inherit property would mean that property might be shifted from one blood line into another. This unwanted result could be avoided and the goal of providing for the survivor implemented either (1) by limiting the surviving spouse to a *life* interest in the wealth of the predeceasing spouse or (2) by limiting the survivor's share to property that had not come to the predeceasing spouse through the latter's family, but was rather the fruit of gainful activities, or (3) by combining a life estate in the inherited property with a share in the acquests. Since acquests were normally made through the activities of the husband, and since he was also the manager of those acquests which might arise out of the wife's activities, it was simple to treat all marital acquests as constituting a single fund which, upon the death of one spouse, would be divided between the heirs of the predeceasing partner and the survivor. In a social system in which inherited wealth consisted primarily of land and in which other forms of property tended to be regarded as relatively unimportant (or as presumptively being acquired by "purchase" rather than by "descent"), it was enough to provide that land owned at the time of marriage would be excluded from the community fund.

Thus, community property has long been a technique of providing for a surviving spouse. The technique of inheritance was also available for this purpose, but that technique seemed abhorrent in societies where the tie between blood and soil was strongly felt. Marriage was no reason for shifting family land from one blood line into another. In the common law systems, the interests at stake were secured by giving the surviving spouse a share or in some cases all of the personal property and, under certain circumstances, a life interest in the real estate of the predeceasing spouse.[163]

The principal modernizing trends in the law concerning the rights of the surviving spouse have uniformly pushed in all countries toward the improvement of the position of the spouse *vis-a-vis* the blood relatives.

A. England

In England, if a predeceasing spouse does not leave a will and his estate is less than £15,000, the survivor is entitled to take it all, over and above certain personal belongings of the decedent including clothing, furniture, jewelry, household goods, and cars. If the estate is larger than £15,000, and issue survives, the surviving spouse takes the personal chattels and £15,000 out-right, plus a life interest in half of the excess over £15,000. [164] The remainder goes to the issue.

As part of the general policy of securing the occupation of the matrimonial home, the law also protects the survivor's right of occupancy whether the home was owned or leased by the decedent. [165] If the decedent was the owner, the survivor may have the home be appropriated to his or her intestate share. If the value of the home is greater than the intestate share (which will be unlikely in most cases,) the survivor, if he or she keeps the home, will be required to pay the difference in value to the estate.

If an English spouse wishes to leave more or less than the intestate share to his partner, he is free to do so by making a will. Unlike the French and German systems, where a parent may not completely disinherit his children, English law permits husband and wife to leave their entire estates to each other even if there are surviving children. Freedom to disinherit the other spouse was at one time limited in English law by the estates of Dower and Curtesy which gave a surviving spouse certain rights for life in the other's real property. But from 1833 to 1938 complete freedom of testation prevailed in England (furnishing Charles Dickens with the plots and sub-plots of many novels). In 1938 this freedom was qualified somewhat by a law providing that the court *may* in its discretion award maintenance to a spouse, or certain other dependents, where the deceased had left a will which deprived them of a "reasonable share" of his property. From 1938 to 1975, the only remedy for a disinherited spouse was to request a court for discretionary "maintenance" out of the decedent's estate. But in 1974 the Law Commission recommended a far-reaching change in this system, and the recommendations were implemented by legislation in 1975. [166] Recognizing the anomaly that existing English law was according greater rights to a divorced spouse than to a surviving spouse, the Law Commission proposed that the court's power to award family provision for dependents on death should be as wide as its power to award provision upon divorce. [167] Thus, the new system is still a system of discretionary court awards, but no longer limits a surviving spouse to "maintenance". He or she can request "reasonable financial provision", on the analogy of the Matrimonial Causes Act of 1973, and the court has the same power as under that Act to award periodic payments or a lump sum or a combination of both, under guidelines similar to those of the 1973 Act. The new act, like the former Family Provision Act, applies to situations both of intestate and testate succession, and like the most recent American legislation, it provides for means to reach *inter vivos* transfers in attempted evasion of the proposed provisions.

The 1975 succession legislation also broadens the categories of persons entitled to claim financial provision upon death in such a way as to blur the distinctions between the legal and *de facto* family. Thus, not only may a legitimate or illegitimate child of the deceased claim provision, but so may any person whom the deceased "treated as a child of the family". Not only may the decedent's surviving spouse or former spouse make a claim, but so may any person who was being "wholly or partly maintained" by the deceased before his death. This latter provision was expressly designed to cover the case where a decedent was cohabiting with someone whose "...moral claim...may be just as great as that of a surviving spouse".[168]

B. United States

In the United States the surviving spouse has clearly become the favorite in inheritance. When a spouse dies without leaving a will, the law of every American state assures the survivor of a substantial share in the estate. In a case where children also survive, the spouse will never take less than a third, often a half, and in some states will, as in England, take a fixed amount plus a fraction, usually one-half, of the balance.[169] The modern trend seems to set this fixed dollar amount high enough so that, as in England, the surviving spouse will take all of a modest estate in the average case.

Studies in the United States have revealed that the desire of the average American spouse is for the survivor to take all of a small or medium-sized estate.[170] The American Uniform Probate Code and the intestate succession laws of numerous states have been drafted with this in mind. The attitude in American community property states appears to be essentially the same as in the non-community property states. A recent study of transmission of wealth at death in the state of Washington shows that community property law has little impact on the disposition that married persons make of their property at death, and justifies the decision which had already been made by the Washington legislature to make the surviving spouse the intestate heir of all of a decedent spouse's interest in the community property regardless of whether other relatives survive.[171]

In the case where a spouse dies leaving a will disinheriting the other spouse, the difference between the law of the American states and that of England is striking: in every American separate property state a widow and usually, but not always, a widower, has fixed and certain property rights which cannot be defeated by will. The major legal techniques by which this is achieved are: dower; indefeasible share; homestead; and family allowances.[172] Except for the indefeasible share, these techniques usually operate also in intestate succession to provide, among other things, a measure of protection for the surviving family against creditors of the decedent. Sometimes these techniques are combined in a single state. Dower is a fixed property interest which attaches upon marriage to the real property of the husband in favor of the wife. In many states dower laws have now been made applicable to both husband and wife. The wife becomes entitled to life-time possessory rights only if she survives her husband and *vice versa*. Several states have recently either abolished the institution of dower, or have eliminated a feature which made it advantageous to the surviving spouse – its immunity to *inter vivos* transfers and encumbrances. It was abolished in England except as to intestate estates in 1833. The principal reasons for the decline of dower are the threat it poses to the security of land titles and its practical ineffectiveness in situations where the deceased owns little or no real property, or where the spouse in need of protection is induced to sign away her dower rights in connection with a sale or security transaction.

Because of the practical difficulties with dower, the states came to see other protective devices as more appropriate to secure to the survivor a share in a deceased spouse's estate. The most popular of these is the simple device, used in many European systems, of securing a minimum share to certain designated takers. This system in American law is in favor of the spouse, rather than in favor of certain groups of descendants and ascendants, as it is in the French system. In some states the forced share is a function of the intestate share; in others it is a fixed sum of money, with or without a fractional share in the surplus. The exact regulation of the forced share in any state will of course reflect the way the legislature of that state balances the policy favoring freedom of testation against the policy in favor of protecting surviving spouses. To Europeans it must seem strange that policies in favor of protecting other dependents play almost no part.

The American system of forced share has some disadvantages, in comparison with the forced share as it is known in the civil law systems. Its principal disadvantage has been that its size depends on the size of the estate. Thus, if the husband, for example, three days before his death, gives away his entire estate the forced share of his wife is defeated. But the Uniform Probate Code of 1969 and a small but steadily increasing number of states have taken steps to protect the surviving spouse by statute against such *inter vivos* transactions. The courts in a minority of states have also developed rules to protect a widow or widower against *inter vivos* transfers by the husband.

A disadvantage of the forced share system, which appears when it is contrasted with the English system, is its lack of flexibility to deal with individual situations. Although the English system of discretionary family provision has been extensively studied in the United States, and considered both as a replacement or supplement to present systems, it has found no acceptance.

The total picture of the protection of the surviving spouse in the United States must include the often generous allowance of support during the administration of the estate, the protection of rights in the marital home through homestead legislation, and finally, but not least, the fact that sharing principles are implicit in the United States federal estate tax scheme which permits an up-to-50% "marital deduction" from the estate of one spouse when it passes to the other.

The net effect of this combination of devices will in the cases of many (but not all) middle-class couples turn out to be very much like an equal division in a traditional system of community of acquests. If the husband dies first, and he had acquired and held most of the couple's property in his name, the American systems will, upon his death, effect a division or even a complete transfer of the acquests and all other property to the wife thus, finally, if belatedly, recognizing her contribution to their acquisition. The American laws will result in a surviving spouse's taking *all* of many small estates, in accordance with the presumed intentions of most married persons. The forced share of an American spouse is computed on the decedent's *total* estate which includes that property which a community system would designate as separate property, whereas in a community of acquests the survivor's one-half is computed on the basis of the acquests alone. Taken together, all these legal devices reveal in the law of the United States the fullest expression to be found in the four countries here examined of the idea of economic sharing in marriage at least so far as the case of marriage termination by death is concerned.

C. *France*

In France where a marriage is terminated by death, the matrimonial regime is dissolved, an inventory is made, a balance sheet drawn up, and the assets and liabilities of the community divided (as in the case of divorce). But this time the division is between the survivior and the estate of the deceased instead of between the two ex-spouses. A surviving spouse has the right to receive from the community fund the funeral expenses, and food and lodging for a period of a year after the death, and then to receive one-half of the remaining community fund.

If the predeceasing spouse owned separate property, his or her estate includes such property as well as his or her half of the community property.

Thus, in certain cases, the rights supplementing the survivor's right to "his own" half of the community are important.

Whether the surviving spouse as such has any rights to the estate of the deceased depends on what other persons rank as heirs of the deceased, and on whether or not the deceased left a will. Under the Code of 1804 the spouse was called to intestate succession only in default of collaterals within the 12th degree. Since that time, the position of the spouse has improved, but not to the point where it is equivalent to that in the other countries studied here. Where the decedent leaves descendants as well as his spouse, the surviving spouse is entitled only to the usufruct of one-quarter of the succession.[173] The usufruct can exist on half the estate if the decedent is survived by brothers and sisters, descendants of brothers or sisters, ascendants or natural children conceived during the marriage.[174] If there are only collaterals in the paternal or maternal line more remote than those just mentioned, the surviving spouse takes one-half of the estate outright.[175] Only if there are no relatives at all, or if the survivors are remote collaterals, does the spouse take the entire estate.[176]

This result is in marked contrast to the situation of an American widow or widower for whose benefit, as we have seen, the law of intestate succession secures at least a third, usually a half, and sometimes all of the estate outright when he or she is in competition with issue of the decedent. But the contrast is mainly in legal techniques. The two situations in the normal case may not be markedly different. The American surviving spouse in non-community property states receives no share of the acquests made by the other spouse during the marriage as such. The effect of giving her one-half of his estate by intestate succession may have much the same effect. There is, however, a marked trend in the United States to award the entire succession in a small estate to the surviving spouse on the theory that this treatment accords with the desires of most couples and makes more sense where the surviving children are minors.[177]

In the area of testate succession French and Anglo-American law differ as well. The difference is partly understandable in the context of the different matrimonial property laws. In every common law jurisdiction, the surviving spouse is protected against disinheritance. In contrast to American and West German law, French law gives the surviving spouse no indefeasible share in the succession. Freedom of testation is limited only in favor of descendants and ascendants. Where the decedent is survived by two children, for example, their reserved share is two-thirds.[178] The remaining one-third is the *quotité disponible*, of which the testator is free to dispose by will as he wishes.

This share, it must be noted, is a share of the entire estate, i.e. one-half of the community fund combined with the entire separate funds of the decedent. A testator who is survived by issue may choose among three alternatives if he wishes to dispose of this share in favor of his surviving spouse. (1) He may give the entire *quotité disponible* to his spouse outright, i.e. where two children survive this would be one-third of his estate; or (2) he may give the survivor one-quarter of his estate outright and the income from the remaining three-quarters; or (3) he may give the survivor the income of the entire estate.[179] The latter two options have been available only since the law of 13 July 1963. Under the prior law, the only alternatives to giving the surviving spouse the *quotité disponible* were to give her one-fourth of the entire estate outright and one-fourth in usufruct; or to give her the usufruct of one-fourth of the entire estate. At the same time that these amounts were increased in favor of the spouse in 1963, the descendants were given the right to have the usufruct converted to an annuity, provided (1) that they give sufficient security to guarantee the annuity and (2) that the property which is subject to the usufruct is not the residence of the surviving spouse nor the furnishings of such a residence.[180]

Thus, since 1963, one can see at work in French law more concern for the surviving spouse at the expense of the traditional concern for heirs in the blood line of the deceased. Nevertheless, the maximum amount available to be willed to the surviving spouse is still far less than that available under the law of the American states where, except in Louisiana, it is the entire estate. The difference between French and American law is less remarkable when it is recalled that the surviving spouse has already received one half of the community fund. Perhaps it is the American failure to secure a forced share to children that ought to appear remarkable.

But on this point it seems clear that the common law reflects the popular American conceptions of how property should be distributed at death. In France, on the other hand, even the very limited expansion of surviving spouses' rights has not been welcomed by everyone. The writer of a 1974 article claims the introduction of forced inheritance by the surviving spouse will encourage divorce. His arguments show that the strength of the blood tie is not a negligible factor in French succession law at the present time:[181]

One must never forget when one speaks of the surviving spouse as a forced heir, that there will always be a fundamental and irreversible difference between the spouse and the other forced heirs. The others are the ascendants and the descendants of the decedent. Their right to a forced share is an intangible right, because it is founded on a blood tie, which no one, not even the future decedent, can destroy. It is different with a spouse. The inheritance rights of a spouse are tied to marriage, in the absence of divorce or legal separation. The protection that one might wish to assure to a surviving spouse can only boomerang against him because of the fragility of the basis of such a right.

On the other hand, the remarkable popularity of the optional regime of universal community as a will substitute among long-married couples ever since it became possible to change a marital property regime by contract in 1965 attests to the changing economic behavior and attitudes of French couples. An opinion survey done in connection with the 1965 reform showed a characteristic ambivalence: most respondents thought existing treatment of the surviving spouse "abnormal", but at the same time were shocked at the thought of property escaping into a strange family, i.e. non-blood relatives.[182]

The gradual improvement of the surviving spouse's position in succession in French law will probably continue, if only because modernization of the French matrimonial property system in 1965 diminished the effectiveness of the community property system itself as the basic means of providing for a surviving spouse.

D. West Germany

The idea that a surviving spouse should share in the other's property can be achieved by giving the survivor a share in the acquests, as in the French system, or by giving him an indefeasible share of the whole estate as in most American states. The latter technique was regarded as simpler and therefore preferable by the parliamentary committee which drafted the final version of the 1957 West German Equal Rights Law which, among other things, reformed West German marital property law.[183] If the spouses have lived under the legal property regime of *Zugewinngemeinschaft*, the law does not extend the technique of the equalization claim used in divorce cases to the case where one spouse dies intestate. The appraisals and calculations necessary for the determination of the equalization claim were regarded as so cumbersome that they would delay the liquidation of a decedent's estate. In the case of intestate death of a spouse under the legal regime, it was resolved that "the equal sharing in the marital increase is to be achieved by increasing, by one-fourth of the estate, the share of the surviving spouse" irrespective of whether or not there has been any difference of increase in the particular case.[184] As this works out, the surviving spouse under the rules of the *Zugewinngemeinschaft*, is entitled to one-half of the estate if there are descendants of the decedent; at least three-fourths if there are parents, descendants of parents or both a grandparent or grandparents and descendants of grandparents; and the entire estate in all other cases.[185]

In addition to his intestate share, the West German law of succession gives the surviving spouse a benefit which resembles the surviving spouse's award in American state laws. If the surviving spouse is intestate heir together with parents, descendants of parents, or grandparents, he is entitled to the wedding gifts and household goods. If he is intestate heir together with descendants, he is entitled to such items if he needs them for the conduct of an appropriate (angemessenen) household. [186]

By increasing the share of the surviving spouse, of necessity the 1957 law reduced the share to which the other intestate successors were previously entitled. The intestate share of descendants for example has been reduced from formerly three-fourths to one-half the estate under the legal regime. For this reason the law has been widely criticized and resort to alternative contractual regimes by propertied persons has been frequent. [187] But the 1957 law is a recognition of the fact that in West Germany as elsewhere in modern industrialized societies the blood tie has been weakening, as has the significance of inherited wealth. According to Müller-Freienfels, this change in the amount received by the surviving spouse, as opposed to the children, is the principal reason that in practice spouses with large fortunes tend to contract out of the statutory marital property scheme.

If the decedent spouse has disinherited the survivor by will, the survivor receives the equalization claim as he would in a divorce case. In addition to the equalization claim, the disinherited spouse is entitled to the reserved share (Pflichtteil) which was his under the prior law. [188] The Pflichtteil of a disinherited spouse is one-half of what would have been due him as an intestate heir. Complex rules apply to cases where the surviving spouse has been partially, but not wholly, disinherited.

E. Summary

In the legal changes in all the countries studied here, the conjugal relationship has increasingly been preferred to blood relationships. But the precise adjustment of the relative positions of spouse and blood relatives varies greatly from France, where blood relatives still have a strong position, to the American states where the surviving spouse not only enjoys a favored position but is everywhere protected against disinheritance.

The uniform trend toward sharing of spouses' property on death is not surprising. The main obstacles to this were feelings about blood ties and inherited wealth which are rapidly changing. Unlike the divorce situation, no force pushes strongly for maintaining independence of the spouses' economic interests here. The trend appears to be related to changes in the nature of wealth, the diminishing of the strength of feelings about blood ties and their relation to property, the emergence of the nuclear, joint and conjugal family, and the tendency to view an amicable marriage, at least, as a pooling of the economic interests of the spouses. These factors are reflected in current testamentary and *inter vivos* gift behavior and in legal changes, both of which reveal a preference for inheritance by the surviving spouse over children of the marriage and also over other blood relatives of the decedent. This preference is weaker in some systems, like the French, and very strong in others, like the American, but in all systems when change has taken place it has been toward expansion and strengthening of the rights of the survivor.

A new problem which is receiving increasing attention is that of pensions, insurance annuities, social security and other such rights. Should a married person's expectation of receiving such payments upon retirement, disability or the death of the other spouse be lost if the marriage is terminated by divorce? Life insurance and pension rights are tending more and more to assume the place of capital savings. In a divorce case the future benefits of a life insurance policy of one spouse can be secured for the other. But if a divorce occurs when the husband is middle-aged, how is one to deal with his future retirement benefits or the pension that will be due to his widow upon his death? The "widow" will of course be the woman to whom he is married when he dies. Shall she have the whole pension while the wife from whom he is divorced receives nothing? Scandinavian laws have described schemes for pension splitting between the widow or widower and the former spouses. An elaborate *"Rentenausgleich"* is contained in the new West German divorce law. That scheme has been criticized for the likelihood that it will result in splitting up pensions into fractions too small to be of help to the recipients. The problem is one to which a generally satisfactory solution has not been found.

IV. State, Law and Family

A. What is Left of Legal Marriage?

In the area of the present Chapter, consequences of dissolution of marriage, one cannot say that legal marriage no longer has legal effects. At first glance legal marriage appears to be firmly established as the basis from which legal consequences flow upon divorce or death of one of the spouses. Support and inheritance rights as such, even in Sweden, accrue only in connection with legal marriage.[189] But a closer look reveals that even here the categories are slipping and are being adjusted to reflect social and economic changes. One can see this in the trend not to accord support, marital property sharing and social security benefits where a marriage has been of short duration. Sometimes a specified period is set out in statutes beyond which a legal marriage must endure in order to have certain property consequences.[190] Thus, alongside the phenomenon of *de facto* marriages of a certain duration being accorded legal effects under social laws, we can place the phenomenon of legal marriages with *no* legal effects, for social security purposes, unless they have lasted a specified period of time.[191]

But just as Chapter 4 showed support law of the on-going marriage moving away from the idea of spouses supporting each other during marriage, as opposed to mutually contributing to household expenses during cohabitation, so all the systems here examined except the English are moving away from the idea that in principle the spouses have a continuing economic responsibility for each other after divorce.[192] The starting point is instead that support payments should be made only in specified cases of need, and should, if possible, be temporary until the payee-spouse can become self-supporting. As for division of marital property, to the extent that these issues are not merged with support issues, the rules pertaining to spouses are becoming similar to those governing the property relations of other cohabitants. Child support, to the extent that it is not merged with spousal support issues, is increasingly being freed from dependence on the existence of legal, as opposed to biological or *de facto* ties. In the background in some countries, out in front in others, the issue is being framed as to whether the economic responsibility for casualties of broken marriages should belong to the ex-spouses or to society as a whole.

At first glance it may seem that there is no common thread running through modern spousal support, child support and marital property law. Levels of "support morality" are different in the different countries,[193] the extent of marriage dissolution is greater in some countries than in others, and the welfare state has assumed more responsibility for the casualties of broken marriages in some countries. But with all the differences in attitudes, behavior and laws, one nevertheless can discern, overall, the continuing process of transformation of the idea of marriage that is being expressed in the law. Just as in the preceding chapter we traced the development of marriage from an indissoluble institution to one terminable at will, so the developments in this chapter show its evolution from an institution which entailed economic responsibility of the husband for the wife, continuing in the case of an "innocent" wife, even after dissolution, to an institution in which both parties are treated as primarily responsible for their own economic welfare.

Thus in the new French divorce law, divorce in principle terminates the duty of support; in the new West German law spouses are expected to be self-supporting; and in the Uniform Act in the United States, as in the proposed reforms in Sweden and Canada, the starting point is no alimony in principle. We have already seen that such laws are unrealistic in that they ignore the facts of post-divorce economic dependency. But they enshrine and perhaps reinforce the sense that the economic problems of divorce are, like illness and unemployment, problems for the society as a whole. The question occurs, however, whether in a time of declining affluence the relatively monogamous majority can or will support the victims of divorce other than, as at present, in a miserly and resentful fashion.

In one area at least the ideology of community and cooperation in husband–wife relationships and the special place accorded to legal marriage seem to rule supreme. This is in the law of succession. Here, not only at the level of symbolism (as was the case with the developments described in the law of the on-going marriage), but in practical economic effect, sharing between the spouses has been implemented and constantly strengthened. Thus if a legal union lasts "until death does them part", the aspirations of society for marriage as expressed through the law are at last and most fully realized.

But even here it has to be noted that while the legal forms may be left standing, or even reinforced in some cases, social and economic developments are emptying them of some of their content. For example, changes in society have gradually brought about a state of affairs in which it can be said that property, in the sense of assets of real or personal property, is less important than individual earning power and public or private benefits based on such labor.[194] Modern matrimonial property law has thus had to become increasingly concerned with rights and obligations concerning income produced by a spouse's labor, and with such relatively modest assets as the family home.[195] In this context, matrimonial contracts, gifts, and succession, while still important for some segments of the population, have yielded the center of attention to legal efforts to deal with the problems of family support and the rights and duties pertaining to income of family members.

Also, while there are economic advantages which normally attach to the legal status of being married, at the same time economic benefits in modern welfare states are increasingly derived from the State on the basis of need, regardless of one's family status. The traditional private law effects of marriage, inheritance and marital property rights, are of less concern to the great numbers of people who consume what they earn, and leave little behind when they die, than are the various forms of social assistance. We must turn to this development, which is changing the whole frame of reference of family law, in the next section of this Chapter.

Finally, even as the forms of legal marriage are being drained of some of
their traditional subject matter by changes in the forms of wealth in society,
they are being flanked by legal developments (reflecting changes in marriage
and family behavior) which assimilate the effects of legal marriage to the
effects of *de facto* family relationships, even in the areas of property and
succession.[196] The achievement of marriage-neutrality in public law affecting
the family, as well as its beginning recognition in private law as described
above in Chapter 3, is not the product of intentional effort on anyone's part to
diminish the significance of legal family ties. For the most part it simply
reflects the fact that certain social problems cannot be affected by traditional
"family law", but have to be got at through laws relating to employment,
social welfare and social insurance, tax laws and education.

B. "Statization"[197]

The private law of the family must be understood in the context of certain
public law developments which have, on the one hand, resulted in the
assumption of certain family functions by the State and, on the other hand,
resulted in the gradual elimination of the distinction between marriage and
non-marriage, legal and *de facto* families in the performance of these State
functions. As in Section II.D. above, reference is made here primarily to the
law of the United States to illustrate how this has worked out in one system.

Public assistance law, generally speaking, has emerged as a separate field of
legal interest and specialization only recently. Programs designed to provide
financial assistance to persons in need have long existed, of course, but
litigation on behalf of recipients has been rare. However, social and economic
developments which go far beyond the matters discussed in this work yet
which profoundly affect them, have brought into being welfare law, consumer law, poverty law, public interest law, environmental law and many
others. These are not "new" areas of law. Most of the underlying rules of
positive law with which they are concerned have long existed. However, the
new titles signify a new way of looking at the law; an enormous increase in
litigation in these areas; and the emergence of specialized interest groups who
bring lawsuits and lobby for statutory change. This activity has in turn
brought about considerable change in the positive law.

Broadly understood, public assistance includes not only direct cash assistance to the poor, but programs which do not apply only to the poor. In a
broad sense, every expenditure of public funds, or publicly required transfer
of private funds, or relief from public monetary liability could be included
here. Thus welfare would include social security benefits for retirement or

disability of wage earners, military and civil service benefits and a host of other measures. Also, it would include programs designed for the poor which do not involve transfer of cash, but rather of goods or housing. The tax law, too, can be looked at as a means of conferring benefits on certain taxpayers (often not the poorer taxpayers) at the expense of the others.

So far as the relationship between the legal family and the informal family is concerned, recent developments in the law governing the administration of the various public assistance programs have tended to purge them of discrimination between the legal and the non-legal family. Traditionally, these laws, dealing mostly with the problems of the poor, tended to provide the occasion for society to try to impose the dominant ideas about sexual morality upon recipients of public aid. But today the emphasis is on factual need and dependency. In the United States, the turning point is marked, once again, by a decision of the United States Supreme Court. Public assistance in the United States is furnished through both federal and state funds, but practically all funds, regardless of source, are administered by the states. It became common for some states to adminster these funds in such a way as to deny aid to members of informal families. But in 1968 the Supreme Court held, as a matter of statutory interpretation, in *King* v. *Smith*[198] that states must dispense federal funds to dependent children in families with a "substitute father" on the same basis as to children in "legitimate" families. In the wake of *King* v. *Smith*, federal regulations were issued to make clear that the presence in a home of a "substitute parent" or "man in the house" would not be an acceptable basis for declaring a child ineligible for aid, or for presuming the availability of additional income.[199] These regulations were upheld by the Supreme Court in 1970.[200] Then, in 1973, the Court held that a state could not even use its own funds to aid legitimate families while denying aid to irregular families.[201] The presence of an unrelated adult in the household is of course still relevant on the question of the actual economic need of the family. In this way, and in many other ways which cannot be described here, the law of public assistance has been brought into conformity with the life styles of welfare clients, by becoming neutral on the question of how their sexual and family lives are organized.

The most important fact about all these American programs is not any particular legal development but their sheer size and pervasiveness. Since 1950, federal spending for social welfare purposes has risen from $10.5 billion to almost $170 billion per year: from less than one fourth of the federal budget to about one half.[202] When comparable state and local programs are included, the figure is $250 billion. The increase from 1950 to 1974, in terms of percentage of national income spent for social-welfare purposes, is from 4%

to 15%. The increase in number and variety of programs is even more telling. In the early 1960s there were about 200 programs, now there are over 1,100. This development has naturally brought with it an army of government workers to administer these programs which pervade almost every aspect of life. As the programs affect more and more groups besides the poor, as those who must deal with the system are increasingly articulate and educated, the more, in other words, that every citizen becomes a welfare client, the more extensive the programs become.

Let us briefly notice how importantly these developments bear on the principal questions with which we are concerned. With respect to the relationship of the State to the family and to individuals, it means that all sorts of functions which were once performed by the family are now performed by the State and its specialized agencies and personnel. But one must not exaggerate this. In the first place certain families are more exposed to the influence of the State and its agencies than others. Also, in the past, as Carbonnier points out, the family has also been supported and controlled by forces external to it: the clan; the church; private benefactors; community organizations.[203] It is the bureaucratization of these functions above all which is new. Furthermore, the evidence seems clear that conditions in families are such that often the government must step in. There is a cause and effect problem here – how much is the institution of the family weakened by being deprived of some of its functions? What types of government action hurt the family more than they strengthen it?

One effect of increased government programs, and increased government workers in public assistance, has been to raise the level of awareness of what the real problems of the clients of the system are, as well as an awareness of their various life styles. The effect of this interaction may be eventually to change the system to conform more closely to the needs and patterns of living of its clients.

In Sweden it seems to be a conscious objective of the government to use marriage and family legislation "...as one of several tools available when we endeavor to create a society where every adult person assumes the responsibility for himself and does not allow himself to be economically dependent on relatives, and where equality between men and women has become a reality".[204] The Alva Myrdal report to the Swedish Social Democratic Party in 1971 states, "Income from one's own job and the modern social insurance system are the two foundation stones upon which the security of the individual will rest in the future."[205] This sentiment has been echoed recently in thoughtful studies of American family policy.[206] But is the Public Household big enough to take in all the refugees from broken families? Will its doors be open?

C. *"Rising Entitlements" and the Decline of Affluence*

The tendency of citizens to look to the government for the solution to all problems, and the United States government's assumption of the role of universal problem-solver since the middle 1960s' "Great Society" programs, has been described by sociologist Daniel Bell as the idea of "the Public Household". [207] The government's assumption of this role has in turn given rise to the feeling that citizens are "entitled" to expect that governmental services and benefits will continue and expand. The U.S. Supreme court has sanctioned this view. [208] Bell has called the appearance of this set of expectations "the revolution of rising entitlements". [209] But, with the growing perception in all segments of society that economic growth can no longer be expected to provide the means of meeting demands for rising entitlements, and the inevitable consequence that if such demands are to be met they must now be met through wealth redistribution, a type of social conflict has arisen which does not neatly fit the model of peaceful, healthy competition; nor the model of a regime of reciprocity with shared, common ends. Social conflict is increasingly being expressed as competition among various interest groups for their shares of the governmental largesse.

One of the manifestations of the revolution of rising entitlements in the area of our concern is the emergence of welfare rights organizations. Their appearance is a demonstration of both branches of Bell's thesis: these organizations, of which many welfare recipients have never heard, and in which lawyers and social workers are important forces, are the means for one competing interest group to enter the fray, which they enter as persons entitled to "income maintenance", not as supplicants for public assistance. [210] Now, while poor families are being championed on the one hand by the welfare rights organizations, they are being ministered to on the other by a vast self-perpetuating bureaucracy which not only dispenses cash assistance, but visits their homes, inquires into their personal lives, teaches them cooking, hygiene, and birth control, and sends out a new emissary every few weeks. These emissaries, too, as Daniel Moynihan has pointed out, partake of the ideology of entitlement because they feel entitled to their jobs. [211] Sundberg has vividly described some other political aspects of what I have described as the replacement of traditional "family law" with "laws affecting the family":

Family law as conceived by the Ministries of Justice [here Sundberg is referring to private law of the family] was replaced by the family law created by the other ministries, the coffin being covered with a flag reading "family policy". Consequently, when the Swedish Minister of Justice...proclaimed the neutrality principle, what he really did was to strike colors. His rivals in the other ministries had already shot the family law conception of the Department of Justice to pieces.[212]

The intensification of social conflict that can be expected in the current period of expanding pressure of population against resources, may bring changes to industrial societies – even the Swedish – and thus to the problems here under consideration, which are impossible to foresee. Some would see in all this a distinctive "contradiction of capitalism": the increased social expenditures are necessary to maintenance of the State, but the State will ultimately be unable to pay the bill. It is no comfort to know that socialist States are confronting similar difficulties. In any event, in times of increasing austerity, it is not likely that the government will completely divest the family of its ancient functions of caring for the young, the sick, the old and the needy. Many of the transformations of marriage and family practices and ideology have been expressions of the life style of the affluent society. The young, the aged, the sick, the insane, the disabled have to be taken care of by somebody. Traditionally, the bearer of this burden has been the family. Now the welfare State is taking over, but the cost of social care provided by the State is higher than that of the care provided by the family. Socialist ideology has called for the substitution of family care with that provided by the State. But when socialists came to power in backward, impoverished Russia, they found that the national product was not yet sufficient to allow the State to take on the immense burden of social security. The strengthening of marriage and the family, after an initial period of non-regulation, became and remained an urgent and prominent aim of Soviet policy. As productivity grows, more and more of the tasks of social welfare are taken over by the socialist States, just as they have increasingly been assumed by the States of the affluent West.

But will affluence continue to increase? If it should not, and if the trend should be reversed, the family in some form will again be as necessary as it was in the long age of scarcity and as it still is in the developing countries. In Western countries a full return to such a pattern is unlikely unless society should be confounded by catastrophe. But even at the present time problems of dependency are still resolved first and foremost within the family. The hope that the society may one day not need to rely upon the "caretaker" function of the family seems utopian. And, even in Robert Nozick's world of optional utopias,[213] it is not certain that many people would choose to live in this one. What the changing family needs is support for its nurturing and caretaker activities. In the case of the one-parent family, this means that the lone parent should neither be pressured to go out to work, nor penalized for choosing to do so.

NOTES

[1] J. Giele, Toward Equality for Women Ch. 4 (to be published in 1977). I rely here primarily on American materials, referring from time to time to relevant materials from other systems. However, the single-parent family trends described here for the United States must be understood in connection with the fact that divorce rates in the United States are significantly higher than in England, France and West Germany:

Table 1

Rates of Divorce Per 1000 Population, 1970–1974

	1970	1971	1972	1973	1974
France	0.79	0.93	0.94	. . . .	0.95
German Federal Republic	1.24	1.31	1.40	. . . .	. . . .
Sweden	1.61	1.69	1.87	2.00	3.11
United Kingdom	1.18	1.51	2.41	2.14	. . . .
United States	3.47	3.72	4.03	4.35	4.58

Source: Demographic Yearbook of the United Nations 1974, Table 13.

Table 2

Raw Number of Divorces Granted, 1970–1974

	1970	1971	1972	1973	1974
France	40,000	47,700	48,354	. . . .	50,000
German Federal Republic	76,520	80,444	86,614	. . . .	. . . .
Sweden	12,943	13,679	15,189	16,292	25,369
United Kingdom	57,421	73,666	118,253	105,199	. . . .
United States	708,000	773,000	839,000	913,000	970,000

Source: Demographic Yearbook of the United Nations 1974, Table 13.

[2] Hayghe, Families and the Rise of Working Wives, Monthly Labor Review, May, 1976, p. 18. See also Ross & Sawhill 11.

[3] Ross & Sawhill 1, 30; Household and Family Characteristics: March 1975, U.S. Census Bureau, Current Population Reports, Population Characteristics, Table 1 (Series P–20, No. 291, 1976); A statistical Portrait of Women in the U.S., U.S. Census Bureau, Current Population Reports, Special Studies, at 15 (Series P–23, No. 58, 1976); Marital Status and Living Arrangements: March 1975, U.S. Census Bureau, Current Population Reports, Population Characteristics, at 5 (Series P–20, No. 287, 1975).

[4] Ross & Sawhill 61–62. According to Marital Status and Living Arrangements, supra n. 3 at 5, three-fourths of the net increase in female-headed families between 1970 and 1975 was accounted for by women who were divorced or separated.

[5] A Statistical Portrait of Women, supra n. 3 at 46; McEaddy, Women Who Head Families: A Socioeconomic Analysis, Monthly Labor Review, June 1976, at 3; Ross & Sawhill 93; Characteristics of Households Purchasing Food Stamps, U.S. Census Bureau, Current Population Reports, Special Studies, Table 10 (Series P–23, No. 61, 1976).

[6] I Finer Report 62.

[7] I Finer Report 244.

[8] Reported in Müller-Fembeck & Ogus, Social Welfare and the One-Parent Family in Germany and Britain, 2 Int. & Comp. L. Q. 382, 383 (1976).

[9] American evidence suggests that most one-parent families there are transitional units which, after an average period of five to six years, are reconstituted as traditional families. *Ross & Sawhill* at 6, 160. The Finer Report states that between two thirds and three quarters of divorced English persons marry again. I *Finer Report* 63.

[10] Especially so far as the inheritance rights of the child born outside legal marriage are concerned, but also to some extent with respect to the attribution of economic effects to *de facto* marriages. See Chapter 3 *supra* at pp. 74 and 97.

[11] Unless otherwise stated, what is said here with respect to divorce also pertains to legal separation and annulment.

[12] *Clark HB* 282–283.

[13] *Rheinstein & Glendon, Int. Encyc.* par. 32.

[14] *Ibid.*

[15] *Carbonnier, Mémoire* at 118.

[16] See *infra* Section a.

[17] *Ibid.*

[18] "Nevertheless he may obtain a payment in an exceptional case if, taking account of the duration of the life in common and his collaboration in the profession of the other spouse, it would appear manifestly contrary to equity to refuse him all monetary compensation following divorce." French C.C. new art. 280–1, line 2.

[19] "The compensatory payment is of a forfeitary nature. It cannot be modified even in case of unforeseen change in the resources and needs of the parties, unless the absence of modification would have consequences of exceptional gravity for one of the spouses." French C.C. new art. 273.

[20] *Lindon* No. 180.

[21] *Id.* at No. 182.

[22] Dean Carbonnier felt the time was not ripe to make this explicit, but it is clear that he did not expect much from the present system: "There is no reasonable question here of that radical liberalization which would consist of treating divorce as a social risk, whose cost should be spread over the society in general. Thus the effort at liberalization today is practically limited to confining itself behind the frontiers of private law which unavoidably impedes its efficacity." *Carbonnier, Mémoire* at 118.

[23] *Lindon* no. 185. This problem was foreseen by Dean Carbonnier, but within the confines described in n. 22, he apparently saw no alternative solution.

[24] See n. 18 *supra*.

[25] See Ch. 5 *supra* at p. 207.

[26] *Ibid.*

[27] French Code de le securité sociale, art. 351–2.

[28] *Ibid.*

[29] French Code de pensions civiles et militaires de retraite, new art. L. 44, L. 45.

[30] *Carbonnier, Mémoire* at 118.

[31] Former French C.C. art. 301.

[32] 1 *Mazeaud* 852.

[33] Cass. Civ. 2me, D. 1960 Jur. 447.

[34] Cass. Civ. 2me, D. 1960 Jur. 447, note by H. Roland 448–453.

[35] *Carbonnier, 2 Droit Civil* 199.

[36] Paris cour d'appel, 4 janv. 1952, s. 52,2,85, note Mazeaud.

[37] Matrimonial Causes Act 1973 s. 25.

[38] Samuels, Financial and Property Provision, 5 Fam. L. Q. 6 (1975); *Cretney* 192.

[39] Matrimonial Causes Act 1973 s. 25.

[40] Samuels, *supra* n. 38 at 9.

[41] *Cretney* 192–193.

[42] *Cretney,* Financial Provision – The New Case Law, 122 New L. J. 24, 25 (1972).
[43] *Cretney* 193.
[44] *Ibid.*
[45] *Rheinstein & Glendon, Int. Encyc.*
[46] *Wachtel* v. *Wachtel* [1973] Fam. 72, 90; noted in 89 L. Q. Rev. 320–322. (1973).
[47] E.g. *Ackerman* v. *Ackerman* [1972] Fam. 1 (C.A.); *Pheasant* v. *Pheasant,* [1972] Fam. 202; *Porter* v. *Porter* [1971] p. 282.
[48] *Rogers* v. *Rogers* [1974] 2 All ER 361, 363.
[49] See *Samuels, supra* n.38.
[50] *Id.* at 9.
[51] I *Finer Report* 95.
[52] *Rheinstein & Glendon, Int. Encyc.* par. 136.
[53] EheG. §58.
[54] *Markovits* 144–146.
[55] EheG. §58.
[56] As under the prior law, if a marriage is found "invalid" or if it is "cancelled" (*aufgehoben*) the property effects are practically the same as those of a decree of divorce.
[57] See *infra* at p. 267.
[58] German C.C., new §1569: "If a spouse cannot take care by himself of his support after divorce, he then has a claim against the other spouse for support according to the following provisions."
[59] German C.C., new §1571.
[60] German C.C., new §1572.
[61] German C.C., new §1570.
[62] German C.C., new §1573, 1574.
[63] See *infra* at p. 262.
[64] German C.C., new §1575.
[65] German C.C., new §1577.
[66] German C.C., new §1579.
[67] *Rheinstein & Glendon, Int. Encyc.*
[68] German C.C., new §1587.
[69] Die Zeit, 23 April 1976 p. 1 (overseas ed.).
[70] Note, *Current Legal Developments, Sweden,* 19 Int. & Comp. L. Q. 164 (1970).
[71] *Sundberg, Louvain Report:* Annex p. 8.
[72] Swedish GB 11:14 (Rheinstein translation in *Rheinstein & Glendon, Int. Encyc.*).
[73] *Sundberg, Louvain Report.*
[74] *Ibid.*
[75] Id. at 17.
[76] *Id.* at 7, 20.
[77] *Id.* at 19.
[78] *Ibid.*
[79] *Sundberg, Marriage or No Marriage* 229.
[80] Pennsylvania and Texas, with the exception, in Pennsylvania, of alimony for an insane spouse.
[81] Citizen's Advisory Council on the Status of Women, The Equal Rights Amendment and Alimony and Child Support Laws at 4 (Department of Labor, Washington, D.C. CACSW Item 23–N 1972).
[12] *Id.* at 1, 4, 5.
[83] *Calderwood* v. *Calderwood,* 327 A.2d 704 (N.H. 1974).
[84] *Rheinstein & Glendon, Int. Encyc.*
[85] *Foster & Freed, Unequal Protection* 206–207.
[86] New York Times, Jan. 15, 1975, at 18 cols. 1–8.
[87] New York Times, April 10, 1975, at 41, cols. 5–8.

88 *Hughes* v. *Hughes* 334 A.2d 379 (N.J. Super. Ct. App. Div. 1975).

89 *Pinkowski* v. *Pinkowski*, 226 N.W. 2d 518 (Wisc. 1975); *Pellegrino* v. *Pellegrino*, 342 A.2d 226 (N.J. Super. Ct. App. Div. 1975).

90 *Blitt* v. *Blitt*, 353 A.2d 340 (N.J. Super. Ct. Chancery Div. 1976).

91 *Kruger* v. *Kruger*, 354 A 2d 340 (N.J. Super. Ct. App. Div. 1976).

92 42 U.S.C. 402(e)(1)(A).

93 See Report of Hearings of Senate Special Committee on Aging, in 2 Fam. L. Rptr. 2013 (1975).

94 UMDA, Draftsmen's Prefatory Note p. 5.

95 New York Times, February 2, 1976, at 41, cols. 1–4.

96 *Rheinstein & Glendon, Int. Encyc.*

97 *Rheinstein, Willamette Symposium* 418.

98 *Id.* at 424.

99 *Rheinstein & Glendon, Int. Encyc.*

100 *Ibid.*

101 UMDA §307 Alternative A.

102 UMDA §307, Draftsmen's Comment.

103 UMDA §307, Alternative A.

104 *Rheinstein & Glendon, Int. Encyc.*

105 *Ibid.*

106 *Ibid.*

107 See Chapter 4 *supra* at p. 161.

108 *Sundberg, Louvain Report.*

109 *Rheinstein & Glendon, Int. Encyc.*

110 *Sundberg, Marriage or No Marriage* 225.

111 See *supra* Chapter 4 at 146–147.

112 The purest example of this kind of system seems to be Scotland, where Clive and Wilson were able to say, in 1974, "In general, so far as property is concerned, the position of a man living with his wife is the same as that of a man living with a mistress." The Law of Husband and Wife in Scotland 289 (1974).

113 *Rheinstein & Glendon, Int. Encyc.*

114 See Chapter 3 *supra* at n. 37.

115 *Jeanmart* 300.

116 *Rheinstein, Willamette Symposium* 420.

117 *Rheinstein & Glendon, Int. Encyc.* According to the American economist, J. Galbraith, the producers of goods have a great, but hitherto largely unrecognized, stake in maintaining the women in their role, or "career" as consumers, users, and maintainers of manufactured goods. According to Galbraith, this "crypto-servant" role assigned to women is essential for the expansion of consumption necessary to modern capitalist economics. Economics and the Public Purpose 29–37, 233–240 (1973).

118 *Stöcker* 553.

119 *Glendon, Separate Property* 327.

120 *Rheinstein, Willamette Symposium* 435.

121 *Ibid.*

122 *Ibid.*

123 *Volid* v. *Volid*, 286 N.E. 2d 42 (Ill. App. 1972).

124 *Dawley* v. *Dawley*, 551 P. 2d. 323 (Cal. 1976).

125 *Rheinstein, Willamette Symposium* 461.

126 *Ibid.*

127 The present discussion will be confined to custody in the narrow sense of the right to keep the child and control its upbringing after divorce. It does not treat such related matters as the management of the child's property or what is called in continental discussions the "parental authority", to the extent that these are separate concerns from custody of the child's person nor

does it treat issues of custody between persons other than the child's parents. See in general, *Stoljar* par. 100.

[128] England: *Bromley* 288–289; France: French C.C., new art. 287; United States: *Clark HB* 584; West Germany: *Beitzke* 209.

[129] *Wheeler* 25; *Foster & Freed, Divorce Reform* 490.

[130] E.g. *State ex. rel. Watts* v. *Watts,* 350 N.Y.S.2d 285 (N.Y. Fam. Ct. 1970). An excellent review of the American cases is Trenker, Modern Status of Maternal Preference Rule or Presumption in Child Custody Cases, 70 A.L.R. 3d 262 (1976).

[131] See Glendon, The French Divorce Reform Law of 1976, 24 Am. J. Comp. L. 199, 221–222. (1976).

[132] *Carbonnier, Mémoire* 121–122.

[133] J. Goldstein, A. Freud, & A. Solnit, Beyond the Best Interests of the Child (1973).

[134] See e.g. the excellent articles by Professor Mnookin: Child Custody Adjudication: Judicial Functions in the Face of Indeterminacy, 39 Law & Contemp. Prob. 226, 232–237 (1975) and Was stimmt nicht mit der Formel "Kindeswohl"? FamRZ 1975, 1.

[135] *Sundberg, Marriage or No Marriage* 236.

[136] *Sundberg, Louvain Report.*

[137] *Ibid.*

[138] Krause, Int. Encyc. pars. 103–114.

[139] *Cretney* 280.

[140] *A.S.* v. *B.S.,* 354 A.2d 100 (N.J. Super Ct. Ch. 1976).

[141] *Supra* n. 37.

[142] Cf. German C.C. new §1582 with EheG. s. 59.1 and 68.

[143] *Foster & Freed, Unequal Protection* 206–207; CACSW Report *supra* n. 81 at 6.

[144] CACSW Report *supra* n. 81 at 8.

[145] New York Times, April 2, 1974 at 34 cols. 1–6.

[146] *Foster & Freed, Unequal Protection* 207.

[147] *Ross & Sawhill* 3.

[148] *Id.* at 62, 160.

[149] Loi No. 75-618 du 11 juillet 1975, relative au recouvrement public des pensions alimentaires (J.O. 12 July p. 7178) was passed as part of the divorce reform legislation. Social Services Amendments Law of 1975, 42 U.S.C.A. §651–660 (Supp. 1975).

[150] *Lindon* at No. 221.

[151] *Supra* at No. 143.

[152] *Lindon* at Nos. 223, 227.

[153] *Lindon* at No. 226.

[154] *Lindon* at No. 227.

[155] *Lindon* at No. 226.

[156] Drinan, Has John Frank Proposed a Radical Reform of Family Law? 47 Tex. L. Rev. 991, 1001 (1969).

[157] Boston Sunday Globe, April 11, 1976, at 1 cols. 2–4.

[158] Money Income and Poverty Status of Families and Persons in the United States: 1974, U.S. Census Bureau, Current Population Reports, Consumer Income (Series P–60, No. 99, 1975).

[159] *Ross & Sawhill* 3.

[160] Drinan put it this way: "Should society begin to admit that divorce, like death and disability, is a fact of existence and that children adversely affected by the divorce should, like other disadvantaged children, receive from society those benefits normally available to all children?" *Supra* n. 156 at 1001.

[161] CACSW Report *supra* n. 81.

[162] E.g. *Ross & Sawhill* 162, 178 and see *infra* section IV.

[163] See in general, *Rheinstein & Glendon, Int. Encyc.*

[164] Administration of Estates Act 1925, 15 & 16 Geo. 5 c. 23 s. 46; as amended by the Intestates'

Estates Act 1952, 15 & 16 Geo. 6 & 1 Eliz. 2 c. 64, and the Family Provision Act 1966, s. 1, and the Family Provision (Intestate Succession) Order 1972, S.I. 1972/916.

[165] *Rheinstein & Glendon, Int. Encyc.*

[166] Inheritance (Provision for Family and Dependents) Act 1975.

[167] The Law Commission, Second Report on Family Property: Family Provision on Death, Law Commission No. 61 (1974).

[168] Mackay, Family Provision on Death, 126 New L. J. 228 (1976).

[169] *Rheinstein & Glendon, Decedents' Estates* 34–38; Schermützki, Die gesetzliche Stellung des überlebenden Ehegatten im Recht der Common Law Staaten der U.S.A. (1967).

[170] See *Rheinstein & Glendon, Int. Encyc.*

[171] Price, The Transmission of Wealth at Death in a Community Property Jurisdiction, 50 Wash. L. Rev. 277, 283–284 (1975).

[172] See generally, *Rheinstein & Glendon, Int. Encyc.*

[173] French C.C. art. 767.

[174] *Ibid.*

[175] French C.C. art. 766.

[176] French C.C. art. 765

[177] *Rheinstein & Glendon, Decedents' Estates* 34 *et seq.*

[178] French C.C. art. 913.

[179] French C.C. art. 1094, 1094–1.

[180] French C.C. art. 1094–2.

[181] Dagot, Conjoint Survivant – Heritier Reservataire? D.S. 1974. Chr. 8.

[182] F. Terré & A. Sayag, Conscience et Connaissance du Droit, Annexes A.13 (1975).

[183] *Rheinstein & Glendon, Int. Encyc.*

[184] German C.C. §1371 par. 1.

[185] German C.C. §1931, 1924, 1925, 1926, 1932.

[186] German C.C. §1932.

[187] See the articles by Müller-Freienfels, Family Law and the Law of Succession in Germany, 16 Int. & Comp. L. Q. 409, 430 (1967) and Equality of Husband and Wife in Family Law 000, 8 Int. & Comp. L. Q. 249, 265 (1959).

[188] See generally *Rheinstein & Glendon, Int. Encyc.*

[189] But, as Chapter 3 has shown, *functional* counterparts of support and inheritance are increasingly accumulating around *de facto* situations.

[190] For example, section 416(c) of the U.S. Social Security Act defines a widow for social security purposes as a "surviving wife of an [insured] individual, but only if...she was married to him for a period of not less than nine months immediately prior to the day on which he dies...". Originally the provision required a marriage of five years. It has been held constitutional in *Weinberger v. Salfi*, 422 U.S. 744 (1975). *Cf.* the presumption of *"Zweckehe"* (marriage for a limited purpose) in West German Reichsversicherungsordnung 594.

[191] I am grateful to Professor Erik Jayme of the University of Munich Law Faculty for pointing out to me the relevance to my analysis of such cases and statutes.

[192] The Law Reform Commission of Canada in 1976 recommended breaking with the English principle, saying in its working paper on maintenance after divorce that the following principle should be established: "Marriage per se does not create a right to maintenance or an obligation to maintain after divorce; a divorced person is responsible for his or her own maintenance." Reported in 2 Fam. L. Rptr. 2563 (1976).

[193] See *Ross & Sawhill* 176.

[194] *Supra* Ch. 4 at 164 *et seq.*

[195] In Sweden, according to *Sundberg,* there are no assets of importance in the estates of many deceased or divorced persons besides pension rights or annuities, *Marriage or No Marriage* 224.

[196] See Chapter 3. The legal development of "step" relationships should be mentioned here as well, see 68 A.L.R.3d 1220 (1976).

[197] I have borrowed this term from Dean *Carbonnier* who uses it to describe the type of phenomenon dealt with in this subsection. *Flexible Droit* 128.

[198] 392 U.S. 309 (1968).

[199] 45 C.F.R. §233.90(a) (1975).

[200] *Lewis* v. *Martin,* 397 U.S. 552, 559 (1970).

[201] *New Jersey Welfare Rights Organization* v. *Cahill,* 411 U.S. 619, 621 (1973).

[202] These and all figures following are from Bell, The Revolution of Rising Entitlements, Fortune, April 1975, at 98 *et seq.*

[203] *Carbonnier, Flexible Droit* 129.

[204] *Sundberg, Louvain Report.*

[205] Quoted in Sage, Dissolution of the Family under Swedish Law, 9 Fam. L. Q. 375, 379 n. 20 (1975).

[206] *Ross & Sawhill* 162; Giele, Family Values and Family Policy, March 25, 1976 (paper delivered at 1976 Groves Conference on Marriage and Family, Kansas City. Mo.). See Generally, D. Moynihan, The Politics of a Guaranteed Income (1973).

[207] Bell, The Public Household, The Public Interest no. 37, at 29 (1974).

[208] *Goldberg* v. *Kelly,* 397 U.S. 254 (1970).

[209] Bell, *supra* n. 202.

[210] "[W]hat must be recognized is that the welfare poor came to form a coherent organization as a consequence of federal intervention in the cities – as a consequence of the Great Society social workers and VISTA volunteers who became the organizers of NWRO groups, of Great Society lawyers who brought NWRO legal suits, and of the Great Society Rhetoric and protection that made attacks on local welfare agencies first imaginable and then feasible." R. Piven & R. Cloward, Regulating the Poor: The Functions of Public Welfare 329 (1972).

[211] Moynihan, The Annals of Politics, The New Yorker, January 13, 1973 at 34; January 20, 1973 at 60; January 27, 1973 at 57.

[212] *Sundberg, Louvain Report.*

[213] R. Nozick, Anarchy, State and Utopia (1974).

STATE, LAW AND FAMILY

[W]hat did you want meddling with the like of us,
when it's a long time we are going our own ways...?
J. M. Synge, *The Tinker's Wedding*[1]

I. Marriage as a Social Institution

"Factual custom everywhere has begotten a feeling of oughtness", said Max
Weber in discussing the transition from custom to law.[2] So it is that we in the
late 20th century take State regulation of marriage and divorce for granted.
But so it is also that, upon reflection, we may be led to wonder how it came
about that custom, in a matter so basic as marriage, became what it is today.
We know that, let us say, Cro-Magnon men and women did not go before a
Registrar to be joined together, nor did they go before a judge to be separated.
With the help of ethologists, anthropologists and sociologists we are gaining
increased understanding of how different mating customs and rituals may
have evolved in different cultures, and over the course of time in each. But
coming back to Weber, we may still wonder how it is that, in the West, the
innovations of *law*, ecclesiastical or secular, could themselves have become,
to a great extent, our marriage customs. How, for instance, did marriage in
the West become indissoluble in principle, or dissoluble only for serious
cause? How did the Church and the State succeed in gaining social acceptance
of rules that persons had to pass before an official in order to be married or
unmarried? To what extent did they succeed?

The answers are to be sought first in a long story of struggles by and among
various worldly institutions, kinship groups, property owners, the Christian
Church (later churches), emperors, kings and nation states. The chief
episodes of that story are recounted here in order to account for the state of
the law as it stood on the eve of the current process of legal change that has
been described in this work, and to bring out the significance of the present
series of changes.

We cannot start the story at its very beginning, for the beginnings of actual regularity and usage in human conduct are shrouded in darkness. No one knows when the evolutionary shift from biological to cultural patterns of mating occurred. Nor, for that matter, does anyone yet know much about what is innate and what is cultural in man. We do know that it is useful to distinguish between marriage and the family, since the importance of marriage in various societies is quite variable, while the same cannot be said of the family.[3] In some societies marriage, as distinct from other sexual relationships, is said to be barely visible, and in some societies marriage is viewed as irrelevant to family formation.[4]

Concerning the Germanic and Roman antecedents of those modern systems which we have examined here, we do know something about how community or kinship group interest in who mated whom manifested itself and about the early forms of rank and status derived from marriage and birth. Marriage existed in the sense of being a definite social status. But the wedding, or marriage rite, itself seems to have been important only under special circumstances, in particular where property was exchanged. The two earliest forms of Roman marriage rites of which we know were a religious rite, used by the patrician class, and a symbolic purchase. Although there are traces of marriage initiated by capture in earliest Germanic laws, the usual form was a purchase marriage.[5] While purchase marriage certainly did not exclude the possibility of turning a profit on the occasion, Pollock and Maitland think its essential function among the Anglo-Saxons was the bargaining by the bride's kinfolk for her honorable treatment as a wife and widow. Among the early Germans, marriage was different from other sexual unions only in that the wife and children of the marriage enjoyed a more secure position in relation to the husband and his kinship group than other women with whom he cohabited and their offspring.[6] The distinction between "legitimate" marriage and other unions which though not disapproved are of lower status appears not only in primitive systems, but also in Roman law and in pre-Tridentine canon law, and in the civil law of France until the 16th century. Only the legitimate wife shared the social rank and status of her husband.

In the widespread custom of high status families to give away their daughters only on assurances of preferred status for the daughter and her children, Max Weber saw the origin of the earliest *legal* characteristics of the legitimate marriage: dowry, the agreement to support the wife and to pay her compensation upon abandonment, and the successoral position of her children.[7] From a sociological point of view, the significance of the legitimate marriage is that it enables the family to function as a status-conferring institution.[8] We shall return to this point after we consider how legitimacy, expressed in social

norms, became, through a long and tortuous process, "legality", expressed in
rules of positive law.

In cultures where marriage is simply the decision of the partners to live
together and raise common children, and involves no exchange of property,
it tends to be dissolved simply by desertion and separation.[9] But as marriage
formation becomes more complex, the procedure for dissolving it does too.
The emphasis on procedures for formation and dissolution seems to vary
with the importance of rank and property. Where these are important, there is
a need to clearly distinguish which sexual relationships will give rise to rights.
The need to justify the dissolution of marriage and to furnish reasons to
neutralize the objections of relatives appears.[10]

This was already beginning to be the case in the earliest periods of Roman
and Germanic customary law of which we have knowledge. It is said that the
early Germanic folk were relatively monogamous, although plurality of
wives was permissible among them; and that for the first 500 years Rome had
a tradition of marital stability, although marriages were dissoluble there. In
the morally strict society of early Republican Rome, a man would incur
disapproval if he repudiated his wife without some cause such as barrenness
or infidelity.[11] Old Germanic law recognized marriage dissolution by agreement between the husband and the wife's relatives. The husband, and eventually the wife, could unilaterally end the marriage for certain causes.[12]

The first point to observe, if we wish to understand the process of juridification of marriage, is that in Roman times, and among the Germanic peoples
by whom the Roman empire eventually was overrun, marriage was not
regulated as such by norms of law but rather by social norms. A second
significant point to keep in mind is that lack of *legal* regulation did not mean
that marriage was unregulated. Nor, in Rome, did lack of legal regulation of
marriage as such mean that the law was indifferent to marriage. The existence
or not of a marriage was indirectly significant for the Roman law when it had
to deal with problems involving membership of the "houses" of which the
body politic was composed, with succession on death, or with allocation of
responsibility for civil wrongs.[13] But in making these determinations,
Roman law contented itself with referring to the mores and accepting as a
marriage whatever was recognized by the mores as such. Roman law also
imposed a kind of political taboo upon marriages between Romans and most
non-citizens, between free persons and slaves and, at one time, between
Senators or other upper-class men with women of lower rank.

But social norms governing marriage varied considerably in the long
period of Roman history of which we have knowledge.[14] In early times,
marriage among the leading class of patricians was initiated by a religious

ceremony, *confarreatio*. Two other forms of marriage also existed: *coemptio*, initiated by a form which is thought by some to be a symbolic purchase; and *usus*, which began with no particular form but existed when a couple had lived as husband and wife for a year. The forms that existed for initiating marriage were, according to Corbett, "in great part legally indifferent" (except to a limited degree in *confarreatio*), in the sense that the validity of the marriage did not depend on their observance. Originally, it seems these three forms of marriage involved the wife coming under the legal control, *manus*, of her husband.

By late Republican times these three kinds of marriage became obsolete. They gave way to the so-called free marriage, marriage without *manus*, in which the man and woman married simply by starting life in common, provided they had *affectio maritalis*, that is, that they regarded each other as husband and wife. Free marriage had been recognized as early as the time of the earliest Roman code of laws, the XII Tables (451–450 B.C.). It became a common practice in the third and second centuries B.C., and was the customary mode of marriage in late Republican times. There was nothing but *affectio maritalis* to distinguish free marriage from any other type of sexual union. If this intention ceased, the marriage was at an end in principle. The free marriage was treated by the law as dissolved when the parties separated, or when one spouse left the marriage and notified the other of his or her intention to terminate the relationship. It may have been that originally only the husband could unilaterally terminate the marriage. But the parties were on an equal footing by the end of the third century B.C., and perhaps from the beginning. The use by both husband *and* wife of this power to terminate a marriage is said to have been common in the first century B.C., almost the only deterrent being rules governing the return of dowry. Thus, in Rome, marriage had become a formless transaction dissoluble at the will of either party, and remained so at the time of the first Christian Emperor, Constantine (285–337 A.D.).

Little that the Christian emperors did changed this situation. From Constantine until Justinian (c. 482–565 A.D.), the Christian emperors confined themselves to punishing unjustified repudiations. If a spouse repudiated the other without some good reason, he might have to give back the marriage portion or lose other property rights; or eventually, he could even be deported, confined within a monastery, or subjected to restrictions on remarriage. But these laws did permit repudiation for cause and did not affect divorce by mutual agreement. Thus, Professor Noonan seems correct in saying that the legislation of the Christian emperors assumes the dissolubility of marriage, with remarriage as the normal sequel to dissolution; and that, at least so long as the sanctions were only property-related, the law's concern was limited to the upper classes.[15] Noonan concludes that it was "...a good question...whether the prohibitions of divorce from Constantine to Anastasius had any teeth to them", if someone was able to pay the price or work out a settlement.[16]

Even the strongly religious Emperor Justinian at first did not disturb the effectiveness of marital dissolution by mutual agreement, declaring in 535 A.D. that "all that has been joined together by man can be separated by man".[17] Later, Justinian broke with Roman tradition and established penalties for mutual consent divorce as well as for unjustified repudiation.[18] According to Corbett, the reason Justinian sought to restrict this kind of divorce was that children had been using divorce or the threat of divorce to defraud parents of their contingent rights in dowries or to hasten the payment of dowries.[19] In any event, Justinian's law was neither well-received nor well-observed, and was repealed in 566 by Justinian's successor, Justin II, in one of his first acts after ascension to the throne.[20]

At the close of the Roman period, then, it can be said that the law took little notice of the social institution of marriage. Marriage itself was formless so far as the law was concerned; the idea of legal regulation of marriage formation or the conduct of married life was unknown; legal regulation of marriage dissolution had been attempted only to a very limited degree by the legislation of the Christian emperors which implicitly accepted the premise of the essential dissolubility of marriage.

Hence in Rome and among the Germanic peoples, marriage was not a legal institution. To find the answers to the questions how marriage became formal, indissoluble and subject to far-reaching state regulation, we must turn to another legal system which, at the time of Christian Roman legislation, was not a legal system at all but only an evolving body of doctrine: the system of Roman Catholic canon law.

II. The Rise of Ecclesiastical Jurisdiction over Marriage Formation and Dissolution

A. The Struggle for Jurisdiction

After the Roman Empire in the West broke down in the course of the 5th century A.D., the Christian Church not only remained intact but became stronger than ever. The new kingdoms had not yet developed those political organizations on the Roman pattern that were later to grow into the new pattern of feudalism. The Church was able to exercise great influence over, and was closely associated with the secular power of, the new Visigothic kings, and the later Merovingian and Carolingian dynasties.[21] Even so, the establishment of the doctrine of indissolubility of marriage and of ecclesiastical jurisdiction over matrimonial matters took centuries.

The Church's claim to exclusive jurisdiction over marital causes and the novel idea that marriage was indissoluble were both closely connected to the new Christian idea that marriage was a sacrament. But the sacramental nature of marriage and the ideal of indissolubility were not settled all at once as matters of firm doctrine. Both ideas had powerful proponents: St. Ambrose (c. 339–397) for indissolubility; and his convert, St. Augustine (354–430), for the sacrament. St. Augustine went on record for indissolubility too, by opposing "adulterous marriages" (remarriage by one who has put aside a spouse even for a grave reason such as adultery). But at the end of his life he returned to the problem dissatisfied. In his *Retractations*, he says "I think that I did not reach a perfect solution of this question."[22] He calls it a "very difficult question" (*difficillimam quaestionem*), and speaks of its "obscurities". All during the period of the development of Roman Law under the Christian emperors described in the preceding section, it has been said that "Christians in good faith could believe that marriage was dissoluble or indissoluble...".[23]

The greatest obstacle to the direct enforcement by the Church of the new Christian ideas about the ethics of sex and marriage arose from the fact that marriage was regarded everywhere in Europe in the first half of the Middle Ages as a personal and purely secular matter, almost entirely outside the scope of law. Conversion to Christianity in the Roman empire and in the lands inhabited by the Germanic tribes did not automatically result in immediate acceptance of Christian sex ethics: of the notions that marriage was strictly monogamous and that all sexual relations outside marriage were prohibited.[24] Nor did the Church insist on this. Marriage matters continued to be governed by social taboos including rules about marriage age, choice of partners, and legitimacy. Sometimes these social rules were grounded in custom and convention, sometimes in ancient pagan religious practices. The story of the rise of ecclesiastical jurisdiction over marriage is in large part one of compromise with, adaptation to and even incorporation of indigenous practices. In the early centuries the Church hardly tried to exercise jurisdiction in its own name.[25] Its mingling in these matters began slowly, as a matter of custom, as with the priestly blessing of marriages of the early Christians. Gradually it was recognized as a matter of right.

The idea of the indissolubility of marriage did not easily gain a foothold in the ancient world, where marriages were dissoluble, (without the intervention of any judge) by mutual consent or by unilateral repudiation, perhaps with payment of a penalty.[26] The indissolubility doctrine, as elaborated by the Church fathers, was based on several sayings of Jesus as reported in the Gospels. If his sayings were correctly interpreted, the doctrine was a novelty. Even within the Church, especially in ancient times, some held the opinion that the sayings of Jesus in the Gospels did not absolutely prohibit divorce, at least in the case of adultery.[27] As ecclesiastical doctrine became more or less fixed, the Church still had to compromise with the firmly established secular customs. The Anglo-Saxons, the Franks, the other Germanic tribes and the Romans, all had permitted divorce. For centuries, when all the Church had to work with was its disciplinary power over Christians, it had to exercise a great deal of tolerance. To some extent, it even accepted divorce and remarriage.[28]

As for the idea that a couple must pass before a priest in order to be validly married, that would have to wait until the Tridentine Decree *Tametsi* in 1563 when the authority of the Church had already begun to wane. The variety of marriage rituals among the Christian nations was great and the Church from the beginning had adapted its own rituals to them. In the view of the Church, marriage was and is formed simply by the exchange of consents between the spouses.[29] No particular form was or is imposed for the exchange, it being permitted even today to exchange consents in any form "sanctioned by praiseworthy custom", as well as in the forms to be found in ritual books of the Church. The custom for Christians to seek a blessing for their marriages seems to have begun as early as the first century, but the Church constantly stressed that the blessing was not the essential factor. Consent sufficed to constitute a valid marriage without the participation of a priest. Even today the parties, not the priest, are the ministers of the sacrament, though his presence as a witness is now obligatory. During the Middle Ages the custom of exchanging vows at the church door developed. Then the Church began to prescribe this public religious ceremony. But where the prescribed form was not followed, no doubt was cast on the validity of the marriage.[30] Thus, until Trent, there were two equally valid sorts of marriage, one public and formal, the other private and informal. For a long time the only type of informal cohabitation among the laity to receive specific condemnation was adulterous or incestuous cohabitation.[31] Only with the Council of Trent was informal marriage made invalid, and even then, as we shall see, the Church compromised with reality.

The Church's long tolerance of and adjustment to secular and pagan customs even when they were at variance with its own evolving doctrine, is thought by some to reflect its concern not to "multiply sins".[32] But in reality we cannot separate the Church's policy of adaptation from the gradual and eventually successful assertion of its total control over regulation of marriage. No wiser course than accommodation could have been chosen. Adaptation to, and blending in of indigenous customs must have contributed significantly to the ultimate success of the Church in establishing and extending its jurisdiction. When the Pope told the first Irish missionaries to England not to be too severe with their new converts so far as incest and marriage prohibitions were concerned, he was helping to assure the success of their missions, just as later Popes made similar concessions to local customs in dealing with other primitive civilizations.[33]

B. *The Canon Law Prior to the Council of Trent*

Full legislative and judicial authority over matrimonial causes and the rudiments of a canon law system were established in what is now France and the Germanies by the end of the 10th century,[34] and in England by the middle of the 12th century.[35] In its long competition with the State for temporal authority, the Church had made its bid for exclusive control of other matters as well, such as succession on death, jurisdiction over all matters pertaining to Church land, and civil and criminal authority over the clergy.[36] But it was only with respect to marital causes that its path was clear and its success was eventually complete. Any exercise of jurisdiction in those times was desirable as a source of "tax" revenue in the form of fees and fines. However, with respect to marriage, it was taken for granted either that this was a matter people could regulate themselves, or that it was an essentially religious matter. The development of the doctrine of sacramental marriage was therefore important as furnishing the theoretical basis for regulation by the Church of matters which previously had not been subject to any kind of systematic official control. The idea that regulation of marriage or adjudication of disputes concerning marriage could or should be conducted by the secular political community was not seriously considered before the 16th century and the Protestant Reformation.

The exercise of jurisdiction by ecclesiastical courts and the application by these courts of the ecclesiastical doctrine which had become a body of canon law was in a sense a remarkable innovation in human history. It was an innovation which had long been impending, yet at the same time one which did not gain immediate acceptance in social life. But while the norm system of the canon law, formulated and systematically organized after the manner of the law of the late Roman empire, may have had little immediate effect on the mores, it had far-reaching and long-lasting effects on all Western marriage law down to the present day.

As Max Weber has demonstrated, canon law grew naturally out of what had gone before. After the Church itself developed a bureaucratic and hierarchical structure, it was not surprising that it also developed a system of courts and procedures and a body of law of the type that has come to be known as "formally rational", radically different from the law of other religious legal systems.[37] Gratian is credited with beginning the application of scholastic methodology to the study of the sources of canon law. His Decretum of 1140 together with the Decretals of Pope Gregory IX of 1292 formed the core of the *Corpus Juris Canonici* which was for centuries the official source of the positive law of the Church.[38]

We now begin to get the answers to some of our questions: how marriage came under any official regulation at all, how it became the subject of legal norms, and how it came to be indissoluble. But we are only beginning, for there is abundant evidence that marriage continued to be considered as basically a private matter even after ecclesiastical jurisdiction was established and canon law had fixed the norm of indissolubility. In other words, even when the Church's authority was successfully established *vis-à-vis* the *political* authority (which had never regulated marriage as such anyway), its norms had not yet fully penetrated the *mores*. The Church bided its time, winning social acceptance of its norms in much the same way as it had gained jurisdiction, through a long patient process of action and interaction with social life. Meanwhile, canon law took the form which was to be of crucial importance for the future, even where and when the authority of the Church much later had been eroded.

Once the rule of indissolubility had been established, an important consequence followed. It had to be spelled out in minute detail exactly which unions were of the type that now could not be dissolved, and outside of which all sexual intercourse was unlawful. "Marriage" had to be defined with more precision than ever before. Out of this need came the whole complex canon law system of marriage impediments and prohibitions. The multiplication of causes of nullity in turn led to the need to investigate whether impediments in fact existed, and thus to the origin of the publication of the banns, the Church's increasing insistence on public marriage, as well as to the elaboration of procedures for declaring marriages invalid. In addition, since marriage between persons not under any impediment was based uniquely on consent, it became relevant to determine whether their consent had been real and free. The result was, of course, that the principle of indissolubility was considerably mitigated by the rules on consent and by the existence of impediments based on blood or marital relationship, spiritual relationship (as between godparents and children), impotence, insanity and nonage. The proliferation of grounds for annulment has been variously interpreted as: following from the necessities of intrinsic logic; related to money and power in the sense that annulments gave the Church a source of revenue and a certain amount of control over families; a humane response to the need of some individuals to escape from intolerable situations and to remarry; and a "safety valve", substituting for the necessary but missing institution of divorce. No doubt all these factors played a role.

The Church's own records, according to recent English and French studies, show the continuation of the habit of contracting marriages informally, and the stubborn persistence of older notions of marriage as a private matter. Helmholtz concludes, on the basis of his study of 13th through 15th century marriage litigation in Church courts in England, that it took a long time for the idea to disappear that people could regulate marriage for themselves.[39] At the same time, he was able to trace a process, equally gradual, of social assimilation of the Church's standards, and to demonstrate considerable room for variety and growth within the canon law itself.

The Church mitigated the harshness of its indissolubility rule in other ways besides through the many causes for annulment. It provided for judicial separation in situations where one spouse had committed adultery, apostasy or heresy, or had deserted or seriously mistreated the other. But unlike annulment, judicial separation did not give rise to permission to remarry. Thus, apart from the avoidance of sin, the main interest in judicial separation must have been in connection with the assignment of support rights to a blameless spouse and denial of them to a blameworthy one. But it is of interest to us in answering one of our questions about the origin of that divorce law which we have come in Western societies to take for granted. Foreshadowed itself by the grounds of justifiable repudiation in the imperial Roman decrees, the canon law of judicial separation prefigures that doctrine of divorce as a sanction for marital misconduct which reappeared in the ideas of the Protestant reformers and which came to dominate Western divorce law until the recent events described in Chapter 5 of this work.

C. *The Tridentine Marriage Law*

So far we have not found the answer to the question of how the formation of marriage has come to require, in nearly all Western legal systems, the presence of an official. Up to the Council of Trent, the Church had shown its interest in this subject only by making the blessing in church a religious duty sanctioned by penance or censure. To find out why the Roman church suddenly insisted on public formal marriage as a condition for the *validity* of marriage in the Trentine Decree *Tametsi*, we must look, not to ecclesiastical doctrine, but to the pressures and events of the secular world.

The Anglican Church, which had taken over the exclusive jurisdiction of matrimonial causes from the Roman Church in England in 1534, continued to recognize informal marriages as valid until 1753. But in continental Reformation Europe, the stress under which the Church found itself, combined with social and economic changes which in certain levels of society pressed for family control over the shifts of wealth and power which marriages could produce, prepared the way for a modification of the time-honored doctrine that Christians formed their marriages by consent alone. This doctrine, it should be noted, had had the beneficial side effect of liberating the individual from constraints which parents, kinship groups or political authority might try to impose on the choice of spouses. But it was this very liberating effect which began to be troublesome in 16th century Europe, especially in France and Spain, in those circles where increasing amounts of money were changing hands upon marriage.

It had undoubtedly always been true that so long as informal marriages were valid, the difficulty of either proving or disproving them would permit some persons to depart from valid marriages, and others to profit by inheritance or otherwise from invalid marriages. But this longstanding potential for abuse does not seem to have been the precipitating cause of reform. Prominent among the proponents of compulsory ceremonial marriage at the Council of Trent were the French and Spanish delegates who (contrary to the Christian idea of marriage as a voluntary union) were also pressing to make parental consent an ecclesiastical marriage requirement.[40] The parental consent proposal found little support, and the question of compulsory ceremonies was a controversial one at the Council. The validity of informal marriage was defended by theological purists who said it was morally neutral in itself.[41] They also pointed out that it had the virtue of protecting the spiritual liberty of the individual to marry or not to marry from interference by others, particularly parents. The advocates of change claimed that informal marriages threatened inheritance rights, preservation of families, social peace and private morality.[42] They won, 133–59.[43] The Decree *Tametsi* provided that henceforth no marriage was valid which had not been celebrated in the presence of a priest and witnesses. This Decree, which also prescribed the publication of banns of marriage and the keeping of official records of marriages, aided families at least to keep up with the marriage plans of their children, and thereby perhaps to exercise some control over marriages. But it did not go so far as the French and Spanish prelates would have liked.

Other contemporary developments are evidence of the strength of the pressures of the times for preventing secret marriages and for supporting parental control of the marriage decision. A French royal edict of 1556 had empowered parents to disinherit children who married without parental consent and it provided punishments for anyone assisting such a marriage.[44] Martin Luther himself had criticized "secret" marriages as enabling strangers to marry into wealthy families without prior parental approval and to obtain a share of estates.[45] Pressures for making couples marry in public resulted in the requirement of a minister's presence in the Reformation ordinances of Geneva (1561); the protestant principality of Württemberg (1553); and the Palatinate of the Rhine (1563).[46] These ordinances all made parental consent a requirement for marriage.

The requirement of parental consent, which had not found acceptance at Trent, was made part of French civil law by the Ordinance of Blois of 1579. In various forms, as we saw in Chapter 2, it came to penetrate Western marriage law generally. England, however, long remained an exception to the parental consent requirement as well as to the ceremonial marriage requirement. In the end, *Tametsi* as such was not promulgated in France. But there the monarchy enacted the Tridentine reforms as civil legislation in the Ordinance of Blois. Through the 17th century French law continued in various ways to try to discourage secret marriages.[47]

As with the Christian Roman marriage legislation it is questionable whether these changes were evidence of anything more than a concern with the marriage practices of the upper class, whose property interests are reflected in the laws they alone were in a position to influence. Even in these circles, and in spite of the pressures operating in favor of parental authority and the maintenance of class lines, Professor Hunt found a persistent

...conflict between public legislation on the one hand and generally accepted popular custom and usage on the other. The edicts and ordinances clearly show that legists recognized the strength of the tradition they were trying to uproot: the continuing belief that cohabitation, simple mutual consent, made a marriage.[48]

So far as the Church was concerned, *Tametsi* itself, by its terms, was not effective where it was not promulgated. Thus informal marriages continued to be valid under canon law in many parts of the world until a decree of Leo XIII in 1892, followed by the decree *Ne Temere*, which went into effect in 1908 and was consolidated in the present Code of Canon law which went into effect in 1918.[49] But the code still preserves the validity of informal marriages in certain circumstances.[50] Also, in the Decree *Tametsi* the church was careful to provide specifically that "if...any laudable customs and ceremonies are in use" besides those prescribed by the decree, "the holy Council of Trent desires that they should be retained".[51]

III. The Protestant Reformation and Secularization of Jurisdiction over Marriage Formation and Dissolution

The history of Canon Law up to the Council of Trent begins to answer the questions posed at the outset of this chapter by showing how marriage became subject to a kind of official and legal regulation, namely, that of the Church courts, applying canon law. It also shows the origin of the idea of legal indissolubility and the beginning of compulsory ceremonial marriage. But how did these matters become concerns of the secular State which previously had been largely indifferent to them? As Rheinstein has pointed out, in the medieval world the State, in in the sense of the omnipresent legal sovereign, did not even exist.[52] Law in those times was not the equivalent of the norm system sanctioned by the State, because the State was not yet the exclusive political organization. Rather, the political organizations of emperor, kings, barons, boroughs, guilds and the Church were all constantly vying with one another for supremacy in various areas of social life.[53]

From the 16th to the 18th century, in great parts of Western Europe, the Catholic Church lost its jurisdiction over marriage: in Protestant regions as a consequence of the Reformation, and in France in connection with Gallicanism and the progress of the monarchy. But in what Esmein calls "a remarkable phenomenon", the law which the Church had created still continued to govern marriage, although it received a new interpretation on certain points.[54] In France from the mid-16th century the State was competing with the Church for jurisdiction of matrimonial causes, and by the 18th century most marital cases were before royal courts. Nevertheless, these courts continued to apply the law developed by the Church.[55]

In Protestant areas, when the Roman Church lost its monopoly over matrimonial causes, the State acquired jurisdiction more or less by default. But to a great extent it simply took over the ready-made set of rules of the canon law, the prior law on judicial separation and maintenance becoming the model for the new secular divorce law.[56] Although Luther and others had claimed that marriage was a proper subject for the civil courts and not subject to exclusive ecclesiastical control, they little dreamed that marriage would one day be regulated by the State according to other than Christian principles. While the reformers held that marriage was not a sacrament, they thought that secular regulations should conform to Christian teaching.[57] Christian teaching was of course reinterpreted by them to permit divorce as a punishment for grave violation of marital duties, for adultery in particular, but gradually for other causes as well. This well-known instance of departure from Roman Catholic doctrine should not, however, obscure the fact that Catholic canon law was still widely applied. Nor should the importance of the introduction of divorce itself be exaggerated, for it was accompanied by a tightening up of nullity which the Church had at times offered rather freely.[58] Protestantism did not return divorce to the private order by any means: no divorce by mutual consent was recognized and divorce for cause had to be granted by an official. Only in the Enlightenment did a true antithesis to the Roman Catholic attitude appear.

IV. The "Enlightened" Absolutist State and Statization of Family Law

The effects of the Protestant Reformation take us further toward understanding how marriage formation and dissolution came under the jurisdiction of the secular State, and thus how some of the law described in Chapters 2 and 5 of this book (marriage formation and dissolution) took shape. However, we have yet to learn how the State came to apply its own secular, as opposed to ecclesiastical, norms of law.

In addition, we still have no answer to the question of how the secular law came to regulate or at least to purport to regulate a matter from which canon and Roman law had abstained, namely, the organization and conduct of married life, the subject considered in Chapter 4. To understand the evolution of this branch of law, account has to be taken of two developments for which the Protestant reformers cannot be held responsible, although in a sense they helped pave the way. These developments are the appearance of the humanistic and individualistic thought of the Enlightenment and the rise of the absolutist State, the *Polizeistaat*.

The developments occurred in different fashion in France and the various regions of Germany, but resulted eventually in unprecedented comprehensive regulation of family relationships there. England, on the other hand, remained in many ways a special case, and so, in consequence, did the United States.

Rulers like Frederick II of Prussia, Joseph II of Austria, Napoleon, and their legal scholars and bureaucratic administrators felt the need for a clear and complete codification of all private law.[59] Further, these rulers were in a position to impose their own ideas as rules of positive law in their Codes.

The new secular law of the Codes drew substantially on the former law, just as the reformed Protestant church had drawn heavily on canon law. But marriage law, cut loose from its Catholic and Protestant religious moorings in the established medieval order, increasingly began to be affected by the

trends of the times, by humanism and individualism, as well as by the
practical concerns and interests of the secular state and the dominant groups
within it. [60] Thus, as Müller-Freienfels has pointed out, the idea of marriage as
a civil contract took a new turn. Consent had been the essence of marriage in
the Church's law. The State, however, shifted its concern to the rights and
duties of the spouses, constructing a network of legal relationships on the
basis of which each spouse had a full set of claims against the other that could
be made the basis of legal action before a judge. [61] In the great codifications, as
we have already seen in Chapter 4, the law intervened in the smallest details of
the most intimate relationships in a way unknown to the Roman and Canon
law. Sometimes these extremes of juridification seem to be in the furtherance
of some interest of the State (as with population-related provisions), or of
dominant groups in society (as with the paternal authority over children).
Sometimes they seem to be merely the result of that urge for completeness so
evident in other aspects of, say, the Prussian General Code of 1794. [62]

In the endeavor not to leave any gap whatever in the codification, the
Prussian Code concerned itself with such matters as when marital intercourse
may be declined, when the absence of a spouse from home is excused, and
how often and how long a baby can be taken into bed and nursed. Professor
Carbonnier describes this legal atmosphere as "panjurism", the idea that
everything is law, or "...at least that law has a vocation to be everywhere, to
envelop everything, and, like a god, to hold up the entire inhabited world". [63]

The development of two important modern marriage institutions dates
from this period: the compulsory civil marriage ceremony in France and
Germany, and the development of comprehensive registration systems of
civil status. Both spread from France to the world.

The compulsory civil marriage is the child of the French Revolution
(which made a great point, as everyone knows, of refusing to distinguish
between legitimate and illegitimate children). The civil marriage ceremony
had been made available in the Calvinist Netherlands and in New England
but was made compulsory by the French revolutionary decree of 20 September 1792. This decree marked the shift in France from secularization to
statization. By the time of the Revolution the royal courts had already quietly
assumed control of marriage cases from the Church without any outright
confrontation, so that by 1789 the jurisdiction of the Church courts was
purely theoretical. [64] All that remained for the Revolution was to substitute,
for the ecclesiastical doctrine still applied by the royal courts, the starting
point that marriage was a civil contract organized by the State. Even so, later
events down to the present time in France show the persistence of canon law
ideas. As we saw in Chapter 5, the Napoleonic Code of 1804 rejected some of

the revolutionary ideas about marriage. What clearly remained of the revolutionary marriage legislation of 1792 was the civil ceremony which spread all over the world, as at least an optional method of marrying, and that system of secular registration of civil status which is now also in world-wide use. Compulsory civil marriage was retained by the Napoleonic Civil Code and was later adopted in various regions of Germany, finally becoming the law of the whole German empire by the Personal Status Law of 6 February 1875, and finding its place in the German Civil Code of 1896. Registration of civil status had been preceded in France and elsewhere first by ecclesiastical record-keeping, then by governmental regulation of church registrations.[65]

Another child of the French Revolution and of the Code of Frederick the Great, unilateral divorce, seems to have been born too soon. But we have seen its rebirth in Chapter 5, as well as the full maturity of mutual consent divorce which had been recognized by the revolutionary law and the Codes of Frederick the Great and Napoleon.

As has already been mentioned, England remained a case apart. Ecclesiastical jurisdiction over marriage survived the Reformation without real disruption until 1857. Briefly under Cromwell, it seems, civil marriage was available and divorce may have been permitted. But civil marriage did not reappear in England until 1836 and then only as an optional system. Informal marriages were valid in England until Lord Hardwicke's Act in 1753 which like the Decree *Tametsi* made an ecclesiastical ceremony compulsory and required publication of the banns.[66] Divorce was available after 1660 but only by special parliamentary act, and then only for adultery. It was expensive, complicated and rarely used. Divorce as such became available only by the Matrimonial Causes Act of 1857, effective in 1858.

In the United States,[67] those areas settled by Protestants had divorce laws from early times, while those with a strong Anglican influence initially had no divorce at all. Legislative divorce survived in many colonies and states into the 19th century. The Western frontier states were more liberal, so that by 1860 migratory divorce had already appeared. With the English background, and in the Southwest[68] with the indulgence of the canon law prior to *Ne Temere*, informal marriage became an established legal institution in some places. "Common law" marriages are still recognized in some 13 states and the District of Columbia. Sweden, interestingly enough, did not finally implement a secular version of the Tridentine requirement of formal marriage until 1915.[69] Thus, the recent rise in informal marriage in Sweden must be viewed against the background of a very late legal acceptance of the compulsory formal marriage.

The processes of secularization and eventual statization of marriage law just described coincided with certain trends in legal thought which were to reach their high point in the 19th century. So far as legislation is concerned, panjurism is probably most fully reflected in the Prussian General Code of 1794. But in 19th century case law and doctrine legal norms and concepts were formalized and expressed in that conceptualistic way which had been typical of revived Roman law and the canon law.[70] Legal rules which often were but the expression of moral value judgments or the resolution of conflicting interests, came to appear to have life of their own, producing "logical" and "necessary" consequences. At the same time, as Max Weber noted, the notion of legitimacy had come to be identified with that of "legality", understood as the quality of enactments which are formally correct and made in the accustomed manner.[71]

In view of all we have seen of the evolution of marriage regulation, this is a rather curious notion. It reminds one of the attachment which infant monkeys in captivity can be induced to have for a rag on a stick. Conduct among primitive people is oriented to ideas of legitimacy expressed in customs, convention and religion. As we have seen, the legal method of regulation appeared rather late in human history. Yet, once it appeared, it interacted with the mores and eventually acquired the force of tradition. Enactments which are formally correct and which have been made in the accustomed manner became themselves the matrimonial customs of the West.

However, much of what has been related in Chapters 2 through 5 of this book can be seen as evidence that we are now experiencing a period of dissociation between legality and legitimacy. Much of the law of formation, organization and dissolution of marriage, which has its origins in social and political conditions different from those of modern society, has long been irrelevant to vast areas of human conduct. Now it seems that behavior and ideology are pulling away from the law. Behavior and ideology can of course be *oriented* to an idea of legitimacy expressed in the law even when the legal norms are not *obeyed*.[72] In the recent past with respect to divorce, for example, it seems to have been necessary for society to go through a period of maintaining strict divorce law on the books, even though divorce in practice was freely available.[73] Presently, as Chapter 5 shows, in many places conduct is no longer even oriented to the ideals of the law, and the legal forms are being repealed or simply ignored.

V. Dejuridification: Marriage as a Social Institution?

It has been one of the purposes of the historical survey presented in this

Chapter to show how the law of marriage came to assume the form it had when the developments described in Chapters 2 through 6 began. We have seen that struggles among Church, State and politically powerful groups; popular customs and practices; and sheer historical accident have all had their part. This last factor in particular seems to account for the fact that in the United States divorces are heard in the same kind of proceedings as are disputes arising out of personal injuries or commercial contracts.[74]

More important from the point of view of this work, however, is the fact that against this background of the gradual establishment and eventual triumph of juridification and official regulation of the social institution of marriage, the present period of change can only be seen as a downward curve of *dejuridification* and *deregulation*, a return to forms of social control other than legal rules concerning the formation, dissolution and organization of married life. As the title of this book indicates, it is my belief that a close look at the discrete elements of the current period of legal evolution reveals a shift in the posture of the State with respect to the family, a shift which is approached in magnitude only by that which occurred in connection with the Reformation in most European countries, when the State acquired jurisdiction over matrimonial causes from the ecclesiastical authorities. Neither that process of juridification of family matters nor the present process of change is characterized by suddenness. In fact, both processes have involved long periods of discontinuity between social and legal phenomena, or as Professor Carbonnier puts it, between law and non-law. In what way has the posture of the State with respect to the family changed? Precisely in redefining what is law and what is non-law.

In the area of marriage formation and especially marriage dissolution, social conduct has for a long time gradually been pulling away from the law, treating the law as irrelevant. Now the law is pulling away from the social conduct, leaving questions of who marries whom and how, what rights and duties the spouses have toward each other, as well as how such unions are terminated, increasingly in the private order.

If we now recall the description of current developments in the formation of legal marriage and the legal treatment of informal marriages described in Chapters 2 and 3, we can see that the modern State has retreated considerably from the role it had assumed by the beginning of the 20th century. The ideas of freedom to marry, of privacy, and of neutrality with respect to different customs and life styles, have been the accompanying strains to which the corporate welfare state has drifted away from interfering with the choice of spouse, the eligibility to marry and the insistence on formalities. Like its predecessor the *Polizeistaat*, however, the State continues to pursue its own interests in population control and record keeping.

With respect to the law of the on-going marriage, it will be recalled from Chapter 4 that these largely symbolic rules had their origin for the most part in the excesses of the codification movements. Now we have seen that the law has either withdrawn completely, in the name of tolerance, or it has replaced the portraits on the wall. Where the hierarchical family headed by husband and father was once depicted, there now hangs a photo of the family composed of equals, all of whom are closely bound together in community but each of whom is a separate independent individual. There is some reason to doubt, as we saw, whether either version was a good likeness. But in the area of Chapter 4, the on-going marriage, perhaps realism is neither necessary nor even of particular virtue.

Finally, in Chapter 5 on divorce, dejuridification was most dramatically apparent. Free divorce has widely appeared in the legal norms, and official regulation through the courts has become perfunctory, often amounting to little more than registration.

Chapters 2 through 5 of this book show in varying degrees in the different countries: marriage by registration, with optional *de facto* marriage on the increase; divorce by registration; and deregulation of the on-going marriage. But, the wheel has not come full circle and we have not returned to Rome. For as the discussion of the effects of marriage dissolution in Chapter 6 showed, the modern State has not ceased to interest itself in the family. Yet since the family law of Chapter 6 is by and large marriage-neutral and unconcerned with legitimacy or illegitimacy of children, we can say that marriage itself seems once more to be becoming a purely social rather than a legally regulated institution.

If this is so, we may well wonder whether and how marriage will be regulated by social norms as it was before legitimacy came to be so strongly identified with legality. Anthropologists and sociologists have insisted on the importance of marriage as a determinant of status, and on its role in distinguishing those persons entitled to derive rank and property through the family.[75] But a survey of the recent law indicates that marriage law seems to be withering away precisely because rank and status, wealth and power, in society are decreasingly determined by family relationships. It would of course be naive to think that family relationships are unimportant with respect to these matters, but certainly they are less important than before.[76]

The significance of marriage was once comprehensive, when society was organized in clans and sibs in which membership depended, wherever the organization was patrilineal, upon descent from the man with whom an individual's mother was married. Marriage then constituted the basic relationship upon which an individual's position in society was determined and upon which the organization of society was based. For centuries a person's entering upon marriage has been regarded as the assumption of a status by which his position in society was fixed in aspects of basic importance. Today, under the impact of the postulate of equality the concept of status is being abandoned; and with the increasing importance of jobs and pensions rather than inherited wealth, the significance of the legitimate family in property matters is reduced. This trend is at once symbolized and advanced by the recent reforms assimilating the legal status of children born outside marriage with that of "legitimate" children. In addition, as the groups to which we belong become more and more heterogeneous, it becomes impossible to define, much less punish, the deviant. Marriage becomes primarily a concern of the individuals involved and is governed by their individual sense of ethics or utility, as the case may be.

From another point of view, however, we might say that the change is not so great as it first seems. Most family law, like most family history of which we have knowledge, has been concerned only or mainly with the upper and, later, the middle classes. In the twentieth century, the law began to take increasing notice of groups which it had previously neglected and they began to take notice of it.[77] There is reason to believe, for example, that in France and Germany the entry into formal as opposed to informal marriages was a way in which the members of the working class gave expression to their aspirations to rise in social status.[78] There is a hint of this kind of motivation in Sarah's character in *The Tinker's Wedding*. As more and more groups were included, and included themselves, under the umbrella of laws devised mainly for propertied groups, the discrepancy between law and mores widened. From this perspective then, we may only be seeing how narrow the application of "law" really was all the time. Like the tinkers Michael and Sarah, most of the travellers through this world have been ignored by the State and its laws made for fine ladies and gentlemen. The Church has usually generously excused them from strict compliance with its more formalistic rules. But when it didn't, then like Michael and Sarah, sure, they must have excused themselves.

VI. Statization and the Family in the Modern Welfare State

It must be admitted here that the theory of delegalization of marriage just sketched glosses over two extremely troublesome problems. If we accept the argument of Chapters 2 through 5 that society, once again, is leaving the

formation, conduct, and dissolution of family relationships to social regulation, is there any reason to think that leaving these matters to regulation by
the norms of custom, ethics, convention and religion means that they will be
subject to any norms at all? Second, the trend just described does not mean
that the theories of those philosophical proponents of the minimal state who
would say marriage and family matters are of no legitimate concern to the
State have suddenly found their terrestrial home. In fact the State is more
heavily involved in such matters than ever before, but in a different way.
Adjusting to the increasing tendency of people to look to the State rather than
the family or any other groups to solve their problems, governmental agencies have become deeply involved with the economic consequences of marriage dissolution and with the welfare of children produced by cohabitation
of a formal or informal kind. Bringing the State into ever more intimate
contact with legal and *de facto* families is the strange and unwieldy edifice of
national and municipal dispensaries of money, food, medicine, advice, comfort, recreation, nursing care and education with their army of bureaucrats. It
seems clear that social conditions are such that this State intervention is often
required. But here is the second problem: how can we tell what kind of State
involvement will shore up and strengthen family life, and what kind will
undermine and weaken it?

These questions are in a sense outside the scope of this book. Certainly no
one has yet furnished their answers. But a few observations with respect to
them may not be out of place, especially since law reform efforts must
proceed on the basis of assumptions, however imperfect, about the probable
effect of law on behavior. Let us first consider the modern statization of
family law. Then, in the concluding section we will turn to those legal
changes which have blurred the distinctions between marriage and non-
marriage, and between legal and informal family relationships.

In considering the posture of the State toward the family as expressed
through its laws, we must peel back and peer behind the slogan of privacy.
Philippe Ariès and others have described how in the 18th century the family
began to hold society at a distance, and to push it back beyond a steadily
expanding zone of private life.[79] The evolution of private life spread from
nobles to the middle class to other social strata until it has come finally to
embrace nearly the whole of society. But, at the same time, the family was
losing many of its functions to a series of impersonal institutions. Thus the
progress of privacy can also be seen as Lawrence Stone sees it:

Its [the family's] legal, political and economic functions declined before the ever-
encroaching march of the institutions of the modern state....

Furthermore, the power of the state undermined the influence of the kin, and thus increased the isolation and privacy of the nuclear family....[80]

The care which the State and its laws once lavished on the protection of private property has now been extended to maintaining the machinery of the social welfare state. Every country with which we have been here concerned, to a greater or lesser extent, has taken over the economic and educational tasks which were once primarily the responsibility of the family. All these countries have systems, varying in detail from each other, for distributing the risks of unemployment, sickness, death of a provider, and for providing security in old age. State concern is currently shifting from providing protection against the worst aspects of insecurity to attempting to provide each individual in society with the minimum wherewithal for a decent level of existence.

By removing the threat of total misery these trends should theoretically provide the conditions for a full and happy family life. But the situation is immensely complicated. Relieved of many of its economic and educational functions, the family seems indeed to have become organized around new ideals. It is supposed to be a private place where satisfying personal relationships between husbands and wives, and parents and children, can flourish. It is supposed to be a refuge from the psychic assaults of society and the disappointments of the world of work. But the refuge seems more and more to be itself the place of disillusion. Partly this may be because too much is expected of marriage and the small modern family. But one also has to consider the influence which society and the family have upon each other. The family shapes the individuals who compose society, but society in turn limits what families can do in forming its members. One might mention, among those aspects of twentieth century life which seem to have an effect on family life, as well as on other areas of human behavior: changes in the nature of work; the increasing number of choices open to individuals in many areas of life; and the tendency for one's activities, such as work, recreation, home life, education and so on, to be divided into different and separate areas, rather than to take place in one area with the same companions.

Testifying in 1973 before the U.S. Senate Subcommittee on Children and Youth, Urie Bronfenbrenner said that the forces of family disorganization

...arise primarily not from within the family itself, but from the circumstances in which the family finds itself and the way of life which these circumstances, in turn, impose. Specifically, when...there is no support or recognition from the outside world for one's role as a parent, and when time spent with one's family means frustration of career, personal fulfillment, and peace of mind – it is then that the development of the child becomes adversely affected.[81]

Pressures originating in social life, together with exaggerated expectations of what the family can provide in the way of compensating for deprivations elsewhere, may have made the ideals of family intimacy and cohesion harder to obtain. At the same time, as families under stress disintegrate, they may be producing the sort of individuals who are ready-made to take their place in Robert Heilbroner's dreadful vision of the authoritarian states of the future.[82] Thus, the banner of privacy may be flying over a wasteland of psychic, and ultimately social, devastation. The ideology of privacy may be in fact nothing more than what we have already seen as tolerance and neutrality sloganized to cover up a constant undermining of conditions that could make privacy meaningful.[83]

Philippe Ariès in France and Kenneth Keniston in the United States are now saying that the attention and importance given to childhood in society since the beginning of the 18th century are beginning to wane; that once again indifference to children, at best, is becoming the norm.[84] More illustrative perhaps than intellectual theorizing about the possible anti-family tendencies inherent in the organization of modern social life is the following letter which appeared in the correspondence section of *Le Nouvel Observateur* of 19 January 1976:

I have read the article by François-Henri de Virieu concerning the birth rate.

Bernadette and I do not want to have children.... She works at the Post-Telephone-Telegraph Service and I am a delivery man. We live in a studio apartment (630 F per month) in a nearby suburb.

Although the majority of people we run into do not understand us, we do not plan to pass the rest of our life like this; that is, with each of us carrying out every day a monotonous task, which is repetitive, without initiative, without responsibility, without real social meaning, and, furthermore, on the physical level, exhausting and numbing.

If we had had one or two children, we would have had to put them in a nursery, then in day care, then in school, which means spending even more time in transportation, and seeing one's children "on the fly" in the evening, with even more work to do around the house. Our salaries do not permit either one of us to stop working. I think that children brought up under present-day conditions will be even more unhappy and disoriented than we are if our mode of living is not changed by reducing the number of working hours. A real family is a family where a common task is carried out every day with the sole aim of making those who survive us happier than we are.

Some optimistic observers suggest that marriage and the family are now merely undergoing a difficult transitional stage, and that better adaptations and accommodations than ever before will eventually be worked out.[85] Thus, a view of the future can be constructed in which the State furnishes individuals and families with minimum economic security, and the society as a whole facilitates participation by men in family life and by women in work life.

But in the long run we have to consider that, with the decline of affluence, the State may not be able to fulfill the task it has set itself and that the family will continue to be the major institution through which society deals with dependence. It is possible too that tolerance of diversity and liberty of the individual will one day be seen as phenomena of affluence. Some may see the trends described in this book as themselves signs of social disintegration. The question becomes more pressing whether and how the State can assist and strengthen the family. As we adjust to a world of diminishing resources and expanding population, we may come to search in family law as elsewhere for mechanisms and models through which we can learn to live in community.

At present, the law, mirroring society and individual families, is filled with tensions and contradictions. With respect to these contradictions, I think it is important to cultivate what John Keats in another context called negative capability – that is, the ability to hold opposed interpretations of the present and visions of the future in our minds without flinching or turning away. We should, in the spirit with which we approach these problems, avoid both the naive optimism according to which family relationships need only to be cleansed of their economic sediment, and the currently fashionable neo-Manichaeism which sees the disintegration of the family and society as imminent. If we are able to do this, we may hope that these same tensions which have the potential to tear a society, an individual or a family apart, can also perhaps generate in legal and social policy that enormous creative human energy that they have been known to generate in art.

VII. Afterword

> "Sit down, the two of you, there before me", said Neary, "and do not despair. Remember there is no triangle, however obtuse, but the circumference of some circle passes through its wretched vertices. Remember also one thief was saved."
> "Our medians," said Wylie, "or whatever the hell they are, meet in Murphy".
> "Outside us," said Neary. "Outside us."
> "In the outer light," said Miss Counihan.
> Samuel Beckett, *Murphy* (1938).[86]

The puzzles of law, behavior and ideology with which we are now left are knotted together, each strand is turned in on itself. No one can foresee how they will be resolved. Yet as they unfold, future developments will be seen to follow naturally from what has been set forth here. This is because, as the political theorist Raymond Aron has put it, complex events are always the simultaneous result of a large number of circumstances, but minute facts can determine the course an important movement will take.[87] Thus, says Aron, we all, in a sense rightly, believe that the past was determined but the future is not.

It is perhaps appropriate to acknowledge here that the theories advanced in this book have a certain hypothetical character. It is necessary to construct and employ concepts and theories in the effort to understand the relationships among law, behavior and ideology. But human reality is not stylized and rationalized. It is complex, obscure and, ultimately, mysterious.

If, however, it is correct to see the present period as one of delegalization, perhaps there is much to be said for leaving the social institution of the family to social regulation. If one adopted without question the slogans of freedom to marry, individual liberty, and tolerance of diverse life styles, one could anticipate with some pleasure the day when all of the encrusted layers of law will finally be peeled away, and the social institution of the family is once again subject to none but social regulation, "free by the laws and restrained by manners", in Montesquieu's phrase. This position is not without difficulty, however. One difficulty is that in modern Western societies we cannot say that a change from what has been rather extensive legal regulation of marriage and family matters to "delegalization", is completely neutral. This is because, in an indefinable but nonetheless real way, much of our law performs educational and hortatory functions. In a society where there are few sources of common inspiration, the law can take on in some instances a sacred character: it can become what the American sociologist Robert Bellah calls a "civil religion".[88] This is particularly true, for example, of the pronouncements of the Supreme Court of the United States or of what is written in the French Civil Code. To the extent that legitimacy is still identified with legality, laws permitting unilateral divorce on demand for example must have a certain, though impossible to quantify, moral significance. Thus, we cannot say in our societies that the law is completely unimportant in comparison with other factors. In fact, it interacts with and reacts back upon social change.

While not dismissing this point, I believe that the effect which changes in marriage and divorce law may have on marriage behavior, under present conditions, is minimal. When the law is in tune with other social forces, when they are all running in the same direction, it is possible that they will enter into a synergistic relationship and that the law will produce a greater effect in combination with other forces than it could on its own. But when the law runs counter to what is happening in society, and legitimacy is decreasingly identified with legality, the effect of law must be small. Rheinstein has shown once and for all the lack of correlation between strict or easy divorce laws and marriage stability or instability.

Thus, I conclude that the possible effect of changes in laws governing marriage formation, dissolution and the conduct of married life is not a reason to struggle against what in any event is probably an inevitable process of deregulation. However, matters are otherwise when we turn from marriage formation, organization and dissolution, to the economic and child-related consequences of marriage dissolution, and when we consider the problems of dependency generally. There the question is not whether the State should intervene, but how and how much.

Another theoretical difficulty which some might have with delegalization is that in modern societies no one can be really sure that leaving marriage and family matters to the norms of convention, ethics, and religion, means that they will be subject to any norms at all. In other words, thinking about delegalization brings us back to the problem that the social institution itself is facing serious challenges. Our wise men tell us that the extent of family disorganization is serious, that we have a disease called alienation, and that our only common value is hedonism.

But, if all this is true (it may be permitted to wonder, since wise men these days often live in such places as California, New York or Paris), it is hard to imagine that enacted norms would succeed where all others have failed. Perhaps there is some comfort in König's observation that while the family changes slowly, new forms of the family are constantly emerging. Perhaps the social institution will adapt to yet another set of challenges.[89]

Finally, although I have here emphasized the diminishing importance of the legal aspects of the family, there is every reason to believe that its other aspects, however frail and faltering they may be, are as important as ever. For most of us, the family remains the theater in which we each realize our full capacity for good or evil. Relationships between husband and wife, parents and children, give rise to crises and tensions, conflicts between love and duty, reason and passion. They also provide the framework for resolving them. For most of us, the family furnishes our one opportunity to aspire to heroism, greatness or even sainthood. On the other hand, as Dostoevsky well knew, it provides most of us with our principal occasions to really do or suffer evil. Even though, after the loosening of legal ties that has been described in this book, the only bonds which remain to unite the family may be the ties of human affection, we can perhaps – if we are hopeful – recognize in those fragile connections analogies for that Love which is the Law that binds all of us together in the Family of Man and the City of God. A note sounded by a player on one instrument may call forth a corresponding note from another; a child, hearing an accordion outside the window, may begin to sing and dance.

NOTES

[1] J. M. Synge, *The Tinker's Wedding*, in The Complete Plays of John M. Synge 180, 207 (1960; orig. publ. 1907).
[2] *Weber* 3.
[3] *König* par. 96.
[4] *Winch* 1.
[5] *Hübner* 593; II *Pollock and Maitland* 364.
[6] *Hübner* 588.
[7] *Weber* 134.
[8] *Winch* 2.
[9] *König* par. 96–97.
[10] *Ibid.*
[11] *Jolowicz* 117–118.
[12] *Brissaud* 142; *Hübner* 613.
[13] *Rheinstein, M.S.D.L.* 15.
[14] In the following discussion of the Roman marriage, I rely on *Corbett* 68–105; 218–248.
[15] *Noonan* 44–46.
[16] *Id.* at 53.
[17] Novel 22.
[18] Novel 117 of 542 A.D.
[19] *Corbett* 242–243.
[20] *Rheinstein, M.S.D.L.* 16.
[21] I *Esmein* 14.
[22] St. Augustine, The Retractations, in LX The Fathers of the Church 247 (1968).
[23] *Noonan* 87.
[24] *Rheinstein, M.S.D.L.* 13–14.
[25] *Bassett* 129.
[26] II *Esmein* 49.
[27] *Id.* 50–51.
[28] *Id.* at 49–50; *Brissaud* 143–144; *Hübner* 614; II *Pollock and Maitland* 392–393.
[29] Canon 1100.
[30] de Reeper, The History and Application of Canon 1098, 14 Jurist 148, 152 (1954).
[31] Buckley, "Concubinage", in IV New Catholic Encyclopedia 120 (1967).
[32] II *Pollock and Maitland* 370.
[33] *Id.* at 366.
[34] *Bassett* 129–130; *Brissaud* 88–89; *Hübner* 614.
[35] II *Pollock and Maitland* 367.
[36] *Rheinstein, M.S.D.L.* 18.
[37] See generally, *Weber* Ch. 8, esp. 250–255.
[38] *Bassett* 130.
[39] *Helmholtz* 5.
[40] *Brissaud* 115; *Gottlieb* 35–37; *Kidd* 104.
[41] *Gottlieb* 59–60; 62–63.
[42] *Gottlieb* 38–39.
[43] *Kidd* 104.
[44] *Hunt* 60.
[45] *Gottlieb* 16.

[46] *Id*. 124–135.

[47] *Hunt* 62.

[48] *Id*. at 63.

[49] *Bouscaren and Ellis* 581–583.

[50] Canon 1098, see Chapter 1 of this book at n. 23.

[51] Thurston, "Marriage, Ritual of", in IX The Catholic Encyclopedia 703, 704 (1910).

[52] *Rheinstein, Int. Encyc.* par. 7.

[53] *Ibid*.

[54] *I Esmein* 34.

[55] *Ibid*.

[56] *Ibid*.

[57] *Rheinstein, M.S.D.L.* 22.

[58] *Id*. at 23.

[59] *Id*. at 25–26.

[60] Müller-Freienfels, Ehe und Recht 18–25.

[61] *Id*. at 20–21.

[62] *Id*. at 22–23.

[63] *Carbonnier, Flexible Droit* 20.

[64] *Brissaud* 91–92.

[65] *Rheinstein, M.S.D.L.* 198; see also Chapter 2 of this book *supra* at 58.

[66] *II Pollock and Maitland* Chapter 7.

[67] See *Clark CB* 7–11.

[68] See generally Baade, The Form of Marriage in Spanish North America, 61 Corn. L. Rev. 1 (1975).

[69] *Schmidt (1970)* 203–204.

[70] *Rheinstein, M.S.D.L.* 19.

[71] *Weber* 9.

[72] *Id*. at 45: "Very frequently the order is violated only in one or another partial respect, or its violation is sought to be passed off as legitimate, with a varying measure of good faith. Or several different interpretations of the order coexist alongside each other. In that case the sociologist will regard each one as valid in exactly so far as it is actually determinative of conduct. It is, indeed, in no way difficult for the sociologist to recognize that several, possibly mutually contradictory, orders are valid within the same group. Even one and the same individual may orient his conduct toward mutually contradictory orders. He can do so successively; such cases can, indeed, be observed all the time; but...[this] can [also] occur with respect to one and the same conduct.... Where, however, evasion or violation of the order (i.e., of the meaning generally ascribed to it) has become the rule, the order has come to be valid in but a limited sense or has ceased to be valid altogether.... Fluid transitions exist between validity and nonvalidity, and mutually contradictory orders can be valid alongside each other. Each one is valid simply in proportion to the probability that conduct will actually be oriented toward it."

[73] *Rheinstein, M.S.D.L.* 247–260.

[74] *Id*. at 20.

[75] See especially, B. Malinowski, Sex, Culture and Myth 63–65, 139–140 (1962), and *Goode* 19–30.

[76] The fact that the family, in a broader sense, contributes to inequality in the sense of providing different life prospects for individuals who may be equally endowed, has troubled John Rawls in his Theory of Justice, 301, 511–512 (1971).

[77] *Rheinstein, Int. Encyc.* par. 14.

[78] *Carbonnier, 2 Droit Civil* 194; *Rheinstein, M.S.D.L.* 301.

[79] *Ariès* 398–404; see also *Braudel* 223–224.

[80] Stone, The Massacre of the Innocents, The New York Review of Books, Nov. 14, 1974, 25, 27.

[81] Hearings on American Families: Trends and Pressures, Subcomm. on Children and Youth,

Senate Comm. on Labor and Public Welfare, 93 Cong., 1st Sess. (1973), reproduced at 119 Cong. Rec. S 18,011 (daily ed. Sept. 28, 1973).

[82] R. Heilbroner, An Inquiry into the Human Prospect (1975).

[83] Christopher Lasch points for example to what he calls the "flight from feeling...rooted in developments that have undermined intimacy and privacy in the family: most obviously, the absence of the father", in What the Doctor Ordered, The New York Review of Books, Dec. 11, 1975, 50, 54. In March 1975, in the United States one out of seven children was living in a family without a father, as compared to one out of ten in March 1970, according to Beverly McEaddy of the Bureau of Labor Statistics: Women who Head Families: A Socioeconomic Analysis, Monthly Labor Review, June 1976, at 3, 6.

[84] Ariès, L'enfant: la fin d'un règne, Autrement No. 3, 169, 171 (1975); Keniston, The Emptying Family, The New York Times, Feb. 18, 1976, p. 33 cols. 2–4.

[85] Giele. Changing Sex Roles and the Future of Marriage, Feb. 13, 1973 (lecture delivered at Wellesley College).

[86] S. Beckett, *Murphy* 213–214 (Grove Press ed. 1957; orig. publ. 1938).

[87] II Main Currents in Sociological Thought 237, 241 (1967).

[88] Beyond Belief, Ch. 9 (1970).

[89] *König* thinks that the fact that the family may be an inheritance from the higher animal species and the family's endurance capacity as demonstrated through the chaos of history permit "a well-grounded statement of doubt as to all the schools of thought that from time to time predict an imminent dissolution of marriage and the family, or believe they can point to a period of decline in our day and age". par. 29. See also par. 55.

INDEX